Global Capitalism and the Crisis of Humanity

This exciting new study provides an original and provocative exposé of the crisis of global capitalism in its multiple dimensions – economic, political, social, ecological, military, and cultural. Building on his earlier works on globalization, William I. Robinson discusses the nature of the new global capitalism, the rise of a globalized production and financial system, a transnational capitalist class, and a transnational state and warns of the rise of a global police state to contain the explosive contradictions of a global capitalist system that is crisis-ridden and out of control. Robinson concludes with an exploration of how diverse social and political forces are responding to the crisis and alternative scenarios for the future.

William I. Robinson is a professor of sociology at the University of California, Santa Barbara, where he is also affiliated with the Latin American and Iberian Studies Program and with the Global and International Studies Program. He has previously published seven books, including the award-winning *Promoting Polyarchy* (Cambridge University Press, 1996), *A Theory of Global Capitalism* (2004), and the award-winning *Latin America and Global Capitalism* (2008). He has published some fifty articles in academic journals such as *Sociological Forum*, *Theory and Society*, *International Studies Review*, *International Sociology*, *Cambridge Review of International Affairs*, *International Relations*, *Global Society*, *Globalizations*, *Race and Class*, *New Political Economy*, *Third World Quarterly*, and *Radical Philosophy* and hundreds of essays, book chapters, and articles in the popular press. He is a member of the editorial board of fifteen academic journals. In 2013 Robinson was elected chair of the Political Economy of the World-System section of the American Sociological Association (ASA). He is a member of the ASA, the Latin American Studies Association, the Global Studies Association, and the International Studies Association. He was a founding writer for and editor of *Pensamiento Propio*, a monthly journal of the Coordinadora Regional de Investigaciones Economicas y Sociales.

Everyone recognizes beauty
  only because of ugliness
Everyone recognizes virtue
  only because of sin

Life and death are born together
Difficult and easy
Long and short
High and low –
  all these exist together
Sound and silence blend as one
Before and after arrive as one

   Tao Te Ching, Verse 2

Global Capitalism and the Crisis of Humanity

WILLIAM I. ROBINSON

University of California, Santa Barbara

CAMBRIDGE
UNIVERSITY PRESS

CAMBRIDGE
UNIVERSITY PRESS

32 Avenue of the Americas, New York, NY 10013-2473, USA

Cambridge University Press is part of the University of Cambridge.

It furthers the University's mission by disseminating knowledge in the pursuit of education, learning, and research at the highest international levels of excellence.

www.cambridge.org
Information on this title: www.cambridge.org/9781107691117

First published 2014

Printed in the United States of America

A catalog record for this publication is available from the British Library.

Library of Congress Cataloging in Publication Data
Robinson, William I.
Global capitalism and the crisis of humanity / William I. Robinson.
pages   cm
Includes bibliographical references and index.
ISBN 978-1-107-06747-9 (hardback) – ISBN 978-1-69111-7 (paperback)
1. Capitalism – History – 21st century.   2. Power (Social sciences)   3. Social classes.   4. Globalization.   I. Title.
HB501R624   2014
330.12'2–dc23   2014019656

ISBN 978-1-107-06747-9 Hardback
ISBN 978-1-107-69111-7 Paperback

Contents

Acknowledgments

All intellectual labor is collective, part of the social labor process. The collective labor behind this study includes literally thousands of people who have contributed to my own intellectual and political development, many of whom I do not know personally. The best I can do to acknowledge my debt is to mention here those people who more immediately provided invaluable assistance in the research and preparation of this study and those who were the most proximate sources of inspiration. To start, I cannot thank enough Mario Barrera and Kent Norsworthy, both of whom carefully read and commented on every chapter. My former undergraduate student Anaiya Mussolini, a bright and multitalented young woman, read the entire manuscript, suggested where I could improve it, and helped me format the notes. Xuan Santos provided important comments on a draft of Chapter 5.

I do not think my graduate students in the doctoral program at the University of California – some of whom have defended their dissertations and are now colleagues – realize just what an inspiration they have been. Among them, I want to extend special thanks (in alphabetical order) to Yousef Baker, Veronica Montes (now Dr. Montes, Research Fellow at the University of Southern California), Steven Osuna, Cesar "Che" Rodriguez, Amandeep Sandhu (now Dr. Sandhu), Xuan Santos (now Dr. Santos, assistant professor of sociology at California State University–San Marcos), Jeb Sprague, and James Walsh (now Dr. Walsh). There are many more, both graduate and undergraduate, whom I cannot mention here.

I would also like to thank friends and colleagues in several professional associations to which I belong. These include the Political Economy of the World-System section of the American Sociological Association; the Global Studies Association (North American chapter); and the Network for Critical Studies of Global Capitalism (this network has a website, http://netglobalcapitalism.wordpress.com/). Among the many colleagues active in these three and other professional associations who have supported my own career over the years, generously extended to me invitations, and stimulated the development of my ideas (even when they are in disagreement), I want to pay special thanks to Christopher Chase-Dunn, who now directs the Institute for Research on World-Systems at the University of California at Riverside; Jerry Harris, organizational secretary of the Global Studies Association (North America); Leslie Sklair, professor emeritus of the London School of Economics; Mark Hrubec, the director of the Center for Global Studies of the Czech Academy of Sciences; Immanuel Wallerstein at Yale University; and the late Giovanni Arrighi. A special thanks to Juan Manual Sandoval and my friends and comrades from the Red Mexicana de Accíon Frente al Libre Comercio (REMALC) and the Seminario Permanente de Estudios Chicanos y de Fronteras (SPECHF) of the National Insitute of Anthropology and History (INAH) of Mexico.

Thanks also, in alphabetical order, to Berch Bergeroglu, Jesse Diaz, Linda Elder of the Foundation for Critical Thinking, FLACSO (Latin American Social Science Faculty) offices in Costa Rica and Guatemala, Sam Gindin, Asafa Jalata, Adam David Morton, Georgina Murray, Radmila Nakarada of Belgrade University, Dawn Paley, Leo Panitch, Marielle Robinson-Mayorga, Manuel Rozental, Saskia Sassen, Jason Struna, Lilian Vega and friends and colleagues at the Central American University in El Salvador, and Deniz Yukseker. My apologies to anyone I have inadvertently failed to include here. Thanks to three anonymous reviewers for Cambridge University Press; to my editor at the Press, Lewis Bateman; to assistant to the editor Shaun Vigil; and to copy editor Russell Hahn. I gratefully acknowledge the Academic Senate Committee on Research of the University of California at Santa Barbara for its generosity in funding, through two grants, important portions of the research involved in this study.

Acronyms

ALEC	American Legislative Exchange Council
APEC	Asia Pacific Economic Cooperation forum
BRICS	Brazil, Russia, India, China, and South Africa
CAFTA	Central American Free Trade Agreement
CCA	Corrections Corporation of America
CIT	computer and information technology
DHS	Department of Homeland Security
EU	European Union
G-7	Group of Seven, referring to the United States, Canada, England, Germany, Italy, France, and Japan (Russia is sometimes included in an expanded "Group of Eight" or G-8)
G-20	Group of Twenty, referring to Argentina, Australia, Brazil, Canada, China, the European Union, France, Germany, India, Indonesia, Italy, Japan, Mexico, Russia, Saudi Arabia, South Africa, South Korea, Turkey, the United Kingdom, and the United States
GATS	General Agreement on Trade in Services
ICC	International Chamber of Commerce
IMF	International Monetary Fund
IT	information technology
MENA	Middle East and North Africa
MNC	multinational corporation
NAFTA	North American Free Trade Agreement
OECD	Organization of Economic Cooperation and Development
OWS	Occupy Wall Street
R&D	research and development
SB1070	Senate Bill 1070 (Arizona anti-immigrant law)
TCC	transnational capitalist class

TNC	transnational corporation
TNS	transnational state
TRIPS	Trade Related Intellectual Property Rights
UN	United Nations
UNCTAD	United Nations Conference on Trade and Development
WB	World Bank
WEF	World Economic Forum
WSF	World Social Forum
WTO	World Trade Organization

Introduction

A Crisis of Humanity

All men will see what you seem to be; only a few will know what you are.

Machiavelli[1]

Our world is burning. We face a global crisis that is unprecedented in terms of its magnitude, its global reach, the extent of ecological degradation and social deterioration, and the scale of the means of violence. This is a time of great upheavals, momentous changes, and uncertain outcomes; fraught with dangers, including the very real possibility of collapse as well as the growing threat of repressive social control systems that serve to contain the explosive contradictions of a global capitalism in crisis. Certainly the stakes bound up in the raging conflicts of our day are too high for the usual academic complacency. I believe that the most urgent task of any intellectual who considers him or herself organic or politically engaged is to address this crisis. If nothing else, we will all agree that global capitalism is a highly unstable and crisis-ridden system. If we are to avert disastrous outcomes we must understand both the nature of the new global capitalism and the nature of its crisis. This book is an attempt to contribute to such an understanding.

In this book I aspire to analyze and theorize the global crisis from the perspective of global capitalism theory. Wide-ranging debate continues on the nature of the twenty-first-century global order and its contemporary crises. I have been centrally concerned with these matters for over two decades, seeking above all to construct a theoretical framework for situating them – specifically, a theory of global capitalism.[2] The world in which Karl Marx analyzed capital

---

[1] Niccolo Machiavelli, *The Prince* (New York: Bantam Books, 1981 [1513]), 63–64. To understand this quote is to understand the distinction between the inner sanctum of power and the outward appearance of power.

[2] See, in particular, William I. Robinson, *A Theory of Global Capitalism* (Baltimore: Johns Hopkins University Press, 2004), William I. Robinson, *Latin America and Global Capitalism* (Baltimore: Johns Hopkins University Press, 2008), Chapter 1.

has radically changed. The global capitalism perspective offers a powerful explanatory framework for making sense of the crisis. Analysis of capitalist globalization not only says something about the nature of the crisis but is also a template for probing a wide range of social, political, cultural, and ideological processes in this twenty-first century. Following Marx, we want to focus on the internal dynamics of capitalism in order to understand the crisis. And following the global capitalism perspective, we want to see how capitalism has qualitatively evolved in recent decades. The systemwide crisis we face is not a repeat of earlier such episodes such as that of the the 1930s or the 1970s precisely because world capitalism is fundamentally different in the twenty-first century.

How, specifically, is world capitalism different now than during previous episodes of crisis? In my view globalization constitutes a qualitatively new epoch in the ongoing and open-ended evolution of world capitalism, marked by a number of qualitative shifts in the capitalist system and by novel articulations of social power. I have highlighted four aspects unique to this epoch. First is the rise of truly transnational capital and a new global production and financial system into which all nations and much of humanity have been integrated, either directly or indirectly. We have gone from a *world economy*, in which countries and regions were linked to each other via trade and financial flows in an integrated international market, to a *global economy*, in which nations are linked to each other more organically through the transnationalization of the production process, of finance, and of the circuits of capital accumulation. No single nation-state can remain insulated from the global economy or prevent the penetration of the social, political, and cultural superstructure of global capitalism.

Second is the rise of a Transnational Capitalist Class (TCC), a class group that has drawn in contingents from most countries around the world, North and South, and has attempted to position itself as a global ruling class. This TCC is the *hegemonic fraction* of capital on a world scale. I will have more to say about the TCC in Chapter 1. Third is the rise of Transnational State (TNS) apparatuses. The TNS is constituted as a loose network made up of trans- and supranational organizations together with national states that functions to organize the conditions for transnational accumulation and through which the TCC attempts to organize and institutionally exercise its class power. I will have more to say about the TNS in Chapters 2 and 3. Fourth are novel relations of inequality, domination, and exploitation in global society, including an increasing importance of transnational social and class inequalities relative to North-South inequalities that are geographically or territorially conceived. I discuss these novel relations in several chapters.

Capitalist globalization is an ongoing, unfinished, and open-ended *process*, one that is contradictory and conflict-ridden, driven by social forces in struggle; it is *structure in motion, emergent*, with no consummated end state. In the dialectic, *emergent* means there is never a finished state, only open-ended process driven by contradictions, in this case by ongoing struggles among contradictory social forces worldwide. If we are to understand global capitalism and its crisis we must in the first instance train our focus on configurations of these contradictory social forces; such a focus must be analytically prior to focusing on the ways in which they become institutionalized and expressed in political, cultural, and ideological processes.

I began writing about globalization in the early 1990s. My ideas have developed through a series of concrete, historical investigations involving much induction rather than more abstract, formalized methods of derivation. Informing my theory of global capitalism is the idea that we cannot understand this new epoch through extant nation-state-centric paradigms that purport to explain world political and economic dynamics as interactions among nation-states and competition among national classes in an interstate system. I have continued to debate with many colleagues and companions the merits of my theoretical claims, demonstrating their explanatory utility through two major empirical-historical studies, both on Latin America, and in diverse journal articles and commentaries focusing on the crisis-ridden nature of the global system.[3]

In 2008, when world capitalism lurched into its most severe recession since the 1930s depression – what some refer to as the Great Recession – I turned my attention more fully to the topic of global crisis, specifically, to the occurrence and significance of *accumulation* and *legitimation* crises in the global system – both of which will be explained in what follows. While the present study discusses my theory of global capitalism including the specific thesis of the TCC and the TNS, I would direct readers to my earlier works for a fuller exposition of this theory. My central objective in this book is to elaborate on and apply this theory in relation to the global crisis. The idea for this book grew out of three essays on the topic of global crisis. The first, published in 2007, *Beyond the Theory of Imperialism*, challenged the notion that resurgent U.S. interventionism in the wake of the September 11, 2001, attacks on the World Trade Center and the Pentagon could be explained as a "new U.S. imperialism" aimed at competing with rivals for Middle Eastern resources and restoring U.S. hegemony in the international system. Instead, I saw this interventionism as a

---

[3] See, inter alia, William I. Robinson: *Transnational Conflicts: Central America, Social Change, and Globalization* (London: Verso, 2003); William I. Robinson, *Latin America and Global Capitalism*, Chapter 1; William I. Robinson, "The Crisis of Global Capitalism: Cyclical? Structural? Systemic?," in Martinj Konings, ed., *The Great Credit Crash* (London: Verso, 2010); William I. Robinson, "Beyond the Theory of Imperialism: Global Capitalism and the Transnational State," *Societies without Borders* (2007), 2: 5–26; William I. Robinson, "Aqui Estamos y No Nos Vamos!: Global Capitalism and the Struggle for Immigrant Rights, *Race and Class* (2006), 48(2): 4–29; William I. Robinson and Mario Barrera, "Global Capitalism and Twenty-First Century Fascism: A U.S. Case Study," *Race and Class* (2012), 53(3): 4–29; William I. Robinson, "Global Capital Leviathan," *Radical Philosophy* (2011), no. 165: 2–6; William I. Robinson, "Globalizacion, Crisis, y Escenarios de Futuro," *Estudios Centroamericanos* (2009), 63(715–716): 331–344; William I. Robinson, "What to Expect from U.S. 'Democracy Promotion' in Iraq," *New Political Science* (2004), 26(3): 441–447.

response to the crisis of global capitalism – in particular, a drive to violently integrate new regions into the global capitalist system and to militarize accumulation in the face of stagnation tendencies. The second, *The Crisis of Global Capitalism: Cyclical, Structural, Systemic?*, published in 2010, argued that underneath the 2008 collapse was a structural crisis of overaccumulation that threatens to become systemic and that the TCC had turned to three mechanisms – militarized accumulation, the raiding and sacking of public finance, and frenzied financial speculation – as outlets to unload surplus as productive outlets dried up. The third, *Global Crisis and Twenty-First Century Fascism: A U.S. Case Study*, written together with Mario Barrera, was published in 2012. We identified three responses to the global crisis in the midst of rising political conflict and polarization worldwide: resurgent leftist, popular, and radical response from below; a reformist impulse from global elites; and a neo-fascist response.[4] These are, stated in broad strokes, the themes I develop at greater length in this book.

The crisis is much talked about these days. Most commentators refer to the economic crisis that they date to the U.S. subprime loan debacle that began in mid-2007 and was followed by the global financial collapse of September 2008 and the Great Recession. The crisis that exploded in 2008 with the collapse of the global financial system springs from contradictions in global capitalism that are expressed in immanent crisis tendencies and in a series of displacements over the past three decades that had served to postpone a "day of reckoning."

A key focus in this book is on what I see as the underlying and causal social-economic (or material) elements in the crisis, or what in Marxist lexicon we call the internal contradictions of the capitalist system. Moreover, because the system is now global, crisis in any one place tends to represent crisis for the system as a whole. I attempt in this work to analyze the causal origins of the global crisis in *overaccumulation* and also in contradictions of *state power*. The system cannot expand because the marginalization of a significant portion of humanity from direct productive participation, the downward pressure on wages and popular consumption worldwide, and the polarization of income have reduced the ability of the world market to absorb world output. At the same time, given the particular configuration of social and class forces and the correlation of these forces worldwide, national states are hard-pressed to regulate transnational circuits of accumulation and offset the explosive contradictions built into the system.

Yet I want to evoke here the concept of global crisis in a broader sense. There are multiple and mutually constitutive dimensions of global crisis – economic, social, political, cultural, ideological, and ecological, not to mention the existential crisis of our consciousness, our values, and even our very being. There is a crisis of social polarization, that is, of *social reproduction*. The system cannot meet the needs or assure the survival of millions of people, perhaps a majority of humanity. There are crises of state legitimacy and political authority, or of

---

[4] See the previous note for full references to these articles.

hegemony and *domination*. National states face spiraling crises of legitimacy as they fail to meet the social grievances of local working and popular classes experiencing downward mobility, unemployment, heightened insecurity, and greater hardships. The legitimacy of the system has increasingly been called into question by millions, perhaps even billions, of people around the world and is facing expanded counter-hegemonic challenges. Global elites have been unable to counter this erosion of the system's authority in the face of worldwide pressures for a global moral economy. And as a canopy that envelops all these dimensions, there is a crisis of sustainability rooted in an ecological holocaust that has already begun, expressed in climate change, peak oil, and the impending collapse of centralized agricultural systems in several regions of the world, among other indicators. Beyond the economic situation we want to explore these different dimensions and to identify how they are interconnected. My notion of global crisis is best captured in the notion of a *crisis of humanity*, by which I mean a crisis that is approaching systemic proportions, threatens the ability of billions of people to survive, and raises the specter of a collapse of world civilization and degeneration into a new "Dark Ages."

GLOBAL CAPITALISM THEORY AND ITS CRITICS: A RESPONSE

There has been a great deal written from a critical and an historical materialist perspective about the crisis of world capitalism.[5] What demarcates my arguments in this book is that they are advanced from the perspective of global capitalism theory as just summarized. Part of my aim here is to take issue with works on crisis that come from extant critical approaches. My propositions on global capitalism have met with debate and criticism from a range of theoretical and political quarters, among them traditional Marxists, world-system theorists, international relations scholars, and colleagues coming from my own critical globalization perspective. Critics have charged, among other things, that: I do away with the nation-state; I do not acknowledge uneven accumulation; I dismiss imperialism and its practice by the U.S. state; I ignore local, national, and regional variation by attributing everything causally to global capitalism and overstate the extent to which globalization has equalized the conditions for the production and exchange of value across space in the global system. These

[5] These works are too numerous to list here. Among those that I have found useful (despite my disagreement with their interpretations) are Konings, ed., *The Great Credit Crash*; Chris Harman, *Zombie Capitalism: Global Crisis and the Relevance of Marx* (Chicago: Haymarket Books, 2010); Michel Chossudovsky and Andrew Gavin Marshall, eds., *The Global Economic Crisis: The Great Depression of the XXI Century* (Quebec: Global Research Publishers, 2010); Christian Marazzi, *The Violence of Financial Capitalism* (Los Angeles: Semiotext(e), 2011); Istvan Meszaros and John Bellamy Foster, *The Structural Crisis of Capital* (New York: Monthly Review Press, 2010); David McNally, *Global Slump: The Economics and Politics of Crisis and Resistance* (Oakland, CA: PM Press, 2010); William K. Tabb, *The Restructuring of Capitalism in Our Time* (New York: Columbia University Press, 2012).

critiques and my responses have been published as exchanges in several journal symposia.[6]

Some critiques cannot be taken seriously, given their misrepresentation and even ignorance of my work, the ideological nature of the criticism, or the zeal to defend paradigms into which critics are deeply invested irrespective of historical and empirical evidence.[7] Some critics, moreover, base their objections on the very conceptual categories and frameworks whose assumptions I challenge, so that the critique remains tautological. Nonetheless, others have put forward important concerns that I attempt to address in the present study. In Chapter 1, I revisit some general themes with regard to global capitalism and transnational capitalists. In Chapter 2 I revisit the topic of TNS apparatuses. These first two chapters are not meant to reiterate the theory of the TCC and the TNS but to serve as complements to what I have previously written on these themes. Chapter 3 takes up the matter of imperialism and the U.S. state as well as that of uneven accumulation. Chapter 4 analyzes the 2008 collapse and its aftermath from a global capitalism perspective. Chapter 5 explores evolving twenty-first-century modalities of domination and social control in the face of challenges to global capitalism from below. Chapter 6 draws some general conclusions and prospects for the future. Readers will find that there are several themes that at the risk of redundancy I have interwoven throughout the book: the transnationalization of capital; the importance of the concept of the TNS; the uneven accumulation of capital; imperialism and the U.S. state; the pitfalls of a nation-state-centric framework of analysis; and the *historical* nature of the world capitalist system. While the reader who wants the full story must read the book from beginning to end, I have designed each chapter so that profit may be gained by reading any one of them on its own.

---

[6] See symposia in the following journals: *Theory and Society*, (2001), 30(2); *Science and Society* (2001–02), 65(4); *Critical Sociology* (2012), 38(3); *Historical Materialism* (2007), 15; *Cambridge Review of International Affairs* (2006), 19(3).

[7] See, e.g., my exchange with the international relations scholar Paul Cammack in *Geopolitics, History and International Relations* (2009), 1(2) (more on this exchange below); my exchange with the political scientist Ellen M. Wood in *Historical Materialism* (2007), 15 (William I. Robinson, "The Pitfall of Realist Analysis of Global Capitalism," 71–93, and Ellen M. Wood, "A Reply to Critics," 143–170); or the sociologist Juan Corradi's ideologically driven discussion of my work, "Review of Latin America and Global Capitalism," *Contemporary Sociology* (2009), 28(5): 396–398. Diane Barahona observes in her review-essay of my *oeuvre* that many of my critics may have read some of my theoretical essays but not my empirical works. "His methodology," she writes, "is to study historical facts, filtering them for their significance through the lens of Marx and Gramsci, and formulate inductive theory from them. Once the theory has been universalized, he goes back and does more research to test how well the theory works, 'unpacking' the theory to see if it 'fits' new sets of facts. In the process of reading these books the reader is confronted with much information to support Robinson's theoretical arguments. The main problem with critics of Robinson's theory is that they have failed to address his supporting case studies." Diane Barahona "The Capitalist Globalization of Latin America," *Critical Sociology* (2011), 37(6): 889–895, quote from p. 892.

In what remains of this introduction I will dispense with several of the more common criticisms of my work and address some methodological and epistemological issues. Those readers wanting to jump right to the topic of crisis with may wish to proceed at this point directly to Chapter 1.

END OF THE NATION-STATE?

Perhaps the most most frequently raised criticism of my work is that I view the nation-state as fading away or as irrelevant to global capitalism. Typical of this charge is the position of British political scientist Paul Cammack, who in one diatribe says that my theory posits "the end of the state," "the end of the national state altogether," "the demise of national states," and that the nation-state is "fated to depart the historic stage at this particular point in time."[8] He advises that I "accept that national states have a changing but continuing role in the global capitalist system" and abandon the idea that capital has become "*extraterrestrial* rather than *spread across numerous territories*" (emphasis in original). I have never used the term "extra-terrestrial." In fact, my argument *is precisely* that as capital has transnationalized it has become spread across numerous national territories through globalized circuits of production. The phrase "supranational space" that I have often evoked refers not to the supersession of space but to supranational space as accumulation across many national territories. Hence, the relation between transnationalizing capital and *particular national territories* needs to be reconceived. More generally, we need to rethink the spatiality of capital. In previous epochs capitalists were largely based in particular national territories and turned to "their own" national states in pursing their class interests. These interests were as much in organizing the conditions for accumulation within their respective national territories and disciplining labor within these territories as in competition with national capitalists from other countries for markets and resources around the world. As capital has gone global the leading groups among national capitalist classes have interpenetrated across national borders through an array of mechanisms and arrangements. This emergent TCC operates across borders in numerous countries and has attempted to convert the whole world into a single unified field for global accumulation.

Another charge frequently raised by my critics is that I believe that transnational capitalists "have no interest in the *local* state in any territory in which they are active."[9] What I have argued is that as transnational capitalists operate in numerous countries they turn to local (national) states of the countries in which they operate. Just as in previous epochs, they require that these local (national) states provide the conditions for accumulation within

---

[8] Paul Cammack, "Forget the Transnational State," *Geopolitics, History and International Relations* (2009), 1(2): 85–98.

[9] See, e.g., Cammack, "Forget the Transnational State."

their respective territories, including disciplining labor. Reciprocally, local managers of the national capitalist state are compelled, just as they were in the past, by the structural power of the capitalist system. The legitimacy of these states and the reproduction of the status of state elites as privileged strata depend on their ability to attract and retain now-globalized accumulation to the territories over which they exercise political authority. Competition among national states to attract transnationally mobile capital becomes functional to global capital and to its ability to exercise a structural power over the direct power of states – that is, over the policymaking process of national states, in the same way that national capital previously exercised what some referred to as the "veto power" of capital over the state. In this way, the continued existence of the nation-state and the interstate system appear to be a central condition for the class power of transnational capital and for the reproduction of global capitalism. Transnational corporations during the early 1990s, for example, were able to utilize the institutions of different nation-states in order to continuously dismantle regulatory structures and other state restrictions on the operation of transnational capital in a process of "mutual deregulation." These are topics that I take up later on; they are central to an understanding of the global crisis, which in part involves the disjuncture between a globalizing economy and a nation-state-based system of political authority.

William Carroll, a sociologist who studies the transnational interlocking of corporate boards of directors, echoes another frequent criticism of my theory. He charges that in my theory locality is transcended and that I do away with place. I advance, he says, an "abstract dualism" between the global and the national/local; I see the global and the national/local as "mutually exclusive."[10] Yet I have harshly criticized global–national/local dualisms and insisted that the global emerges out of contradictions arising *within* the local/national and the system of nation-states, that it is nested in the national. "Far from the 'global' and 'national' as mutually-exclusive fields," I have asserted, "the global becomes incarnated in local social structures and processes."[11] I have shown how the global and the local/national are interpenetrated and mutually constitutive, how trajectories of integration into global capitalism are conditioned by and emerge from particular local, national, and regional histories and by contingency, and how local agents and processes shape the trajectory of global processes in dialectic interplay as much as the global affects the local or the national. Regarding local variation in the global system, I stated in my 2003 study of Central America, among other places:

> The transition from the nation-state to the transnational phase of capitalism involves changes that take place in each individual country and region *reciprocal* [emphasis in original] to, and in dialectical interplay with, changes of systemic importance at the

[10] William Carrol, "Global, Transnational, Regional, National: The Need for Nuance in Theorizing Global Capitalism," *Critical Sociology* (2012), 38(3): 365–373.
[11] Robinson, *A Theory of Global Capitalism*, 110.

level of the global system. A critical focus of a renewed transnational studies should be exploration into the dynamic of change at the local, national, and regional levels in tandem with movement at the level of the global whole. The concern should be about how movement and change in the global whole are manifest in particular countries or regions, but with the focus on the dialectical reciprocity between the two levels.... [G]lobalization is characterized by related, contingent and unequal transformations. To evoke globalization as an explanation for historic changes and contemporary dynamics does not mean that the *particular* [emphasis in original] events or changes identified with the process are happening all over the world, much less in the same way.... It does mean that events or changes are understood as a consequence of globalized power relations and social structures. [I]n the study of development and social change in Central America ... the locus of analysis is the mediation of distinct social forces in the dialectic of transformations taking place at the level of the global system and transformations in particular nations and regions. It is not possible to understand anything about global society without studying a concrete region and its particular circumstances; a part of a totality, in its relation to that totality. All knowledge is historically situated and ... requires a synthesis of nomothetic and ideographic. The general is always (and only) manifested in the specific; the universal in the particular.[12]

The charge that I dismiss the nation-state is usually reactive – a response to my critique of *nation-state centrism* or a *nation-state framework of analysis*. Nation-state centrism refers to both a *mode of analysis* and a *conceptual ontology of world capitalism*. In this ontology, which dominates the disciplines of international relations and political science, world-systems theory, and most Marxist approaches to world dynamics, world capitalism is made up of national classes and national states existing in a flux of competition and cooperation in shifting alliances. These nation-state paradigms see nations as discrete units within a larger system – the world-system or the international system – characterized by external exchanges among these units. The key units of analysis are the nation(al) state and the international or interstate system. Nation-state/ interstate paradigms place a particular template over complex reality. Everything has to fall into place *within* the template – its logic, the picture it portrays. Explanations cannot be *outside* the template. In this sense, nation-state-centric paradigms are blinders. Facts, we know, don't "speak for themselves." These blinders prevent us from interpreting facts in new ways that provide greater explanatory power with regard to novel developments in the late twentieth- and early twenty-first-century world.

The template also organizes how we collect and interpret data. Most data on the global economy, for instance, comes from national data collection agencies and has been disaggregated from a larger totality (the global economy) and then reaggregated into nation-state boxes. This is precisely the mistake made by Hirst and Thompson in their oft-cited study, *Globalization in Question* (they also

[12] William I. Robinson, *Transnational Conflicts: Central America and Global Change* (London: Verso, 2003), 55–56.

make the mistake of defining globalization in terms of trade rather than production relations).[13] As Dicken observes:

> The conventional unit of analysis of the global economy is the country. Virtually all
> the statistical data on production, trade, investment and the like are aggregated into
> national 'boxes.' Indeed, the word 'statistics' originally denoted facts collected
> about the 'state.' However, such a level of statistical aggregation is less and less
> useful in light of the changes occurring in the organization of economic activity. . . .
> [B]ecause national boundaries no longer 'contain' production processes in the way
> they once did, we need to find ways of getting both below and above the national
> scale – to break out of the constraints of the 'national boxes' – in order to under-
> stand what is really going on in the world. One way is to think in terms of
> production circuits and networks. These cut through, and across, all geographic
> scales, including the bounded territory of the state.[14]

The critique of nation-state-centrism does not refer to evocation of the evident
political organization of world capitalism into discrete nation-states that engage
with each other in the interstate system. What is the nature or meaning of these
discrete units and of their engagement, and has the meaning of that engagement
changed? To say that globalization involves the supersession of the nation-state
as the organizing principle of capitalist development does not mean the end of
the nation-state or that the state is now irrelevant. What it does mean is that we
need to return to an understanding of the nation-state as an *historical* rather than
an immanent category, an institution that came about as a result of the particular
form in which capitalism as an historical system developed. The kind of catego-
rical thinking that plagues nation-state paradigms ends up reifying the nation-
state, so that, for instance, the categories of core and periphery, as the opposite
ends of polarized accumulation, must necessarily correspond to territorially
defined nation-states. Nation-state paradigms are unable to grasp the transnational character of many contemporary processes and events such as world
trade, international conflicts, and uneven development – processes that I analyze
in this volume from a global capitalist perspective – because they box transnational phenomena into the nation-state/interstate framework.

These paradigms face the pitfall of *theoreticism*. What I mean by theoreticism
is developing analyses and propositions to fit theoretical assumptions. Since
received nation-state paradigms establish as their frame an interstate system
made up of competing national states, economies, and capitals, twenty-first-
century reality must then be interpreted so that it fits into this frame one way or
another. As I will discuss in Chapter 3, such theoreticism in the study of globalization has forced many, at best, to follow Harvey's schizophrenic dualism of
economic and political logics: capital is economic and globalizes, while states are
political and pursue territorially based political-state logic.[15] Theory needs to

---

[13] Paul Hirst and Graheme Thompson, *Globalization in Question*, 3rd ed. (Cambridge: Polity, 2009).
[14] Peter Dicken, *Global Shift*, 5th ed. (New York: Guilford, 2007), 13.
[15] See David Harvey, *The New Imperialism* 2nd ed. (New York: Oxford University Press, 2005).

illuminate reality, not make reality conform to it. Theories shape researchers' thinking processes, lay the foundations for their analytical frameworks, guide their research propositions and hypotheses. They lead researchers to adopt certain methodologies, to focus on certain data sets and empirical facts and to bypass others, or to interpret these data sets in particular ways. Critical inquiry involves the ability to step out of or beyond established paradigms that may be taken for granted even as the social and historical conditions that gave rise to them undergo transformation.

Nation-state-centric approaches reify institutions by substituting them for social forces and then giving them a *fixed* character in causal explanations, so that, for instance, national states are bestowed with agency in explaining global political and economic dynamics. Institutions such as states, however, are not actors with an independent life of their own; they are the products of social forces that reproduce as well as modify them and that are causal in historical explanations. Social forces operate through multiple institutions in complex and shifting webs of conflict and cooperation. We need to focus not on states as fictitious macro-agents but on historically changing constellations of social forces operating through multiple institutions, including state apparatuses that are themselves in a process of transformation as a consequence of collective agencies.

Deductive reasoning and the logical exposition and critique of theoretical concepts and propositions is only half of the process of scientific theory production. The other half is inductive empirical research. When empirical data and historical events do not correspond to the predictions of theories, we need to question the validity of our theories. For instance, according to the predictive logic of world-system, Marxist, and other critical theories of world political dynamics, we should have witnessed in recent years inter-imperialist rivalry and growing protectionism, yet we have seen neither. Similarly, these theories are at a loss to explain why the United States in the aftermath of its occupation of Iraq opened up that country to investors from all over the world rather than sealing it off under the canopy of occupation to investors from the United States. My main point of contention with these theories and other radical interpretations of the world historic moment is that they take historically contingent and specific categories such as nation-state, national capital, and imperialism and make of them a fixed, immutable structure, in the process reifying them.

To get beyond nation-state-centric ways of thinking we need to keep in mind that a study of globalization is fundamentally *historical analysis*. When we forget that the nation-state is a historically bound phenomenon, we *reify* the nation-state and by extension the interstate system or the world system founded on nation-states. To reify something is to attribute a thinglike status to what should more properly be seen as a complex and changing set of social relations that our practice has created, one that has no ontological status independent of human agency. When we forget that the reality to which these concepts refer is our own sets of social relations that are themselves in an ongoing process of transformation and instead attribute some independent existence to them, then we are reifying. States are sets of institutionalized practices and power relations; "congealments" of class/social relations, to evoke Poulantzas's terminology. The question is, how do we understand the social and class relations embedded in the states? How may these social and class relations become embedded in institutions or networks beyond national states, in institutions and networks that are trans- or supranational? How do social and class groups that operate transnationally or globally pursue their interests through institutions?

As global capitalism now sinks into its most serious crisis in decades, an accurate understanding of the nature of the system has become a burning political matter if we are to respond effectively to the depredations that the crisis has unleashed on broad swaths of humanity. Such an understanding requires a paradigmatic break with nation-state-centric modes of conception, and warrants brief comments here on the matter of methodology and conception or ontology.

THE NEED FOR A HOLISTIC APPROACH AND NOVEL CONCEPTS: STRUCTURAL AND CONJUNCTURAL ANALYSIS

Reality is multidimensional; our study of it must involve many different levels of analysis. The goal of our study should be to simplify complex reality in a way that helps explain patterns and outcomes, so long as we take into account the problems of inference that may result from our simplifications. As Chase-Dunn puts it, "there is no point in making a map which is as complicated as the territory."[16] Global capitalism, like social reality in general, is always a complex synthesis of multiple determinations and of historical conjunctures. By "conjunctures" I mean historical moments, all of which are unique, that bring together particular and contingent circumstances, including human agency and consciousness, in an infinite variety of mixtures with underlying structural processes. The world capitalist system is *structure in motion*, constantly evolving in an open-ended way that involves as much the pulse of cycles, patterns, and regularities as contingency and agency. Structure and agency is not an antagonistic binary but a unity that must be brought together in our methodologies and ontologies of inquiry into the world through historical and conjunctural analysis. The conjunctural specificity of much of what goes on in the world does not negate but is informed by the deeper structures that stamp and circumscribe conjunctures. We want to distinguish between structural and conjunctural dimensions in a given situation *within* the internal unity of that situation. The structural is that which cannot be altered by a given agent or set of agents during a given time period – ceteris paribus – while the conjunctural is that which can be altered by a given agent or set of agents during that period.[17]

[16] Christopher Chase-Dunn, *Global Formation: Structures of the World-Economy* (Lanham, MD: Rowman and Littlefield, 1998), 215.

[17] On this point, see the discussion by Jessop in *The Capitalist State* (Oxford: Martin Robertson, 1982), 253.

Social outcomes (the concrete) are the complex synthesis of multiple determinations, and the "laws" of capitalism are abstract principles subject to
complex mediations. This is to say, as I have insisted throughout my work,
the general is manifest only in the particular, or the real historical, so that
causal tendencies (the spread of capitalist relations, dynamics of accumulation,
etc.) located beneath surface appearance are manifested through complex
mediations and contingencies that are not predetermined and are driven by
agency interacting with structure. There *is* reciprocal movement between the
general and the particular – for example, we *can* find similar transformations
wrought by globalized capitalism in various countries and regions, such as the
rise of transnationally oriented fractions of the elite, the transnationalization of
the state, novel economic activities tied to the global economy, social polarization, and so on. But such movement does not obey laws as much as historical
conjunctures through which laws are manifested in limitless possible and
unpredictable ways. For instance, striving to maximize profit is a law of
accumulation, but what this striving actually means in a particular historical
context can take on an infinite number of forms. In our analysis of such
historical situations we want to avoid the conflation of conjunctural and
structural elements.

Contingency, agency, and conjunctures involving the coming together in
unique ways in each historical circumstance of multiple causal chains make
historical outcomes open-ended and not as predictable as positivists assume.
However, at the level of deep structure there is an underlying determination,
that is, the process of social production and reproduction that is our "species
being" and the material foundation of our existence. More generally, historical
materialism *as method* attempts to understand the dialectical relationship
between the particularities of our existence (as a species, as a collective inhabiting the planet) and the underlying structural conditions and processes that
link these to the general and the universal. We want to understand how
concrete particulars are constituted by more general and abstract social forces.
The global economy – that is, globalized processes of social production and
reproduction – does exercise an underlying structural determination at this
level of deep structure. To study deep structure means to study capitalism, its
underlying laws and dynamics, which at the abstract level of analysis have not
changed in this epoch of globalization. The task of good macro–social science
is to uncover the kaleidoscope of articulations between deep structure, structure, and conjuncture as distinct levels of analysis that are causal to open-ended
social change.

It is not an easy task to identify the dialectic of structure and agency. It is
important to avoid treating political and ideological processes as the outcome of
relations among subjects endowed with consciousness and free will to the neglect
of the social (structural) relations that drive these political and ideological
practices and that constitute subjects engaged in them. To focus only on the
conjunctural is to mistake surface appearance for essence; to focus only on the

structural is reductionism.[18] My own approach has emphasized multiple determinations and distinct levels of analysis – in particular, the articulation of
structural and conjunctural (that is behavioral/agency) levels via a mediating
structural-conjunctural level of analysis that mediates "forward" to agency and
"backward" to structure.[19] The agency of individuals and groups is shaped and
enabled by social structures. In the present study, as elsewhere, I strive to center
the analysis at the structural-conjunctural level and to move "backward" and
"forward" from that center.

This must be an historical undertaking, in the sense not that there are no
underlying structural regularities but that they are always and only manifest in
real historical circumstances in which contingency and agency come into play.
World capitalism is a singular process. A holistic approach starts with the global
system and sees subparts or smaller units, such as the nation-state, as part of the
larger whole. We also need to distinguish between the existence of a unit (in an
historical and empirical sense as well as in an analytical sense) and the varied
ways which that unit fits into the larger whole over time. As I have pointed out
previously, a biological analogy is useful to illustrate how a particular attribute
or feature of a system may continue to exist as it changes its functions, for
example, nation-states and the interstate system. The task is to analyze not
only the social and class forces and agencies that operate through these subunits,
without reifying the state, but also changes in the larger system at the level of
world capitalism or the global whole that frame (and limit) the possible constellations of social and class forces.

It is during moments not of equilibrium but of crisis that the intervention of
agency can be most effective in bringing about structural change. Crises are key
conjunctures when significant structural – and in rare historic moments, systemic – change becomes possible, that is, when all things are *not* equal as the
fault lines of structure are revealed. Exploration of the global crisis involves
conjunctural analysis nested in an historical approach and informed by structural analysis. Our undertaking requires the new conceptual tools of the TCC,
the TNS, and global (as distinct from world) capitalism in order to grasp the
evolution of capitalism in recent years, comprehend the twenty-first-century

---

[18] We cannot conflate the determinacy of the real world with determinacy as a property of a given
theoretical system, as Jessop observes, lest we explain the former in terms of the latter. This error
forms the basis, in Jessop's view, for three methodological miscarriages: *reductionism*, or invoking
one axis of theoretical determination to explain everything about the state and politics; *empiri-
cism*, or mistaking a synchronic description or historiographic account of an actual event for an
explanation of that event; and *subsumption*, or subsuming a particular description or history of
this kind under a general principle of explanation as one of its many instantiations (see Jessop's
excellent discussion in *The Capitalist State*, 211–220).

[19] See my discussion on methodology in the introduction to William I. Robinson, *Promoting
Polyarchy: Globalization, U.S. Intervention, and Hegemony* (Cambridge: Cambridge University
Press, 1996).

global system and the transnational processes at work, and intervene as effectively as possible to avert catastrophe.

Finally, one caveat: this is not intended to be an exhaustive study of the global crisis. That would involve much more than can be accomplished in this brief work; indeed, it would require many volumes and many years. I am forced as a result into inevitable simplifications. There is as well much literature that I am unable to engage with. My hope is to make a modest contribution to our understanding of, and to advance a very broad collective research agenda on, the contemporary crisis.

I

Global Capital and Global Labor

> [Foxconn] has a workforce of over one million worldwide and as human beings are also animals, to manage one million animals gives me a headache.
>
> Terry Gou, chairman of Foxconn, talking to Chin Shih-Chien, director of the Taipei Zoo, regarding how animals should be managed, and prior to announcing plans to replace one million workers with robots[1]

> The solution to the sanitation crisis – at least as conceived by certain economics professors sitting in comfortable armchairs in Chicago and Boston – has been to make urban defecation a global business. Indeed, one of the great achievements of Washington-sponsored neoliberalism has been to turn public toilets into cash points for paying off foreign debts – pay toilets are a growth industry throughout the Third World slums.
>
> Mike Davis, in *Planet of Slums*[2]

Capitalism goes through regular crises about once a decade, what we call *cyclical crises*. But the crisis that exploded in 2008 with the global financial collapse and the Great Recession points to a deeper *structural crisis*, such as we faced in the 1970s, and before that in the 1930s, meaning that the system can no longer continue to function in the way that it is structured. These types of crises are therefore *restructuring crises*. They must result in a restructuring of the system if there is to be any resolution to the crisis. Yet in such a conjuncture the structural crisis has the potential to become *systemic*, depending on how social agents respond to the crisis and on the unpredictable element of contingency that always plays some role in historical outcomes. A systemic crisis is one in which only a change in the system itself will resolve the crisis.

---

[1] Henry Bloget, "CEO of Apple Partner Foxconn: Managing One Million Animals Gives Me a Headache," *Business Insider*, January 19, 2012, http://www.businessinsider.com/foxconn-animals-2012–1#ixzz2WGi7e4Hw.

[2] Mike Davis, *Planet of Slums* (London: Verso, 2007), 141.

The twenty-first-century global crisis shares a number of aspects with earlier structural crises of the world economy of the 1970s and the 1930s, but there are also several features unique to the current situation:

1. The system is fast reaching the ecological limits of its reproduction. We may have already reached a point of no return – what environmental scientists refer to as a "tipping point" beyond which the planet becomes destabilized. The ecological holocaust under way cannot be underestimated – peak oil, climate change, the extinction of species, the collapse of centralized agricultural systems in several regions of the world, and so on.[3]

2. The magnitude of the means of violence and social control is unprecedented, as is the concentration of the means of global communication and symbolic production and circulation in the hands of a very few powerful groups. Computerized wars, drones, bunker-buster bombs, Star Wars defense systems, and so forth, have changed the face of warfare. Warfare has become normalized and sanitized for those not directly at the receiving end of armed aggression. At the same time we have arrived at the panoptical surveillance society and the age of thought control by those who manage global flows of communication, images, and symbolic production.

3. Capitalism is reaching apparent limits to its *extensive* expansion. There are no longer any new territories of significance that can be integrated into world capitalism, de-ruralization is now well advanced, and the commodification of the countryside and of pre- and noncapitalist spaces has intensified; that is, they are being, converted in hothouse fashion into spaces of capital, so that *intensive* expansion is reaching depths never before seen. Capitalism must continually expand or collapse. How or where will it now expand?

4. There is the rise of a vast surplus population inhabiting a "planet of slums,"[4] alienated from the productive economy, thrown onto the margins, and subject to sophisticated systems of social control and to destruction – to a mortal cycle of dispossession–exploitation–exclusion.

5. There is a disjuncture between a globalizing economy and a nation-state-based system of political authority. The incipient transnational

---

[3] See, inter alia, Christian Parenti, *Tropic of Cancer: Climate Change and the New Geography of Violence* (New York: Nation Books: 2012); Gwynne Dyer, *Climate Wars: The Fight for Survival as the World Overheats* (Oxford: Oneworld, 2010); John Bellamy Foster, Brett Clark, and Richard York, *The Ecological Rift: Capitalism's War on Earth* (New York: Monthly Review Press, 2011); Bill McKibben, "Global Warming's Terrifying New Math," *Rolling Stone*, August 2, 2012, http://www.rollingstone.com/politics/news/global-warmings-terrifying-new-math-20120719?print=true.

[4] The phrase is from Mike Davis's excellent study, *Planet of Slums*.

state (TNS) apparatuses have not been able to play the role of what social scientists refer to as a "hegemon," or a leading nation-state that has enough power and authority to organize and stabilize the system.

There are the many outward manifestations of the global crisis: raging wars, collapsing states, state and nonstate "terrorism" (such an ill-defined and ideologically charged term that, stripped of particular and competing political contents, is nearly useless as a social scientific concept), pandemics of crime and interpersonal violence, insecurity, social decay, and the degeneration of ecosystems everywhere. There are the alienation and mass pathologies brought on by the cultural banalities and extreme individualism of global capitalism – such as the fact that some thirty million people in the United States are prescribed antidepressants (the sheer number of people on these drugs should be alarming, as should the fact that the medical-pharmaceutical complex medicalizes a social pathology). There is the ever-throbbing crisis of hunger and poverty for billions of people, and so on.

The immediate causes of these manifestations can be analyzed. In 2007 and 2008 food prices spiked around the world, for instance, triggering "food riots" in dozens of countries and pushing the number of people who suffered from chronic hunger beyond the one billion mark. The spike in prices was not due to any significant drop in world food production or to shortages in food stocks worldwide. Rather, financial investors moving hundreds of billions of dollars turned to frenzied speculation in global food and energy markets, especially futures markets, thereby encouraging hoarding and other practices that caused the price of food to climb beyond the reach of many people. In turn we can analyze the causes of escalating financial speculation in the global economy, as I will do in Chapter 4, and we can study the structure of the global food system – the increasing iron grip of transnational corporate control over the system, the displacement from the land of hundreds of millions of farmers, and so on, all processes associated with capitalist globalization.

Yet we must also examine the structural causes and the systemic origins of these dimensions of crisis that in their outward manifestations afflict humanity on a daily basis and at so many lived levels. We must not forget that beneath the manifest violence that is so visible around the world and that draws the attention of the global media is the less visible structural violence of the system in which we live, what philosopher Slavoj Žižek calls "objective" violence – "objective violence is precisely the violence inherent to this 'normal' state of things" and is typically invisible to those who do not suffer it.[5] It is structural violence when 85 percent of the world's wealth is monopolized by just 10 percent of the world's people while the bottom half of adults worldwide owns barely 1 percent of the total (actually, the top 2 percent within the top 10 percent own half the planet's

[5] Slavoj Žižek, *Violence: Six Sideways Reflections* (London: Profile Books, 2008), 8.

wealth),[6] when food stocks are thrown into the oceans even as millions go hungry, when billions of dollars are spent on plastic surgery and cosmetics even as billions of people go untreated for easily curable diseases, and when more money is spent on prison-industrial complexes than on educational facilities.

I will take up a more rigorous analysis of the global crisis and its varied dimensions in subsequent chapters. In this chapter I focus on global capital and global labor.

GLOBAL CAPITAL

> I live the worldsourced life. As CEO of Lenovo, I am an American CEO based in Singapore. Our chairman, who is Chinese, works from North Carolina. Other top executives are based around the globe. A meeting of my company's senior managers looks like the United Nations General Assembly. My company is like some of the world's most popular consumer products. It may say 'Made in China' on the outside, but the key components are designed and manufactured by innovative people and companies spread across six continents. The products of companies that practice worldsourcing may be labeled 'Made in Switzerland' or 'Made in the USA' or 'Made in China,' but in the new world in which we all now live, they should more truthfully be labeled 'Made Globally.' In today's world, assessing companies by their nation of origin misses the point.
> – William J. Amelio, president and CEO of Lenovo,
> a leading global PC firm[7]

The restructuring of the global economy and the anatomy of the emergent global production and financial system are well-researched topics.[8] The *globalization of production* has involved the fragmentation and decentralization of complex production processes, the worldwide dispersal of the different segments and phases in these processes, and their *functional integration* into vast chains of production and distribution that span the globe. There has been a shift from international market integration to global productive integration. Global capitalism is not reducible to a collection of discrete national economies, national capitals, and national circuits of accumulation connected through an international market. Such national economies have been dismantled and then reconstituted as component elements of this new globally integrated production and financial system, a world economic structure qualitatively distinct from that of previous epochs, when each country had a distinct national economy linked to others through trade and financial flows.

The global decentralization of production and services has been going on for several decades and is one of the key empirical processes that led researchers to

---

[6] David Rothkopf, *Superclass: The Global Power Elite and the World They Are Making* (New York: Farrar, Straus and Giroux, 2008), 37.

[7] William J. Amelio, "Worldsource or Perish," *Forbes*, August 17, 2007, http://www.forbes.com/2007/08/16/lenovo-world-sourcing-ooped-ex.

[8] The best study on the anatomy of the global economy continues to be the geographer Peter Dicken's *Global Shift*, 5th ed. (New York: Guilford, 2007).

develop the concept of globalization. The process continued to accelerate in the first decade of the twenty-first century and took new turns that underscored the open-ended nature of world economic structuring and the development of new forms in the face of changing conditions. If General Electric (GE) was already a global corporation by the 1970s in terms of its globalized direct and subcontracting production networks and its service and financial operations, for instance, the company seemed to undergo a new burst of transnationalization in the face of the imperative of integrating production and market circuits in new ways. In 2004, GE had 165,000 employees in the United States and 142.000 elsewhere. By the end of 2008 the preponderance had been reversed, with 152,000 in the United States and 171,000 elsewhere.[9] The multibillion-dollar bailout provided to the U.S.-based branch of General Motors (GM) by the U.S. government in the wake of the 2008 collapse led to media and academic portrayals of the company in nation-state-centric terms as a sick corporate giant symbolizing the decline of the United States as the dominant economic power. Yet GM had divisions in dozens of countries around the world and was healthy and vibrant in many of these divisions, including the one in China, where its car sales, produced in a partnership with Chinese firms, and investment in China were booming. This accelerated transnationalization of both production and marketing involved not only giant corporations but also small manufacturing firms. The network structure of the global economy and the globalized nature of production and service chains mean that even small firms are able to globalize and, moreover, *need* to do so in order to remain competitive. Global corporations organizing production of globally marketed goods and services are able to integrate production and marketing circuits in new ways as the whole world comes to resemble a flexible and open field for organizing accumulation.

Capitalist globalization has been driven, at the strictly technical level, by new information technologies and organizational innovations in capitalist production that have modified how value is created, circulated, and appropriated around the world. Values now cross borders seamlessly as they move swiftly – often instantaneously – through new global financial circuits. The development of computer and information technologies (CIT) in the latter decades of the twentieth century represented a new "Scientific and Technological Revolution" that triggered explosive growth in productivity and productive capacities (as illustration, the entire industrial revolution enhanced productivity by a factor of about a hundred, whereas the CIT revolution enhanced it by a factor of more than a million in just the first few years of its introduction),[10] a disproportionate increase in fixed capital, and also the means for capital to go global – to

---

[9] Don Lee, "Era of Global Consumer May Be Dawning," *Los Angeles Times*, October 4, 2009: A1, A24.

[10] This is reported by A. Sivanandan, *Communities of Resistance: Writings on Black Struggles for Socialism* (London: Verso, 1990), 27, who in turn is making reference to Robin Murray writing in the U.K. journal *New Times* (no reference given).

coordinate and synchronize a globalized system of production, finances, and services, in distinction to a globalized market for goods and services that dates back centuries. CIT also revolutionized warfare and the modalities of state-organized militarized accumulation, including the military application of vast new technologies and the further fusion of private accumulation and state militarization.

In my earlier research on globalized production and the rise of a transnational capitalist class (TCC) I drew on classical power structure and Marxist methods of class analysis to identify a number of mechanisms involved in the increasing transnational interpenetration of national capitals. Others social scientists have continued to research these mechanisms, and there is now a considerable and rapidly growing body of empirical evidence that in the latter part of the twentieth century the giant corporate conglomerates that drive the global economy ceased to be corporations of a particular country and increasingly came to represent transnational capital.[11] Some of the mechanisms of TCC formation are: the

---

[11] For summaries and assessments of this evidence, see, inter alia, Robinson, *A Theory of Global Capitalism*; Leslie Sklair, *The Transnational Capitalist Class* (Oxford: Blackwell, 2001) and *Globalization: Capitalism and Its Alternatives* (New York: Oxford University Press, 2002); Jeffrey Kentor, "The Growth of Transnational Corporate Networks, 1962 to 1998," *Journal of World-Systems Research* (2005), 11(2): 262–286; Kentor and Yong Suk Jang, "Yes, There Is a (Growing) Transnational Business Community," *International Sociology* (2004), 19(3): 355–368; United Nations Conference on Trade and Development (UNCTAD), *World Investment Report* (Geneva: United Nations, various years); Peter Dicken, *Global Shift*, 5th ed. (New York: Guilford, 2007); William Carroll and Colin Caron, "The Network of Global Corporations and Elite Policy Groups: A Structure for Transnational Capitalist Class Formation?," *Global Networks* (2003), 3(1): 29–57; Caroll and Meindert Fennema, "Is There a Transnational Business Community?," *International Sociology* (2002), 17(3): 393–419; William K. Carroll, *The Making of a Transnational Capitalist Class: Corporate Power in the 21ˢᵗ Century* (London: Zed, 2010); Clifford L. Staples, "Cross-Border Acquisitions and Board Globalization in the World's Largest TNCs, 1995–2005," *The Sociological Quarterly* (2008), 49: 31–51; Cliff Staples, "Board Interlocks and the Study of the Transnational Capitalist Class," *Journal of World-Systems Research* (2006), 12(2): 309–319; Staples, "The Business Roundtable and the Transnational Capitalist Class," in Georgina Murray and John Scott, eds., *Financial Elites and Transnational Business: Who Rules the World?* (Camberley, UK, and Northhampton, MA: Edward Elgar Publishing Ltd, 2012). See also other entries in *Financial Elites and Transnational Business*. A number of these studies place major emphasis on interlocking corporate boards of directors as the almost exclusive empirical indicator of a TCC. This is especially so for Carroll, *The Making of a Transnational Capitalist Class*. In reviewing the growth of transnational corporate board interlocks, Carroll finds that "transnational interlocking became less the preserve of a few internationally well-connected companies, and more a general practice in which nearly half of the world's largest firms participate" (98). While these growing interlocks are important, I have criticized this position in both substantive and methodological terms in a symposium on my work published in *Critical Sociology* (2012), 38(3). It is interesting to note that there has in recent years been acceleration in U.S. elite participation in transnationally interlocking boards of directors, including, importantly, in the financial sector. Freeland writes: "America's business elite is something of a latecomer to this transational community [but] the number of foreign and foreign-born CEOs, while still relatively small, is rising. The shift is particularly evident on Wall Street; in 2006, each of America's eight biggest banks was run by a

spread of TNC affiliates; the phenomenal increase in cross-border mergers and acquisitions; the increasing transnational interlocking of boards of directors; increasingly cross- and mutual investment among companies from two or more countries and transnational ownership of capital shares; the spread of cross-border strategic alliances of all sorts; vast global outsourcing and subcontracting networks; and the increasing salience of transnational peak business associations. These patterns of capital transnationalization simply did not exist in earlier decades and centuries. The failure to distinguish between international trade (exchange) relations and globalized production and financial relations leads many commentators, such as Hirst and Thompson, to claim there is little new in the current epoch and that there was a "first" period of globalization in the late nineteenth and early twentieth centuries, when international trade relations expanded rapidly.[12]

There are other, less researched mechanisms that spur on TCC formation, such as the existence of stock exchanges in most countries of the world linked to the global financial system. The spread of these stock markets from the principal centers of the world economy to most capital cities around the world, combined with twenty-four-hour trading, facilitates ever-greater global trading and hence transnational ownership of shares. There are now stock exchanges in some 120 countries, from Afghanistan and Vietnam to Bangalore in India, from Botswana and Nigeria to the capitals of all five Central American republics. While many of them are limited in their offerings, these exchanges are integrated with one another either directly or indirectly. An Argentine can channel investment via the Buenos Aires stock exchange into companies from around the world, while investors from around the world can channel their investments into Argentina via the Buenos Aires stock exchange.

Beyond stock exchanges, investors anywhere in the world need no more than internet access to invest their money through globalized financial circuits into mutual and hedge funds, bonds markets, currency swaps, and so on. The global integration of national financial systems and new forms of money capital, including secondary derivative markets, as I will discuss later, have also made it easier for capital ownership to transnationalize. In addition to its centrality in facilitating the transnational integration of capitals, the new globally integrated financial system allows for incredibly increased intersectoral mobility of capital and hence plays a major role in blurring the boundaries between industrial, commercial, and money capital. The network of stock exchanges, the computerized nature of global trading, the integration of national financial systems into a single global system, and so on, allow the almost frictionless movement of

native-born CEO; today, five of those banks remain, and two of the survivors – Citigroup and Morgan Stanley – are led by men who were born abroad." Chrystia Freeland, "The Rise of the New Global Elite," *The Atlantic*, January/Febraury 2011: 9, http://www.theatlantic.com/magazine/archive/2011/01/the-rise-of-the-new-global-elite/8343/.

[12] Paul Hirst and Graheme Thompson, *Globalization in Question*, 3rd ed. (Cambridge: Polity, 2009).

capital in its money form through the arteries of the global economy and society. One needs to conceptualize creatively the extent to which networks, patterns, and mechanisms of capital formation link capitals in manifold ways across the planet – that is, to think beyond the most conventional ones, such as interlocking boards of directors or the country of domicile of a particular company. For instance, the private investment firm Blackstone Group, one of the largest financial organizations in the world, is a clearinghouse that integrates capitalist groups and often state elites from every continent. By 2008 Chinese state companies had invested over $3 billion in Blackstone.[13] In turn, Blackstone had in that year investments in over 100 TNCs around the world, as well as numerous partnerships with Fortune 500 companies, thus enabling Chinese elites to acquire a stake in this web of global corporate capital and, more generally, in the success of global capitalism.

There has been an historically unprecedented concentration of wealth and power in a few thousand global corporations, financial institutions, and investment funds. The extent of the *concentration* and *centralization* of capital in the hands of the TCC and the TNCs it controls is truly astounding. The concentration of capital is understood as the expansion of capital as it is reinvested. The centralization of capital is understood as the amassing of many capitals into fewer capitals and as ever-greater control by fewer capitals. Unlike earlier epochs in the history of world capitalism, this concentration and centralization involves the amassing and growing power not of national but of *transnational* capitalist groups. A 2011 analysis of the share ownerships of 43,000 transnational corporations undertaken by three systems theorists at the Swiss Federal Institute of Technology identified a core of 1,318 TNCs with interlocking ownerships. Each of these core TNCs had ties to two or more other companies, and on average they were connected to twenty. Although they represented only 20 percent of global operating revenues, these 1,318 TNCs appeared to own collectively through their shares the majority of the world's largest blue chip and manufacturing firms, representing a further 60 percent of global revenues – for a total of 80 percent of the world's revenue.[14]

"When the team further untangled the web of ownership, it found much of it tracked back to a 'super-entity' of 147 even more tightly knit companies – all of their ownership was held by other members of the super-entity – that controlled 40 percent of the total wealth in the network," observed one analysis of the study.[15] In effect, less than one percent of the companies were able to control 40 percent of the entire network. Revealingly, the top fifty were mostly major global

---

[13] Rothkopf, *Superclass*, 46–47.
[14] Stefania Vitali, James B. Glattfelder, and Stefano Battiston, "The Network of Global Corporate Control," *PLOS ONE* (2011), 1–36, http://www.scribd.com/doc/70706980/The-Network-of-Global-Corporate-Control-by-Stefania-Vitali-James-B-Glattfelder-and-Stefano-Battiston-2011.
[15] Andy Cohglan and Debora MacKenzie, "Revealed – the Capitalist Network that Runs the World," *New Scientist*, October, 24, 2011: 1, http://www.newscientist.com/article/mg21228354.500-revealed–the-capitalist-network-that-runs-the-world.html.

financial institutions – among them the Goldman Sachs Group, JP Morgan Chase, and Barclays Bank – and global financial institutions and insurance companies dominated the top fifty. The study shows the incredible concentration and centralization of global capital as well as the inextricable interpenetration of capitals worldwide in vast connected clusters. As Coghlan and MacKenzie observe in their analysis, previous studies that found the leading TNCs to own or control major chunks of the global economy included only a limited number of corporations and omitted indirect ownerships.[16] The study also shows transnational financial capital to be the dominant (hegemonic) fraction of capital on a world scale. Third, although the study did not discuss the political implications of these findings, it should be clear that such an extraordinary concentration of economic power in pursuit of common global corporate interests exerts an enormous structural power over states and political processes, notwithstanding competition among transnational corporate clusters.[17]

The TCC and Transnational Competition

There are those who remain obstinately resistant to the TCC thesis. This has been particularly so for scholars coming from a traditional or orthodox Marxist perspective. While I will discuss this perspective in more detail in Chapter 3, what is important here is that Marx and the leading Marxist theorists who followed him saw the capitalist (and working) classes as developing within the nation-state (as *national* capitalist classes) and in rivalry with other national capitalist classes. This may have been so in the nineteenth and much of the twentieth century. But these latter-day critics of the TCC thesis tend to take Marx's analysis of world capitalism in the nineteenth century, or Lenin's analysis in the early twentieth century, less as historical moments in the ongoing and open-ended evolution of this system than as fixed features of the system.

The political scientist Ellen M. Wood is typical of this resistance among orthodox Marxists to the idea of transnational capital. She insists that "the national organization of capitalist economies has remained stubbornly

---

[16] Ibid.

[17] There is in this regard an inverse movement to the astonishing concentration than involves the decentralization of formal political/administrative power to local, state, provincial, and municipal governments in many countries around the world. This decentralization is often carried out in the name of greater democracy or local self-governance. Yet it serves to facilitate the control of capital over even the smallest localities where production and consumption take place and to absolve the centralized national-state of responsibility for collective rights and social reproduction. It allows TNCs to bypass central national states and intensifies competition among local communities. The increasing dictatorship of transnational capital involves as well a tremendous increase in control over the means of intellectual production, the mass media, the educational system, and the culture industries, a much more profound and complete penetration of capital and its logic into the spheres of culture and community, indeed, into the life world itself.

persistent,"[18] although she – like most such critics of the TCC thesis – offers no evidence to back up her claim or to refute the argument of capital transnationalization. One need only glean daily headlines from the world media to discover endless reams of anecdotal evidence to complement the accumulation of systematic data on transnationalization. IBM's chair and CEO, Samuel Palmisano, affirms in a June 2006 article in the *Financial Times* of London, for instance, that use of the very phrase "multinational corporation" suggests "how antiquated our thinking about it is." He continues:

> The emerging business model of the 21st century is not, in fact 'multinational.' This new kind of organization – at IBM we call it 'the globally integrated enterprise' – is very different in its structure and operations. ... In the multinational model, companies built local production capacity within key markets, while performing other tasks on a global basis. ... American multinationals such as General Motors, Ford and IBM built plants and established local workforce policies in Europe and Asia, but kept research and development and product design principally in the 'home country.'

The spread of multinationals in this way constituted internationalization, in contrast to more recent transnationalization:

> The globally integrated enterprise, in contrast, fashions its strategy, management and operations to integrate production – and deliver value to clients – worldwide. That has been made possible by shared technologies and shared business standards, built on top of a global information technology and communications infrastructure. ... Today, innovation is inherently global.[19]

In turn, IBM is one of the largest investors in India, which has become a major platform for transnational service provision to the global economy. If the decentralization and dispersal around the world of manufacturing processes represented the leading edge of an earlier wave of globalization, the current wave involves the decentralization and global dispersal of services. Data processing, insurance claims, phone operators, call centers, software production, marketing, journalism and publishing, health and telemedicine, medical and legal transcriptions, advertising, banking – these and many other services are now undertaken through complex webs of outsourcing, subcontracting, and transnational alliances among firms. IBM went from 9,000 employees in India in 2004 to 43,000 (out of 329,000 worldwide) in 2006, and this does not include thousands of workers in local firms that have been subcontracted by IBM or by Indian IBM partner firms. Some of IBM's growth in India has come from mergers between IBM and companies previously launched by Indian investors as outsourcing firms, such as Dagsh eSErvices of New Delhi, which went from 6,000 to 20,000 back-office employees after its merger with IBM.[20] In this way,

---

[18] Ellen Meiksins Wood, *Empire of Capital* (London: Verso, 2003), 23.
[19] Samuel Palmisano, "Multinationals Have Been Superseded," *Financial Times*, June 12, 2006: 19.
[20] Saritha, Saritha Rai, "I.B.M. India," *New York Times*, June 5, 2006: A1.

and in countless other examples across the globe, national capitalist groups are swept up into global circuits of accumulation and into TCC formation.

As the hegemonic fraction of capital on a world scale, transnational capital increasingly integrates local circuits into its own; it imposes the general direction and character on production worldwide and conditions the social, political, and cultural character of capitalist society worldwide. The increasing levels of material/social integration brought about by globalization tend to undermine the bases for more national, local, or autonomous political, social, and cultural-ideological processes. A rich sociology of globalization has shown the mutually constitutive complex of material and cultural global processes. Culture may be more deeply embedded or more resilient than socioeconomic structures, although the argument can be made that cultural practices are more functional to these structures and the changes they undergo than cultural theorists would concede. Nonetheless, it is difficult to see how culture, however defined, has acted to impede the socioeconomic transformations associated with global capitalism. Vijay Prashad, an Indian historian and professor of international studies, argues contra global capitalism theory that "the nation-state or regional containers [are] fundamentally important as zones of economic and political activity."[21] This may well be true, yet these zones have for over five centuries been articulated to a larger world capitalist system. The nature of these articulations has continuously evolved over the centuries in conjunction with the development of world capitalism, and they are now experiencing transformation associated with global capitalism. This involves transformations in the economic and social structures and class relations of particular nation-states and regions. In what proportion or in what magnitude transnational capital and its social agents predominate around the world, and to what extent local capitalist groups are integrated into global circuits, will depend, in part, on the particular historical and contemporary circumstances of distinct countries and regions.

Critics such as the Marxist economist William Tabb caricature the idea of a TCC. According to Tabb, I and other theorists from the global capitalist perspective see the TCC as a "single, unified class." Our conception of the TCC, according to Tabb, is that it operates around the world and has "global perspectives and interconnections."[22] In this way, Tabb can claim that capitalist competition around the world proves that it is not a single unified class. He can claim that since global perspectives and interconnections have existed for centuries, then so too has a TCC. But these are straw men. I and other TCC theorists such as the sociologist Leslie Sklair do not define the TCC by its global perspective and interconnections. Tabb and other such critics fail to appreciate the distinction between participation by capitalists in the world market, which dates back hundreds of years, and participation in a globalized production and

[21] Vijay Prashad, "World on a Slope," *Critical Sociology* (2012), 38(3): 402.
[22] William K. Tabb, "Globalization Today: At the Borders of Class and State Theory," *Science and Society*, 73(1): 34–53 (the quote is from p. 36).

financial system, which is a phenomenon of recent decades. Tabb suggests that the shareholders of the Dutch East India Company were members of the TCC.[23] That company may have operated around the world, but its capitalists were tied to the Dutch state/nation-state and competed with merchant capitalists tied to rival nation-states. At the core of this type of criticism is the failure to distinguish between exchange and production relations in the world capitalist system.

Capitalist globalization creates new forms of transnational class alliances across borders and new forms of class cleavages, both globally and within countries, regions, cities, and local communities, in ways quite distinct from the national class structures and international class conflicts and alliances of earlier epochs in world capitalism. Another group of critics of global capitalism theory are international relations scholars who have traditionally analyzed world social and class relations in terms of how they are organized and mediated by nation-states and the interstate system, which are master concepts for the field of international relations. In this vein, the British international relations scholar Alexander Anievas, among others, misreads my argument by associating it with Karl Kautsky's earlier "ultra-imperialism" or "superimperialism" thesis.[24] Kautsy was a German Marxist who in his 1914 essay *Ultra-Imperialism*[25] assumed that as the capitalist system developed, capital would remain *national* in its essence. He suggested that these *national* capitals would eventually come to *collude internationally* instead of competing, and he termed this "ultra-imperialism." In fact, however, my global capitalism approach shares little or nothing with Kautsky's thesis. In my approach conflict among capitals is endemic to the system, yet in the age of globalization that competition takes on new forms not necessarily expressed as national rivalry. Competition dictates that firms must establish global as opposed to national or regional markets. The global economy is both competitive and integrated. There is conflict between national and transnational fractions of capital as well as fierce rivalry and competition among transnational conglomerations that turn to numerous institutional channels, including multiple national states, to pursue their interests. Nor does the TCC thesis suggest there are no longer national and regional capitals, or that the TCC is internally unified, free of conflict, and consistently acts as a coherent political actor.

The TCC has established itself as a class group without a national identity and in competition with nationally based capitals. The TCC does not identify with particular nation-states, but this does not prevent local fractions from utilizing

---

[23] Ibid.

[24] Alexander Anievas, "Theories of a Global State: A Critique," *Historical Materialism* (2008), 16: 190–206.

[25] Karl Kautsky's original essay was published in the September 1914 edition of *Die Neue Zeit*, reprinted on line, http://www.marxists.org/archive/kautsky/1914/09/ultra-imp.htm. As should be clear from the discussion, my position is also quite distinct from hypotheses of a new "alliance capitalism" put forth, e.g., by John H. Dunning, *Alliance Capitalism and Global Business* (New York: Routledge, 1997).

national state apparatuses to advance their agendas, nor does it prevent particular national and regional contingents of the TCC from drawing on particular ethnic identities and cultural practices to achieve their interests. Nonetheless, the national bases of TCC groups are not autonomous or in competition with one another but interconnected and interpenetrated. Transnational capital is heterogeneous and internally divided and has no unambiguous boundaries demarcating it as a specific fraction other than its distinction in an ideal-type construct from particular national capitals, insofar as the former is grounded in global circuits of accumulation and the latter in national ones. Alongside conflict between national and transnational fractions of capital is the rivalry among transnational conglomerations that turn to numerous institutional channels, including multiple national states, to pursue their interests. For instance, IBM and its local Indian shareholders and partners compete for service outsourcing contracts, explains Rai, with Cognizant Technology Solutions, a company based in Teaneck, New Jersey, and one of IBM's chief rivals in the Indian subcontinent. The rivalry between IBM and Cognizant cannot be considered competition between national capitals of distinct countries, and both groups turn to the U.S. and the Indian state to seek advantage over competitors.

Tabb observes that in 1987 the European Union (EU) adopted a GMS standard for cell phones that spread to the rest of the world and forced "American companies" into a competitive disadvantage. "Are these conflicts within a transnational capitalist class or competitive maneuvering of competing [national/regional] blocs of capital," asks Tabb, in defense of the latter interpretation.[26] Tabb *starts* with the *assumption* that capitals are nationally organized – although he offers no evidence for this – a template though which competition beyond borders *must* then be interpreted as competition among rival national or regional blocs of capital. But what do he and others who assign the world's global corporations to one or another nation-state mean by an "American" or a "European" company? When we study these companies we find that the only thing "American" or "European" about them may be their legal domicile or their country of original establishment. They bring together shareholders from around the world, both individual and institutional; have merged, cross-invested, and undertaken joint ventures and alliances with other companies from around the world, organized transnational boards of directors, and so on. Let us look more closely at the claim of U.S.-EU telecommunications competition.

Until the early 1990s telecommunication services were typically provided by national companies, often as monopolies and often state-owned. "The few instances of transnational activity in that industry were generally limited to State-owned developed country firms operating in the markets of developing countries within their home countries' sphere of influence, typically those of

[26] Tabb, "Globalization Today," 39.

colonies and former colonies," observe Clegg and Kamall in their detailed study.[27] But three events in the 1990s facilitated rapid transnationalization as well as increasing concentration of the industry in giant TNCs. In 1996 the U.S. government deregulated the telecommunications industry. A year later the WTO Telecommunications Agreement resulted in the deregulation and liberalization of national telecommunications markets. And the 1998 integration of the EU involved deregulating and liberalizing the industry. All these measures were enacted within the larger context of neo-liberal globalization around the world. Here is an instance of TNS apparatuses – the U.S. state, the WTO, and the EU – facilitating the transnationalization of capital, and doing so, as Clegg and Kamall note, under pressure from capitalists from the industry itself; exactly the type of (transnational) capital–(transnational) state relations I have theorized. These measures resulted in a wave of mergers and acquisitions, often cross-border, an escalation of FDI in the industry, and a burgeoning of transnational cross-investments, joint ventures, and alliances.[28] By the twenty-first century it was simply impossible to speak of "national" telecommunications companies. What have come about – and this is characteristic as regards the commanding heights of the global economy – are *webs of transnational capital*.

There ensued fierce competition, but *not* among national companies or among regional blocs. A wave of mergers and joint ventures took place within the EU, so that what were national companies in Europe became transnational EU companies, but in turn these "European" TNCs undertook mergers, cross-investments, joint ventures, and alliances with extra-regional TNCs and also extended their own activities globally. For instance, the UK's BT formed a joint venture with Banco Santander in Spain to provide telecommunications services in competition with Telefónica, which itself had joint ventures with foreign companies. Here, competition was not between national capitals but among groups of transnational capitals. In the late 1990s, a triad pattern of competition emerged among what Clegg and Kamall termed "global service alliances," each of three such alliances bringing together TNCs originating on both sides of the Atlantic and from elsewhere around the world. One of these, Uniworld,

> was an alliance of two separate alliances: WorldSource and Unisource. At its core, Unisource NV [a Netherlands-domiciled holding company] owned 60% and AT&T [U.S.-domiciled] owned 40% of Uniworld. In turn, Uniworld owned 20%, AT&T 40%, Singapore Telecom 16%, and KDD of Japan 24% in AT&T WorldPartners. The members of WorldPartners Company distributed Worldsource Services. It was a partnership of AT&T, KDD, Testra of Australia and Singapore Telecom. Unisource is

---

[27] Jeremy Clegg and Syed Kamall, "The Internationalization of Telecommunications Service Firms in the European Union," *Transnational Corporations* (1998), 7(2): 39–96 (the quote is from p. 40).

[28] On these details, see Ibid. and also Myeong-Cheol Park, Dong Hoon Yang, Changi Nam, and Young-Wook Ha, "Mergers and Acquisitions in the Telecommunications Industry: Myths and Reality, *ETRI Journal* (2002), 24(1): 56–64.

a partnership of Telia of Sweden, the Swisscom, the Swiss PTT and KPN of the Netherlands. Unisource NV joined the WorldSource alliance by becoming an equity owner in the WorldPartners Company in June 1994. WorldSource Services in 1998 were distributed through the following member companies: AT&T Canada, Alestra of Mexico, Telebras of Brazil, Telstra of Australia, Hongkong Telecom, VSNL of India, Indosat of Indonesia, KDD of Japan, Korea Telecom, Telekom Malaysia, Telecom New Zealand, PLDT of the Philippines, Singapore Telecom, Chunghaw Telecom of Taiwan, Communications Authority of Thailand, Bezeq International of Israel and Telkom of South Africa.[29]

Research from other regions of the world reveals a similar pattern of waves of mergers and acquisitions, in the global telecommunications industry, joint ventures and heightened concentration that result in the emergence of transnational capitalist conglomerates involved in fierce competition with one another.[30] We must recall as well that investors around the world can operate through the global financial system to acquire shares of these TNCs, so that real ownership relations and the class relations that they indicate are many times more complex than simply tracing the relations among the TNCs themselves. In sum, my critics notwithstanding, the debate at this point is not whether or not there is a TCC but the nature of this class fraction and the extent to which the totality of capital as a global relation may now be considered transnational.

The TCC in the South

In 1957, Paul Baran, a Russian-born U.S. Marxist, published *The Political Economy of Growth*,[31] one of the first texts of the post–World War II period to discuss the effects of the colonial system in distorting the economic and class development of the Third World. Baran specifically identified structures of "backwardness" generated by colonialism that resulted in the drainage of surplus from the colonies and former colonies to the metropolitan centers. He argued that the import-substitution industrialization strategy that most Third World countries pursued in the postwar era was futile because the economies of these countries had developed to the stage of "monopoly capitalism," so that the dominant class interests in these countries would block the social

---

[29] Clegg and Kamall, "The Internationalization of Telecommunications Service Firms," 86. If these global service alliances belie the claim of national capitalist competition in the dynamics of the global telecommunications industry, neither can they be understood in terms of regional bloc competition. "These global service alliances (GSAs) are strategically distinct from the area-focused regional service alliances (RSAs)," observe Clegg and Kamall. "Global alliances cater for transnational clients' demand for global network coverage. They represent the transnational response to the transnational business customer calls' market, while RSAs are used to enter foreign domestic and regional markets" (85).

[30] See summary discussion in Kevin J. O'Brien, "Telecom Industry Ripe for Consolidation," *New York Times*, March 28, 2010, http://www.nytimes.com/2010/03/29/technology/companies/29iht-telco.html?pagewanted=all.

[31] Paul A. Baran, *The Political Economy of Growth* (New York; Monthly Review Press, 1957).

transformations necessary to bring about development. Baran's study laid a framework for later critical theories of development and underdevelopment, but his claim that the dominant classes had become capitalist and integrated into the international class structure generated great debate at the time. While Baran may have overstated the case for the 1950s, it is clear that the former Third World by the end of the twentieth century was becoming rearticulated to and integrated into global capitalism in a new way, so that its internal class structure was becoming transnationalized and its leading capitalist strata were becoming part of the TCC.

Third World elites in the postcolonial world capitalist system needed to figure out how to corral and organize an exploitable labor force and put it to productive use so that a surplus could be extracted from it. In this context, the move to consolidate agriculture, as Prashad has observed, "had the net effect of trying to *control* the peasantry. . . . [P]easant production in the Third World would now be made subservient to the dynamics of world trade (and imperialism) rather than the subsistence needs of the localities that could have governed their development" [emphasis in original].[32] Extracting surplus from the peasantry by subordinating peasant production to the world market and/or by tying the peasantry to landlords who organized cash crop production was one major source of class formation by the dominant groups in the postcolonial era. At the same time, industrial, commercial, and financial elites and urban property barons flourished during the initial decades of import-substitution industrialization. With the onset of globalization, dominant groups in pursuit of their own class interests had to develop new accumulation strategies by inserting themselves and the working classes of their countries into the emergent globalized production and financial system. These new strategies laid the basis for TCC formation in the South.

Given that Baran dedicated the major portion of his historical focus to India and the effects of British colonialism there, it is worth exploring capitalist globalization in that country and the rise of a powerful TCC group. India began to abandon its post-independence strategy based on the development of national industry and agriculture with initial neo-liberal reform in 1991 under the guidance of Finance Minister Manmohan Singh, who went on in 2004 to become prime minister. Over the next five years imports doubled, exports tripled, and foreign capital investment quintupled.[33] Twin dimensions of the country's globalization have been liberalization of agriculture and investment policies and the development of an information technology industry. The initial years of liberalization unleashed the telltale social polarization so characteristic of global capitalism as a whole – in

[32] Vijay Prashad, *The Darker Nations: A People's History of the Third World* (New York: New Press, 2007), 197.

[33] Steve Derne, "Globalization and the Making of a Transnational Middle Class: Implications for Class Analysis," in Richard P. Appelbaum and William I. Robinson, eds., *Critical Globalization Studies* (New York: Routledge, 2005), 178.

the 1990s malnutrition increased and average caloric intake declined in India among the poor[34] – but liberalization also unleashed the process of capital transnationalization. In conjunction with the transnationalization of the Indian state, an Indian contingent of the TCC quickly emerged. One arena of such class formation was among Indian companies tied to the information technology industry, at first as business process outsourcing (call centers, data processing, etc.) and later as informatics companies in their own right. Another arena was among corporate conglomerates that had developed in previous decades and went transnational starting in the 1990s, sourcing capital from various countries and agents, especially from non-national Indians abroad. The sequence appeared to be a major influx of foreign TNC investment in the 1990s, followed by the integration of local transnationally oriented investors into the emerging IT industry and then the rise of major Indian corporate conglomerates that, driven by global competition, began to go global in the late 1990s and the new century, setting up subsidiaries and offices in various countries around the world and adopting (in fact excelling in) "global best practices." The IT industry experienced a compound annual growth rate of 50 percent in the 1990s and by 2004 revenues approached $16 billion and exports $12.5 billion, some 20 percent of total export earnings.[35]

"The larger companies such as Infosys also started to move up the value chain by offering turnkey projects, end-to-end business solutions, and consultancy rather than only low value added services. Infosys, became in 1999 the first India-based company to be listed on the Nasdaq," notes Upadhya.[36] Accordingly, its CEO, Akshaya Bhargava, pushed the transnational agenda inside the country, pressing the government to sign on to "trade related intellectual property rights" (TRIPS) provisions of the WTO. By the twenty-first century the IT-based TCC groups in India were integrated into an increasingly dense transpacific U.S.-India corridor as well as India-EU and India-Asia corridors. Much of the venture capital that jump-started the IT industry came from non-resident Indians who had accumulated considerable wealth as tech entrepreneurs during the boom years of California's Silicon Valley. Similar to the Chinese experience, ethnic networks served as enablers of transnational class development. "The entry of venture capital, the growing involvement of NRI entrepreneurs and financiers in the Indian IT industry, and the transnational structure of the new generation of start-ups, all point to the emergence of complex transnational connections within the industry and of a new transnational business class," notes Upadhya. "This class includes, apart from NRI

---

[34] Raj Patel, *Stuffed and Starved: The Hidden Battle for the World Food System* (New York: Melville House, 2007), 127.

[35] Carol Upadhya, "A New Transnational Capitalist Class? Capital Flows, Business Networks and Entrepreneurs in the Indian Software Industry," *Economic and Political Weekly* (2004), 39(48): 5141–5151. Citations are from the online version, 1–12, http://www.nias.res.in/docs/caro lepw04.htm.

[36] Ibid.

(non-resident Indians) tech entrepreneurs and venture capitalists, the founders and top executives of large and medium-sized Indian IT companies, top managers of MNC software centers in India, and entrepreneurs of the new breed of high-end start ups."[37] Moreover, the industry exhibited a pattern of interlocked boards of directors across the transpacific corridor.

During this time, Indian witnessed the struggle between nationally oriented and transnationally oriented elites over control of the state and its policies. The transnationally oriented elites in India "differ sharply in their ideological orientation from the established business class, many of whom (represented by the Bombay Club) opposed unbridled globalization," observes Upadhya. "In contrast to the old bourgeoisie, the IT business class emerged within the global economy and a liberalized environment."[38] The IT industry, she states, "has produced a new kind of transnational capitalist class in India":

> Most of the founders of software firms have come from the 'middle class,' building on their cultural capital of higher education and social capital acquired through professional careers. This class, and the IT industry to which it belongs are also distinguished by their global integration and relative autonomy from the 'old' Indian economy dominated by the public sector and a nationalist capitalist class. The entry of multinationals into the IT industry has produced synergies that have helped it to grow and for these reasons the IT business class is also one of the most outspoken votaries of globalization.[39]

A second pattern of TCC formation in India has involved the transformation of companies previously inserted into protected national circuits, such as Wipro, Arcelor Mittal, and most illustrative, India's leading global corporation, the Tata Motor Group. As part of the neo-liberal opening, the Reserve Bank of India (RBI) authorized up to 49 percent foreign investment in stock exchanges, depositories, and clearing corporations, and *The New York Times* reported in 2010 that "India has become a destination of choice for financial investors. In the first nine months of the year, foreigners invested $28.5 billion in Indian stocks and bonds – more than twice what they invested in the comparable period of 2009."[40] This inflow of FDI – one side of the transnationalization equation – was matched by an outflow of FDI from India to other regions of the world. By 2011, the Tata group ran more than 100 companies in 80 countries. It had become the single biggest manufacturer in the United Kingdom – the old colonial power in India – having bought Jaguar, Land Rover, Corus (formerly British Steel), Tetley Tea, Brunner Mond (chemicals), and other holdings. According to *The Economist*, its UK holdings account for 60 percent of the conglomerate's

---

[37] Ibid, 6.
[38] Ibid, 9.
[39] Ibid, 1.
[40] Vikas Bajaj, "India a Hit for Foreign Investors," *New York Times*, October 13, 2010, http://www.nytimes.com/2010/10/14/business/global/14indiastox.html?scp=3&sq=percentage%20of%20foreign%20investors%20in%20world%20stock%20markets&st=cse

revenues.[41] But even if Tata were an exception, there is more than meets the eye, as there are connections that transnationalize class groups that at first blush may appear to be national.

It may be true, as Prashad suggests,[42] that most Indian capitalists invest their money in Indian-domiciled companies. But the domicile of a transnational corporation does not tell us very much because of the complex webs and onion-like layers of transnational ownership of these companies, including institutional investors, mutual fund investment, and so forth, which in turn bring together other sets of individual and institutional investors from around the world. General Motors is domiciled in the United States, but that hardly means it is a "U.S." company. Anyone in the United States who invests in GM is investing in networks of capital spanning the globe and involving a circuitry of finance capital that is utterly impossible to disentangle along any national lines. The individuals who invest in a Chilean institutional investor group that in turn invests in GM, in a mutual fund managed on Wall Street (really, it is managed in cyberspace), or in global bond markets will appropriate values that are gener-ated in transnational circuits of accumulation and hence are inserted into trans-national class relations. The domicile of a TNC tells us very little about identity and class interests. It does not allow us to ascertain where a TNC's production circuits are located or where its products are marketed. Prashad states that exports make up only a quarter of the world's economy. But this tells us little about transnational class relations. If, for instance, much of what is traded locally in a single country is produced in whole or in part by TNCs, either directly or through chains of subcontracting, outsourcing, partnerships, and alliances, these are global economy products produced and marketed locally.

Research from around the world points to similar processes of TCC forma-tion in the global South. I have discussed at some length TCC formation in Latin America. Baker has researched the process in Iraq, Hanieh for Palestine, and Harris for Russia, China, Brazil, and the Gulf states.[43] Senner finds that as Turkey has integrated into global capitalist circuits since it first launched neo-liberal reform in 1980, a new transnational capitalist class has arisen through association with TNCs that have invested in the country and through the integration into theses circuits of previously nationally oriented, often family-owned companies. With this came a sharpening of polarization between Turkish

---

[41] "Tata for Now," *The Economist*, September 10, 2011: 61.

[42] Vijay Prashad, "World on a Slope," *Critical Sociology* (2012), 38(3): 402–404.

[43] Robinson, *Latin America and Global Capitalism* and *Transnational Conflicts: Central America, Social Change, and Globalization*; Yousef Baker, "Global Capitalism and Iraq: The Making of a Neo-Liberal Republic," paper presented at the international conference *Global Capitalism and Transnational Class Formation*, Center of Global Studies, Czech Academy of Sciences, September 16–18, 2011; Adam Hanieh, "The Internationalisation of Gulf Capital and Palestinian Class Formation," *Capital and Class* (2011), 35(1): 81–106; Jerry Harris, "Emerging Third World Powers: China, India, and Brazil," *Race and Class* (2005), 46(3): 7–27; Harris, "Statist Globalization in China, Russia and the Gulf States," *Science and Society* (2009), 73(1): 6–33.

capitalists and elites and rising professional and middle strata, on the one hand, and a deterioration of conditions for the poor and working majority, on the other. These former groups, he shows, increasingly have more in common (in terms of their consumption patterns, cultural practices, worldview, and identity) with their counterparts around the world than with their fellow nationals. Most of the elites, managers, and technocrats he interviewed regarded themselves as "world citizens" first and foremost over national and other identities.[44]

"Davos Man" or "Global Capitalist Man"?

To be sure, global capitalism remains characterized by wide and expanding inequalities when measured *among* countries in North-South terms, and grossly asymmetric power relations adhere to *interstate* relations, as I will discuss later. But this cannot blind us to analysis that moves beyond a nation-state/interstate framework. Even if elites that originate in historically metropolitan countries predominate in a snapshot of the TCC and the transnational elite, these elites and others from around the world are rapidly joining the ranks of what some have called "Davos Man," in reference to the Swiss town that is the annual meeting place for the World Economic Forum (WEF), the peak business and political forum of the TCC and the global elite. These metropolitan elites do not accumulate their capital, nor do they reproduce their status and power, from older national economies or circuits of accumulation but from new transnational ones that are open to investors from around the world and from which spring forth dense networks. If metropolitan elites utilize their disproportionate power in the global system the significant questions are: to what end? in whose interest? who (what class and social groups around the world) benefits from the wielding of that power? I suggest that the interests being met are those of transnational capital. The Group of Eight meetings of the most powerful countries in the international system attempt to stabilize global capitalism, which is in the interests of those social and class groups around the world who are integrated from above into global capitalism and whose own reproduction depends on a stable, open, and expanding global economy. This is in distinction to older anticolonial, ISI, and nationalist elites whose interests often stood in contradiction to those of metropolitan capital, and later on of transnationalizing capital. Third World elite groups in the previous epoch of world capitalism had to utilize local states and promote local accumulation in order to fulfill their aspirations for core social status or to acquire capital and power. This was so because of the structure of the world capitalist system in previous epochs, a structure generated by the particular form in which capitalism spread outward from its original heartland through colonialism and imperialism.

---

[44] Tilmaz Meltem Sener, "Turkish Managers as Part of the Transnational Capitalist Class," *Journal of World-Systems Research* (2008), 13(2): 119–141.

Transnational capitalists and globalizing elites in the former Third World, *and* from the former First World, can increasingly aspire to detach themselves from local dependency – the need to generate a national market, to assure the social reproduction of local subordinate groups, and so forth – and instead utilize the global economy to accumulate capital, status, and power. This does not resolve, and indeed aggravates, the legitimacy crises of local states in both North and South; such is the contradictory and crisis-ridden nature of global capitalism. Yet British and U.S. elites no longer need to build up a domestic labor aristocracy in pursuit of their class and group interests. The fact is that the Mexican multibillionaire Carlos Slim, one of the richest men in the world, has inconceivably more social power than the mass of U.S. workers, as do the Middle Eastern and Chinese elites that control sovereign wealth funds, and so on.

In objecting to my global capitalism theory, Tabb, Prashad, and other critics point to what they sees as fundamental contradictions between the G-7 countries and the BRICS (Brazil, Russia, India, China, and South Africa) countries. The BRICS are what world-systems and other theorists refer to as semiperipheral countries, or countries that occupy an intermediary position between core and peripheral states within a world hierarchy of nation-states, and are presumably attempting to move up in this hierarchy into the core. The BRICS came together as a group in 2006, have held regular summits since 2009, and exercise growing political and economic clout in the international system. "Growing rivalry resulting from the rise of states of the semi-periphery, led by the BRIC countries ... have important significance," says Tabb. "Such states, political and economic alliances, regional groupings, and other counters to U.S. hegemony are numerous and intended to increase leverage against the global hegemon. They are hardly fraternal divisions within some transnational capitalist class but instances of traditionally understood rivalries based on national interests."[45] Nonetheless, a fundamental distinction we want to make in the social sciences, one essential to understanding global capitalism, is between surface phenomena and underlying essence. We must move from the surface-level dynamics of interstate political relations in order to get at the underlying meaning of G-7/ BRICS dynamics. We must not overemphasize political jockeying in the arena of international relations. The relationship between politics and economics is complex. Latin American Marxists have understood a number of left-populist revolutions in that region in the 1960s and the 1970s, such as that led by Juan Velasco Alvarado in Peru in 1968, less as anticapitalist challenges than as movements to bring about more modern class relations in the face of the tenacity of the antiquated, often semifeudal oligarchies, and thus to renovate and free up

---

[45] William K. Tabb, "Globalization Today: At the Borders of Class and State Theory," *Science and Society* (2009), 73(1): 41–42. On Prashad's criticism and my response, see Prashad, "World on a Slope," and William I. Robinson, "Capitalist Globalization as World Historic Context: A Response," *Critical Sociology*, 38(3): 405–416.

capitalism from atavistic constraints on its full development.[46] In a similar way, the BRICS politics aim to force those elites from the older centers of world capitalism into a more balanced and integrated global capitalism. China repeatedly proposed in the wake of the 2008 collapse not that the yuan become the new world currency but that the IMF issue a truly world currency not tied to any nation-state.[47] Such a move would help save the global economy from the dangers of continued reliance on the U.S. dollar, an atavistic residue from an earlier era of U.S. dominance in a world system of national capitalisms and hegemonic nation-states.

There is nothing in BRICS politics and proposals that have stood in any significant contradiction to global capitalism. On the contrary, by and large the BRICS platform pushes further integration into global capitalism. Brazilian and southern opposition to the subsidy regime for agriculture in the North constituted opposition not to capitalist globalization but precisely to a policy that stood in the way of such globalization. BRICS politics sought to open up further the global system for elites in their respective countries. Some of these efforts do clash with the G-7, but BRICS proposals would have the effect of extending and contributing to the stabilization of global capitalism and, in the process, of further transnationalizing the dominant groups in these countries. This is not a case of the old anticolonialism and cannot be explained in the context of earlier First World–Third World contradictions that do not capture the current dynamics. Prashad misreads the economic and political protagonism of BRICS elites. Far from indicating a polarized confrontation or antagonistic interests, this protagonism has for the most part been aimed at constructing a more expansive and balanced global capitalism.

Let us look at this matter further. Brazil has led the charge against northern agricultural subsidies in several international forums in the first decade of the twenty-first century. Its argument was that such subsidies unfairly undermined the competitiveness of Brazilian agricultural exports. Brazil was seeking *more*, not *less*, globalization: a global free market in agricultural commodities. Who in Brazil would benefit from the lifting of northern agricultural subsidies? Above all, it would benefit the soy barons and other giant agro-industrial exporters that dominate Brazilian agriculture. And who are these barons and exporters? A study of the Brazilian economy reveals that they are agribusiness interests in Brazil that bring together Brazilian capitalists and land barons with the giant TNCs that drive global agribusiness and that themselves, in their ownership and cross-investment structures, bring together individual and institutional investors from around the world, such as Monsanto, ADM, Cargill, and so forth.[48] Simply put, "Brazilian" agricultural exports are transnational capital agricultural exports. Adopting a nation-state-centric framework of analysis makes this

[46] See, e.g., discussion in Robinson, *Transnational Conflicts*.
[47] See, e.g., "Yuan Small Step," *The Economist*, July 11, 2009: 71.
[48] Patel, *Stuffed and Starved*, 197–200.

look like a Brazilian national conflict with powerful northern countries. If Brazil got its way it would not have curtailed but have furthered capitalist globalization and would have advanced the interests of transnational capital. (Brazil, in fact, took its case against U.S. farm subsidies and EU sugar subsidies to the WTO, which ruled in Brazil's favor, suggesting that the WTO, far from an instrument of U.S. or European "imperialism," is an effective instrument of the TNS.) What appear as international struggles for global hegemony or struggles of the South against the North are better seen as struggles by emerging transnational capitalists and elites outside of the original transatlantic and trilateral core to break into the ranks of the global elite and develop a capacity to influence global policy formation, manage global crises, and participate in ongoing global restructuring. The BRICS's national economic strategy is structured around global integration. Nationalism becomes a strategy for seeking space in the global capitalist order in association with transnational capital from abroad.

Those who posit growing international conflict between the traditional core countries and rising powers in the former Third World point most often to China and its alleged conflict with the United States over global influence. Geopolitical analysis as conjunctural analysis must be informed by structural analysis. The policies of the Chinese (as well as those of the other BRICS states) have been aimed at integration into global production chains in association with transnational capital. Already by 2005 China's stock of FDI to GDP was 36 percent, compared to 1.5 percent for Japan and 5 percent for India, with half of its foreign sales and nearly a third of its industrial output generated by transnational corporations.[49] Moreover, the giant Chinese companies – ranging from the oil and chemical sectors to automobiles, electronics, telecommunications, and finance, have associated with TNCs from around the world in the form of mergers and acquisitions, shared stock, cross-investment, joint ventures, subcontracting, and so on, both inside China and around the world. Inside China, for instance, some 80 percent of large-scale supermarkets had merged with foreign companies by 2008.[50] There is simply no evidence of "Chinese" companies in fierce rivalry with "U.S." and other "Western" companies over international control. Rather, the picture is one of competition among transnational conglomerates, as discussed earlier, which integrate Chinese companies. That Chinese firms have more secure access to the Chinese state that other firms does not imply the state conflict that observers posit, since these firms are integrated into transnational capitalist networks and access the Chinese state on behalf of the amalgamated interests of the groups into which they are inserted.

Similarly, these same observers point to a growing U.S. trade deficit and an inverse accumulation of international reserves by China and then conclude that

[49] Harris, "Emerging Third World Powers," 10–11.
[50] "Lawmaker Says Monopolistic M&As Threaten China's Economic Security," Xinjua news agency, cable dated March 10, 2008, http://www.gov.cn/english/2008-03/10/content_916121.htm.

the two states are locked in competition over international hegemony. But we cannot possibly understand U.S.-Chinese trade dynamics without observing that between 40 and 70 percent of world trade in the early twenty-first century was intrafirm or associational, that some 40 percent of exports from China came from TNCs based in that country, and that much of the remaining 60 percent was accounted for by associational forms involving Chinese and transnational investors. These *transnational class and social relations* are concealed behind nation-state data. When we focus on the production, ownership structures, class and social relations that lie behind nation-state trade data we are in a better position to search for causal explanations for global political and economic dynamics.

The international division of labor characterized by the concentration of finance, technology, and research and development in traditional core countries and low-wage assembly (along with raw materials) in traditional peripheral countries is giving way to a global division of labor in which core and peripheral productive activities are dispersed as much within as among countries. Contrary to the expectations of nation-state-centric theories, TNCs originating in traditionally core countries no longer jealously retain their research and development (R&D) operations in their countries of origin. The United Nations Conference on Trade and Development (UNCTAD) dedicated its 2005 annual World Investment Report to the rapid internationalization of R&D by transnational corporations.[51] Applied Materials, a leading solar technology company head-quartered in California, shifts components for its solar panels all over the world and then assembles them at distinct final market destinations. The company decided in 2009, however, to open a major R&D center in western China that is the size of 10 football fields and employs 400 engineers.[52] Moreover, many companies that previously produced in the traditional core countries are investing in new facilities in these "emerging economies" in order to achieve proximity to expanding local markets.

This does not mean that there are no political tensions in international forums. These forums are highly undemocratic and are dominated by the old colonial powers as a political residue of an earlier era. But these international political tensions – sometimes geopolitical – do not indicate underlying structural contradictions between rival national or regional capitalist groups and economic blocs. The transnational integration of these national economies and their capitalist groups have created common class interests in an expanding global economy. And besides, as I have already observed, capitalist groups from these countries form part of transnational conglomerates in competition with one another. The inextricable mixing of capitals globally through financial

---

[51] UNCTAD, *World Investment Report 2005: Transnational Corporations and the Internationalization of R&D* (New York and Geneva: United Nations, 2005).

[52] Don Lee, "China Pushes for Bigger Role in Reshaping the World Economy," *Los Angeles Times*, April 2, 2009: A1.

flows simply undermines the material basis for the development of powerful national capitalist groups in contradiction to the global capitalist economy and the TCC. Interstate conflict in the new era is more likely to take place between the centers of military power in the global system and those states where nationally oriented elites still exercise enough control to impede integration into global capitalist circuits, such as in Iraq prior to the 2003 U.S. invasion or in North Korea, or in those states where subordinate classes exercise enough influence over the state to result in state policies that threaten global capitalist interests, such as in Venezuela and other South American countries that turned to the left in the early twenty-first century.

Breaking with nation-state-centric analysis does not mean abandoning analysis of national-level processes and phenomena or interstate dynamics. It does mean that we view transnational capitalism as the world-historic context in which these play themselves out. It is not possible to understand anything about global society without studying a concrete region and its particular circumstances – a part of a totality, in its relation to that totality. Globalization is characterized by related, contingent, and unequal transformations. To evoke globalization as an explanation for historic changes and contemporary dynamics does not mean that the *particular* events or changes identified with the process are happening all over the world, much less in the same ways. It does mean that the events or changes are understood as a consequence of globalized power relations and social structures. As each country transforms its social relations and institutions, it enters a process conditioned by its own history and culture. Thus uneven development determines the pace and nature of local insertion into the global economy. The key becomes their relationship to a transnational system and the dialectic between the global and the local. Distinct national and regional histories and configurations of social forces as they have historically evolved mean that each country and region undergoes a distinct experience under globalization. Moreover, these social forces operate through national and regional institutions. China's integration into global capitalism generates news sets of tensions among classes and groups inside China, including those between the rising elites and the masses of workers and peasants subject to the harsh vagaries of global capitalist exploitation and rising insecurity as a socialist safety net is dismantled, and between elites tied to older national and new transnational forms of accumulation and sections of the state, including state assets, tied to one or another.

State Capitalism or Capitalist Colonization of the State?

The legacy of the postcolonial struggles and the ISI era meant that many former Third World countries entered the globalization age with significant state sectors. Neo-liberal programs involved the privatization of many of these former state holdings in the late twentieth and early twenty-first centuries, but some sectors, often oil and finance, have remained state-held in a number of countries.

At the same time, several countries, such as China and the oil exporters of the Middle East, have set up "sovereign wealth funds" (SWFs) – that is, state-held investment companies – that involve several trillion dollars. Many argued that the rise of such powerful state corporations in the international arena signaled a "decoupling" from the U.S. and Western economy. Yet Harris observes that these state corporations have not turned inward in order to build up protected national or regional economies but have thoroughly integrated into transnational corporate circuits. The SWFs have invested billions buying stocks in banks, securities houses, and asset management firms, among them Barclays, Blackstone, Carlyle, Citigroup, Deutsche Bank, HSBC, Merrill Lynch, Morgan Stanley, UBS, the London Stock Exchange, and NASDAQ. He terms this phenomenon "transnational state capitalism" – the activities of the SWFs and other state corporations underscore "the statist nature of the Third World TCC."[53] These state corporations undertook a wave of investment in "emerging market" equities and in other investments abroad. In researching these global investment patterns, Truman points out that globalization "has had the effect of loosening the 'home bias' of individual, institutional, and governmental investment portfolios."[54] For his part, Harris observes:

> [There comes about] a merger of interests between transnational capitalists from both statist and private sectors that takes place over an array of joint ventures. It is not simply competition between state and private transnational capitalists (although that is one aspect), but rather the integration of economic interests creating competitive blocs of transnational corporations seeking to achieve advantage in a variety of fields and territorial regions.[55]

He adds that many of these SWFs have invested in stock exchanges in the United States, Europe, and elsewhere: "The drive to combine stock markets responds to the financial needs of the TCC, who want to trade shares anywhere, invest across asset classes and do it faster." The case of China, contra those claims that China is competing with Western capitalists, is revealing. Transnational capital is heavily co-invested in China's leading state corporations. In 2007, for instance, Warren Buffet had $500 million invested in the China National Petroleum Corporation (CNPC), the world's fifth-largest oil producing company. The CNPC had co-investments and joint ventures around the world with virtually all the major private transnational oil companies and was able to enter the Iraqi oil market with the assistance of the U.S. occupiers.[56] Importantly, there has

[53] Harris, "Statist Globalization," 6–33.
[54] Edwin Truman, "Sovereign Wealth Funds: The Need for Greater Transparency and Accountability," Peterson Institute for International Economics, Policy Brief PB07-6, August 2007: 2.
[55] Harris, "Statist Globalization," 13.
[56] Harris, "Statist Globalization"; on Iraq, see Baker, "Global Capitalism in Iraq," and Carola Hoyos, "Burning Ambition," *Financial Times*, November 4, 2009: 9. Harris notes: "Contemporary competition is not simply an internal affair among rival Chinese interests or

been a fusion of Chinese and transnational financial capital. In the early twenty-first century, transnational banks became minority holders in major Chinese financial institutions, and conversely, Chinese banks invested in private financial institutions around the world.[57] These same webs of association with transnational capital hold true for Russian state (as well as private) corporations.

What we see is a fusion of capitals from numerous national origins through multiple and overlapping mechanisms and networks into *webs of transnational capital*, what former Goldman Sachs CEO Richard Gnodde refers to as "the ecosystem of global capital."[58] In this ecosystem blocs emerge where countries in the global South that share a desire for expansion in the global economy find solidarity in their opposition to Western institutional and political dominance. "But at the same time they are part of an integrated chain of finance, production and accumulation in which overall class interests are merged with the West," notes Harris, in which alliances most often appear in combinations of TNCs that have nothing to do with national origin or regional membership, "reflecting the constant search for competitive advantage among the TCC."[59] Certainly the TCC in the former Third World needs the state for its class development and in order to enter competitively into global circuits. Yet the picture that emerges is less one of the state controlling capital or of the old state capitalism than of transnational capital colonizing the state in new ways.

In sum, the global capitalist system developed out of the historical structures of world capitalism. That system's centuries-long expansion out of its European birthplace and later on out of other metropolitan centers means that emerging global structures are disproportionately dominated by agents from those regions. What concerns me are: 1) the direction of change; 2) the qualitative changes and discontinuities associated with the epochal shift from nation-state to transnational capitalism from the 1970s onward. Regarding the first, there is no doubt that Davos Man is moving toward an ever greater integration of transnationally oriented elites from across the globe. The World Bank reports that the South-to-North share of cross-border mergers and acquisitions rose from 4 percent to 17 percent between 2003 and 2010, and that southern firms now account for more than one-third of worldwide foreign direct investment (FDI) flows.[60] *The Economist* reported in 2008 that "global business investment now flows increasingly from south to north and south to south, as emerging economies invest in the rich world and in less developed countries," that

among nation-states, but includes all the complex ties to transnational capital that have spread throughout the economy. Export production, outsourcing to local companies, inward and outward investments and join ventures all act to bind Chinese capitalism to transnational accumulation, integrating both private and state economic actors with the TCC" (16–17).

[57] Sundeep Tucker and Jamil Anderlini, "Citic Confirms Appetite for Expansion into America," *Financial Times*, October 17, 2007: 19.

[58] Richard Gnodde, "New Actors Play a Vital Role in the Global Economy," *Financial Times*, November 12, 2007: 11.

[59] Harris, "Statist Globalization," 29.

[60] "South-North FDI: Role Reversal," *The Economist*, September 24, 2011: 19.

companies such as Brazil's Embraer, Mexico's Cemex, India's Tata and Mittal, and China's Lenovo, among others, are global corporations with operations in the hundreds of billions of dollars that span every continent.[61] Cemex is in fact the largest producer of cement in the world, and Mittal is the largest steel producer in the world, with more than 330,000 employees in 60 countries and factories on 5 continents (Mittal himself was in 2007 the fifth-richest man in the world).[62] The WEF is qualitatively different in this regard from earlier northern transnational elite forums such as Bilderberg and the Trilateral Commission. Davos Man is disproportionately European (and vastly disproportionately male). Yet this is less Colonial Man of yesterday than Global Capitalism Man of today.

The Social Cohesion of the Transnational Elite

> The rich of today are ... different than the rich of yesterday. Our light-speed, globally connected economy has led to the rise of a new super-elite [whose] members are ... becoming a transglobal community of peers who have more in common with one another than with their countrymen back home. Whether they maintain primary residences in New York or Hong Kong, Moscow or Mumbai, today's super-rich are increasingly a nation unto themselves.[63] (Chrystia Freeland writing in *The Atlantic*, 2011)

The TCC is comprised of the owners of transnational capital, that is, the group that owns the leading worldwide means of production as embodied principally in transnational corporations and private financial institutions. The TCC, therefore, can be located in the global class structure by its ownership and/or control of transnational capital. The TCC is not coterminous with the transnational (or global) elite. How to conceive of elites is a contentious matter in political sociology. Much debate has centered on the relationship between classes and elites and on whether or not these are commensurate analytical categories. By "elites" I mean dominant political, socioeconomic, and cultural strata and, in particular, capitalists and landlords, along with top-level managers and administrators of the state and other major social institutions and leadership positions

---

[61] "The Challengers: A New Breed of Multinational Company Has Emerged," *The Economist*, January 12, 2008: 61.

[62] Rothkopf, *Superclass*, 42. The Mexican case is illustrative. In his study on the TCC in Mexico, Alejandro Salas-Porras finds that the transnationally oriented fraction of the Mexican corporate and political community has integrated increasingly into regional and global corporate networks since the 1980s, and that leading Mexican transnational capitalists sit on numerous boards of directors of corporations from elsewhere in the world. He notes: "Their [these Mexican transnational capitalists] fate depends increasingly on the performance of such firms in global markets and not necessarily on the Mexican market. As the domestic market loses strategic interest for some Mexican corporations, they also lose interest in the corporate network and become more interested in global interlocking." Alejandro Salas-Porras, "The Transnational Class in Mexico: New and Old Mechanisms Structuring Corporate Networks (1981–2010)," in Murray and Scott, eds., *Financial Elites and Transnational Business*, 173.

[63] Freeland, "The Rise of the New Global Elite," quote from p. 2.

in the political system. Capitalists are elites who own or manage means of production as capital. Elites who are not necessarily capitalists occupy key decision-making positions in institutions, whether in private corporations, the state, political parties, or culture industries. However, in my view the status of elites who are not capitalists proper is dependent on the reproduction of capital. It is important to distinguish between capitalists and elites, even when individuals and groups overlap, and also to combine the two – and other social categories – into analyses of broader social configurations of power, such as when we evoke Gramsci's concepts of an historic bloc, the extended state, and organic intellectuals; Poulantzas concept of the power bloc; or the notion of global elites and of a transnational elite.

Here I want to highlight two interrelated aspects of TCC and transnational elite formation. First is the notion that there exists among global elites an "inner circle," to use the phrase coined by the sociologist Michael Useem,[64] or a politicized stratum among transnational capitalists and state elites that engages actively in global affairs. This core of what in Gramscian terms are *organic intellectuals* attempts to secure the common interests of the dominant groups as a whole and the stability of the global capitalist system. In their political engagement they try to identify and resolve tensions and contradictions that threaten the long-term stability of the system, to problematize the art of ruling and the construction and maintenance of hegemony. Transnational capital, either as specific corporate conglomerates or as a whole, is not an autonomous free-willed subject. Such a conception would reify capital as an agent rather than as a relation (as *value in motion*) and as a structure in motion. Moreover, to see transnational capital in this way would be to lose sight of the mediations between the economic and the political as well as between the micro, mezo, and macro levels of analysis. Here we need to move between structural and agency levels of analysis. How do global elites as the agents of transnational capital develop a consciousness of collective conditions and interests and a capacity for political action? Second is the idea that class formation involves both objective and subjective dimensions. Classes are groups that are objectively located in the structures of production, that occupy identifiable positions in the social relations of production. But as E. P. Thompson so elegantly argued in his classical study, *The Making of the English Working Class*, classes are groups that have forged a collective identity through common historical experience, who are *aware* of themselves as a class – their common interests and conditions of existence.[65]

In the next chapter I focus on the TNS. Here I want to spotlight the TCC in relation to transnational elite civil society organizations, and to discuss specifically the idea of the increasing social cohesion of the TCC and the transnational elite. Capitalists from different countries increasingly have the opportunity to

---

[64] Michael Useem, *The Inner Circle* (New York: Oxford University Press, 1984).
[65] E. P. Thompson, *The Making of the English Working Class* (New York: Vintage, 1966).

interact as they work together to run the world's largest corporations, and it is out of such interactions, in the first instance, that a TCC emerges. However, the conception of a TCC also involves other forms of subjective, cultural, political, and strategic interactions that come from the involvement of transnational capitalists in an expanding network of organizations in global civil society, such as the WEF, other policy planning organiztions, the International Chamber of Commerce, and other transnational business associations, as well as in TNS institutions – whether as formal representatives or as informal lobbies and shadow participants – including the IMF and the G-20. Here Gramsci's "extended state" as "political society + civil society" constitutes the ground upon which transnational capitalist networks develop and TCC formation takes place. We want to focus on the importance of such networks in congealing a TCC with regard to the subjective dimensions of class formation, including transnational class identity, consciousness, and solidarity.

Theories of capitalist class formation include social analysis as a subfield of power structure research that involves these subjective dimensions of class formation, including cultural and social interaction, shared lifestyles, and so forth. Although such mechanisms of collective identity formation as private clubs, intermarriage, boarding schools, galas, and so forth are considerably more dense at the national than the international level, there is already considerable literature on experiences among transnational elites with regard to increasingly shared cultural sensibilities and lifestyles and on the formation of transnationally oriented technocrats at a handful of global elite universities such as Harvard, Cambridge, and Tokyo University. We can identify an increasing social and cultural cohesion of the TCC alongside its political identity. There is an aristocracy of global capitalism that engages in conspicuous consumption and in organized social enclosure practices, that moves through the same global elite universities such as Harvard, and that accumulates universally recognized cultural capital. These intraclass mechanisms of social and cultural integration are at work transnationally despite centrifugal tendencies generated by national histories, cultures, and polities. In any event, the social integration of national capitalist classes was (is) itself an ongoing process taking place over many generations. Managerial elites of the TNS move in and out of corporate board-rooms and posts in national state and supranational organizations in a way similar to that described in earlier literature on national elites, which revealed "revolving doors" and institutional interlocks that bound together national elites into ruling groups that moved about through the dominant organs in civil society and the state. Expanding transnational networks of this nature come to constitute vehicles for global elite integration and institutional bases for the field of transnational power.

The extent to which the TCC has become socially cohesive and self-reproducing in the ways that national capitalist classes have experienced is an important area for ongoing research. Yet there is already a significant literature on the growing social cohesion of global elites, to wit:

Sklair has studied the cosmopolitan lifestyle, cultural practices, educational patterns, and ideological awareness of the TCC. "Integral to this process are exclusive clubs and restaurants, ultra-expensive resorts in all continents, private as opposed to mass forms of travel and entertainment and, ominously, increasing residential segregation of the very rich secured by armed guards and electronic surveillance."[66] Cox has emphasized the socialization that world-class business schools and management training programs provide to new entrants into the values, lifestyles, language, business practices, and worldview.[67] Micklethwait and Wooldrige have coined the term *cosmocrats* to describe transnational capitalists and elites, "the people who attend business school weddings around the world, fill-up the business class lounges at international airports, provide the upper ranks of most of the world's companies and international institutions, and through their collective efforts, probably do more than anyone else to make the world seem smaller." Members of the transnational elite converge around a collective *habitus*, to evoke the concept developed by Bourdieu in reference to the social and cultural conditioning and experiences that bring about a homogeneity among particular social groups, their practices and outlook.

David Rothkopf, a former high-level U.S. government official and Kissinger associate, interviewed several hundred of the top global elite for his study *Superclass* and found considerable evidence for increasing social and cultural integration of global elites.[68] What he calls the "superclass" is the top echelon of the transnational elite. This echelon often coincides with the politically engaged and most class-conscious cluster of the transnational elite, the "elite within an elite" or politicized leadership strata. "A global elite has emerged over the past several decades that has vastly more power than any other group on the planet," he observes, from a power elite perspective in the tradition of C. Wright Mills, author of the classic *The Power Elite*. "Each of the members of this superclass has the ability to regularly influence the lives of millions of people in multiple countries worldwide. Each actively exercises this power, and they often amplify it through the development of relationships with others in this class." Describing his participation in the annual WEF retreats in Davos, Switzerland, Rothkopf notes that "[e]ven the casual observer in Davos would

---

[66] Leslie Sklair, *The Transnational Capitalist Class* (New York: Wiley-Blackwell, 2000), 20–21.

[67] Robert W. Cox, *Production, Power, and World Order: Social Forces in the Making of History* (New York: Columbia University Press, 1987).

[68] Rothkopf, *Superclass*. This is certainly not the first such study; the literature is actually quite extensive. Two works that stand out in the development of my own ideas in this regard are Richard J. Barnet and Ronald E. Muller, *Global Reach: The Power of Multinational Corporations* (New York: Touchstone, 1976), and Richard J. Barnett and John Cavanagh, *Global Dreams: Imperial Corporations and the New World Order* (New York: Touchstone, 1995). See also Leslie Sklair's *The Transnational Capitalist Class* and sections in William K. Carroll, *The Making of a Transnational Capitalist Class*, that discuss what Carroll terms the "transnational corporate-policy network."

have to conclude that had [C. Wright] Mills been writing today, he would have turned his attention from the national elite in America to a new and more important phenomenon: the rise of a global power elite, a superclass that plays a similar role in the hierarchy of the global era to the role that the U.S. power elite played in that country's first decade as a superpower."[69] He goes on:

> Something powerful is happening among the powerful. There have always been national elites, like Mill's 'power elite' in the United States. There have always been connections between the elites of different countries, but they were typically 'foreign relations' – connections between distant power centers, discrete alliances between sovereigns. For several decades now, though, a new community has been forming, at the same time that economies are spilling across borders, global entities are proliferating, and the world is, well, flattening.[70]

This "superclass" is a politically engaged global elite. "The debutante halls and hunts and regattas of yesterday may not be quite obsolete," observes Freeland in another study, "but they are headed in that direction. The real community life of the 21st century plutocracy occurs on the international conference circuit."[71] Freeland profiles several of the most politically engaged among the global elite, among them the UK-born financier George Soros, the Ukrainian entrepreneur Victor Pinchuk, New Zealander Stephen Jennings, and Mohamed ElErian, the CEO of the world's largest bond manager, Pimco, who, Freeland wryly notes, is the son of an Egyptian father and a French mother, educated at Cambridge and Oxford and heading a U.S.-based company that is owned by the German financial conglomerate Allianz SE. The circuit includes a host of elite forums, such as the World Economic Forum, the transatlantic Bilderberg Group, the Boao Forum for Asia, the Clinton Global Initiative, the TED conferences, and the Sun Valley gathering. Carroll has used network analysis to study the interlocks between TNC boards, policy planning bodies, and other civil society forums. What he terms "transnational corporate networks" emerge from these interlocks and play a key role in enabling business communities to construct consensus across borders and exercise influence in political and cultural domains. The network "shrinks the social space of the global corporate elite" and comprises "a field of global policy formation." Its "inner circle of cosmopolitans consists of 105 corporate directors whose corporate affiliations span national borders, or link global policy boards to each other."[72] Gill observes that as capital has rapidly globalized, global policy planning organizations have become crucial elements in a transnational historic bloc bringing together elite policy-planning organizations, transnational corporations, and global-governance

---

[69] Rothkopf, *Superclass*, 9.
[70] Ibid, 11.
[71] Freeland, "The Rise of the New Global Elite," quote from p. 5.
[72] Carroll, *The Making of a Transnational Capitalist Class*, 41, 47.

institutions that has promoted and consolidated a hegemonic project of neo-liberal globalization.[73]

In sum, it is in the elite forums in transnational civil society that global elites forge a common consciousness and identify common concerns, share analyses, coordinate their local, regional, and group-specific pursuits, debate courses of action, develop agendas, and attempt to stabilize the system. But members of the TCC and elites from private foundations, civic associations, the media, academia, and the culture industries also interact with representatives of states and international governmental organizations, such as the IMF and the World Bank. In this way, the global elites come together in both the organs of transnational civil society and TNS apparatuses, developing a self-consciousness and exercising an agency through Gramsci's "extended state" – in this case an *extended transnational state*.

GLOBAL LABOR

The TCC has received the lion's share of attention in research on transnational class formation. However, capital is not a "thing" but a relationship; we cannot speak of global capital outside of its dialectical relationship with global labor. Capital exists only in relationship to labor, and vice versa, if we mean by labor not the social labor of human beings that is our species being but the condition of alienation from the means of life, atomization, and unity with capital as labor power for sale in the capitalist system. It is the globalization of the production process that provides the basis for the transnationalization of classes, understood as groups of people who share a common relationship to the process of social production and reproduction and are constituted relationally on the basis of social power struggles. The TCC has emerged in an antagonistic unity with the global working class; the transnationalization of capital has proceeded in conjunction with a transnational labor regime in which the circuits of global capital and of global labor intersect and reinforce one another.

The fact that TNCs account for some two-thirds of world exports of goods and services, that approximately one-third of total world trade is intrafirm, and that such trade rose from 22 percent to 33 percent of world trade from 1996 to 2008[74] should alert us to the extent to which accumulation worldwide takes place in a *globally integrated* circuit, in which the relationship among classes and social groups around the world is an internal one. In Marxist terms, if constant circulating capital has been international in nature since the inception of the world capitalist system, it is within the matrix of globally networked TNCs that fixed constant capital as well becomes transnational. "The only factor of

---

[73] Stephen Gill, "Globalization, Market Civilization and Disciplinary Neoliberalism," *Journal of International Studies*, 24(3): 399–423.

[74] Dicken, *Global Shift*, 38. The 22 to 33 percent figure is from "International Trade: Boxed In," *The Economist*, September 8, 2012: 69.

production remaining that can be considered national is the worker herself," affirms Struna. However, "given the fact that the variable capital is transnational and the constant capital is transnational, the *relations of production* – regardless of the nationality or cultural affinity of the worker – *are transnational as well*" (emphasis in original).[75]

The idea of a global working class – distinct from that of an international working class of earlier epochs – has begun to take hold, and studies such as the journalist Paul Mason's *Live Working or Die Fighting: How the Working Class Went Global* have become best sellers.[76] How should we conceive of and identify a global working class? For one, the growth of such a class is reflected in the escalation of wage remittances, which quadrupled in the first decade of the twenty-first century, surpassing $500 billion in 2011, according to the World Bank. "The most remarkable thing about remittances today is their continued growth year after year, despite the global economic crisis," observes Dilip Ratha, head of migration and remittances at the World Bank.[77] The migrant worker is a representative of the global working class par excellence, but workers in the global economy are hardly limited to this category of labor. The Progressive Policy Institute has estimated that the number of global workers, defined as those making goods for export or who have migrated for their work, tripled from 225 million in 1980 to 900 million in 2005.[78] Yet neither is working for the global

---

[75] Jason Struna, "Toward a Theory of Global Proletarian Fractions," *Perspectives on Global Development and Technology* (2009), 8: 230–260, 246.

[76] Paul Mason, *Live Working or Die Fighting: How the Working Class Went Global* (Chicago: Haymarket Books, 2010).

[77] "Remittance Corridors: New Rivers of Gold," *The Economist*, April 28, 2012: 77.

[78] As cited in Tessa Mayes, "Is There a New Global Working Class?," *Institute of Contemporary Arts*, November 20, 2007: 1, posted on December 4, 2007, at *Culture Wars* website, http://www.culturewars.org.uk/2007-12/workingclass.htm.

I cannot here adequately discuss transnational labor migration and new global labor markets. It is important to note, however, that in addition to the estimated 200–225 million immigrant workers defined as individuals who depart from their country of origin in search of employment in other countries, there is the relatively new category of "third country nationals," or TCNs. These are workers who are recruited by labor recruitment divisions of TNCs, and especially those of regional companies subcontracted by global corporations. For instance, an "invisible army of cheap labor" was brought into Iraq by the companies that poured into the country in the wake of the U.S. invasion in 2003. These workers were brought in from the Philippines, India, Pakistan, Sri Lanka, Colombia, Turkey, and other countries. David Phinney reports that subcontracted companies that provide labor and other services to TNCs, in Iraq and elsewhere, have experienced explosive growth. TCNs made up 35,000 of the 48,000 workers employed in Iraq by KBR, a division of Halliburton that received multibillion-dollar contracts from the U.S. government for reconstruction and other projects in the occupied country. These TCNs labored in slavelike conditions. Phinney writes: "Numerous former American contractors returning home say they were shocked at conditions faced by this mostly invisible, but indispensable army of low paid workers. TCNs frequently sleep in crowded trailers and wait outside in line in 100 degree plus heat to eat 'slop.' Many are said to lack adequate medicate care and put in hard labor seven days a week, 10 hours or more per day, for little or no overtime pay." See David Phinney, "Blood, Sweat & Tears: Asia's Poor Build U.S. Bases in Iraq," *Corpwatch*, October 3, 2005,

economy limited to laboring in the global factories, farms, mines, and service complexes – the most visible and direct production sites in global circuits of accumulation. It involves as well those who engage in productive activities that feed into these circuits, such as subcontracted supply and input networks and ancillary services. And it would be very difficult to find working-class communities anywhere who are not dependent on these globalized circuits for their social reproduction.

Yet the global proletariat remains "under-explained and under-theorized," observes Struna. The global working class is highly heterogeneous, just as are workers in national contexts; this heterogeneity does not imply that such a global working class does not exist:

> The relationship of the worker to transnationally produced objects of production is a transnational relation. Thus, even workers who do not cross borders still participate in transnational relationships relative to one another, and relative to capital as well. . . . [T]he fact that some workers are not transnational either physically or by virtue of their participation in a transnational production chain does not preclude their belonging to the global working class. Whether or not a worker is excluded or only partially articulated into the global system does not indicate that a worker is not dominated by the system. Generalized systemic diffusion indicates a worldwide proletariat. Thus, some fractions of the global proletariat remain local in nature.[79]

Struna has advanced a theory of "global proletarian fractions" based on a six-fraction typology of the global working class, comprised of three "global" fractions and three "local" fractions. The global proletariat in this typology is fractionated "on the basis of workers' physical mobility relative to nation-states and regions, as well as the geographic scope of workers' labor-power expenditure relative to the circuits of production in which they are engaged." The *dynamic global fraction* is composed of workers whose productive activities and products are geographically diffuse relative to firms and nation-states. "This fraction of the global proletariat is a transnational fraction: in the simplest formulation, the worker flexibly moves to the point of production." The *static*

---

http://www.corpwatch.org/article.php?id=12675. While one recalls such international labor recruitment practices under the old colonial (and semicolonial) system, such as the recruitment by U.S. companies of Chinese "coolie" labor in the nineteenth century, these contemporary global labor recruitment practices take place under the conditions of global capitalism. TCNs are not an aberration but the face of the new transnational proletariat, clustering along global production chains.

[79] Jason Struna, "Toward a Theory of Global Proletarian Fractions," *Perspectives on Global Development and Technology* (2009), 8: 230–260, 233–234. Struna writes: "In the global system, variable capital is constituted transnationally; variable capital confronts the worker as something literally foreign, but at once familiar. It does not matter that the wages paid to a worker derive from capital from a different geographic region than the one in which the worker is employed – the market in which the two parties make contracts remains a market, though it now transcends national boundaries. It also does not matter that the worker knows or does not know the national source of wages (transformed variable capital): the relation itself remains transnational even if it is not apparent to one of the parties" (244).

global fraction is composed of workers whose productive activities are geographically fixed relative to nation-states but whose products are geographically diffuse relative to firms – for example, assembly line workers in *maquiladoras*, or global factories. For this fraction, "labor-power is expended by stationary workers at single points in a transnational production chain in coordination with workers at other points in that transnational production chain." The *diasporic global fraction* is composed of workers whose productive activities are geographically diffuse as a consequence of cross-border migration, and whose products may or may not be geographically diffuse relative to firms and nation-states. "Like the dynamic-global fraction, the activity of this fraction is characterized by cross-border movement, but unlike the dynamic-global fraction, diasporic-global workers do so without the full legal rights or flexibility afforded the former." The members of the *dynamic local fraction* are workers whose productive activities and products are geographically diffuse relative to firms within nation-states, that is, within national production chains. The *static local fraction* is composed of workers whose productive activities and products are geographically fixed relative to firms and nation-states. And finally, the *diasporic local fraction* is composed of workers whose productive activities and products are geographically diffuse relative to the nation-state. "Insofar as the production process is transnationalized," concludes Struna, "class antagonism is transnationalized. ... [F]ractions based on spatial-productive relations should be seen not as the introduction of new theoretical conditions for class analysis, but as the extension of concepts central to class itself into new global contexts."[80]

Much research into the global working class remains to be done, both in the objective and subjective dimensions of its formation. As noted, the global working class labors in the factories, farms, mines, banks, and commercial and service centers of the global economy. These global economy workers do not need to physically cross borders in order to participate in transnational circuits of accumulation – and indeed, the vast majority does not. Yet workers do not enjoy the transnational mobility that capital and capitalists have achieved. National borders are mechanisms for controlling global flows of labor, disaggregating the global working class into national contingents, and fragmenting both the political mobilization and subjective consciousness of workers. It is clear, as I have argued, that globalization acts in this sense as a centripetal force for the TCC, which is increasingly a "class-in-itself" and a "class-for-itself" insofar as this class group has developed a subjective consciousness of itself. Yet the process acts as a centrifugal force for a global working class that exists objectively – structurally, or as a "class-in-itself" – but has not developed a subjective consciousness of itself or shared cultural practices and sensibilities as a collective actor or organizational forms that would give greater coherence to transnational agency as a "class-for-itself."

[80] These citations are from p. 230, 247, 249, and 255 of Struna's article.

Formal and Real Subsumption and Surplus Humanity

Proletarianization worldwide has accelerated through new waves of primitive accumulation as billions of people have been dispossessed and thrown into the global labor market. The global wage-labor force doubled from some 1.5 billion in 1980 to some 3 billion in 2006, as "workers from China, India and the former Soviet bloc entered the global labor pool," observes Freeman. "Of course, these workers had existed before then. The difference, though, was that their economies suddenly joined the global system of production and consumption."[81] This process involves both the *formal* and the *real* subsumption of labor by capital across the planet. In simplified terms, formal subsumption refers to the process by which people are separated from their means of survival or production, such as land, so that they are forced to work for capital. Even when peasant producers do not lose formal title to their land, they have been thrown into export-crop production for the global market and made dependent on transnational capital for credit, supplies, marketing and so forth – reduced, in effect, to proletarians on their own land. Real subsumption refers to the subordination of workers into the capitalist production process as it is directly controlled by capital in the factory, and also on the capitalist plantation or service sector, their total corporeal discipline, oppression, and domination, so that the worker loses whatever is left of individual power and autonomy, incorporated, in Marx's words as a "living appendage" into the production process. This is the case for the hundreds of millions of workers who labor in Chinese sweatshops, Latin American *maquiladoras*, outsourced service work in India, or transnational corporate agribusiness plantations in California, Kenya, and the Philippines.

Formal and real subordination is closely related to the concepts of *real economic possession* by capital, which refers to capital's control over the labor process, and *real economic ownership* by capital, which refers to control over the organization or goals of production and appropriation of surpluses. Under capitalist globalization there has been an acceleration of these processes of subsumption and of possession. Transnational capital has subordinated virtually the entire world's population to its logic and its domination through these processes. In this sense the world's people live under a dictatorship of transnational capital (in the literal sense of the word, such that transnational capital *dictates*) – a dictatorship more powerful, omnipresent, and deadly than any in history.

At the core of these processes associated with capitalist globalization are new capital-labor relations based on deregulated, informalized, flexibilized, part-time, immigrant, contract, and precarious labor arrangements. These arrangements have involved the ongoing withdrawal of the state from protection of

---

[81] Richard Freeman, "The Great Doubling: The Challenge of the New Global Labor Market," *The Globalist* online magazine, March 5, 2010, http://www.theglobalist.com/StoryId.aspx?StoryId=4542

labor and the erosion of reciprocal obligations to labor on the part of the state and capital, or even any notion that social reproduction of the worker is a part of the labor contract. Workers are increasingly a naked commodity to be integrated into and expelled from circuits of accumulation just like any other input. Working-class contingents around the world find themselves destabilized and thrust into crises. The International Labor Organization reported that 1.53 billion workers around the world were in such "vulnerable" employment arrangements in 2009, representing more than 50 percent of the global workforce.[82]

We need to be clear with regard to the causal origins of these arrangements. In Sivanandan's view, "Capital emancipated [itself] from labor on the basis of the revolution in productive forces made possible by the communications revolution." But capital cannot, by definition, emancipate itself from labor lest it cease being capital – one side of an antagonistic unity with labor. Rather, global capital has come to subject and exploit global labor in new ways. Sivanandan *is* correct that "capital no longer needs living labor *as before*; not in the same numbers, in the same place, at the same time" (my emphasis).[83] Similarly, technology may have made globalization *possible*, but it has not *caused* the process. Globalization is rooted in changes that took place in the relations of production starting in the 1970s, when the world economy entered a period of stagnation and crisis. The process evolved out of the response of distinct agents to the 1970s *crisis of Fordism-Keynesianism*, or of *redistributive capitalism*. Let us examine these matters in more detail.

"Fordism" refers to a way of organizing the economy that was associated with a large number of easily organizable workers in centralized production locations, mass production through fixed, standardized processes, and mass consumption. It was known as "Fordism" because it became generalized following the lead of the automobile tycoon Henry Ford. Ford argued that capitalists and governments should stabilize the national industrial capitalist systems that had emerged in the previous century by incorporating workers into the new society through higher salaries, benefits, and secure employment coupled with tight control and regimentation of the workforce (although Ford himself was a bitterly anti-union industrial tyrant). Ford's initial shop-floor changes grew into Fordism as a "class compromise" between workers and capitalists mediated by the state, involving government measures to regulate capitalist competition and the class struggle. Fordism combined with Keynesianism in the post–World War II social order. John Keynes had broken with the assumption of classical economic theory that the natural state of the capitalist economy was an equilibrium brought about by market forces allowed to operate unimpeded. Keynes

---

[82] International Labor Organization, *Global Employment Trends 2011: The Challenge of Job Recovery* (Geneva: ILO, 2011).

[83] A. Sivanandan, "All That Melts into Air Is Solid: The Hokum of New Times," *Race and Class* (1990), 31(1): 8.

observed that the market on its own could not generate sufficient aggregate demand and argued that such demand had to be fomented in order to avoid more crises like the 1930s depression. His demand-side economic strategy emphasized such measures as state intervention through credit and employment creation, progressive taxation, and government spending on public works and social programs to generate demand, along with other mechanisms for regulating (and therefore stabilizing) accumulation. In this way governments could overcome crises, assure long-term growth and employment, and stabilize capitalist society.

The Keynesian revolution swept through the industrialized capitalist world and formed the basis for economic policy for much of the twentieth century. It also played a key role in the rise of populist and import-substitution industrialization projects in the Third World. Fordism-Keynesianism or redistributive capitalism took a wide range of forms around the world in the twentieth century, referred to in its diverse manifestations and in popular parlance as "New Deal capitalism," "welfare capitalism," "social capitalism," "social democracy," "Third World developmentalism," and so on. The key point here is that Fordism-Keynesianism involved a *logic of redistribution* that fundamentally conditioned the process of the worldwide accumulation of capital in the twentieth century. In the first place, this redistribution came about not because of the generosity of capital but because of fierce social and class struggles as well as anticolonial and national liberation struggles around the world that "forced" capital into a "class compromise," putting a check on the unbridled power of capital over labor and the popular classes as mass popular struggles heated up around the world in the 1960s and 1970s.

It was in the wake of the 1970s crisis that capital went global as a strategy of the emergent TCC and its political representatives to reconstitute its class power by breaking free of nation-state constraints on accumulation. These constraints – the so-called class compromise – had been imposed on capital through decades of mass struggles around the world by nationally contained popular and working classes. In the late twentieth century emergent transnational capital was able to take advantage of newfound mobility and new forms of globalized spatial organization of social processes to break the power of territorially bound organized labor, to develop new capital-labor relations based on the fragmentation and flexibilization of labor, and to shift the worldwide correlation of class and social forces in its favor. On this basis transnational capital achieved enhanced class power over nationally based working classes and extraordinary structural influence over state managers. During the 1980s and 1990s globally oriented elites in most countries around the world captured state power or came to determine state policies in favor of capitalist globalization, and globalization and neo-liberal policies opened up vast new opportunities for transnational accumulation.

Neo-liberalism as a policy prescription for worldwide restructuring through globalization rested on the assumptions of neo-classical economics that eclipsed

Keynesianism. Neo-classical economics, with its doctrines of laissez-faire, comparative advantage, free trade, and efficiency, became hegemonic in universities and governments across the First World. Neo-liberalism was implemented experimentally in Chile following the 1973 coup d'etat that brought the dictatorship of Agusto Pinochet to power. But it was the governments of Ronald Reagan in the United States (1981–89) and Margaret Thatcher in the United Kingdom (1979–90) that catapulted neo-liberalism to the center stage of world capitalism, and international financial agencies such as the International Monetary Fund and the World Bank that imposed the model on much of the Third World through structural adjustment programs in the 1980s and 1990s.

It was not so much that the ideas or ideology of neo-liberalism converted it into the dominant model as it was that the concrete program it prescribed was perfectly functional for transnational capital at the particular historic moment in which the major combines of capital worldwide were transnationalizing and seeking to develop new methods of accumulation and to impose new social relations of production. Neo-liberalism is a concrete program and also an ideology, a culture, a philosophical worldview that takes classical liberalism and individualism to an extreme. It glorifies the detached, isolated individual – a fictitious state of human existence – and his or her creative potential that is allegedly unleashed when unencumbered by state regulation and other collective constraints on "freedom." With the death of the collective, "there is no society, only the individual," as Margaret Thatcher was to famously declare. Neo-liberalism as an ideology legitimates individual survival, everyone for him- or herself, and the law of the jungle. The means of survival are to be allocated strictly on a market basis – in its ideological construct, neo-liberalism sees these markets not as created and structured through state and societal relations of power and domination but as products of nature. Followed to its logical conclusion, neo-liberalism as a prescription for society would mean the end of social reciprocity, of collective redistribution of the social product, an end to the family and eventually to the species itself.

The globalization of exchange and production mandates a convergence in economic policies and institutions, of socioeconomic systems. Apart from its ideological and philosophical dimensions, programmatically global neo-liberalism involved twin dimensions, rigorously pursued by global elites with the backing of a powerful and well-organized lobby of transnational corporations. One was worldwide market liberalization and the construction of a new legal and regulatory superstructure for the global economy. The other was the internal restructuring and global integration of each national economy. The combination of the two was intended to create a "liberal world order," an open global economy and a global policy regime that breaks down all national barriers to the free movement of transnational capital *across* borders and the free operation of capital *within* borders in the search for new productive outlets for excess accumulated capital. Economic restructuring programs sought to achieve within each country the macroeconomic equilibrium and liberalization required by transnationally mobile capital and to integrate each nation and region into globalized circuits of accumulation. The model attempted to harmonize a wide range of fiscal, monetary, industrial, labor, and commercial policies among multiple nations, as a requirement for mobile transnational capital to function simultaneously, and often instantaneously, across numerous national borders. The program called for the elimination of state intervention in the economy and of the regulation by individual nation-states of the activities of capital in their territories.

Economic integration processes and neo-liberal structural adjustment programs are driven by transnational capital's campaign to open up every country to its activities, to tear down all barriers to the movement of goods and capital, and to create a single unified field in which global capital can operate unhindered across all national borders. Neo-liberal policies typically include the liberalization of trade and finance, deregulation of capital (but not an end to state intervention to assist capital in its accumulation activities), the privatization of formerly public spheres, and austerity programs that involve, among other things, the lifting of state subsidies on popular consumption, lay-offs in public employment, and cuts in social programs such as welfare, public health, education, and so forth. By synchronizing each national economic environment to an integrated global economic environment, neo-liberalism has served as the policy "grease" of global capitalism that keeps the gears of the system in synch. Greased by neo-liberalism, global capitalism tears down all nonmarket structures that have in the past placed limits on, or acted as a protective layer against, the accumulation of capital. Deregulation made new zones available to resource exploitation; privatization opened up public and community spheres, ranging from health care and education to police and prison systems, to profit making. Nonmarket spheres of human activity – public spheres managed by states and private spheres linked to community and family – are broken up, commodified, and transferred to capital. As countries in the South integrated into global capitalism through neo-liberal restructuring they became "emerging markets" that provided new market segments, pools of labor, and opportunities for transnational investors to unload excess capital, whether in productive or financial investment. By prying open and making accessible to transnational capital every layer of the social fabric, neo-liberalism disembeds the global economy from global society.

In sum, neo-liberal globalization made possible a major extensive and intensive expansion of the system and unleashed a frenzied new worldwide round of accumulation that offset the 1970s crisis of declining profits and investment opportunities. It is the struggle among class and social forces that is causal to globalization. But the development of science and technology has recursive effects on social forces in struggle. The revolution in computer and information technology (CIT) and other technological advances helped emergent transnational capital to achieve major gains in productivity and to restructure, flexibilize, and shed labor worldwide. In the United States, for instance, worker productivity doubled from 1979 to 2012, while wages remained largely stagnant and even declined for a significant portion of wage earners.[84] This, in turn, undercut wages and the social wage and facilitated a transfer of income to capital and to high-consumption sectors around the world that provided new market segments fueling growth.

As globalization has advanced there has been a dual process in the subordination of global labor. One the one hand, a mass of humanity has been dispossessed, marginalized, and locked out of productive partic- ipation in the global economy. On the other hand, another mass of humanity has been incorporated or reincorporated into capitalist produc- tion under new, precarious, highly exploitative capital-labor arrange- ments. The global surplus population now involves as much of a third of humanity – those dispossessed from the means of production yet denied the possibility of meaningful wage work. This is central to the story of global capitalism and global crisis: a mass of humanity involving hundreds of millions, if not billions, of people who have been expropriated from the means of survival yet also expelled from capitalist production as global supernumeraries or surplus labor, relegated to scraping by in a "planet of slums" and subject to all-pervasive and ever-more sophisticated and repressive social control systems.

Marx argued in *The Grundrisse* that at a certain point in the development of production, science and technology become qualitative forces of production that can increasingly generate value independent of "living" human labor (e.g., through automation). Crisis provides transnational capital with the opportunity to accelerate this process of forcing greater productivity out of fewer workers. The largest employers in the United States "have emerged from the economy's harrowing downturn loaded with cash thanks to deep cost-cutting that helped drive unemployment into double digits ... and [resulted in] huge gains in worker productivity," observed one report on the aftermath of the 2008 crisis.[85] The ongoing rise in the organic composition of capital through investment in con- stant capital intended to increase the rate of exploitation and/or to undercut worker resistance eventually results in a qualitatively new situation in which value-generating technology makes the labor power of large swaths of the working class superfluous, a situation that goes beyond what is traditionally considered a Reserve Army of Labor, as I will discuss later.

In the larger conception of social class, marginalized and surplus workers belong to the global working class insofar as they have been alienated from the means of production and have nothing to sell but their labor

---

[84] *Economic Report of the President, 2012*, Washington, DC: United States Government Printing Office, downloaded on August, 31, 2012, http://www.gpo.gov/fdsys/pkg/ERP-2012/pdf/ERP-2012.pdf.

[85] Tom Petruno, "Corporate Giants Awash in Cash as Economy Picks Up," *Los Angeles Times*, March 24, 2010: A1, A8.

power.[86] They are *idle* labor, what Davis calls an "outcast proletariat."[87]
This global army of superfluous labor is caught up in what I characterize as a
mortal cycle of dispossession-exploitation-exclusion. But if these "supernumeraries" are of no *direct* use to capital, in the larger picture such a surplus
labor force is crucial to global capitalism insofar as it places downward
pressure on wages everywhere – especially to the extent that global labor
markets can be tapped and labor can be mobilized throughout the global
economy – and allows transnational capital to impose discipline on those
who remain active in the labor market. On the other hand, unrest, spontaneous rebellion, and organized political mobilization among the structurally
unemployed and marginalized pose a threat to the system and must be
controlled and contained. Criminalization of the structurally marginalized
is one major mechanism of preemptive containment, especially in instances
where marginalization is highly racialized or ethnicized, as in the United
States, as I will discuss in Chapter 5.

Crises, as I have emphasized, are moments in which political agency may
prevail over structural determinants, depending on the elements of contingency
and agency and on shifting correlations of social and class forces. Crises may
therefore present opportunities for capital to utilize unemployment and hardship
to carry out further dispossession. In this respect, the 2008 financial crisis was a
major turning point. The multibillionaire Warren Buffet, chairman of Berkshire

---

[86] Hardt and Negri write: "The composition of the proletariat has transformed and thus our
understanding of it must too. . . . The fact that under the category of proletariat we understand
all those exploited by and subject to capitalist domination should not indicate that the proletariat
is a homogenous or undifferentiated unit. It is indeed cut through in various directions by differences and stratifications. Some labor is waged, some is not; some labor is restricted to within the
factory walls, some is dispersed across the unbounded social terrain; some labor is limited to eight
hours a day and forty hours a week, some expands to fill the entire time of life; some labor is
accorded a minimal value, some is exalted to the pinnacle of the capitalist economy. . . . [A]ll of
these diverses forms of labor are in some way subject to capitalist discipline and capitalist relations
of production. This fact of being within capital and sustaining capital is what defines the
proletariat as a class." Michael Hardt and Antonio Negri, *Empire* (Cambridge, MA: Harvard
University Press, 2000), 52–53. As should be clear from my discussion here, I concur largely with
Hardt and Negri's expanded conception of the new global proletariat but do not agree that merely
being subject *indirectly* to capitalist exploitation, as they claim (52), qualifies someone as a
member of the proletariat. It would seem that in their conception a small-scale rural producer
who owns a parcel of land but is bound and exploited by the capitalist market is a proletarian. I
prefer to define the global working class as all those who have become alienated and have nothing
to sell but their labor, which would include those employed and also the unemployed, and so on.
The more expansive conception for me is that of the *popular classes*, which includes the global
proletariat along with other class and social groups subject directly and indirectly to capitalist
exploitation. My work has sometimes been associated with that of Hardt and Negri. While there
are significant convergences, there are also some important ways in which I diverge from their
Empire thesis. The sociologist Jeb Sprague has discussed these convergences and divergences in
"Empire, Global Capitalism and Theory: Reconsidering Hardt and Negri," *Current Perspectives
in Social Theory* (2011), 29: 187–207.

[87] Davis, *Planet of Slums*.

Hathaway and one of the richest men in the world, famously stated in 2006 that "There's class warfare, all right, but it's my class, the rich class, that's making war, and we're winning."[88] In fact, the global crisis has provided the TCC with an opportunity to intensify this war. As the crisis spread it generated the conditions for new rounds of massive austerity worldwide, greater flexibilization of labor, steeply rising under- and unemployment, and so on. The crisis allowed transnational capital to squeeze more value out of labor, directly through intensified exploitation and indirectly through state finances. Social and political conflict escalated around the world in the wake of 2008, including repeated rounds of national strikes and mass mobilization in the European Union, uprisings in North Africa, and so on. While the TNS failed to intervene to impose regulations on global financial capital, it did intervene to impose the costs of devalorization on labor, as I will discuss later.

A Global Middle Class?

Alongside the global working class, new global middle classes, professional and intermediate strata, both North and South, have emerged in the past few decades. These middle layers – although often part of the working class in a technical sense, in that they sell their labor to capital – constitute the major market segment for global capitalism worldwide and also its real and potential social base, or part of a would-be global capitalist historic bloc. If in the 1980s and 1990s countries such as India and China were seen by transnationalizing capitalists as important new sites for tapping cheap labor and unloading investible surplus, they became as the twenty-first century progressed major markets for global corporations. By the end of the first decade of the new century there were some 300 million people in China who had become integrated into global markets as consumers, making this "middle class" more numerous in China than in the United States.

In the Marxist conception class is a relational category grounded in production relations. Traditional middle classes are those groups who own their own means of production and who live by the labor they expend on those means of production, while new middle classes are those professional and managerial strata that occupy locations between the capitalist and the working class proper, such as managerial elites who do not own the means of production but do control labor power on behalf of capital in exchange for higher status and income.[89] In my view, however, much of what the academic literature and popular discourse terms "middle class" is actually constituted by more privileged strata of the working class that enjoy higher incomes and consumption

---

[88] As quoted in Carroll, "The Making of a Transnational Capitalist Class," 1.

[89] For discussion, see, e.g., Albert Szymanski's classic study, *Class Structure: A Critical Perspective* (New York: Praeger, 1983), and various works by Eric Olin Wright, among them *Classes* (London: Verso, 1994).

opportunities, and often more autonomy in the labor process. One of the narratives of globalization in the popular imagination is the "death of the middle class," in the sense that these privileged strata of the working class in the First World have experienced declining wages and living conditions, heightened insecurity, and downward mobility.

In distinction, Weberian class analysis is based on market or exchange relations. Weber saw middle classes as status groups defining themselves in relation to others through cultural practices associated with consumption. Much of the literature on class and globalization from a Weberian perspective emphasizes the cultural, ideological, and aesthetic dimensions of a new global middle class.[90] In inciting consumption, "the transnational capitalist class ends up creating a transnational middle class, which is oriented to cosmopolitan consumption and which makes up the primary consumers fueling the global economy," observes the sociologist Steve Derne in his study on India. With economic liberalization in India, members of this class can draw on new high-paying jobs oriented to the international market and can buy international products previously restricted by foreign-exchange controls. In distinction to the old Indian middle class that is oriented to local markets for consumption and employment, members of the transnational middle class have high incomes, college degrees, English-language skills, and global connections; can afford televisions, refrigerators, music systems, and computers; and can dine at a Pizza Hut or buy Nike shoes:

> Affluent Indians' perception of themselves as a transnational middle class located between the Indian poor and consumers in rich counties is generated by both structural and cultural factors. Since economic liberalization accelerated in 1991, affluent Indians today are more located on a global field. Their lifestyles can aspire to those of consuming classes in rich countries precisely because global goods are more available.[91]

While cultural, ideological, and aesthetic dimensions are important, I wish to highlight here both the structural location of these class groups and strata in the global system and their functionality to transnational accumulation. The emergent global middle classes tend to possess certain cultural capital and work in skilled and semiskilled, as well as in supervisory, positions within the global economy, such as bilingual call center workers in the Philippines and Costa Rica, software programmers in India, and R&D engineers and technicians in China. These workers are often absorbed into the culture and business sensibilities of global capitalism in order to perform their jobs and can culturally negotiate

[90] See, inter alia, Steve Derne, "Globalization and the Making of a Transnational Middle Class: Implications for Class Analysis," in Richard P. Appelbaum and William I. Robinson, eds., *Critical Globalization Studies* (New York: Routledge, 2005), 177–186; Derne, *Globalization on the Ground: New Media and the Transformation of Culture, Class, and Gender in India* (Thousand Oaks, CA: Sage, 2008).

[91] Steve Derne, "Globalization and the Making of a Transnational Middle Class," 179.

across borders. They are themselves swept up into transnational cultural and consumption patterns through their work and attendant lifestyles.

Credit is a central condition for transnational middle classes. For many years the United States played the role of a "market of last resort" for the global economy, based on sustaining high levels of working- and middle-class consumption fueled by consumer credit and spiraling household debt, as I will discuss in Chapter 4. But the global financial meltdown of 2008, the subprime mortgage crisis, and the severe recession suggested the credit-debt mechanism that underpinned this role may have reached exhaustion and highlighted the dwindling capacity of the United States to act as the market of last resort within the system. U.S.-based companies, according to one 2009 report, were looking increasingly to China, Indian, Brazil, and other so-called emerging economies in the wake of the 2008 collapse, not primarily as cheap labor for re-export but as "potential consumers for American produced goods and services." This shift, "which has been underway for several years but has intensified sharply during the downturn, comes as vast numbers of families in these emerging economies are moving into cities and spending like never before to improve their living standards."[92] The tendency toward a global decentralization of consumer markets reflects a "rebalancing" of the global economy in which consumer markets are less concentrated in the North and more geographically spread around the world. This does *not* mean that the world is becoming less unequal but rather, as I have consistently argued, that North and South refer increasingly to social rather than geographic locations, in terms of transnational class relations rather than membership in particular nation-states.

One of the most notorious outcomes of globalization is an alarming widening of the gap between the global haves and have-nots. The annual *World Wealth Report* published by Merrill Lynch and Capgemini identifies what it terms High-Net-Worth Individuals, or HNWIs, those people who have more than $1 million in free cash, not including property and pensions. The 2011 report identified some ten million of these HNWIs in 2010, concentrated in North America, Europe, and Japan, with the most rapid growth among the group taking place in Asia-Pacific, Latin America, Eastern Europe, Africa, and the Middle East. The collective wealth of the HNWIs surpassed $42 trillion in that year, well over double what it had been ten years earlier, and 10 percent higher than the previous year. For its part, a 2005 Citigroup report advised that "the world is dividing into two blocs – the Plutonomy and the rest:

> In a plutonomy there is no such animal as 'the U.S. consumer' or 'the UK consumer,' or indeed the 'Russian consumer.' There are rich consumers, few in number, but disproportionate in the gigantic slice of income and consumption they take. There are the rest, the 'non-rich,' the multitudinous many, but only accounting for surprisingly small bites of the national pie.[93]

[92] Don Lee, "Era of Global Consumer May be Dawning," *Los Angeles Times*, October 4, 2009: A1.
[93] As cited in Freeland, "The Rise of the New Global Elite," 2.

Beyond the growth of the superrich, however, is social polarization between some 20 percent of humanity who have been able to enjoy the fruits of the global cornucopia and some 80 percent who have experienced downward mobility and heightened insecurity and lie outside what McMichael refers to as "global consumer networks."[94] The World Bank defines extreme poverty as living on less than $1.25 per day and relative poverty as living on less than $2 per day. In 2010, nearly half the world's population lived on less than $2.50 a day.[95] The 20 percent who constitute the consuming segments of the global social structure are increasingly not concentrated territorially in traditional core countries but scattered globally. Whole sectors of countries become successfully integrated into global capitalism through high-paid employment with TNCs or other forms of advantageous participation in new transnational circuits of accumulation, internet communications, credit cards, high consumption patterns, and so forth. The ability to manipulate space in new ways and new police and social control systems pave the way for heightened spatial apartheid. Writing about Istanbul and Turkey's other major cities, the sociologist Meltem Sener describes the globalization of Turkey from the 1980s through neo-liberal policies, outward-oriented economic restructuring, and the massive entrance of transnational corporate capital:

> Multinational firms which did not have connections to Turkey in the previous periods started to make investments and establish branches in Turkey with the liberalization of the Turkish economy. ... The branches of foreign banks, exchange offices, leasing and insurance firms started business one after another. Following the foreign banks and firms, luxurious hotels were built in Istanbul. Later, the shopping malls and stores which targeted the people in high income levels appeared. The new shopping malls were no different from the ones in the other world cities. To the upscale European restaurants were added the Chinese, Japanese, Korean, Indian, Mexican ones. [The] entertainment sector has also prospered tremendously. ... [G]roups of villas ... were built to be sold to high income groups. These spaces offered the people 'a world of privileges': sports complexes, fitness centers, cinemas, restaurants, night clubs creating self sufficient mini-cities. A buyer of these residences bought not only houses but also certain lifestyles."[96]

This is the same pattern I have discussed in detail for Latin America[97] and that I have observed anecdotally during my travels in Asian and African countries in recent years, as is the rise of new residential zones and gated communities for those who belong to the "global consumer networks."

[94] Philip McMichael, *Development and Social Change: A Global Perspective*, 4th ed. (Thousand Oaks, CA: Pine Forge Press, 2007).

[95] Merrill Lynch and Capgemini, *World Wealth Report, 2011*, http://www.ml.com/media/114235.pdf.

[96] Meltem Tilmaz Sener, "Turkish Managers as Part of the Transnational Capitalist Class," *Journal of World-Systems Research* (2008), 13(2): 125–126.

[97] William I. Robinson, *Transnational Conflicts: Central America, Social Change and Globalization* (London: Verso, 2003); Robinson, *Latin America and Global Capitalism* (Baltimore: Johns Hopkins University Press, 2008).

The Unequal Accumulation of Capital: I

"While all societies have experienced development," wrote Walter Rodney in 1972, "it is equally true that the rate of development differed from continent to continent, and within each continent different parts increased their command over nature at different rates."[98] I came of age intellectually and politically while living, working, and studying in Africa in the late 1970s. I became immersed in the anticolonial and development literature alongside my involvement in the struggles against the remaining colonial and apartheid situations and emerging neo-colonial realities. Franz Fannon's *The Wretched of the Earth* and Walter Rodney's *How Europe Underdeveloped Africa*, the classical docudrama *The Battle of Algiers*, Immanuel Wallerstein's *The Modern World System*, the writings of Karl Marx and of early twentieth-century Marxists such as V. I. Lenin and Rosa Luxembourg – these were all beacons for my awakening. The problematic back then was the external relations among distinct societies, the principles and laws that came to govern these relations within a single world market and an international division of labor, and how such arrangements determined the development of some countries and regions and the underdevelopment of others. Leon Trotsky developed his theory of combined and uneven development on the basis of what Marxists consider the law of the uneven accumulation of capital. This law has been seen as *spatial*; capital accumulates unevenly in space, unevenly across geographic or territorial spaces, and these spaces have typically been seen as countries or as regions in the world capitalist system. Uneven accumulation is in the first instance a social relation; what type of spatial expression this social relation takes is an historical and a contingent matter. Under globalization what were relationships among distinct societies in an integrated world market become internal relationships in an integrated global economy and society. Some of the harshest criticism of my theory of global capitalism has revolved around my refusal to see uneven accumulation as a territorial process. I will touch on the matter briefly here; in subsequent chapters I will address my critics and explore the matter of space and accumulation.

Uneven accumulation is immanent to the capital-labor relation. That relation is founded on the extraction and appropriation of value from one end of the pole in this antagonistic unity (labor) by the other end (capital), together with the set of conditions (material, institutional, cultural, ideological, etc.) through which this extraction and appropriation take place. For much of the history of world capitalism the capital-labor relation expressed itself, in part, as a territorial or a geographic relation. The creation of the world market in the formative years of the world capitalist system was mediated through competition among capitals. In their struggles for profits capitals turned to available means for promoting their interests, among them the appropriation of "their" national states for

---

[98] Walter Rodney, *How Europe Underdeveloped Africa* (Washington, DC: Howard University Press, 1982), 8.

extra-national competition. This led to multiple centers of accumulation in the core areas of world capitalism organized around nation-states. The outward expansion of capitalism from its original European heartland, colonialism, imperialism, the creation of a world market, and an international division of labor – all this involved the exploitation of the majorities in the colonial world by ruling groups in the metropolitan heartlands. But this geographic and territorial structure of worldwide capital-labor relations that forms the foundations for the major critical theories of world political economy in the twentieth century, such as world-system, underdevelopment, and imperialism theories, is *not logically immanent to capitalism; it is historical.*

The principal contradiction on a world scale is one of class. But political intervention in uneven development from the original centers of world capitalism gave that contradiction a geographic core-periphery dynamic. The anticolonial struggle *was* primary precisely because it was the sharpest underlying class contradiction on a world scale, the domination by a metropolitan bourgeoisie of the popular classes of the colonized world, and because of the ability it gave that bourgeoisie to attenuate class antagonism in the metropoles via redistribution (e.g., labor aristocracies) and attendant racial ideologies and hierarchies, both within these metropoles and in the larger world system. This particular geographic or territorial form that uneven accumulation took for much of the history of world capitalism led critical theorists to a state-centric view of exploitation. Nation-states became in these theories reified macro-agents that exploit other nation-states. Such a state/nation-state-centric view of exploitation on a world scale obscures the underlying class and social relations. The geography of an ever-more fluid global economy is one of multiple poles of intensive accumulation around the world that are magnets for transnational investors and migrant labor. Under global capitalism there is a shift from a sharply geographically demarcated global economy to one more balanced in *geographic-territorial terms* at the same time that social demarcations are intensifying and becoming less identifiable in clear geographic terms.

But if I am calling for us to move away from a nation-state and state-centric conception of uneven accumulation or development, where does this leave the matter of the state? Let us now turn to the matter of the state.

2

Notes on Transnational State Apparatuses

> The fundamental problem of the social science is to find the [historical] laws according to which any state of society produces the state which succeeds it and takes its place.
>
> John Stuart Mill[1]

Any understanding of the global crisis requires an inquiry into how the reproduction of global capitalism is possible – or indeed, *if* it is possible at all. An examination of the mechanisms of such reproduction involves analysis of the institutions in global society that make it possible, in actuality or in theory. How are the class relations of global capitalism institutionalized? What are the system's institutional and political authority structures? How can we understand the political constitution of the dominant classes in global society – in particular, the TCC? How does the TCC organize itself in order to pursue its interests around the world?

Institutions are social interactions systematized – that is, institutionalized – by a system of norms and rules enforced by distinct coercive mechanisms, while structures organize sets or matrices of institutions. Hence social practices take place through institutions, and social groups and classes organize themselves through institutions; all but the most entirely coincidental social relations are institutionalized. One of the most important of these institutions is the state. Political institutions have secured economic reproduction ever since human beings moved beyond communal societies. The rise of the state in conjunction with the appearance of significant surpluses and the division of society into classes constitutes the central political instance in the development of class societies. There is therefore a historically constituted inner connection between

[1] John Stuart Mill, *A System of Logic* (London: Longmans, Green and Co., 1889), 595, as cited in John Bellamy Foster, Brett Clark, and Richard York, *The Ecological Rift: Capitalism's War on the Earth* (New York: Monthly Review Press, 2010), 25.

state forms and production processes that we want to analyze with respect to capitalism and its transnational phase.

Marxist theories of the state have observed that neither the capitalist system nor the capital-labor relation that is at the core of that system can be reproduced through market relations alone. Capitalism requires the state in order to secure its own reproduction – indeed, in the view of many the capitalist state emerged in function of the initial genesis of capital. There is a long-standing debate in historical sociology and political economy on the origins of the capitalist state that I cannot delve into here. In Wallerstein's view mercantile states imposed capitalist production relations, while in my view emerging capitalist production relations redounded on and transformed the form of the state. In his ambitious theoretical study, the international relations scholar Hannes Lacher proposes that the particular national form of the capitalist state is an historic legacy from precapitalist (absolutist feudal) development that subsequently became constitutive of capital's concrete existence and was internalized by the capitalist system. Such a view reaffirms what I have emphasized here: the entirely historical and contingent nature of state forms.[2] Yet Lacher's mistake is to assume that because this state form emerged independent of capitalism, it continues to retain some independent logic.[3]

Regardless of its particular origins, this inner connection between state form and production processes means that, in Poulantzas' words, "the political field of the state has always, in different forms, been present in the constitution and reproduction of the relations of production,"[4] which is to state that the market is not self-regulating and that the contradictions of the system generate crises

[2] See, inter alia, Perry Anderson, *Lineages of the Absolutist State* (London: New Left Books, 1974); Immanuel Wallerstein, *The Modern World System* (New York: Academic Press, 1974); Joseph R. Strayer, *On the Medieval Origins of the Modern State* (Princeton, NJ: Princeton University Press, 2005); Hannes Lacher, *Beyond Globalization: Capitalism, Territoriality and the International Relations of Modernity* (New York: Routledge, 2006). While Lacher concurs with me that this national form of the state is historical and neither inevitable nor immutable, he rejects the notion of a transnational state form – more generally, he caricatures globalization theory, largely reducing it to its liberal, pluralist variants – and leans toward a view of the current world political conjuncture as moving toward a U.S.-based "imperium." Even if the nation-state form of the political organization of world capitalism has its origins in feudal absolutist states and not in capitalist relations, as Lacher argues, the fact is that this state form became a *capitalist* state form. It would not be the first time that a particular form has changed its functions (or content) as an inherited form has proved to be quite functional to a new set of circumstances. Indeed, the ruling monarchies under feudalism became constitutional monarchies under capitalism, performing ceremonial functions and legitimating the capitalist class system. In any event, Lacher's thesis on the feudal origins of the capitalist state does not have much explanatory purchase in understanding the dynamics of global capitalism.

[3] In a co-authored article, Lacher and Teschke claim that "since the latter [capitalism] emerged within the former [the nation-state form and the system of multiple states], their interrelation is not structurally determined by any 'logic of capital'." Benno Teschke and Hannes Lacher, "The Changing 'Logics' of Capitalist Competition," *Cambridge Review of International Affairs* (2007), 20(4): 565.

[4] Nicos Poulantzas, *State, Power, Socialism* (London: Verso, 1980), 17.

that the state must attempt to resolve. This is as much an historical and empirical observation as a theoretical proposition. In his classical study, *The Great Transformation*, Polanyi showed how the market on its own would tear apart society and make capitalism unworkable. More recently, social scientists from the "social structure of accumulation," the "regulation," and related schools have noted that, to cite Jessop, capitalism requires "supplementary modes of reproduction, regulation, and governance – including those provided in part through the operation of the state."[5]

The globalization literature has engaged in a not-very-useful debate as to whether the nation-state is declining in significance or disappearing in the face of global processes. The state has always been indispensable to the reproduction of capital; at the same time, capitalist society and its institutions experience ongoing transformations as material conditions change and as social groups and classes exercise their collective agency. Capitalism is (and has always been) a globally constituted social relation. The state is not external to capital and capitalism; it is constitutive of capitalist social relations, both theoretically (logically) and historically. The state has been caught up in a process of transformation in concert with the restructuring of world capitalism. The epochal shift from nation-state to transnational or global capitalism has involved the rise of expansive transnational institutional networks that I refer to as TNS apparatuses.

My original theoretical formulation in 2001 suggested that we can conceptualize a TNS apparatus as a loose network comprised of inter- and supranational political and economic institutions *together with* national state apparatuses that have been penetrated and transformed by transnational forces, and have not yet acquired and may never acquire any centralized form. The formulation involved a threefold argument:

1. Economic globalization has its counterpart in transnational class formation and in the emergence of a TNS brought into existence to function as collective authority for a global ruling class.
2. The nation-state is neither retaining primacy nor disappearing but becoming transformed and absorbed into this larger structure of a TNS.
3. This emergent TNS institutionalizes new class relations between global capital and global labor – the new class relations and social practices of global capitalism.[6]

---

[5] Karl Polany, *The Great Transformation* (Boston: Beacon Press, 1944); Bob Jessop, *The Future of the Capitalist State* (Cambridge, MA: Polity Press, 2002), quote from p. 11. See also Michel Aglietta, *A Theory of Capitalist Regulation* (London: Verso, 1979); David M. Kotz, Terrence McDonough, and Michael Reich, eds., *Social Structures of Accumulation: The Political Economy of Growth and Crisis* (Cambridge: Cambridge University Press, 1994).

[6] William I. Robinson, "Social Theory and Globalization: The Rise of a Transnational State," *Theory and Society*, 30(2): 157–200.

Expanding on this formulation, here is what I stated in 2004 in *A Theory of Global Capitalism*:

> The TNS is a particular constellation of class forces and relations bound up with capitalist globalization and the rise of a TCC, embodied in a diverse set of political institutions. These institutions are transformed national states plus diverse supra-national institutions that serve to institutionalize the domination of this class as the hegemonic fraction of capital worldwide. Hence, I submit, the state as a class relation is becoming transnationalized. The class practices of a new global ruling class are becoming "condensed," to use Poulantzas' imagery, in an emergent TNS. According to Poulantzas, the state "is the *specific material condensation* of a relationship of forces among classes and class fractions" [emphasis in the original]. What distinguishes the TCC from national or local capitalist fractions is that it is involved in globalized production and manages global circuits of accumulation that give it an objective class existence and identity spatially and politically in the global system above any local territories and polities. The TNS comprises those institutions and practices in global society that maintain, defend, and advance the emergent hegemony of this global bourgeoisie and its project of constructing a new global capitalist historical bloc. . . . The rise of a TNS entails the reorganization of the state in each nation – I will henceforth refer to these states of each country as *national states* – and it involves simultaneously the rise of truly supranational economic and political institutions. These two processes – the transformation of national states and the rise of supranational institutions – are not separate or mutually-exclusive. In fact, they are twin dimensions of the process of the trans-nationalization of the state. Central to my argument is that under globalization the national state does not "wither away" but becomes transformed with respect to its functions and becomes a functional component of a larger TNS.[7]

Extrapolating from these earlier statements, it is important to underscore that an emergent TNS apparatus does not and need not have a centralized form as historically developed in modern nations; it may exist both in transnational institutions and in transformed national states. It is multilayered and multi-centered, functionally linking together institutions that have different histories and trajectories and that have been tied to distinct structures and regions, and should not be confused with the notion of a constituted "global state." Transnational bodies such as the IMF and the WTO have worked in tandem with national states to rearticulate labor relations, financial institutions, and circuits of production into a system of global accumulation. What is crucial is a shift in the role of national states to promoting the interests of global over local accumulation processes. The TNS can be seen as an "institutional ensemble" or network of institutions loosely unified in function of capitalist globalization and the imperatives of its reproduction. The TNS does not attempt to control terri-tory per se but rather to secure the conditions that allow capital to freely accumulate in and across all territories.

---

[7] William I. Robinson, *A Theory of Global Capitalism* (Baltimore: Johns Hopkins University Press, 2004), 99–100.

This notion of a TNS is an *analytical abstraction* that allows us to make sense of transnational social practices that are central to shaping global capitalism and to the exercise of class power by the TCC. We want to explore how social relations refract into state processes and into interstate and transnational state relations. As I will show later in this and in other chapters, as a concept the TNS provides considerable explanatory power with regard to contemporary world dynamics, including the crisis. Indeed, I will show how its explanatory power is superior to nation-state/interstate approaches to these contemporary world dynamics. Global capital and global labor face one another directly around the world and through multiple institutional mediations that cannot be packaged into the outdated narrative of the nation-state and the interstate system as the underlying organizational logic through which these mediations are effected.

My theory of the TNS has generated varied criticism. Most frequently heard is the charge that I negate the continued significance of the nation-state and of the interstate system, a charge that I have replied to in the Introduction to this book (among other places). The international relations scholar Kees Van der Pijl, who has conducted important research into transnational class relations, charges that the TNS as a concept remains abstract, whereas the concept claims to denote concrete realities.[8] Relatedly, for others, I fail to demonstrate the actual functioning of the TNS and hence its usefulness as a concept. The sociologist Jason Moore believes that my concepts of the TCC and the TNS are based on an "abstract placelessness," whereas capital's "global moment depends on particular places." The economist William Tabb criticizes TNS theory for seeming "to privilege class and capital logic over state theory."[9] These charges are typical of the academic criticism of my thesis on the TNS. I have responded elsewhere to many of these criticisms (see, e.g., the Introduction to the present study and the references cited therein).

In this and the next chapter I want to expand on several of my propositions with regard to TNS apparatuses in light of the global crisis. In doing so, I reply further to several of my critics and illustrate why I view the transnational perspective on state and class as superior in terms of its explanatory power.

[8] See Kees van der Pijl, *The Making of an Atlantic Ruling* Class, 2nd ed. (London: Verso, 2012 [first published 1985]); van der Pijl, *Transnational Classes and International Relations* (New York: Routledge, 1998). The problem in van der Pijl's account is manifest in the title of this latter volume: *inter*-national relations are his frame for *trans*-national classes.

[9] On Cammack, see the Introduction to this volume. Kees Van der Pijl, "A Theory of Global Capitalism: Feature Review," *New Political Economy*, 10(2): 273–277, quote on p. 274; Jason W. Moore, "Capital, Territory, and Hegemony over the Long Duree," *Science and Society*, 65(4): 476–484, quote from p. 481; William K. Tabb, "Globalization Today: At the Borders of Class and State Theory," *Science and Society* (2009), 73(1): 39.

THE TNS AS FOMENTER OF GLOBAL ACCUMULATION

The State as a Product of Class Relations

Critical theories of the state in capitalism posit two related questions: 1) *how* does the state represent the interests of the capitalist class?; 2) *why* does the state serve the interests of capital? The "state debate" is a long-standing one in the social sciences and remains inconclusive.[10] Nonetheless, there are three closely related observations to be drawn from Marxist and neo-Marxist state theorizing that are critical to my conceptualization of the TNS.

First, the state tends to advance the interests of the capitalist class because the capitalist class is dominant in civil society and political economy. The state arises out of the configuration of class and social forces in civil society and expresses the class relations embedded therein. Capitalism – or, more specifically, capitalist production relations, or the capital-labor relation – throws up a capitalist state as institutionalized class relations.[11] State forms evolve in consonance with the evolution of world capitalism, and the particular forms of the capitalist state are historical. To the extent that they posit the nation-state system as an *ontological* feature of world capitalism, extant approaches risk reifying the nation-state. The state does not have a form independent of the constellations of class and social forces that configure the state. Logical categories cannot subsume historiography. The nation-state is entirely historical, an historical form of capitalism, not immanent and derived not from the logic of capitalism but from the particular history of world capitalism. Reifying categories leads to realist analyses of state power and the interstate system. The underlying realist assumption is that states have particular interests and compete with one another through the international system in pursuit of those interests. The organizational realism that predominates in studies of international relations and world politics advances a territorial/geographical conception of the state that cannot account for the transnational processes associated with globalization. Why else, for instance, would the U.S. state promote the relocation abroad of U.S.-based capital? Why would the U.S. state propose in 2012 a "Trans-Pacific Partnership" trade pact between the United States and eight Pacific nations that would allow foreign corporations operating in U.S. territory to appeal key regulations to an international tribunal that would have the power to override U.S. law? Why would states, more generally, deregulate national financial and

---

[10] See Simon Clarke, *The State Debate* (London/New York: Palgrave McMillan, 1991).

[11] I cannot take up here up the debate over the origins of the capitalist state, or as to whether mercantile states imposed capitalist production relations, as Wallerstein and others suggest, or whether emerging capitalist production relations redounded on and transformed the form of the state, as I believe. But see, inter alia, Perry Anderson, *Lineages of the Absolutist State* (London: New Left Books, 1974); Immanuel Wallerstein, *The Modern World System* (New York: Academic Press, 1974); Joseph R. Strayer, *On the Medieval Origins of the Modern State* (Princeton, NJ: Princeton University Press, 2005).

other markets in ways that result in capital flight and in a contraction, sometimes a drastic one, of the national state's tax base?

What concerns me here are twin problematics. The first problematic is Weberian versus Marxist conceptions of the state.[12] The former reifies the state as a "thing," an entity with an independent existence as expressed by a set the institutions and the managers or cadre that administer these institutions. The latter views the state as a set of institutionalized class and social power relations. The second problematic is the separation of the economic and the political under capitalism. This separation is taken as natural or organic in liberal ideology and in Weberian sociology; political and economic structures are seen as separate spheres, each with its own innate laws and dynamics, the first pursuing power and the second wealth.

In historical materialist approaches this *formal* or apparent separation under capitalism of the political and economic spheres of a larger social totality is not real; it is illusory. It is founded on capitalist production relations involving a differentiation of political and economic *forms* of power. The analytical distinction between political and economic structures or spheres corresponds to their institutional separation under capitalism. The economy becomes a "private" sphere in which the power to expropriate the social product, to extract surplus value, has been privatized, and people are decidedly unequal and subordinated to the market. This economic sphere is removed from the "public" sphere and appears to relate externally rather than internally to the "public" sphere of the state, in which people are equal juridical citizens. Under capitalism one does not vote for who will own what or for how property is to be distributed; such material (economic) relations are removed from the public sphere. Moreover, this public sphere is not directly implicated in the private appropriation of the surplus product. Yet the state is charged with organizing the general conditions of accumulation, for its existence is dependent upon the reproduction of capitalist production relations, or the capital-labor relation. The state exercises its autonomy from the directives of capitalists *as individuals, as groups or as fractions*, but it is *not autonomous from those relations*. Herein lies the *underlying unity* of politics and economics as well as the institutional separation of the political and the economic spheres – that separation being a very consequence of the establishment of capitalist production relations.[13]

This separation takes the expression of the separation of the "public" from the "private," the former seen as the state proper, or what Gramsci referred to as "political society," and the latter as what Gramsci referred to as "civil society." In his essay "State and Civil Society," Gramsci critiques the conception of the

[12] See my discussion on this matter in Robinson, *Transnational Conflicts*, and Robinson, *A Theory of Global Capitalism*.

[13] Ellen Meiksens Wood gives detailed treatment to the matter of the separation of the economic and the political under capitalism in *Democracy against Capitalism* (Cambridge: Cambridge University Press, 1995).

state developed by ideologues of capitalist society as derived from the separation of politics and economics and "conceived as a thing in itself, as a rational absolute."[14] This results, in Gramsci's view, in a reified or fetishistic view, in which individuals "are led to think that in actual fact there exists above them a phantom entity, the abstraction of the collective organism, a species of autonomous divinity that thinks, not with the head of a specific being, yet nevertheless thinks, that moves, not with the real legs of a person, yet still moves." Gramsci criticizes this view of the state as a "thing-in-itself," as an entity unto itself in political society, as "statolatry." Instead, the state is "the entire complex of practical and theoretical activities with which the ruling class not only justifies and maintains its dominance, but manages to win the active consent of those over whom it rules."[15] Here the state becomes the "integral" or "extended" state, in Gramsci's formula, encompassing political plus civil society, a conception aimed at overcoming the illusory dualism of the political and the economic.

As we shall see in the next chapter, the dualist notion of class/capital and state reflects an underlying dualism of the economic and the political, or, as it is posed in the sociological and international relations literature, of "state and society" or "states and markets" – formulations that fail to grasp how class relations configure the state and that see the state as an amalgamated actor or macro-agent. As Jessop observes, a key methodological guideline in formulating a Marxist conception of the state is a rejection of all attempts to distinguish between "state power" and "class power."[16] More theoretically, the concept of the capitalist state should be equated not with the historical form of the national state but rather with the separation of capitalist reproduction into economic and political processes. We want to ask, what is the relationship between the economic and the political under global capitalism? How do we think about the political management – or *rule* – of global capitalism? How do we understand the exercise of political domination in relation to the institutions available to dominant groups and sets of changing historical relations among social forces in the extended state?

Second, the state is not a "thing" but a *relation* – class relations played out as a set of institutionalized social power relations, struggles, and practices.[17] The state in capitalism is a *capitalist state*, or the institutionalization of the capital-labor relation.[18] This is to say that capitalism would have to be superseded – the logic of capital accumulation would have to be subordinated to a social logic, or

---

[14] Antonio Gramsci, *Prison Notebooks* (New York: International Publishers, 1971), 210–276, and also see 117 and 12–13.

[15] Gramsci, *Prison Notebooks*, 244, 268–269.

[16] Bob Jessop, *The Capitalist State* (Oxford: Martin Robertson, 1982).

[17] For summaries on Marxist and other critical theories of the state, see, inter alia, Clyde W. Barrow, *Critical Theories of the State: Marxist, Neo-Marxist, Post-Marxist* (Madison: University of Wisconsin Press, 1993); Clarke, *The State Debate*; Jessop, *The Capitalist State*.

[18] I concur here with Lacher: "Capital as a social relation encompasses not only the market, but also the state. To go even further: the autonomous political form of the state is a *relation of*

exchange value to use value – in order for the state to be other than capitalist. How the state as a class relation becomes institutionalized and through what patterns is an historical matter and contingent upon episodes of struggle that take place among class and social forces. This means, among other things, that the relationship between capital and the state is not external; we will see in the next chapter the fallacy of assuming that the state and capital stand in external relation to one another. If we want to study the nature of the state we must analyze the constellation of class and social forces during particular historical periods, and more specifically, how these forces, acting in and out of states and, more broadly, sets of institutions, engage as collective historical agents.

Class power in capitalism resides in capitalist relations of production (or property relations) and the attendant political, social, and cultural-ideological processes that help reproduce and legitimate these relations. Hegemony is forged in civil society. Social power, in the first instance, flows "up" to the state, where it is institutionalized and then reproduced as state power flowing "down" to society. The class power of the TCC is anchored in global capitalist relations of production, in its domination over the world's resources – over the global means of production, markets, and the global media and culture industries. This is the starting point for any understanding of the TNS.

Third, the state serves the interests of capital *both* because of the direct and indirect *instrumental* manipulation of the state apparatus by capitalists and their agents and allies *and* because of the *structural* dependency of the state on capital. There emerged out of the theoretical debates over the state in the 1960s and early 1970s two broadly distinct, although not necessarily incompatible, views on how and in what ways (through what mechanisms) the state actually does represents the interests of dominant groups. One held that the state was "instru-mentalized" directly by representatives of the dominant groups in order to shape

---

production. ... Production refers not just to the production of material goods, but to the production of the social relations, institutions and ideas which make it possible for material goods to be produced in a specific historical form, in particular social relations, and which, in turn, are reproduced through 'economic' production." Lacher, *Beyond Globalization*, 39. But Lacher fails to analyze the transnationalization of capital or to draw out its implications for his theory of the political in the international system. As a consequence, despite his claim to the contrary, he is ultimately unable to move beyond realism in his account of contemporary international relations. "The world market cannot be understood directly in terms of the economic competition between individuals or firms and the social conflicts between capital and labor over property, production and distribution," states Lacher. "Class identities always have a transnational dimension in capitalism, but the territoriality of political authority means that particular amalgamations of class interests and 'national interests' will be of decisive importance in shaping the historical geography of capitalism in any given conjuncture. It valorizes the territorial state as the basic spatial point of reference. In important respects, capital constitutes itself as 'national capital'" (114). Lacher takes quite a leap of faith in assuming that because political authority is nationally fragmented, capital must then be shaped by this fragmentation into "national" capital. Yet as we have seen in Chapter 1, capital "in" particular countries is not just capital "from" many different countries but capital that has interpenetrated and intertwined beyond the point where it could be meaningfully identified in terms of national origins.

policies in their interests. The other held that dominant groups did not necessarily instrumentalize the state directly; rather, the very structure of capitalist society forced the state to implement policies that advanced the interests of these dominant groups. This became known as the "instrumentalist versus structuralist" debate. One of the key insights to emerge from it was the concept of the "relative autonomy of the state" as developed above all by Poulantzas.[19] What is meant by this is that even if we understand the state to be an instrument that serves the interests of particular groups and classes, there is not necessarily any direct manipulation of the state in trying to fulfill these interests. That is, the state may act with autonomy relative to different groups in society. This does not mean, however, that there is a state logic independent of society and the composition of social forces therein.

In Poulantzas's view *state power* is the capacity of a social class to realize its objective interests through the state apparatus. State institutions are not simply repositories of state power, in Poulantzas's reading, but structural channels for the realization of class power. This structural reading of the state gives us important insights into the dynamics of class and power in the global system, especially the separation of state power from the state apparatus, insofar as TNS apparatuses have no power per se as institutions, but merely channel the social power that is constituted in globalized relations of production. This is to say, it is not that TNS functionaries determine the class nature of the TNS. It is the pursuit by the TCC of its class interests through TNS apparatuses that gives the TNS its class character.

Crucial here is the notion of the structural power of transnational capital. The class power of the TCC is constituted on the extensive and intensive enlargement in recent decades of capitalism, on the more fully and completely capitalist nature of the world capitalist system, and on the unprecedented control and domination that transnational capital exercises over the global means of production and over global labor. But this class power is exercised through the TNS. Global corporations could not reproduce their control if it were not for national state apparatuses that provide for property rights, arbitration, and social control, and that open up national territories to TNCs. The TCC could not exercise its class power if the IMF did not impose structural adjustments on countries, if the World Bank did not make its lending conditional on the reform of labor laws to make workers flexible, if the WTO did not impose worldwide trade liberalization, and so on. Insofar as the TNS creates, maintains, and restores such conditions for global capital accumulation, it is a *transnational capitalist state*.

The institutions of the TNS are not in the abstract a repository of transnational state power. Rather, they must be seen as constituting a *network that provides structural channels through which the TCC and its political agents attempt to exercise their class power*. The TCC and transnational elites have been able to instrumentalize TNS institutions, and they have been able to do so

[19] Nicos Poulantzas, *Political Power and Social Classes* (London: Verso, 1968).

because they have behind them the structural power of transnational capital and of global markets over the direct power of national states and over popular classes. The fiscal functioning of national states is dependent on the global capitalist economy and specifically on global financial markets, and national state legitimacy is dependent on these same global market forces. This dependency – that is, the structural power of transnational capital – is *not* limited to the countries of the South; the U.S. government is as much dependent on transnational financial capital as are countries in the South. Ernest Mandel noted long ago that the dependence of states on financial markets is "a golden chain" between the state and capital.[20] In the age of globalization, this "golden chain" is between national states and transnational capital.

The global mobility of capital under globalization and especially its ability to move money almost frictionlessly and instantaneously through the circuits of globally integrated financial markets has allowed it to extend the mechanism of capital flight, or its "veto" or "strike" power, to the planet as a whole. This power is enhanced many times over to the extent that the global economy is financialized and material assets are securitized and can be traded as financial instruments. This mechanism is, *in content*, a class power of transnational capital over that of popular classes worldwide. It is a class power that is exercised, *in form*, over the direct power of national states. It is crucial to stress "in form" because transnational power resides *within* each national state, not external to it; the national state is part of a more expansive TNS apparatus. This class power of transnational capital could not be exercised outside of the state power of the TNS.

Hence the TNS is a transnational *capitalist* state because its own reproduction is dependent on reproducing the circuits of transnational accumulation. This is so for a majority of the organs that make up the TNS network, in particular, national states networked into larger international forums, such as UN agencies, the G-20, the IMF, and the WB. But it is also true in a broader sense that individual national states, to the extent that the countries in question are integrated into the circuits of global capital, must promote accumulation within their borders in order to reproduce themselves and the social formations within their territorial jurisdictions. Competition among national states to attract and retain transnationally mobile capital is an important political dynamic in the global system. To the extent that inter- and supranational institutions promote such competition – "competitive states" – they promote conditions favorable to transnational capital and act as agents of global capitalism. This competition, moreover, serves to justify imposing on national working classes austerity, deregulation, and deunionization. However, we must recall that transnational power structures are localized within each nation by concrete social forces that are materially and politically part of an emergent transnational power bloc.

---

[20] Ernest Mandel, *Late Capitalism* (London: Verso, 1978).

But structuralist analysis of the state has limitations. Structural analysis and *structuralism* are not coterminous. Structuralism is generally identified with the approach developed by Louis Althusser and reduces human agency to "bearers of structures."[21] The teleology of classical state structuralism in which effects explain causes reflects a more general flaw of structuralism: its negation of agency and the role of social forces in struggle as historical agents that shape and reshape structures that they have created. There are no institutions and structures that are not mediated by historical agency. Structures are not predetermined and are contingent. Structuralist approaches replace the dialectic of structure and agency with a one-sided determination of structures. There is no dichotomy between structural determinations and those of historical agency. Agency conceived separate from structure reduces social classes and groups to voluntary interpersonal relations – a conspiratorial and strictly contingent view of the world.

Yet structure that is conceived as separate from agency is a reification. Structures institutionalize patterns of social interaction – including the material and ideological power relations involved in that interaction – within the bounds set by nature and those generated by collective agents. Structure operates "behind the backs" of agents and often contravenes the intentions of the most powerful agents in generating unintended consequences of social action. The collapse of the global financial system in September 2008 was just such an unintended structural outcome. Yet that outcome was the result of multiple collective agencies, such as the speculative activity of investors seeking to make profit. The response of the state to the needs of capitalist reproduction is not automatic, guaranteed, or immediate (as it is assumed to be in functionalist approaches). It is the job of social analysis to identify the processes of mediation through which collective agencies identify their circumstances and undertake action on that basis. Our focus must be on how social relations and processes are played out through institutions – including states – that are created and constantly recreated by collective agents, even if those institutions have in turn a recursive effect on the development of social forces. Of particular import here is the role of organic intellectuals – academics, journalists, charismatic politicians, technical functionaries, and so on – as key agents that mediate between the economic, the political, and the cultural-ideological level.

Derivationist readings of the state in the 1970s and 1980s that emphasized the "logics of capital and class struggle" placed agency and the contradictions of capitalism back into structuralist theories, including the observation that there is no guarantee that the state can secure the long-term stability and reproduction of capitalism.[22] Writing in the late 1970s and the 1980s, the derivationist school

[21] See, e.g., Louis Althusser, *Lenin and Philosophy and Other Essays* (New York: Monthly Review Press, 2001 [originally published in 1965]).

[22] See, e.g., John Holloway and Sol Picciotto, eds., *State and Capital: A Marxist Debate* (Austin: University of Texas Press, 1978), and, for summaries, Barrow, *Critical Theories of the State*.

proposed four phases or state forms in the historical development of capitalism: 1) an "absolutist state" form as a strong centralist state capable of subduing precapitalist ruling classes (corresponding, in my reading, to the mercantile era); 2) a "competitive capitalist state" form that assumes a background role of policing and adjudicating market transactions (corresponding, in my reading, to the era of competitive capitalism); 3) a "state capitalism" form in which a more interventionist state takes over some private activities and actively promotes accumulation (corresponding, in my reading, to the late nineteenth- and early twentieth-century era of national corporate capitalism); 4) a "world capitalism" form in which internationalization results in crises for states that must defend national capital and also adopt policies favorable to international capital. Writing on the eve of globalization and anticipating a TNS form, Picciotto and Radice suggested that the crisis of the state can be resolved only through the creation of transnational federations and international institutions, since transnational capital requires ever-larger state units to perform the essential political and economic functions of capital accumulation.[23]

The TNS as Promoter of Global Accumulation

Just as the national state is seen to secure the general conditions for accumulation at the national level, the TNS attempts to secure the general conditions for such accumulation at the level of the global economy. Capitalism could not function if the political and the economic were not formally separated because economic decision making is by definition accrued to property ownership under capitalism, which, also by definition, excludes the mass of wage laborers but also precludes the state from exercising authority over production or controlling it. The state is reduced to inducing private accumulation. The national state found it increasingly difficult to perform this function in the wake of the restructuring crisis of the 1970s. As capital went global the national state's efforts to induce transnational accumulation converged with the transformation of existing international and supranational institutions, such as the Bretton Woods institutions and organizations belonging to the UN system, and the creation of new institutions, such as the WTO and the European Union (EU). These diverse institutions would increasingly network around the task of generating the conditions for transnational accumulation and opening up global markets. The TNS generates such juridical and political conditions for the global valorization and accumulation of capital through numerous mechanisms, ranging from lifting national restrictions on the cross-border circulation of capital, to imposing new labor laws on countries, privatizing state and public assets, negotiating free trade agreements that displace peasants and turn them into proletarians, breaking up cooperatives and collectively held lands where collective ownership impedes

---

[23] As cited and discussed in Barrow, ibid, 84.

their commodification, and so forth.[24] The TCC and its agents utilize these TNS apparatuses, and at the same time these apparatuses organize the TCC.

Stated in different terms, the state must have the capacity to keep private capital in motion in accordance with prevailing conditions, organizational and political opportunities. This is indeed the capacity that the TNS has been developing, if not to the extent or in the same way that national states have historically developed. One way in which the TNS exhibits these capacities is by promoting (imposing) economic adjustment programs that generate in "adjusted" countries the macroeconomic conditions necessary for transnational capital to accumulate within and across its borders. Another is the creation of a global environment necessary for the global economy to function that includes free trade agreements, intellectual property rights, military interventions, multinational arbitrage mechanisms, and so on. The TNS actively seeks to promote investor confidence in the global economy, to respond to crises that generate instability and undermine access to resources and markets, and to promote policy uniformity. Former UN secretary general Kofi Annan observed in an address to the WEF that "the business of the United Nations involves the businesses of the world." It is worth quoting Annan at length:

> Technical standard-setting in areas such as aviation, shipping and telecommunications provides the very foundation for international transactions. . . . Our efforts to eradicate poverty create new markets and new opportunities for growth. Our peacekeeping and emergency relief operations in war-torn nations bring the stability needed to regain the path to long-term development. Our untiring efforts to build societies based on the rule of law promote regulatory consistency and peaceful change. We also help countries to join the international trading system and enact business-friendly legislation. . . . Creating wealth, which is business's expertise, and promoting human security in the broadest sense, the UN's main concern, are mutually reinforcing goals. Thriving markets and human security go hand in hand. . . . Markets do not function in a vacuum. Rather, they arise from a framework of rules and laws, and they respond to signals set by Governments and other institutions. Without rules governing property rights and contracts; without confidence based on the rule of law; without an overall sense of direction and a fair degree of equity and transparency, there could be no well-functioning markets, domestic or global. The UN system provides such a global framework, an agreed set of standards and objectives that enjoy worldwide acceptance. A strong United Nations is good for business.[25]

Another UN branch, the United Nations Conference on Trade and Development, or UNCTAD, was by the twenty-first century producing investment guides for global conglomerates so that they could have "comparative information on investment opportunities" in the global South.[26] And the WB's

---

[24] Robinson, *A Theory of Global Capitalism* and *Latin America and Global Capitalism*.
[25] Kofi Anna, "The UN and the Private Sector: 'Markets for a Better World'," *The Economist*, March 28–April 3, 1998: 24.
[26] See Prashad, *The Darker Nations*, 240–241.

International Financial Corporation has set up equity funds for global investors, in which the Bank acts as "global connector," in the words of former WB president Robert Zoellick, linking investors looking for high returns with investment opportunities around the world.[27]

Reciprocally, the TCC exercises its class power through TNS apparatuses. The International Chamber of Commerce, perhaps the premier transnational business association, develops in conjunction with UN agencies programs for liberalization and free market reform around the world. In doing so, it imposes its class power through the institutions of the TNS. In 1998, for instance, the office of the UN secretary general signed a joint statement with the International Chamber of Commerce (ICC) declaring that the UN and the ICC would "forge a close global partnership to secure greater business input into the world's economic decision-making" and would seek to establish "an effective regulatory framework for globalization." The ICC website explains that the Chamber "has established the G20 Advisory Group, comprising business leaders and CEOs from major global corporations, to effectively target G20 policy development on a global scale":

> In this context, the work of the G7/G8 has been a natural focal point for ICC to promote robust and unfettered global trade and to ensure that government policy is aligned with core business goals of open trade and investment, economic growth and job creation. Since the Houston G8 Summit in 1990, ICC's Chairman has been received by the G8 host Head of State – enabling us to present policy recommendations on behalf of world business. [More recently] the work of the G20 is a natural focal point for ICC's unique international policy stewardship – and presents an opportunity for global business to establish an enduring mechanism to engage with the Group of 20 governments and provide regular input into the G20 policy process.[28]

Beyond the G-8 and the G-20, the ICC "has engaged in a broad range of activities with the United Nations, the World Trade Organization, the World Intellectual Property Organization, and many other intergovernmental bodies." It has represented business in major global forums, such as the World Summit on Sustainable Development, the UN Framework Convention on Climate Change, and the Internet Governance Forum.

> ICC, as the world business organization, has a close working relationship with the WTO, supporting its work on trade. In 2011, ICC launched the business World Trade Agenda, an initiative proposing that business works together with governments to drive more effective trade talks, answering a call from G20 leaders for new approaches. ... ICC also participates in the WTO Expert Group on Trade Finance, which has become an important forum during economic crises, holding regular

[27] Robert B. Zoellick, "The End of the Third World? Modernizing Multilateralism for a Multipolar World," speech by Zoellick at the Woodrow Wilson Center for International Scholars, April 14, 2010, http://web.worldbank.org/WBSITE/EXTERNAL/NEWS/0,,contentMDK:22541126~pagePK:34370~piPK:42770~theSitePK:4607,00.html.

[28] See http://www.iccwbo.org/global-influence/g20/advisory-group/G20-advisory-group/

meetings with partners from commercial banks, the Berne Union, regional development banks, and other multilateral export credit and specialized agencies.[29]

Such examples of the role that the TNS plays in opening up opportunities for
TNC investment abound.[30] We see a functional fusion of TNS organs with
TNCs and business associations in policy development and implementation.
This appears to be a structural feature of global capitalism, one that mirrors
the relationship that has developed between the state and capital at the nation-
state level. It is through a TNS apparatus that global elites attempt to convert the
structural power of the global economy into supranational political authority.
TNS cadres utilize this structural power to impose global capitalist relations,
including loans and credit ratings. The TNS is in this sense a lever for the flow of
transnational investment. Core or "hard" national states, as components of a
larger TNS apparatus, play key roles in global restructuring. Transnational
fractions among dominant groups are able to use these core states to mold
transnational structures. This helps us to understand the preponderant role of
the U.S. national state in advancing capitalist globalization (about which I will
have more to say in the next chapter).

Just as the capitalist national state presents itself as the representative of the
general interests of the people and the nation, key organs of the TNS present
themselves as universalizing instances representing the common interests of
humanity by promoting development, defending human rights, pursuing justice,
resolving conflicts, and so forth. Yet such programs as World Bank micro-
financing, IMF structural adjustment loans, the United Nations Compact,
Millennium Development Goals, and peacekeeping operations – not to mention
the U.S.-led invasion of Iraq (see the following chapter) – seek to generate the
broader social and political conditions that allow global accumulation to proceed. The TNS insofar as it fosters the conditions for a globally integrated
market and globalized circuits of accumulation can be seen to impose the
"general will of capital" on global society. If the national form of the state, as
conceived in prevailing Marxist theories of the state and of international relations, implies that the state sets about to constitute the "general interest" of
capital on a national basis, then the emergent transnational form of the state is
that which attempts to achieve this "general interest" – presented as the common
interests of humanity – on a global basis.[31]

[29] Ibid.
[30] See, e.g., The European Corporate Observatory (http://www.corporateeurope.org/), a research
website on global corporate lobbying in the EU, which is full of examples.
[31] The "capital relation" approach of the so-called Open Marxist school associated with a group of
British scholars, among them Peter Burnham, John Holloway, Sol Picciotto, Simon Clarke, and
Werner Bonfeld, has made important contributions to our understanding of the state. Yet these and
other Marxists refuse to contemplate the transnationalization of the capitalist class, as I will discuss
in the next chapter, so that the competition among individual capitalists that the state mediates at the
national level becomes competition at the international level among national capitalist classes, yet

The UN's Millennium Development Goals, for example, were promulgated with much fanfare in 2000 at the United Nations Millennium Summit and with the participation of so-called civil society representatives. The Millennium Development Goals put forth a set of eight development goals to be achieved by 2015, among them a reduction by half in the percentage of people living in extreme poverty and who suffer from hunger; universal primary education; a reduction by two-thirds in the mortality rate among children under five and by three-quarters in the maternal mortality rate; halting and reversing the incidence of major diseases; promoting gender equality and the empowerment of women, and so on. However, the prescription put forth to achieve these lofty goals was based on a more thoroughgoing privatization of health and educational systems, further freeing up of the market from state regulations, greater trade liberalization and more structural adjustment, and the conversion of agricultural lands into private commercial property – in other words, an intensification of the very capitalist development that has generated the social conditions to be eradicated.[32]

The TNS is concerned with the problem of the cohesion of global society and with the political and ideological practices necessary to achieve that cohesion. Many of the programs of transnational institutions such as the United Nations, the G-8, and the G-20 seek to develop forums for generating consensus and collective solutions to problems that threaten the stability and reproduction of the global capitalist system. Poulantzas closely followed Gramsci's notion of hegemony in developing his concept of the power bloc. In such a bloc the interests of the dominant classes are constituted as the "general interest," so that corporate struggles are transposed to an alleged universal plane and dominant class unity is secured through an alliance of classes and fractions in which one – in this case, the TCC – is dominant. The state is the political organizer of the power bloc, and Poulantzas called the conglomerate of classes whose political interests are upheld by the state the "power bloc." The power bloc is comprised of various fractions of the capitalist class as well as other economically powerful classes or class fractions such as the landed aristocracy, elements of the petite bourgeoisie, and so on. In global capitalist society, the TCC is the dominant fraction of the capitalist classes worldwide and brings into the power bloc local capitalists, urban and rural landlords, transnationally oriented state

this competition is not mediated by the national state. Rather, it becomes the source of national competition and international conflict. Typical is Burnham: "Competition between capitals ... is not confined within a domestic economy. The accumulation of capital within the domestic economy depends on the accumulation of capital on a world scale. The role of the capitalist state is to express the 'general interest' of capital. However the national form of the state implies that the state can only constitute this 'general interest' on a national basis. Nation-states therefore have a similar relation of conflict and collaboration as individual capitals." See Peter Burnham, *The Political Economy of Postwar Reconstruction* (London: MacMillan, 1990), 185.

[32] See the critique by Samir Amin, "The Millennium Development Goals: A Critique from the South," *Monthly Review* (2006), 57(10), published online at http://monthlyreview.org/2006/03/01/the-millennium-development-goals-a-critique-from-the-south.

managers and other elites, and high-consumption middle layers. I will return shortly to the matter of the transnational power bloc.

The TNS as an Organizer of the TCC

Do global corporate and political/institutional elites constitute a coherent ruling class as distinct from a loose agglomeration of groups? Corporate elites are by themselves incapable of organizing into coherent class actors, beyond the immediate pursuit of profits, that is, beyond individual and corporate accumulation strategies. Keeping in mind the distinction between particular capitals and capital in general, we are concerned with how particular capitals are organized and how they form part of capital in general through varied mediations and articulations, and especially through the state.

One of the fundamental contradictions in the current global order is that a globalizing economy unfolds within a nation-state-based system of political authority. This poses great challenges for both popular classes and ruling groups. For popular classes, the challenge is how to transnationalize social and class struggle, how to accumulate beyond national borders the class power necessary to challenge global capital. For ruling groups, the challenge is how to develop instruments and institutions that allow global capitalism to be stabilized through the distinct sets of instrumental, supervisory, and regulatory processes that were previously more effective at the nation-state level. In part, the impetus to develop TNS apparatuses comes from above as an effort to assure instruments of rule, or domination, and mechanisms for stabilizing the volatile global order.

But if the inability of the TNS to impose coherence and regulation on transnational accumulation is due in part to the underdevelopment of TNS apparatuses – in particular, to the problem of multiple jurisdictions and lack of enforcement capacity – it is also due to the vulnerability of the TCC as a class group in terms of its own internal disunity and fractionation, and its blind pursuit of immediate accumulation – that is, of its immediate and particular interests over its long-term or general interests. The TCC does not have the political capacity to rule directly in its own name *as a class*, or in its own long-term interests. The politicized strata of the TCC and transnationally oriented elites and organic intellectuals, including those who staff TNS institutions, attempt to define these long-term interests and to develop policies, projects, and ideologies to secure these interests. Since the specific interests of the various components of the power bloc are divergent, it is the state's role to *unify* and *organize* the various classes and fractions in order to uphold their long-term political interests against the threat of the exploited and oppressed classes, argues Poulantzas. The power bloc "can in the end only operate under the hegemony and leadership of the component that cements it together in the face of the class enemy."[33]

---

[33] Poulantzas, *State, Power, Socialism*, 135.

The members of the TCC and transnational managerial elites operate through the dense network of institutions that comprise a TNS apparatus as they manage their investments and pursue their political concerns around the world. And it is out of such networking that a politicized strata has been able to engage transnationally. The TNS is a web of decentered institutions, a fragmentary apparatus that lacks supranational enforcement mechanisms or institutional cohesion. There is certainly no systemic unity in an organizational sense. The U.S. national state is the closest thing to a center within the TNS. There is no central coordinating mechanism. But the degree of centralized cohesion is *not* what determines whether the network constitutes a TNS; rather, *it is the ability of the TCC and transnational elites to operate institutionally through this network to coordinate policies and practices across borders in the effort to achieve their class interests, exercise class power at a transnational level, and develop a field of transnational power.*

Global capitalists and elites operate in conjunction with one another across borders *through* national states and institutions as well as through inter- and supranational organizations. Discussing his research into the global "superclass," Rothkopf describes how his team participated in the joint annual meetings of the IMF and the WB and in meetings of the regional development banks. "At such events, we watched as a few hundred bankers and finance ministers worked together on global financial issues: bailing out failed countries at breakfast, forming alliances over canapés, funding deals at cocktail hour," and so on.[34] Rothkopf then goes on to observe:

> The complication in the era of the superclass is that political institutions, for the most part, are linked to nation-states. Those seeking to win or use political power on a transnational basis must chose between working with comparatively weak international institutions and contending with a vast array of uncoordinated, often competitive or conflict-divided national political systems. One of the considerable strengths of the superclass is its ability to build political potency on a cross-border basis, and to do so with both those internationalized elites that also operate within the global economy, and national elites that are important within individual countries. In the absence of global political institutions, the best path to influencing global outcomes is building networks of individuals and organizations that have influence in key countries. This is the special strength of the superclass given its positions, resources, and global orientation, and it is part of the reason that gatherings of these elites are so important – they become hubs at which ideas can be advanced globally. Thus unable to lobby or serve in a global government, the superclass effectively employs a global political strategy the only way possible, via influencing the influencers.[35]

Let us examine more closely this idea of global elites influencing national-state managers – and recall that these global elites are not just on the outside looking in; they are also influencing national-state apparatuses from the inside. This

[34] Rothkopf, *Superclass*, xviii.
[35] Rothkopf, *Superclass*, 85–86.

influence is a key nexus in the exercise of TNS power. The state has never been a unitary macro-agent, even in the heyday of the Westphalian order. National states have always been fragmentary and multilayered; distinct agencies and ministries are sites of conflict and competition and are linked to distinct combinations of social and class forces in civil society. One salient dimension of the transnationalization of the state has been the relative increase in power and influence of those agencies and ministries tied to the global economy, especially finance, trade, and foreign ministries and central banks. Indeed, as a number of authors have noted, the movement toward the independence of central banks has been crucial to globalization policies and pressures from within national states.[36]

Social scientists who study the state tend to focus either on the individual national state or on the interstate or international state system. While the latter is of great importance to the study of global capitalism, I am concerned here with the institutional forms or apparatuses of the TNS that are emerging, in part, *out of* the system of national states. The world capitalist system is not made up of an aggregation of compartmentalized units. It is a single system in which state power has historically been allocated between territorial entities. In practice, exclusive jurisdiction is impossible to define. With the increasing transnational integration of capitalist social relations the network of overlapping and interlocking jurisdictions becomes denser. On the other hand, ironically, the fragmentary and highly emergent nature of a TNS apparatus means that it has more political ability than national capitalist states to act independently of specific transnational corporate groups and "special interests" and more political ability to (attempt to) act in the general interests of the global capitalist system. Yet it has less material ability to defend those interests, given the dispersal of formal political authority across many national states and the lack of enforcement mechanisms, and the loose nature of a TNS apparatus with no center or formal constitution.

In exploring this contradiction, it is important to distinguish analytically – for methodological purposes – between the state and civil society – between TNS institutions such as the UN, the IMF, the WB, the EU, the WTO, the APEC, and so on, and private transnational elite forms such as the WEF, the Trilateral Commission, and the ICC. However, the two are subsumed under the larger category of social forces and the institutional matrices that these forces create and through which they operate – in what Gramsci refers to as the *extended state* as "political society + civil society." No state exhibits clear-cut boundaries between its institutions and others in a social formation. The boundary between state and civil society is an artificial conceptual line that is "drawn within an

---

[36] On the spread worldwide of Central Bank independence, see Marco Arnone, Bernard J. Laurens, and Jean-Francois Segalotto, *"Measures of Central Bank Autonomy: Empirical Evidence for OECD, Developing, and Emerging Market Economies,"* IMF Working Paper, WP/06/228 (IMF: Washington, DC, 2006).

unbroken network of institutional mechanisms through which a certain social and political order is maintained."[37] Both formal state institutions and the myriad of associations in civil society are grounded in the class relations of political economy. The TNS, as I have conceived it in analytical abstraction, is comprised of a network of trans- and supranational organizations together with national states or parts of national states that link national to transnational social structures. The TCC organizes itself increasingly through transnational associations that constitute part of global civil society – the WEF, the ICC, and so forth – just as at the national level these transnational civil society organizations interpenetrate with the TNS.

Conceptually, what takes place is a process of mutual constitution; the TNS is brought about by the transnational activities of the TCC, yet the TNS organizes the transnational power bloc. The varied organizations, arrangements, treaties, and so forth of the TNS are forums that generate coordination among national state managers and with the global corporate community. The formal meetings and the countless working groups and activities of such organizations as the Organization for Economic Cooperation and Development (OECD), the IMF, the World Bank, the APEC, and the G-20 play a crucial integrative function for cadre of the TNS and for the TCC. The organs of the TNS operate as well in close coordination with TCC organizations, such as the WEF and the ICC, and with informal forums such as the Trilateral Commission that form part of transnational civil society yet interface closely with the TNS, building consensus among the transnational elite. The attempt to manage global capitalism takes place through kaleidoscopic contacts across components of the TNS, private TCC organizations, foundations, and what can best be called public-private forums such as the WEF, which bring together representatives from the global corporate community with national state managers, cadre from TNS institutions, and organic intellectuals in the service of global capitalism.

For Van der Pijl the theory of global capitalism, including the concept of the TNS, "remains abstract whereas they claim to denote concrete realities."[38] It is true that in order for the concept of the TNS to acquire validity we must be able to demonstrate, using concrete empirical research, specific TNS forms and practices and to demonstrate the exercise of TNS power in specific conjunctures. I have done so in several empirical-historical studies. To summarize but one example, in *Transnational Conflicts* I demonstrated the rise of new economic activities in Central America that now constitute the core of accumulation in that region, including *maquiladora* industrial production, transnational tourism and financial services, and new agro-industrial operations. I then documented how the locally dominant economic groups shifted a good portion of their investments into these new accumulation activities, which involved a major interpenetration of these local groups with transnational corporate capital and as

---

[37] Barrow, *Critical Theories of the State*, 144.
[38] Van der Pijl, "A Theory of Global Capitalism: Feature Review," 276.

well increasing extra-regional investment by these local groups in transnational corporate circuits.

As local Central American capitalists shifted into these new activities and transnational investment outlets, so too did they organize politically in their respective countries through existing parties or the creation of new parties and corporate political associations. Operating through these political vehicles, these new transnationally oriented elites in the region were able in the 1980s and 1990s to capture local states in elections and to place their representatives into key ministries, in particular, Central Banks and economic and foreign ministries. From these positions they pursued sweeping deregulation, liberalization, and integration into the global economy; they dismantled earlier multiclass developmentalist coalitions; they reoriented local market production to the global market; they made labor flexible; they negotiated free trade agreements, and so forth. Reciprocally, local political and state elites came to recognize that their own status would require promoting these new economic activities and patterns of accumulation in alliance with the transnationally oriented capitalists. In all of this, the supranational agencies such as the WB, the U.S. Agency for International Development, and the Inter-American Development Bank liaised through numerous mechanisms with local Central American states and elites in promoting the new transnational model of accumulation. In short, a new power bloc emerged in Central America that brought transnational corporate and political functionaries from outside the region together with new economic and political elites inside the region into the global capitalist bloc.

The Case of Free Trade Agreements

Such concrete empirical and historical examples of the exercise of TCC power through TNS apparatuses abound. The problem is not that the concept remains abstract but that the concrete realities it denotes, such as those I have been discussing, are blind-sighted out of analyses whose framework is the traditional nation-state/interstate system. This framework, for instance, views trade liberalization in North-South national terms, so that regional agreements such as the North American Free Trade Agreement (NAFTA) and the Central American Free Trade Agreement (CAFTA) in the Americas, or multilateral WTO negotiations, are interpreted as instances of northern or core country domination and exploitation of the South. Free trade agreements have indeed opened up the world to transnational corporate plunder, further concentrating power in the hands of the TCC, dispossessing local communities, and deepening polarization of the rich and the poor within and across countries. But these agreements were also promoted by powerful agents within the South who were just as much a part of the global power structure and who benefitted as much from liberalization as their northern counterparts. U.S. and EU government reluctance to eliminate agricultural subsidies during WTO negotiations in recent years over the liberalization of the global agricultural system were seen as attempts by the North to protect its own agricultural producers while gaining access to southern agriculture and markets and hence to maintain domination in the international system.

Yet farmers in the North did not benefit from free trade agreements and faced the same takeover by the leviathan-like transnational agro-industrial corporations that have come to dominate the world food system from laboratory to farm to supermarket – such as Cargill, Monsanto, and ADM – as did their southern counterparts. And southern governments such as Brazil and India that in calling for an end to Northern agricultural subsidies supposedly championed the interests of the South over the North were no more protecting the interests of small farmers and local rural communities in their own countries than were northern states. These same governments had steadily facilitated as part of capitalist globalization the transformation of their national agricultural systems into corporate-dominated capitalist agriculture. Brazil, for example, is the second largest exporter of soy in the world, and its soy industry is thoroughly enmeshed in the global corporate agro-industrial complex, in the hands of large-scale producers, suppliers, processors, and exporters who themselves are part of the global corporate food system. In fact, these governments were not pushing for a more democratic international order but for a *more complete and balanced corporate globalization.*

Cargill is the largest exporter of U.S. *and* of Brazilian soybeans. Cargill, ADM, and Argentine-based Bunge finance 60 percent of the soy produced in Brazil, while Monsanto controls soy-seed manufacturing in both countries.[39] Brazilian-based capitalists, in turn, are heavily invested in these companies. This globalized soy agro-industrial complex uses Brazil as a base from which to conquer and control world soy markets. The Brazilian government's aggressive program of agricultural trade liberalization, waged through the WTO (in particular, through the Cairns Group of countries that rely heavily on agricultural exports) is not in defense of "Brazilian" interests against northern or imperial capital but on behalf of a transnationalized soy agro-industrial complex.[40]

In India, another member country of the Cairns Group, powerful transnationally oriented Indian capitalist interests have pushed hard for the Indian state to sign on to WTO "trade related intellectual property rights" (TRIPS)

---

[39] Raj Patel, *Stuffed and Starved: The Hidden Battle for the World Food System* (Brooklyn: Melville House, 2007), 199.

[40] One U.S. soy farmer and activist with the U.S.-based National Family Farm Coalition has explained: "[F]armers [from different countries] need to understand why they're competing against each other. The thing that made me realize this most is that Cargill is not only the largest exporter of U.S. soybeans but also the biggest exporter of Brazilian soybeans. So then what's the conflict of trade rules about? Farmers need to understand that every independent producer of tradable commodities in every country is being squeezed by the same companies – the big traders, processors, and retailers – and that the root of the problem is the corporate structure of the global agricultural economy, not one country's subsidies or another country's environmental practices." The farmer and activist is Emelie Peine, as quoted in Patel, *Stuffed and Starved*, 197.

agreements, which allows corporations to claim legal ownership and patent over knowledge and ideas such as software, trademarks, entertainment, genetically modified organisms, and farming knowledge – that is, to convert these into intangible capital. Within India, as Patel explains, the TRIPS that would benefit the capitalists in the information technology and other transnationally oriented sectors would further devastate small farmers, whose farming techniques and knowledge are under threat of being appropriated and patented by transnational agribusiness corporations. In one widely cited case, the W.R. Grace Company attempted in the 1990s, under the banner of intellectual property rights, to win a patent on the Indian neem tree because it had discovered that the tree is a powerful natural pesticide. Indian farmers who had had such knowledge of the tree's properties for two thousand years would have been forced to pay W.R. Grace for use of the tree if the patent had actually been approved.[41]

NAFTA was interpreted by many of its leftist critics as a U.S. takeover of Mexico along the lines of classical dependency theory.[42] Much has been written on NAFTA as a casebook study of the ravages of capitalist globalization on the popular classes in the countryside, including what remains of the peasantry proper, of small- and medium-market producers and rural communities. An estimated 1.3 million families were forced off the land in the years after NAFTA went into effect in 1994 as the Mexican market was flooded with cheap corn from the United States. U.S. farmers did not reap the benefits of NAFTA; transnational corporate agro-industry did, along with a handful of powerful economic agents on both sides of the border. From approval of NAFTA into the twenty-first century, Mexican agro-export businesses grew rapidly. In Mexico, the winners were the Mexican members of the TCC. Patel has shown how urban (and rural) consumers in Mexico did *not* benefit from cheaper corn imported from the United States. Rather, the price of tortillas – the Mexican staple – actually *rose* in the wake of NAFTA even as bulk corn prices dropped. This was because NAFTA helped Mexican transnational capitalists to gain monopoly control of the corn-tortilla market. Just two companies, GIMSA and MINSA, together control 97 percent of the industrial corn flour market.[43] GIMSA, which accounts for 70 percent of the market, is owned by Gruma SA, a multibillion dollar Mexican-based global corporation, which also dominates the tortilla market in the United States under the label Mission Foods. Alongside the displacement of millions of small producers the Mexican government increased its subsidies for these large ("efficient") corn millers and simultaneously scaled back credit for small rural and urban producers and social programs involving food subsidies for the poor, who traditionally consume local hand-made tortillas.

---

[41] Patel, *Stuffed and Starved*, 132–133.
[42] See, e.g., James M. Cypher and Raul Delgado Wise, *Mexico's Economic Dilemma: The Developmental Failure of Neoliberalism* (Landham, MD: Rowman and Littlefeld, 2010).
[43] Patel, *Stuffed and Starved*, 53.

In sum, the corn-tortilla circuit went from one based on small, local corn and tortilla producers to a transnational commodity chain involving industrially produced and U.S.-state-subsidized corn and industrially produced and Mexican-state-subsidized tortilla production and distribution on both sides of the border. We can see here how transnational conglomerates of corn production and processing on both sides of the border were the beneficiaries of NAFTA, while both the U.S. and the Mexican state acted to facilitate transnational accumulation through the approval of NAFTA, the subsidization of transnational corporate production, the conversion of peasant agriculture into transnational agribusiness, and neo-liberal austerity. This is not a picture of U.S. colonization of Mexico as much as it is one of transnational corporate colonization of both countries, facilitated by the two national states functioning as we would expect from TNS apparatuses.

The Mexican state and political system were wracked by fierce and even bloody struggles between national and transnational fractions of the elite in the 1980s and 1990s as the country integrated into the global economy.[44] During these struggles, transnationally oriented fractions were broadly supported by global elites from outside Mexico and by TNS institutions in their effort to gain control of the Mexican state and to become the reigning group in control of the then-ruling party, the Institutional Revolutionary Party (PRI). This transnational fraction of the Mexican elite triumphed definitively with the election to the presidency of one of its key representatives, Carlos Salinas de Gortari, in the fraud-tainted vote of 1988. These class dynamics constituted the broader context for the Mexican state's promotion of NAFTA, which was above all aimed at the transformation of the Mexican agricultural system – which had come into existence with the Mexican revolution of 1910 and which involved a significant portion of peasant, collective, and small-scale production for the domestic market – into a globally integrated system based on large-scale export-oriented capitalist agriculture. It is noteworthy that NAFTA itself was heavily pushed by transnational groups within the Mexican business and political elite. The North American Group of the Trilateral Commission, which played a key role in designing and governing NAFTA, included twelve Mexican members.[45]

Transnationally oriented Mexican state managers ensconced in power starting in 1988 called on the World Bank – simultaneous with their negotiation of the NAFTA – to assist them in drafting policies to accomplish this transition.[46] In fact, as both Babb and Centeno show in their respective studies,[47] the original

---

[44] On these details, see Robinson, *Latin America and Global Capitalism*.

[45] Alejandro Salas-Porras, "The Transnational Class in Mexico: New and Old Mechanisms Structuring Corporate Networks (1981–2010)," in Georgina Murray and John Scott, eds., *Financial Elites and Transnational Business: Who Rules the World?* (Cheltenham, UK: Edgard Elgar Publishing, 2012), 169.

[46] Patel, *Stuffed and Starved*, 55.

[47] Miguel Centeno, *Democracy within Reason: Technocratic Revolution in Mexico* (Philadelphia: Pennsylvania State University, 1997); Sara Babb, *Managing Mexico: Economists from Nationalism to Neo-Liberalism* (Princeton, NJ: Princeton University Press, 2001).

impetus for Mexico's globalization came from transnationally oriented technocrats from within the Mexican state under the Salinas administration in consort
with supranational organizations such as the World Bank. Subsequently they
mobilized powerful economic groups among the Mexican business community,
who were able to make the shift from national into transnational circuits of
accumulation and who would go on to lead powerful Mexican-based transnational corporations. TNS apparatuses in such cases actually take the lead in
organizing and globalizing dominant local groups. This transnationalization of
the Mexican state and of significant portions of the Mexican capitalist class is a
process that cannot be understood in terms of outdated neo-colonial analyses of
U.S. imperialism and Mexican dependence.

The agricultural trade liberalization pushed by northern states and the transnational agro-industrial corporate lobby shifts value not to First World farmers
but to transnational capital, to the giant corporations that control marketing
and agro-industrial processing, while also reorganizing the value structure in
such a way that cheap processed foods are available to better-off urban strata in
both North and South. As peasant subsistence agriculture has increasingly given
way to incorporation into the global capitalist agricultural system, several
models have emerged, ranging from large-scale and corporate plantation agriculture to the subordination of smaller producers to the market via dependence
on agro-industrial inputs (e.g., seeds – often genetically modified – fertilizers and
pesticides, etc.) and on marketing agents. This latter category can be seen as a
process of subsuming these groups more fully into capital's orbit. While it is true
that U.S. "farmers," for instance, may enjoy a higher standard of living than
many of their Third World counterparts, they have no more security and are
completely controlled by corporate dictates. They are more accurately seen as
employees of the corporate agribusiness giants or as rural workers – since capital
exercises indirect control over the means of production, determining what must
be produced, how it must be produced, and under what terms output is to be
marketed – than as independent farmers. This, of course, when their land is not
itself foreclosed. Producers who actually perform the labor of planting and
harvesting – even when these are not wage-earning farm workers but those
who formally own land – are not meant to be the winners in trade liberalization.

One Mexican analyst of the global food crisis reveals the schizophrenic
thinking generated by a nation-state/interstate framework of analysis. The
author observes that the steep rise in food prices in 2010–11 as a result of
investor speculation in commodity markets "also affects the poorest U.S. citizens. Currently there are some 40 million people in the United States who exist
under conditions of food poverty, in that their income does not even allow them
to cover basic food necessities." She continues: "These people live in conditions
of extreme poverty similar to that of the Third World. ... [I]s it not the same
when one digs through the garbage dump for food in Beverly Hills, California, as
it is when one does so in Haiti? Poverty has globalized; it is no longer just
spreading in the poor countries as it did in the 1980s." Nonetheless, immediately

after making these observations the commentator insists that "the United States continues to be the principal hegemonic power that benefits from the food crisis," and that in Mexico "authorities undertake policies that unconditionally benefit U.S. agribusiness interests. ... The food crisis is a part of the struggle among states for hegemony in the world market."[48]

The TNS as an Instrument of Coercion and Labor Control

TNS apparatuses have exercised economic and extra-economic coercion in order to impose new labor regimes worldwide. TNS practices have unequal and asymmetric effects on the ability of different social forces to realize their interests through political action. Corporate lobbies, for instance, are invited into the inner chambers of IMF or WB annual meetings and send delegations to G-8 and G-20 meetings, while those who wish to make known their opposition to global capitalism at these forums are locked out and their protests subject to police repression. But more central to the labor and social control functions of the TNS is its structural power, that is, as I discussed previously, the coercive discipline of the global market, whose levers can be pulled by the IFIs and the core national states of the G-8 to open up space for global accumulation within each nation and region. As we have seen, states are subject to this structural power of transnational capital and the coercive discipline of the global economy even when transnationally oriented groups are unable to instrumentalize states directly. This coercive economic power is superimposed on local political conflicts and social struggles in order to subordinate local labor and undermine opposition to global capitalism.

The TNS has played a key role in imposing the neo-liberal model on the old Third World and therefore in reinforcing a new capital-labor relation. Structural adjustment and austerity programs imposed by the IMF, the WB, the EU, and other transnational financial institutions that open up a given country to the penetration of transnational capital, the subordination of local labor, and the extraction of wealth by transnational capitalists are operating as a TNS institution to facilitate the exploitation of local labor by global capital. IMF, WB, EU, and other TNS lending and bailouts are conditioned on austerity, deregulation, and flexibilization of local labor markets, among other measures that impose the new capital-labor relation on the particular country and in the process fundamentally transform local labor markets and class and power relations. These structural pressures bolster the political action capacity of transnationally oriented elites and dampen that of the popular classes.

Functionaries of the TNS are quite conscious of their role in subordinating global labor to global capital in order to reproduce the new capital-labor

---

[48] Nydia Egremy, "Mexico y Grandes Regiones del Mundo, en Riesgo de Hambrunas," *Rebelion*, online magazine, February 2, 2011: 1–10, quotes from pp. 2–3, http://www.rebelion.org/noticia. php?id=122471&titular=m%E9xico-y-grandes-regiones-del-mundo-en-riesgo-de-hambrunas-.

relations. For instance, in a major policy address in 1984, then IMF Director Jacques de Larosiere explained:

> Over the past four years the rate of return on capital investment in manufacturing in the six largest industrial countries averaged only about half the rate earned during the late 1960s. . . . Even allowing for cyclical factors, a clear pattern emerges of a substantial and progressive long-term decline in rates of return on capital. There may be many reasons for this. But there is no doubt that an important contributing factor is to be found in the significant increase over the past 20 years or so in the share of income being absorbed by compensation of employees. . . . This points to the need for a gradual reduction in the rate of increase in real wages over the medium term if we are to restore adequate investment incentives.[49]

How is extra-economic compulsion or direct coercion organized and deployed under global capitalism, and how does it combine with economic compulsion? Weber's classic definition of the state consists of two interrelated propositions. First, what distinguishes the state is its claim to a legitimate monopoly of violence. Second, this legitimate monopoly of the exercise of violence is limited to the territorial boundaries of nation-states. Like Weber, Martin Shaw argues in his study, *Theory of the Global State*, that the state is best understood as institutionalized political authority backed up by legitimate violence. Such an institutionalized authority has now become transnationalized and incarnated in the "Western state," which refers to the major capitalist nation-states of the West and the "worldwide web of authoritative relations" that the Western state has spun.[50] Cast in the light of TNS theory, we can observe that the U.S.-led TNS attempts to achieve a Weberian legitimate exercise of state violence at the global level, for example, through UN Security Council resolutions sanctioning "peace-keeping" or "humanitarian" occupations, "no fly-zones," bombing campaigns, and so on, as those in Serbia, Haiti, Lybia, Iraq, Afghanistan, and Somalia. Such bodies as NATO, the African Union, and United Nations blue-helmet forces join the United States as incipient networks of global extra-economic compulsion. As I will discuss in the next chapter, the U.S. invasion of Iraq imposed a property regime that gave free reign to transnational capital in the occupied country and promoted integration into global capitalism, in this way internalizing global capitalist relations in the occupied country. Both economic coercion by the TNS apparatus – IMF practices, for example – and extra-economic compulsion of these apparatuses – for example, UN interventions in Serbia and Haiti and the U.S.-organized invasion and occupation of Iraq – are instances of *TNS practices*.

As capitalism has developed, the state, alongside its repressive control functions, has increasingly acquired the function of integrating subordinate classes

---

[49] As cited in Howard M. Wachtel, *The Money Mandarins: The Making of a New Supranational Economic Order* (New York: Pantheon, 1986), 137.

[50] Martin Shaw, *Theory of the Global State: Globality as an Unfinished Revolution* (Cambridge: Cambridge University Press, 2000), 193. For my critique of Shaw's study, see my book review in *American Political Science Review* (2001), 95(4): 1045–1047.

into the dominant social order. This integrative function is carried out not only through a myriad of cultural and ideological processes, including shaping the means of communication, cultural and ideological production, and discursive practices, but also through material and political incentives that come to be structured into historically impermanent social arrangements such as historic blocs and social structures of accumulation. The state, that is, remains Machiavelli's centaur, or half-man and half-beast, coercion and consent. The TNS is no different in this regard, although its capabilities and limits, its modalities, and the level of regularity, organization, and coherence with which its organs attempt to fulfill these functions is quite distinct from the national-state level. The Millennium Goals, antipoverty programs, ideologies of universal human rights and international justice, and so forth are all part of these "integrative functions" of the TNS. But *intent* is not *ability*; there are severe limits on the ability of the TNS to stabilize global capitalism, much less resolve the system's crisis.

GLOBAL CRISIS AND THE CONTRADICTIONS OF TNS POWER

We now have global financial markets, global corporations, global financial flows. But what we do not have is anything other than national and regional regulation and supervision. We need a global way of supervising our financial system. . . . [W]e need very large and very radical [political, institutional] changes.
— British Prime Minister Gordon Brown following an emergency G-8 meeting in 2008 on the global financial collapse[51]

"For much of the controversy about the state makes sense only on the false assumption that the state has a definite unity because it is a subject or because it performs a specific pre-given function or functions in capitalist reproduction," Jessop has observed. "But there are no valid grounds for presupposing the essential class unity of the state and various arguments suggest that it is necessarily fragmented and fissured. The state comprises a plurality of institutions (or apparatuses) and their unity, if any, far from being pregiven, must be constituted politically."[52] If this is true for the national state, it is even truer for the TNS. Theoretical conceptualization of the state takes on renewed relevance in this new epoch, but now in the context not of the nation-state but of global economy and society. Structural readings of the state have observed that the structural limitations of the state are marked by its inability to supersede the functional constraints (i.e., the contradictions) of the capitalist system.

The global crisis forces the capitalist state to intervene in an attempt to stabilize the system and prevent its collapse. Poulantzas stated famously in his treatise *Political Power and Social Classes* that the state functions as "the

[51] Jeremy Brecher, Tim Costello, and Brenda Smith, "The G-20 vs. the G-6 Billion," *Znet*, Nov. 20, 2008, http://www.zmag.org/znet/viewArticle/19707.

[52] Jessop, *The Capitalist State*, 222.

regulating factor" in capitalism's "global [meaning "overall," not "planetary] equilibrium as a system," and that it fulfills this function by "constituting the factor of cohesion between levels of a social formation."[53] But global (planetary) crisis presents a new level of complexity because the TNS cannot play this role – or, to use structural language, it cannot fulfill this function. A fundamental contradiction in the global system, to reiterate, is a globalizing economy within a nation-state-based system of political authority, legal enforcement, and legitimation. One of the chief obstacles to any resolution of the global crisis from above – no matter how temporary – is precisely the lack of more fully developed TNS machinery that could actually impose its political authority over global capital. The TNS *has* been able to impose its domination over the world's popular classes in the interests of transnational accumulation. But it has not been able to impose such authority over transnational capital or in the general and long-term interests of global capitalism. Money's increasing circulation as globalized stateless money, in the form of transnational financial capital, in particular, presents hitherto unprecedented problems for the institutional regulation of the circuits of accumulation (see Chapter 4).

Bound up with global capitalism are contradictory and conflictual processes of transnationalization *both* of the state and of capital; the crisis (or crises) of global capitalism involves a crisis of transnational capital *and also* a crisis of the interstate system. As globalization advances there are overlaps and conflicts of jurisdiction to regulate capital, especially among the most powerful national states, as became apparent in the series of emergency G-8 and G-20 meetings held in the wake of the September 2008 collapse of the global financial system, and as insinuated by Gordon Brown in the quotation that opens this section. These are not "inter-imperialist" conflicts. They are of a very different nature. Intra-elite political battles at the international level are not over national competition or rivalry but over how to stabilize and relegitimate global capitalism, how to achieve a "relative autonomy" of the TNS.

The TNS has functioned to open up the world to transnational capital and to develop a multitude of political strategies aimed at containing rebellion from below – such as the Millennium goals, fostering organizations in global civil society and bringing the more moderate among them into the networking activities of TNS apparatuses. But it cannot resolve the fundamental contradictions of global capitalism. Among these contradictions is that between the capitalist state's accumulation function and its legitimation function. This contradiction is not new to the epoch of globalization. However, the conditions of capitalist globalization have aggravated this contradiction to the extent that states are unable to regulate previously national circuits of capital that are now transnationalizing. *The national state's accumulation function is now transnational, while its legitimation function remains national.* The neo-liberal national state must assure national integration into the global economy and generate the conditions for transnational accumulation within its particular

---

[53] Nicos Poulantzas, *Political Power and Social Classes* (London: Verso, 1973), 44.

territorial jurisdiction. At the same time, its legitimation function remains national. To state this more theoretically, there is a "complex and contingent" articulation of the socially necessary and the class function of the state.[54] This articulation – or multiple forms of articulation – achieved during the nation-state era of world capitalism is being undone by the forces of globalization.

The state, as Offe has noted, must compensate for market failures without infringing on the primacy of private accumulation, yet it cannot undertake this compensation without undermining the dominance of the capital-labor relation through the extension of noncommodity forms.[55] These contradictions were managed for a time during the post–World War II period through Fordist-Keynesianism, but globalization undermined these arrangements and unleashed the neo-liberal "counterrevolution." The invasion and commodification of what were noncommodified spaces has ranged from outsourcing more and more public activities (including war itself) to private companies, the privatization of health and education, and so forth. This juggernaut of the commodification of everything has aggravated crises of social reproduction, undermining the social bases for more stable forms of consensual domination and providing further impetus for more coercive forms of social control.

Worldwide class and social conflict in the 1960s and 1970s brought into sharp relief the incompatibility of the state's accumulation and legitimation functions, leading to spiraling fiscal and legitimation crises.[56] Capitalist restructuring in response to these crises involved a shift from the social welfare to the social control state. National states turned from providing means of social reproduction for the growing surplus population to repressing this population. The "neo-liberal revolution" unleashed by globalization marked a transition from the Fordist-Keynesian social structure of accumulation to a savage global capitalism that entailed 1) a redisciplining of labor through globalization, flex-ibilization, high un- and underemployment, and the dismantling of welfare systems, *and* 2) the development of vast new social control systems, including prison-industrial complexes and transnational immigrant labor supply and control systems.

The state responds to those expelled from the labor market and locked out of productive labor not with expanded social welfare and protection but with abandonment and with repressive social control and containment strategies, including a vicious criminalization of the marginalized, often racialized and ethnicized, and the mobilization of the "culture industries" to dehumanize the victims of global capitalism as dangerous, depraved, and culturally degenerate Others, as criminal elements posing a threat to society. At the same time, the

---

[54] For further discussion on this point, see Jessop, *The Capitalist State*.
[55] Claus Offe, "Structural Problems of the Capitalist State," in K. Von Beyme, ed., *German Political Studies*, vol. 1 (London: Sage, 1974), 31–57.
[56] See James O'Connor, *The Fiscal Crisis of the State* (Piscataway, NJ: Transaction Publishers, 2001); Juergen Habermas, *Legitimation Crisis* (Boston: Beacon Press, 1975).

culture of global capitalism attempts to seduce the excluded and abandoned into petty consumption and fantasy as an alternative to placing social or political demands on the system through mobilization. These ideological campaigns deflect attention from the sources of social deprivation and channel the insecurities associated with capitalist globalization onto the marginalized groups. Within the nation-state the marginalized and/or superexploited become scapegoats, which helps the political representatives of the ruling groups to organize electoral coalitions and construct consensus around the new order (e.g., anti-immigrant and get-tough-on-crime campaigns). Internationally, the Third World victims of abandonment – viz, Somalia, Haiti, the Congo – are portrayed, at best, as passive and incompetent victims eliciting paternal sympathy, if not as inferiors to be dismissed and relegated to oblivion.

In sum, the state's ability to function as a "factor of cohesion" within the social order breaks down to the extent that capital has globalized and the logic of accumulation or commodification penetrates every aspect of social life – the "life world" itself – so that "cohesion" requires more and more social control – gated communities, policing, panoptical surveillance, spatial apartheid, prison-industrial complexes, and so on – in the face of the collapse of the social fabric. This is a topic I will discuss in detail in Chapter 5. The point to highlight here is that the shift from social welfare to social control states is less a question of public policy, in the first instance, than of class relations; the liberation of emergent transnational capital from the nation-state has undermined the material basis of the capitalist redistributive state. This liberation has altered the relative power of popular classes and of capital that had congealed in the redistributive state.

Redistribution is still possible at the nation-state level when popular class and social forces take control of, and transform, the neo-liberal national state (as in Venezuela). Even then, however, the larger global system and the structural power that transnational capital is able to exercise over the direct power of national states severely constrains redistributive projects at the nation-state level. As social forces struggle in, for, and against national states within particular countries, these *are* transnational struggles, to the extent that countries are integrated organically into global capitalism. The starting point of struggles from below by subordinate groups is the local and the national, but even when national states are captured by these groups, projects of popular transformation from below can hope to succeed only as part of more expansive transnational projects.

The struggle for hegemony in the global system should not be seen in terms of a dispute *among* nation-states but in terms of transnational social and class groups and their struggles to develop hegemonic and counterhegemonic projects. The class relations of global capitalism are now so deeply internalized *within* every nation-state that the classical image of imperialism as a relation of external domination is outdated. As I will take up in the next chapter, nation-state-centric analyses of inter- and transnational relations fail to appreciate the integrative character of global capitalism. The TCC has been attempting to position itself as a new ruling class worldwide since the 1980s and to bring some coherence and stability to its rule through emergent TNS apparatuses. The world politics of this would-be global ruling class is not driven, as it was for national ruling classes, by the flux of shifting rivalries and alliances played out through the interstate system but by the new global social structure of accumulation.

If the TCC is able to accrue considerable structural power, exercised in part through TNS apparatuses, the TNS simply does not have the capacity to penetrate the ideological and cultural systems of the civil societies of multiple countries. An expansive hegemony will remain illusive to the global capitalist bloc. The TNS is better equipped to forge ideological and political consensus among transnationally oriented elites. In this sense, the TCC exercises a structurally inscribed political domination but not an ideological hegemony over the poor majority of global society; its hegemony is within dominant strata – capitalist class groups and elites around the world. The transnational elite has been unable to forge a stable global capitalist historic bloc.

In modern conditions, Gramsci argues, a class maintains its dominance not simply through a special organization of force, but through *hegemony*, that is, because it is able to go beyond its narrow corporative interests, exert moral and intellectual leadership, and make compromises, within certain limits, with a variety of allies who are unified in a social bloc of forces that Gramsci calls the historic bloc. The bloc represents the basis of consent for a certain social order, in which the hegemony of a dominant class is created and re-created in a web of institutions, social relations, and ideas. No emergent ruling class can construct an historic bloc without developing diverse mechanisms of legitimation and securing a social base. Such a bloc involves a combination of consensual integration through material reward for some, and the coercive exclusion of others whom the system is unwilling or unable to co-opt. The acute social polarization generated by capitalist globalization and the expanding crises of survival for the poor majority of humanity make it exceedingly difficult for the transnational elite to forge an historic bloc.

Instead it has forged a more restricted power bloc – a *global capitalist power bloc*. Here I diverge from Poulantzas's somewhat ambiguous conception of the power bloc, in particular, his inability to clearly distinguish his conception from Gramsci's concept of the historic bloc. The power bloc attempts to establish the hegemony of the dominant fraction within the dominant groups and to advance through the state the divergent interests of these groups, yet it is not necessarily able to bring in subordinate majorities through consensual domination. This is to say that within an historic bloc there is a power bloc (or shifting power blocs), yet a power bloc may come into being absent an historic bloc. As a would-be global capitalist historic bloc began to unravel in the late 1990s, what was left in its place was a power bloc centered on the TCC, and especially transnational finance capital – a dictatorship of transnational finance capital in the literal sense of unrestrained power to dictate. This power is structural; it is neither coercive (directly, although "legitimate" transnational coercion through the TNS is an increasing occurrence) nor hegemonic. During the 1980s and 1990s the transnational elite and TNS organs forged consensus among the leading dominant groups in most countries around the world and weaved together a global capitalist power bloc, but it was unable to secure a more expansive hegemony or base of "active consent" among subordinate majorities around the world. This further complicates attempts from above to resolve the global crisis.

In this chapter I have responded to some of the critique of my thesis of the TNS by replying specifically to several of my critics and also by elaborating on the thesis itself. I have shown how the TNS as an analytical abstraction may provide a superior explanation for such world dynamics as BRICS activism and international trade agreements. However, perhaps the most vociferous criticism of the TNS thesis – and of the theory of global capitalism more generally – is based on the notion that the global system is organized as a U.S. empire and that the great world events of our day can best be understood in terms of U.S. imperialism or world domination. It is to this subject that I now turn.

3

Beyond the Theory of Imperialism

> As in the case of democracy, which is used in a positive sense to describe, from particular positions, radically different and consciously opposed political systems, *imperialism*, like any word which refers to fundamental social and political conflicts, cannot be reduced, semantically, to a single proper meaning. Its important historical and contemporary variations of meanings point to real processes which have to be studied in their own terms.
>
> Raymond Williams, *Keywords*[1]

Theories of a "new imperialism" proliferated in the years following the September 2001 attack on the World Trade Towers and the Pentagon and the subsequent U.S. invasions of Afghanistan and Iraq. These theories argued that the United States set about to renew a U.S. empire in order to offset a decline in its hegemony amid heightened inter-imperialist rivalry.[2] So popular were new imperialism theories that they came to be seen as common sense; critics were seen as heretics or nut cases, and

---

[1] Raymond Williams, *Keywords: A Vocabulary of Culture and Society* (New York: Oxford University Press, 1976), 132.

[2] See, inter alia, David Harvey, *The New Imperialism*, 2nd ed. (New York: Oxford University Press, 2005); Ellen Meiksins Wood, *Empire of Capital* (London: Verso, 2003); John B. Foster, "The New Age of Imperialism," *Monthly Review*, 55(3): 1–14, and Foster, *Naked Imperialism: U.S. Pursuit of Global Dominance* (New York: Monthly Review Press, 2006); Peter Gowan, *The Global Gamble: Washington's Bid for World Dominance* (London: Verso, 1999); Alex Callinicos, *Imperialism and the Global Political Economy* (Cambridge: Polity, 2009), and Callinicos, *Bonfire of Illusions: The Twin Cries of the Liberal World* (Cambridge: Polity, 2010); Ray Kiely, "United States Hegemony and Globalisation: What Role for Theories of Imperialism?," *Cambridge Review of International Affairs* (2006), 19(2): 205–221; Gonzalo Pozo-Martin, "A Tougher Gordian Knot: Globalisation, Imperialism and the Problem of the State," *Cambridge Review of International Affairs* (2006), 19(2): 223–242; Walden Bello, *Dilemmas of Domination: The Unmaking of the American Empire* (New York: Henry Holt, 2005); Michael Klare, "The New Geopolitics," *Monthly Review*, 55(3): 51–56; Giovvani Arrighi, "Hegemony Unraveling I" and "Hegemony Unraveling II," *New Left Review* (2005), 2(32/33, March–April and May–June): 23–80 and 83–116; Robert Brenner, *The Boom*

99

alternative explanations nearly disappeared from the intellectual and political radar. Yet these theories rested on a crustaceous bed of assumptions that must be peeled back if we are to get at the root of twenty-first century global social and political dynamics. The *lynchpin* of "new imperialism" theories is the assumption that world capitalism in the twenty-first century is made up of "domestic capitals" and distinct national economies that interact with one another and a concomitant realist analysis of world politics as driven by the pursuit by governments of their "national interest." Realism of this sort sees each national economy as a billiard ball banging back and forth against the others. This billiard image is then applied to explain global political dynamics in terms of nation-states as discrete interacting units (the interstate system). The realist paradigm that dominated the study of international relations during the post–World War II period lost much of its luster as globalization unfolded in the 1980s and 1990s, but then made a powerful comeback following the events of the 2001 and renewed U.S. interventionism.

In one of the most popular of the "new imperialism" studies, *The Global Gamble: Washington's Bid for World Dominance*, Gowan, for instance, refers incessantly to an "American capitalism," a "German capitalism," an "Italian capitalism," a "French capitalism," and so on, each a discernible and discrete economic system featuring distinctly organized national capitalist classes involved in sets of national competitive relationships.[3] In another leading treatise of this nature, *Empire of Capital*, Ellen Meiksins Wood similarly avows the continued existence and causal centrality of national capitals. Asserting that "the national organization of capitalist economies has remained stubbornly persistent," she repeatedly refers to "U.S." capital, to other competing national capitals, and to economic competition among core nation-state rivals. Over and again the "new imperialism" literature stubbornly refuses to address the reality of transnational capital as discussed in Chapter 1, and instead insists on the existence of "U.S." capital and on U.S. imperialism as a bid to secure the advantage of "U.S. capital" over rival national capitals and to shore up, in Wood's words, "*its own domestic capital*," to "compel other economies to serve the interests of the imperial hegemony in response to the fluctuating needs of *its own domestic capital*," and so on.[4] World-system theorists take a similar position. "The logic of competition and conflict in the interstate system (geopolitics) and the logic of competition in the world market ... [are] interdependent determinants of the dynamics of capitalist development," argues a leading world-systems theorist, Chris Chase-Dunn.

> Capitalist states have always tried to protect the capitalists who control them. States act to expand markets or to destroy barriers to market competition when their own capitalists will benefit because they enjoy a competitive advantage. The interstate system, centered on powerful core states which contend with one another

---

and the Bubble: The U.S. in the World Economy (London: Verso, 2002); *Monthly Review* (July–August 2003), 55(3): special issue titled "Imperialism Now."

[3] Gowan, *The Global Gamble.*

[4] Wood, *Empire of Capital*, 33, my emphasis.

for hegemony, is an important structural basis of the continued competition within the world capitalist class.[5]

Wood, Gowan, and others *assume*, although they provide not a shred of empirical evidence, that capital remains organized, as it was in earlier moments of the world capitalist system, along national lines and that the development of capital has stopped frozen in its nation-state form. Since for "new imperialism" theorists world capitalism is made up of "domestic capitals," world politics must be driven by "national interests." What does "national interests" mean? Marxists have historically rejected notions of "national interests" as an ideological subterfuge for class and social group interests. Yet the interstate/nation-state framework obliges "new imperialism" scholars to advance this unproblematized notion of "national interests" to explain global political dynamics. What is a "national economy"? Is it a country with a closed market? protected territorially based production circuits? the predominance of national capitals? an insulated national financial system? No capitalist country in the world fits this description. The key figures who developed the theory of imperialism in the early twentieth century empirically *tested* and *demonstrated* their propositions as the starting point of analysis. But "new imperialism" theories assume precisely that which needs to be demonstrated.

"New imperialism" theories are grounded in the classical statements of Lenin, Bukharin, and Hilferding and are based on this assumption of a world of rival national capitals and economies, conflict among core capitalist powers, the exploitation by these powers of peripheral regions, and a nation-state-centered framework for analyzing global dynamics. Hilferding, in his classic study on imperialism, *Finance Capital*, argued that national capitalist monopolies turn to the state for assistance in acquiring international markets and that this state intervention inevitably leads to intense political-economic rivalries among nation-states. There is a struggle among core national states for control over peripheral regions in order to open these regions to capital export from the particular imperialist country and to exclude capital from other countries. "Export capital feels most comfortable ... when its own state is in complete control of the new territory, for capital exports from other countries are then excluded, it enjoys a privileged position," observed Hilferding.[6] Lenin, in his 1917 pamphlet *Imperialism: The Latest Stage of Capitalism*, stressed the rise of

---

[5] Christopher Chase-Dunn, *Global Formation: Structures of the World-Economy* (Lanham, MD: Rowman and Littlefield, 1998), 34, 36, 41.

[6] Rudolf Hilferding, *Finance Capital: A Study of the Latest Phase of Capitalist Development* (London: Routledge, 1981 [1910]), 322. Similarly, Nikolai Bukharin, in the chapter titled "World Economy and the 'National' State" in his classic study, *Imperialism and World Economy* (New York: Monthly Review Press, 1973 [1929]), states: "There is a growing discord between the basis of social economy which has become world-wide and the peculiar class structure of society, a structure where the ruling class (the bourgeoisie) itself is split into 'national' groups with contradictory economic interests, groups which, being opposed to the world proletariat, are competing among themselves for the division of surplus value created on a world scale" (106).

national financial-industrial combines that struggle to divide and redivide the world among themselves through their respective nation-states. The rivalry among these competing national capitals leads to interstate competition, military conflict and war among the main capitalist countries.

Hilferding, Lenin, and others analyzing the world of the early twentieth century established this Marxist analytical framework of rival national capitals that was carried into the latter twentieth and early twenty-first centuries by subsequent political economists via theories of dependency and the world system, radical international relations theory, studies of U.S. intervention, and so on. As we have seen, capitalism has changed fundamentally since the days of the classical theorists of imperialism, yet this outdated framework of competing national capitals continued to inform observers of world dynamics in the early twenty-first century. The following 2003 assertion by Klare was typical:

> By geopolitics or geopolitical competition, I mean the contention between great powers and aspiring great powers for control over territory, resources, and important geographical positions, such as ports and harbors, canals, river systems, oases, and other sources of wealth and influence. Today we are seeing a resurgence of unabashed geopolitical ideology among the leadership cadres of the major powers. ... [T]he best way to see what's happening today in Iraq and elsewhere is through a geopolitical prism.[7]

Such thinking provided the scaffolding for the torrent of "new imperialism" literature. Some argued that unilateral U.S. interventionism belied earlier claims that we are moving toward a globalized world order and that this intervention refuted "misguided" theories of globalization.[8] According to Bello:

> What was seen, by many people on both the left and the right, as the wave of the future – that is, a functionally integrated global economy marked by massive flows of commodities, capital and labor across the borders of weakened nation states and presided over by a 'transnational capitalist class' – has retreated in a chain reaction of economic crises, growing inter-capitalist rivalries and wars. Only by a stretch of the imagination can the USA under the George W. Bush administration be said to be promoting a 'globalist agenda.'[9]

The actual empirical data, some of which we have seen in Chapter 1, however, made clear that only by a stretch of the imagination could one ignore the profound intensification of economic globalization – including, precisely, escalating flows of commodities, capital, and labor across the borders of nation-states, – that took place in the first decade of the twenty-first century, prior and *subsequent* to the events of September 2001. And the Bush government did

---

[7] Michael Klare, "The New Geopolitics," *Monthly Review*, 55(3): 51–56.

[8] See, e.g, Doug Henwood, *After the New Economy* (New York: The New Press, 2003); Pozo-Martin, "A Tougher Gordian Knot."

[9] Walden Bello, "The Capitalist Conjuncture: Over-Accumulation, Financial Crises, and the Retreat from Globalization," *Third World Quarterly* (2006), 27(8): 1345–1367, quote from p. 1346.

indeed promote the globalist agenda of intensified globalization. What evidence has there been of "growing inter-capitalist rivalries" among nation-states? There were no trade wars or military tensions among the major capitalist powers during that decade but rather attempts, desperate at times, on the part of their governments to collectively manage the system and its crisis tendencies. New imperialism theories failed to make the distinction between conjunctural analysis and structural causation, and mistook surface appearance – for example, public statements by policymakers – for underlying essence.

In this and the next two chapters I will offer an alternative explanation for heightened U.S. interventionism in recent years from the perspective of global capitalism theory. U.S. interventionism is *not* a departure from capitalist globalization but a *response to its crisis*. The U.S. state has taken the lead in imposing a reorganization of world capitalism. But this does not mean that U.S. militarism and interventionism seek to defend "U.S." interests. As the most powerful component of the TNS, the U.S. state apparatus attempts to defend the interests of transnational investors and the overall system and to confront those political forces around the world that, in one way or another, threaten those interests or threaten to destabilize transnational capitalist processes. In the larger picture, there is a new relation between space and power that is only just beginning to be theorized and that requires that we revisit the matter of uneven accumulation.

REIFICATION, THEORETICISM, AND DUALISM IN "NEW IMPERIALISM" THEORIES

The Antinomies of David Harvey

Some "new imperialism" theorists see globalization as synonymous with the genesis of capitalism and its outward expansion, so that there is little or nothing new about the system in the twenty-first century.[10] But most acknowledge to varying degrees that changes have taken place, and particularly, that capital has become more global. Yet capital in these accounts has not been transnationalized; it has been "internationalized." These accounts are concerned with explaining the *inter*-national order, which by definition places the focus on interstate dynamics. The need to accommodate the reality of transnationalizing capital within a nation-state-centric framework for analyzing world political dynamics leads "new imperialism" theories to a dualism of the economic and the political.

This dualism is epitomized in perhaps the landmark treatise among this literature, *The New Imperialism*. In it, the urban geographer and Marxist theorist David Harvey argues that capital is economic and globalizes but that states are political and pursue a self-interested territorial logic. Harvey's theory starts with the notion that

[10] See, e.g., Henwood, *After the New Economy*.

the fundamental point is to see the territorial and the capitalist logic of power as distinct from each other. ... The relation between these two logics should be seen, therefore, as problematic and often contradictory ... rather than as functional or one-sided. This dialectical relation sets the stage for an analysis of capitalist imperialism in terms of the intersection of these two distinctive but intertwined logics of power.[11]

Harvey's approach, however, is *not* dialectical but mechanical. Dualist approaches such as Harvey's view the parts under analysis as externally related, whereas the hallmark of a dialectical approach is recognition that relations between different parts – processes, phenomena – are *internal* relationships. An *internal relation* is one in which each part is constituted in its relation to the other, so that one cannot exist without the other and has meaning only when seen within the relation, whereas an *external relation* is one in which each part has an existence independent of its relation to the other.[12] The different dimensions of social reality in the dialectical approach do not have an "independent" status insofar as each aspect of reality is constituted by, and is constitutive of, a larger whole of which it is an internal element. Distinct dimensions of social reality may be *analytically distinct* yet are *internally interpenetrated* and *mutually constitutive* of each other as internal elements of a more encompassing process, so that, for example, the economic/capital and the political/state are *internal* to capitalist relations.

It is remarkable that Harvey and others who adhere to such a mechanical dualism propose such a separation, since the history of modern critical thought – from Polanyi to Poulantzas and Gramsci, among others, not to mention half a century of historical materialist theorizing on the state – has demonstrated both the *formal* (apparent) separation of the economic and the political under the capitalist mode of production and the illusion that such a separation is organic or real.[13] This separation has its genealogy in the rise of the market and its apparently "pure" economic compulsion. This separation appears in social thought with the breakup of political economy, the rise of classical economics and bourgeois social science, and disciplinary fragmentation.[14] Weber, in particular, advanced the dualist notion of the state as an independent political sphere staffed by cadre that interacts externally with capital in pursuit of its own territorial/institutional interests. Weber saw the competitive interstate system as a necessary structural condition for the emergence and reproduction of capitalism. He argued:

---

[11] Harvey, *The New Imperialism*, 29–30.
[12] Bertell Ollman, *Alienation*, 2nd ed. (Cambridge: Cambridge University Press, 1976).
[13] For discussion, see, inter alia, William I. Robinson, *Promoting Polyarchy: Globalization, U.S. Intervention, and Hegemony* (Cambridge: Cambridge University Press, 1996), Chapter 1.
[14] See, inter alia, Goran Therborn, *Science, Class and Society: On the Formation of Sociology and Historical Materialism* (London: Verso, 1985, first published in 1976); Irving M. Zeitlin, *Ideology and the Development of Sociological Theory*, 7th ed. (Englewood Cliffs, NJ: Prentice Hall, 2000).

The competitive struggle [among nation-states] created the largest opportunities for modern western capitalism. The separate states had to compete for mobile capital, which dictated to them the conditions under which it would assist them in power. Out of this alliance of the state with capital, dictated by necessity, arose the national citizen class, the bourgeoisie in the modern sense of the word. Hence it is the closed national state which afforded to the capitalist its chance for development – and as long as the national state does not give place to a world empire capitalism also will endure.[15]

The separation of the economic from the political was a hallmark of the structural functionalism that dominated much of mid-twentieth-century social science. Structural functionalism followed Weber in separating distinct spheres of the social totality and conferring a functional autonomy to each subsphere, which was seen as *externally* related to other subspheres in a way similar to Harvey's notion of separate territorial and capital logics that may or may not coincide. It is to this dualism that Harvey now turns to explain the "new imperialism."[16]

Harvey offers no explicit conception of the state, but he acknowledges that state behavior has "depended on how the state has been constituted and by whom."[17] Yet dual logics of state and capital ignore the real-world policymaking process in which the state extends backward, is grounded in the forces of civil society, and is fused in a myriad of ways with capital itself. To the extent that civil society – social forces – and capital are transnationalizing, the analysis of the state cannot remain frozen at a nation-state level. The essential problematic that should concern us in attempting to explain phenomena associated with the "new imperialism" is the political management – or rule – of global capitalism. The theoretical gauntlet is to understand how the political and the economic become articulated in new ways in the current era. This requires a conception of agency and institutions. The agency of historically situated social forces is exercised through institutions that they themselves have created and constantly recreate. We need to focus not on states as fictitious macro-agents but on historically changing constellations of social forces operating through multiple institutions, including state apparatuses that are themselves in a process of transformation as a consequence of collective agencies.

---

[15] Max Weber, *Economy and Society* (Berkeley: University of California Press, 1978 [1922]), 354.

[16] The dualist economic-capital/political-state framework has also had a tenacious presence in world-systems studies and in international political economy (IPE). Giovanni Arrighi's influential 1994 world-system study, *The Long Twentieth Century*, traced the evolution of world capitalism over five centuries as the intersection of independent territorial and capitalist logics of power: Giovanni Arrighi, *The Long Twentieth Century: Money, Power, and the Origins of Our Time* (London:Verso, 1994). In sociology, state-centric theories of international affairs became popular in the 1980s following the publication of *Bringing the State Back In* by Evans and his colleagues: Peter B. Evans, Dietrich Rueschemeyer, and Theda Skocpol, eds., *Bringing the State Back In* (Cambridge: Cambridge University Press, 1985).

[17] Harvey, *The New Imperialism*, 91.

The Reification of Space and of Territory

But instead of offering an ontology of agency and how it operates through historically constituted institutions, much of the "new imperialism" literature reifies these institutions. When we explain global dynamics in terms of institutions that have an existence or agency independent of social forces, we are reifying these institutions. As the Gramscian School in international political economy and critical state theories[18] have shown, the story starts and ends with historically situated social forces as collective agents. It is this reification that leads to realist analyses of state power and the interstate system. Instead, one must look *beneath* an interstate/nation-state framework – at historical social forces, the evolving structures they create, and the changing institutional configurations through which they operate – and *beyond* an interstate/nation-state framework in order to capture what is taking place in the world today.

The state, says Harvey, in reverting to the realist approach, "struggles to assert its interests and achieve its goals in the world at large."[19] But Harvey does not stop with this reification of the state. He introduces an additional territorial reification, so that territorial relations become immanent to social relations. "The wealth and well-being of particular territories are augmented at the expense of others," writes Harvey.[20] This is a remarkably reified image – "territories" rather than social groups have "wealth" (accumulated values) and enjoy "well-being." In this way Harvey gives space an independent existence as a social/political force in the form of territory in order to advance his thesis of the "new imperialism." It is not how social forces are organized, either in space or through institutions, that is the focus. Rather, for Harvey, territory acquires a social existence of its own, an agentic logic. We are told that "territorial entities" engage in practices of production, commerce, and so on. Do "territorial entities" really do these things? Or is it not that in the real world, individuals and social groups engage in production, commerce, and so on? And *they do so via institutions* through which they organize, systematize, and demarcate their activities as agents. Social groups became aggregated and organized in the modern era through the particular institutional form of the territorially-based nation-state. But this particular institutional form does not acquire a life of its own, and neither is it immutable. Nation-states continue to exist, but their nature and meaning evolve as social relations and structures become transformed – particularly, as they transnationalize.

Space is a social relationship. To see space as territory is to reify space. Space is not a thing any more than a commodity is a thing. As a social relationship, space is a social process that is historical – that is, evolving along temporal axes

[18] See, in particular, Robert W. Cox, *Production, Power, and World Order: Social Forces in the Making of History* (New York: Columbia University Press, 1987).
[19] Harvey, *The New Imperialism*, 26.
[20] Ibid., 32.

of history – and is determined by relations among social groups and classes, including the contradictions and antagonisms among them. There is nothing in the theory of global capitalism that implies that capital does not accumulate unevenly with regard to space and place. Sassen suggests that in the age of globalization space needs to be rescaled "downward" to the subnational and "upward" to the transnational and the global.[21] While I concur, my concern here is not such rescaling but a more fundamental epistemological shift that involves the de-reification of space and place. To see a given organization of space in terms of territory or geography, involving socially constructed borders (e.g., national borders) as fixed or immanent to world capitalism is to reify space. This much is not particularly polemical. The problem, however, is the view or assumption that the process of uneven accumulation, which *is* immanent to capitalism, takes a definite and even fixed territorial or geographic expression, which is to confuse a social relation with a territorial relation. Spatial orders are abstractions of social relations. The particular territorial or geographic expression that spacial relations took in the evolution of world capitalism – which has been referred to as core and periphery, or North and South – was entirely historical. Logical boundaries (e.g., core and periphery) and systemic contradictions (antagonistic poles in a dialectical unity) should not be conflated with spatial boundaries and spatial contradictions. That the two are, or have been, coeval is historical rather than immanent.

It is true that the social does not exist outside of the spatial and that human beings experience the world in time and space, with space as distance measured in time. It is equally true that space is relative and experienced subjectively, as Lafebvre observes.[22] Drawing on insights from Lafebvre, Marx, Luxemburg, and others, Harvey earlier introduced the highly fertile notion of spatial (or spatial-temporal) fixes to explain how capital momentarily resolves contradictions (particularly, crises of overaccumulation) in one place by displacing them to other places through geographic expansion and spatial reorganization. Following Marx's famous observation that the expanded accumulation of capital involves the progressive "annihilation of space through time," he also coined the term "time-space compression" in reference to globalization as a process involving a new burst of such compression in the world capitalist system.[23]

But "places" have no existence or meaning in and of themselves. It is people living in particular spaces who do this dis-placing (literally), these spatio-temporal fixes. The "asymmetric exchange relations" that are at the heart of Harvey's emphasis on the territorial basis of the "new imperialism" must be, for Harvey, territorial exchange relations. But not only that: they must be nation-state territorial exchanges. But exchange relations are social relations, exchanges

[21] Saskia Sassen, *A Sociology of Globalization* (New York: Norton, 2007).
[22] Henri Lefebvre, *The Production of Space* (Oxford: Blackwell, 1991).
[23] David Harvey, *The Limits to Capital* (London: Verso, 2006 [1982]), and Harvey, *The Condition of Postmodernity* (London: Blackwell, 1990).

among particular social groups. There is nothing in the concept of asymmetric exchanges that by fiat gives them a territorial expression, no reason to *assume* that *uneven exchanges* are *necessarily* exchanges that take place between distinct territories, much less specifically between distinct nation-states. That they do or do not acquire such an expression is a matter of historical, empirical, and conjunctural analysis. Certainly spatial relations among social forces have historically been mediated in large part by territory; spatial relations have been territorially defined relations. But this territorialization is in no way immanent to social relations and may well be fading in significance as globalization advances.

If most of the people in one place that we can call a territory or nation-state achieve "wealth" and "well-being" by having displaced contradictions to most of the people in another place, then we may be able to justify the view that social relations acquire a territorial expression – hence the territorial (nation-state) basis of classical theories of colonialism and imperialism and later world-system and related theories of geographically defined core and periphery. But we know that under globalization masses of people in core regions such as Los Angeles and New York may suffer the displacement of contradictions offloaded to them from people physically contiguous to them in the very same city, whereas rising middle-class and affluent sectors in India, China, Brazil, and South Africa may benefit as much as their counterparts in First World global cities from spatio-temporal fixes that offload crisis to the global poor through neo-liberal mechanisms.

Any theory of globalization must address the matter of place and space, including changing spatial relations among social forces and how social relations are spatialized. This has not been satisfactorily accomplished, despite a spate of theoretical propositions, ranging from Castell's "space of flows" replacing the "space of place" to Giddens's "time-space distanciation" as the "lifting" of social relations from territorial place and their stretching around the globe in ways that may eliminate territorial friction.[24] This notion of ongoing and novel reconfigurations of time and social space is central to a number of globalization theories. It in turn points to the larger theoretical issue of the relationship of social structure to space, the notion of space as the material basis for social practices, and changing relationships under globalization among territoriality/ geography, institutions, and social structures. The crucial question here is the ways in which globalization may be transforming the spatial dynamics of accumulation and the institutional as well as political arrangements through which it takes place. *The subject – literally, that is, the agents/makers of the social world – is not global space but people in those spaces.* What is central, therefore, is a spatial reconfiguration of social relations beyond a nation-state/

[24] Manuel Castells, *The Rise of the Network Society, Vol. I: The Information Age: Economy, Society, Culture* (Oxford: Blackwell, 1996); Anthony Giddens, *The Consequences of Modernity* (Cambridge: Polity, 1990).

interstate framework, if not indeed even beyond territory. I will return to this matter later in this chapter.

States are institutionalized social relations and territorial actors to the extent that those social relations are territorialized. Nation-states are social relations that have historically been territorialized but those relations are not by definition territorial. To the extent that the United States, and other national states promote deterritorializing social and economic processes, they are *not* territorial actors. The U.S. state can hardly be considered a territorial actor when it promotes the global relocation of accumulation processes that were previously concentrated in U.S. territory. Harvey's approach is at a loss to explain such behavior, since by his definition the U.S. state must promote its own territorial aggrandizement. Harvey observes that as local banking was supplanted by national banking in the development of capitalism, "the free flow of money capital across the national space altered regional dynamics."[25] In the same vein we can argue that the free flow of capital across global space alters these dynamics on a worldwide scale. But Harvey's nation-state/interstate-centric analysis prevents him from contemplating such a possibility.

Let us return to the question: why would Harvey propose separate logics for the economic and the political – for capital and the state? By separating the political and the economic he is able to claim that globalization has indeed transformed the spatial dynamics of accumulation – hence that capital globalizes – but that the institutional and political arrangements of such global accumulation remain territorial as nation-states. The state has its own independent logic that brings it into an external relation to globalizing capital. Here we arrive at the pitfall of theoreticism. If one *starts* with the theoretical assumption that the world is made up of independent, territorially based nation-states and that this particular institutional-political form is something immanent to the modern world – Wood makes the assumption explicit, a *law* of capitalism; for Harvey it seems implicit – then by theoretical fiat the changing world of the twenty-first century *must* be explained in these terms. Reality must be made to conform to the theoretical conception of an immutable nation-state-based, interstate political and institutional order. But since Harvey acknowledges the reality of globalizing capital, he is forced to separate the logic of globalizing capital from that of territorially based states; he is forced either to abandon the theoretical construct altogether or to build it upon a dualism of the economic and the political, of capital and the state.

As I observed in the Introduction, the pitfall of this *theoreticism* is to develop analyses and propositions to fit theoretical assumptions. Since received theories establish a frame of an interstate system made up of competing national states, economies and capitals, twenty-first century reality must be interpreted so that it fits into this frame one way or another. Such theoreticism forces theorists of the "new imperialism" into a schizophrenic dualism of economic and political

[25] Harvey, *The New Imperialism*, 106.

logics. In any event, Harvey has trapped himself in a blind alley that underscores the pitfall. Despite his acknowledgement of capital's transnationalization, he concludes that the U.S. state's political/territorial logic is now driven by an effort to open up space vis-à-vis competitor nation-states for unloading national capital surplus, hence the new U.S. imperialism. So in the end he reduces global-izing capital to national capitals operating internationally, and by explaining U.S. state behavior in terms of its functionality to capital he actually contradicts his earlier theoretical construct by painting an internal relationship between capital accumulation and the state.

The Uneven Accumulation of Capital: II

For Neil Smith, as for his mentor Harvey, "uneven development is the hallmark of the geography of capitalism."[26] While that geography under globalized capitalism, has yet, in my view, to be adequately theorized or analyzed, the matter of uneven development or accumulation is central to the classical theory of imperialism and to new imperialism theories. The British international rela-tions scholars Alexander Anievas, Adam Morton, and Alex Callinicos have claimed in their respective critiques that Trotsky's "law of uneven and combined development" shows that capitalism inherently develops unevenly and that this uneven development belies my thesis on the TNS.[27] Capital does indeed accu-mulate unevenly. But these critics do not argue just that uneven accumulation is

---

[26] Neil Smith, *Uneven Development: Nature, Capital and the Production of Space* (Cambridge, MA: Basil Blackwell, 1990 [1984]).

[27] Alexander Anievas, "Theories of a Global State: A Critique," *Historical Materialism* (2008), 16: 190–206; David Adam Morton, *Unravelling Gramsci: Hegemony and Passive Revolution in the Global Economy* (London: Pluto Press, 2007); Alex Callinicos, "Does Capitalism Need the State System?," *Cambridge Review of International Affairs* (2007), 20(4): 533–549. Morton's critique of the TNS thesis (see pp. 140–148) is particularly misleading. Among other critiques, he states that I view national states as mere "transmission belts" for the diffusion of global capitalism and ignore the "internalization of [transnational] class interests within the [national] state." Yet I have argued consistently and at great length that national states – and the social and class forces operating therein – act proactively from within to promote capitalist globalization; precisely that the neo-liberal national state internalizes the class interests of transnational fractions of capital and elites. He reduces my notion of the TNS to supranational institutions that supersede nation-state institutions. In fact, I argue that nation-state institutions are not superseded but *incorporated* into a more expansive network conceived in analytical abstraction as a TNS. He conflates the TNS thesis with the matter of uneven development with the claim that "conditions of uneven develop-ment are flattened out by the assumptions of the transnational state thesis" (147). In general, it is hard to make heads or tales of Morton's critique as it so misconstrues my argument. Consider the following convoluted affirmation: "A key feature, it is argued, of the epoch of globalization is therefore not only the transformation of the state but its supersession ... by a transnational state apparatus consisting of transnational class alliances involving everything from transnational corporations; to the expansion of foreign direct investment; to cross-national mergers, strategic alliances, capital interpenetration, interlocking directorates, worldwide subcontracting and resourcing; to the extension of economic zones and other forms of economic organization"(141). Clearly, Morton has conflated the notion of the TNS with that of the TCC and processes of TCC

immanent to capitalism, with which I entirely agree; they insist that this uneven accumulation must, by the nature and logic of the system, take the form of uneven development among nation-states. "The central question then is whether there is anything inherent to capitalism which would perpetuate a territorial configuration of class interests and state power," states Anievas. "The answer lies in what Trotsky termed the 'law of uneven and combined development.'"[28]

Lenin and Hilferding theorized an historical moment in world capitalism on the basis of an application of the laws of capitalist development, specifically, the manifestation of the outward expansion of competing capitals as imperialism. Trotsky, similarly, applied the laws of capitalist development – the uneven accumulation of capital as a consequence of the competition among capitals – to the world of the early twentieth century that he was analyzing. The historical forms that are thrown up by the laws of motion of a social order are just that: *historical* and therefore subject to transformation as the system evolves. The center-periphery division of labor created by modern colonialism reflected a particular spatial configuration of the law of uneven development that is becoming transformed by globalization. There is nothing in the concept of asymmetric exchanges that by fiat gives them a territorial, much less a nation-state, expression. Globalization reconstitutes the speciality of world capitalism. I concur with Sassen on the historicity of scale and on the need to recode national and local processes as "instantiations of the global," without assuming, as she observes, that if processes or conditions are located in national institutions or national territory, they must be national.[29]

According to Anievas, "another central factor perpetuating this uneven development, manifested in territorialized and geographical forms, is the construction of spatially-embedded physical infrastructures (e.g. transport and communication technologies) necessary for the expanded reproduction of capital. Investments in built environments come to define regional spaces for the circulation of capital." As a result, he argues, "capital demonstrates a clear tendency towards concentrating in specific regions at the expense of others, thereby producing a somewhat porous but nevertheless identifiable 'territorial logic of power' – regionality – inherently arising out of the process of capital accumulation in space and time."[30] Political economists have long observed what is known as agglomeration dynamics, or the tendency for capital to concentrate in particular built environments. But there is nothing in this theory

---

formation in the global economy. Similarly, Morton makes the absurd claim that I place "the totalizing assumption of depeasantization at the hub of the transnational state thesis" (144). I do indeed argue that one feature of global capitalism is accelerated depeasantization and proletarianization worldwide, but this certainly is not at the "hub" of the TNS thesis; indeed, what at all it has to do with the TNS thesis is entirely unclear. Morton himself is still fixated on the national-international axis.

[28] Anieves, "Theories of a Global State," 200.
[29] Saskia Sassen, *A Sociology of Globalization* (New York: Norton, 2007).
[30] Anieves, "Theories of a Global State," 201.

of agglomeration economies that would suggest that these spaces must be *nation-state spaces*, and in fact a great deal of empirical evidence indicates an ongoing erosion of the correspondence of national space with such economies and the accumulation circuits and levels of social development that adhere to them. The literature on global cities,[31] for instance, shows how capital accumulates unevenly in space and time, resulting in sharp social and spatial polarization within agglomeration economies nested in metropolitan, local, subnational, cross-border, and other spaces that do not correspond to nation-state spaces in an interstate logic.

These and other studies show that uneven accumulation tends increasingly to unfold in accordance with a social and not a national logic. Different levels of social development adhere from the very sites of social productive activity, that is, from *social*, not geographic, space. Moreover, privileged groups have an increasing ability to manipulate space so as to create enclaves and insulate themselves through novel mechanisms of social control and new technologies for the built environment (see the following discussion and Chapter 5). The persistence, and in fact *growth*, of the North-South divide remains important for its theoretical and practical political implications. What we must ask is whether the divide is something innate to world capitalism or a particular spatial configuration of uneven capitalist development during a particular historic phase of world capitalism, and whether tendencies toward the self-reproduction of this configuration are increasingly offset by countertendencies emanating from the nature and dynamic of global capital accumulation.[32]

Spatial relations, like all structures of society, are a result of historically specific and contingent processes. What made uneven development spatial in the sense understood by theories of imperialism is that value was generated in one political space and moved to another political space. What made this

---

[31] On global cities, see, esp., Saskia Sassen, *The Global Cities: New York, London, Tokyo*, 2nd ed. (Princeton, NJ: Princeton University Press, 2001), and, for a summary of the global cities literature, see William I. Robinson, "Saskia Sassen and the Sociology of Globalization," *Sociological Analysis* (2009), 3(1): 5–29. Regarding my case studies, see Robinson, *Transnational Conflicts*, and *Latin America and Global Capitalism*.

[32] The notion of a world economy divided into core and peripheral *countries* defined by an international division of labor in which high-wage and high-value-added activities are concentrated in core countries and low-wage, low-value-added activities in peripheral countries has been integral to the world-systems paradigm. Yet this international division of labor has given way to a global division of labor in which core and peripheral productive activities are dispersed as much within as among countries. In a departure from his earlier geographical-territorial conception of core and periphery, Immanuel Wallerstein has recently acknowledged that core and periphery are a relation, so that "core-like and peripheral processes" are to be found in the same geographic space. Immanuel Wallerstein, "Robinson's Critical Appraisal Appraised," *International Sociology* (2012), 27(4): 524–528. Nonetheless, Wallerstein remains committed to a realist analysis of world political dynamics. See William I. Robinson, "Globalization and the Sociology of Immanuel Wallerstein: A Critical Appraisal," *International Sociology* (2010), 26(6): 723–745.

national is that value was generated in one nation or national territory and appropriated as surplus flows to another nation or territory as a result of the particular colonial and imperial history of the world capitalist system. This movement of values through space or the appropriation of surplus by some social groups may be immanent to capitalism, but what is not is that this space is by definition national space. Under global capitalism, values are generated in particular spaces, but they can be and are circulated almost instantaneously through the money form to other spaces that may be anywhere in the globe and, moreover, these values are permanently restless; they do not stay in any one place, that is, they do not accumulate continuously at one point of what is the open space of global capitalism. To explain the movement of values between different "nodes" in globalized production, we clearly need to move beyond nation-state-centric approaches and apply a theory of value to transformations in world spatial and institutional structures (the nation-state being the central spatial and institutional structure in the history of world capitalism).

It is in the nature of global capitalism to create uneven spaces, if only because of the mapping of functions onto space within the system. The law of uneven and combined accumulation postulates that the unevenness or inequality between regions together with their combination in a single international division of labor underlies capital accumulation. The spatial distribution of unequal development between North and South (or center and periphery) as a particular territorial feature of the world system was determined in large part by the role of states as instruments of territorially bound classes and by the distinct socio-economic and historical conditions that capitalism confronted in its genesis and worldwide spread. The reality of capital as a totality of competing individual capitals, and their concrete existence as a relation within specific spatial confines determined geographically as nation-states, worked against a trans- or supranational unifying trend. Now globalization reconfigures these spatial relations of accumulation.

Capitalists regardless of their national origin are able to use the uneven accumulation of capital and distinct spaces and political jurisdictions to their advantage in pursuing accumulation strategies. The continued existence of distinct or unequal conditions across nations is a function to global capitalism and allows transnational capital to establish distinct base areas for accumulation activities. Transnational capitalists of *Mexican* origin, for instance, are served as much as are transnational capitalists of U.S. or German origin by the particular conditions or advantages provided by labor and other political and factor cost considerations in Mexican territory. The Mexican multibillionaire Carlos Slim and his Grupo Carso conglomerate, for instance, have operations that span all six continents. The conglomerate utilizes the Mexican and U.S. states as well as state agencies and managers in many other countries where it operates, taking advantage of uneven accumulation between Mexican and U.S. territorial spaces in pursuing its own transnational accumulation strategies. The Grupo Carso has no intrinsic interest in "developing" Mexico and no intrinsic aversion to uneven accumulation across national and other spatial boundaries; to the contrary, these often work to its advantage.

Global capitalism, it is clear, has a global social base; it is a relation internal to virtually all countries and regions of the world. North-South contradictions are a consequence of the historical development of world capitalism. In perhaps the most detailed analysis of the core-periphery structures that emerged from the historical development of world capitalism through imperialism and colonialism, Samir Amin has argued that there is a fundamental distinction in the structure of the developed and underdeveloped worlds. Whereas core capitalism experiences what he terms "auto-centric" accumulation, revolving around the production of capital goods and mass consumption, "peripheral capitalism" revolves around production for export and the consumption of luxury goods.[33] But Amin is describing an *historical* structure, one that was imposed by metropolitan capital in an earlier epoch of world capitalism and that no longer describes the globalized economy.

There remain significant regional differences in relation to global accumulation and particular histories and configurations of social forces that shape distinct experiences under globalization. Moreover, these social forces operate through national and regional institutions. Hence there is variation in the process of globalization and concomitant processes of institutionalization of the new social relations and political structures of global capitalism. But this does not mean that national and regional competition is causal to processes of uneven accumulation. Instead, we want to see how transnational social forces from above are able to reproduce and utilize regional distinctions to serve global accumulation and how transnational social forces from below continue to operate politically through local and national institutions in struggles against global capitalism. The North-South or core-periphery contradiction is complicated by capitalist globalization. The fundamental social contradiction in global society is between subordinate and dominant classes in a transnational setting.

The crisis of global capitalism is resulting in an accelerated decline of social conditions in the United States, including an erosion of wages and living standards for much of the working class, the decay of the educational and health systems, deteriorating infrastructure, unemployment, underemployment, job instability, and ever-greater social inequalitiy. The national state cannot resolve these contradictions of globalized capitalism. Powerful or core national states previously "displaced" the most explosive contradictions to the colonial and formerly colonized world through imperialism. The end of the welfare states in the North and new waves of austerity in the wake of the 2008 crisis underscore the brutal "Thirdworldization" of working classes and the poor in the traditional heartlands of world capitalism – a displacement that is more social than

---

[33] Samir Amin, *Accumulation on a World Scale: A Critique of the Theory of Underdevelopment* (New York: Monthly Review Press, 1974), and Amin, *Unequal Development: An Essay on the Social Formations of Peripheral Capitalism* (New York: Monthly Review Press, 1977).

territorial. Indeed, a 2005 study on global inequality by the United Nations reported that parts of the United States are as poor as the Third World.[34]

There are indeed distinct spatial scales to uneven accumulation, among them the international, but this international scale, no matter how important historically, is not immanent to world capitalism; the spatial reorganization under globalization is making apparent the social (as opposed to territorial) and contingent nature of uneven accumulation. Capitalist globalization results in an accelerated *social* concentration and centralization of capital but not in a *spatial* centralization. To the contrary, it results in its opposite, a spatial *decentralization*. In this regard, I part ways with Smith, who identifies the centralization of capital as spatial and as pivotal to uneven development.[35] The meaning of space is ever more imbricated in its social construction – in the type of sharp social polarization that we are seeing in transnational class terms. The rise of affluent zones and gated communities alongside the marginalized and ghettoized can be seen around the world; gentrification and homelessness side by side in every urban center. Dickens's *Tale of Two Cities* is today a tale of two worlds inhabiting distinct social spaces in the same places. Writing twenty-five years after the publication of his seminal study, *Uneven Development*, Smith alluded to the shifting scalar nature of uneven development:

> The theory of uneven development suggested a see-saw movement of capital already evident in a gentrification process which has today ballooned into a global and systemic rather than local and incidental event, but the meteoric economic expansion of China, India, Brazil, Korea and various other economies of South America and Asia ... would seem to bear out this argument at other scales too. .... The remaking of Beijing, Shanghai and Mumbai, and of other cities in Asia and elsewhere suggests a global scale gentrification of cities that could not really have been imagined in New York, London, Sydney or Philadelphia as late as the 1990s. Gentrification is a central part of this localization of uneven development and of global struggles, yet this process has itself transformed (and not just through an increase in scale). Gentrification today has blossomed into a full-blooded global city-building strategy ... [and is now] a vehicle of capital accumulation. The resulting patterns of uneven geographies at the local scale are very different from those observable three decades ago.[36]

Smith does not take the point far enough. The reconstruction of core and periphery into social spaces across the globe is evident beyond the older and now the newer global cities that Smith mentions. As I discussed previously, global social polarization has cut across national and North-South spaces and is expressed in a restructuring of space made possible by new globalizing technologies, the ability of affluent sectors to insulate themselves from the slums that surround them, introduce medical, health, and utility services,

[34] United Nations Development Program, *Human Development Report 2005* (New York: United Nations, 2005).
[35] Smith, *Uneven Development*.
[36] Neil Smith, "Uneven Development Redux," *New Political Economy* (2011), 16(2): 262–264.

shopping, and recreation into these reconstructed spaces, buffered by the politics of inequality and social control – global "Green Zones," in allusion to the security buffer that U.S. forces set up in Baghdad. What Smith describes now seems quite generalizable to much of the world.[37]

For Smith, the logic of uneven development

> derives specifically from the opposed tendencies, inherent in capital, toward the differentiation but simultaneous equalization of the levels and conditions of production. Capital is continually invested in the built environment in order to produce surplus value and expand the basis of capital. But equally, capital is continually withdrawn from the built environment so that it can move elsewhere and take advantage of higher profit rates.[38]

The essence of uneven development for Smith is this spatial search by capital for higher profit rates through physical relocation. This is the process that leads many to insist that the law of combined and uneven development gives a (fixed/nation-state) territorial dimension to accumulation. But capital's moving elsewhere does not necessarily mean its moving from one country to another or even from one city to another. Differentiation and equalization as spatial phenomena are a social relation whose particular territorial or geographic expression is historical, contingent, and not predetermined to be international. Consider the following: Unicor, a public company that uses inmates from U.S. federal prisons to produce goods and services for government procurement, was authorized in 2012 to partner with private sector firms to produce for the open market. In other words, private corporations could now co-invest with Unicor to tap into prison labor that is paid US$0.23 per hour up to a maximum of US$1.15 per hour – a rate competitive with Mexico, India, and China – to work in prison call

---

[37] Steven Graham writes in his revealing study, *Cities Under Siege: The New Military Urbanism* (London: Verso, 2010), 5–6: "[Urban landscapes around the world are] now populated by a few wealthy individuals, an often precarious middle class, and a mass of outcasts. Almost everywhere, it seems, wealth, power and resources are becoming ever more concentrated in the hands of the rich and the super-rich, who increasingly sequester themselves within gated urban cocoons and deploy their own private security or paramilitary forces for the tasks of boundary enforcement and access control. 'In many cities around the world, wealth and poverty coexist in close proximity,' wrote Anna Tibaijuk, director of the UN's Habitat Program, in October 2008. 'Rich, well served neighborhoods and gated communities are often situated near dense inner-city slum communities that lack even the most basic of services'." To the observation of private security forces we need to add that the state deploys its own repressive apparatus to protect the private property and security of the well-off, and to repress real or potential threats to these social class relations from the mass of the dispossessed and marginalized, whether those threats are "criminal" or political in nature (and, as we shall see in Chapter 5, political challenges to global capitalism are now systematically criminalized).

[38] Smith, *Uneven Development*, xv. Smith is careful not to identify uneven development between a global core and a global periphery as intrinsic to capitalism. However, Smith does not depart from the notion of a territorial "geography of capitalism." To be clear, I do not argue that there are no territorial dimensions to global accumulation; my concern is to critique the notion that uneven accumulation is by fiat territorial and pertaining to nation-states in an international system.

centers and sweatshops producing everything from textiles, electronics, and optical equipment to furniture, printing services, and vehicle equipment. The company advertised these opportunities as follows:

> After years of providing quality goods and services to federal agencies, UNICOR now has the authority to partner with private sector firms who are sending the work offshore, or in lieu of sending the work offshore. Companies expanding into new areas of business can also take advantage of UNICOR's unique outsourcing alternative. With more and more call center work being outsourced, UNICOR can provide call center support at a highly competitive rate, and do it right here in the USA. Imagine ... [a]ll the benefits of domestic outsourcing at offshore prices. It's the best kept secret in outsourcing! ... Let's face it, outsourcing offshore can be a hassle. There are language barriers, varying monetary exchange rates, time differences, and simply visiting your call center can involve a transoceanic flight. When you outsource with UNICOR, your call center is located in the United States, and those issues disappear. Your company will enjoy all the benefits of a domestic operation, with the cost savings of going offshore.[39]

Capital has always developed its capacity to extend its operations in time and space. This involves the capacity, especially during times of crisis – or in response to crisis – to escape the particular structural constraints of historically constituted arrangements. Attempts to circumvent such constraints can take place through the manipulation of *time* with regard to accumulation and appropriation – increasing turnover time, creating futures markets, derivatives, and so on, as I will discuss in the next chapter – as well as *space* – capital flight, extraterritorial expansion, the spatial reorganization of production, and so on. Historically such spatial expansion has taken place through colonialism and imperialism, which has involved not only waves of outward expansion from the original centers of capitalism but also the often-violent conversion of new zones to the commodity form (primitive accumulation).

The Unicor example, one of countless we could point to, suggests that the spatial reorganization of accumulation in response to crisis is not necessarily one that involves outward expansion or territorial relocation. The contradictory processes of differentiation and equalization, depending on prevailing technological, political, and social conditions, may not take an international or even a geographically significant expression. The increasing use of caged (prison) labor – itself largely the consequence of state repression of surplus labor, as I will discuss in Chapter 5 – places downward pressure on uncaged labor. Here the U.S. state generates the conditions for U.S.-based labor to be competitive with labor anywhere around the world and therefore offsets the strictly territorial/international dimensions of equalization pressures. As we shall see in Chapter 5, the politics of global crisis and the transition from social welfare to social control or police states generate the political and social conditions propitious to equalization in terms of exploitable labor pools that cut across the traditional core-periphery international divide.

---

[39] This quote is taken from the Unicor web page, http://www.unicor.gov/services/contact_helpdesk/.

The Crisis of Global Capitalism and the U.S. State

The inconsistencies in Harvey's argumentation reflect a general contradiction in the "new imperialism" literature: the dualism of the economic and political, of capital and the state is negated by the claim that the state functions to serve (national) capital. How does Harvey view U.S. foreign policy? "If, for example, the US forces open capital markets around the world through the operations of the IMF and the WTO," he says, "it is because specific advantages are thought to accrue to US financial institutions."[40] Hence foreign policy is a function of financial interests (what a "U.S." financial institution actually refers to in the twenty-first century is not specified). More generally, "new imperialism" theories analyze U.S. foreign policy in relation to the realist assumption of competition among national capitals and consequent political and military rivalry among core nation-states. The United States engages in heightened interventionism to offset its hegemonic decline, says Arrighi.[41] "Intercapitalist rivalry remains the hub of the imperialist wheel," claims Foster. "In the present period of global hegemonic imperialism the United States is geared above all to expanding its imperial power to whatever extent possible and subordinating the rest of the capitalist world to its interests."[42] Henwood insists that U.S. foreign policy in recent years has been singularly aimed at the restoration of the relative strength of "American" capitalists[43]; and "[t]he European Union," writes Wood, "is potentially a stronger economic power than the U.S."[44]

Yet, as we saw in Chapter 1, empirical study of the global economy reveals that *trans*national corporations operate both inside as well as outside the territorial bounds of the EU, that transnational investors from all countries hold and trade in trillions of euros and dollars each day, that share ownership has been significantly transnationalized, and that European investors are as deeply integrated into transnational circuits of accumulation that inextricably pass through the "U.S." economy as are U.S. investors into such circuits that pass through the "EU" economy. These transnational capitalists operate across U.S.-EU frontiers and have a material and political interest in stabilizing the "U.S." and the "EU" economy and "their" financial institutions. Once we belie the realist notion of a world of national economies and national capitals, the logical sequence in "new imperialism" argumentation collapses like a house of cards, since the whole edifice is constructed on this notion. By coming to grips with the reality of transnational capital we can grasp U.S. foreign policy in this new epoch in an

---

[40] Harvey, *The New Imperialism*, 32.
[41] Arrighi, "Hegemony Unraveling I" and "Hegemony Unraveling II"; Immanuel Wallerstein, "An American Dilemma of the 21st Century?," *Societies without Borders* (2006), 1(1): 7–20.
[42] John Bellamy Foster, "The New Age of Imperialism," *Monthly Review* (2003), 55(3): 1–14.
[43] Henwood, *After the New Economy*.
[44] Wood, *Empire of Capital*, 156.

organic, if not merely functional, relation to the actual structure and composition of the dominant social forces in the global capitalist system.

During a July 2004 visit to Chile I came across a report that Chilean capitalists had invested the previous year some $40 billion around the world in diverse pension funds, securities, and other financial outlets. An IMF report that same month explained that Malaysian, German, Russian, Japanese, and U.S. investors were among the thousands of holders of Argentine bonds who had demanded from the IMF and the Group of Eight that the Argentine government reverse its default and honor these bonds. Hence, when the U.S. state, the IMF, or the G-8 pressure the Argentine government to honor its debt to private capitalists from around the world, including from Chile, is this a case – as Wood, Henwood, Foster, Arrighi, Harvey, and the rest would have it – of the U.S. state serving the interests of "its own domestic capital" or the even more amorphous "interests of the imperial hegemon?" Or is it that the U.S. state, together with the IMF and the G-8, is serving the interests of transnational capital and the interests of global capitalist circuits over those of specifically local or national circuits? The July 2004 *Le Monde Diplomatique* reported that Thailand's largest corporate conglomerate, the Charoen Pokphand Group (CPG), employed 100,000 people in 20 countries in operations ranging from poultry and other food production to seeds, telecoms, feed, and franchises on Seven-Eleven retail shops.[45] Clearly, whenever U.S. or IMF pressures open up any of those twenty countries to the global economy, CPG and its investors are just as much the beneficiaries as are transnational investors from the United States, the EU, Chile, and elsewhere. And surely the CPG would be pleased to sell its cut chicken pieces (for which it is best known) in a new Iraqi market opened up by the 2003 U.S. invasion.

Let us return to the case of IBM in India first discussed in Chapter 1. It is no surprise that the Indian government went from being a fierce opponent of the General Agreement on Trade in Services (GATS) in 2001 to being one of its most enthusiastic backers in 2006.[46] The GATS has been discussed as part of continued WTO negotiations and specifically would lift all state control over, and cross-border restrictions on, transnational service sector activity. As India has become a leading global platform for transnational services an increasing number of Indian political and economic elites, along with professional and middle-class strata, have become transnationally oriented and provide the social base for the dramatic turnaround in the government's position toward the GATS. By promoting the GATS the Indian state is in effect promoting the globalization of

[45] Isabelle DelForge, 'Thailand: The World's Kitchen,' *Le Monde Diplomatique*, July 2004: 5; International Monetary Fund, "Independent Evaluation Office (IEO) of the IMF, Report on the Evaluation of the Role of the IMF in Argentina, 1999–2001," June 30, 2004. http://www.imf.org/external/np/ieo/2004/arg/eng/index.htm.

[46] Benny Kuruvilla, "Services Industry Drives Indian GATS Negotiations," *Focus on Trade*, June 2006: 121, Focus on the Global South electronic bulletin from http://www.focusweb.org/content/blogsection/9/60/.

service sector accumulation activities; it is fomenting the transnationalization of capital, the integration of India into the global economy, and acting as a component of the TNS. One would be hard-pressed to see the global political battles around the GATS in nation-state-centric terms; support and opposition to it must be interpreted in transnational class terms. Either we must recognize that the picture emerging is less one of international competition among national capitals than one of global competition among transnational capitals (and other social groups), or we must sever the economic from the political in the way Harvey and others do, by erecting a dualism in an attempt to salvage a nation-state-centric view of the world and a realist reading of global politics.

Wood, among other "new imperialism" theorists, dismisses the proposition that a "global state" apparatus may be coming into existence because, in her view, any such argument is based on the idea that the territorial state is increasingly obsolete. No one beyond a few commentators[47] suggests that the nation-state is disappearing, or that capital can now, or ever has been able to, exist without a state. There are vital functions that the national state performs for transnational capital – among them, formulating local economic policies aimed at achieving macroeconomic equilibrium, the provision of property laws and infrastructure, and of course, social control and ideological reproduction. However, there are other conditions that transnational capitalists require for the functioning and reproduction of global capitalism. National states are ill equipped to organize a supranational unification of macroeconomic policies, create a unified field on which transnational capital can operate, impose transnational trade regimes, provide supranational "transparency," and so forth. The construction of a supranational legal and regulatory system for the global economy in recent years has been the task of sets of transnational institutions whose policy prescriptions and actions have been synchronized with those of neo-liberal national states that have been captured by local transnationally oriented forces.

We cannot, as Wood does, simply shrug off the increasingly salient role of a transnational institutional structure in coordinating global capitalism and imposing capitalist domination beyond national borders. "New imperialism" dogma reduces IMF practices to instruments of "U.S." imperialism. Yet I know of no single IMF structural adjustment program that creates conditions in the intervened country that favor "U.S." capital in any special way, rather than opening up the intervened country, its labor and resources, to capitalists from any corner of the world. This outcome is in sharp distinction to earlier imperialism, in which a particular core country sealed off the colonized country or sphere of influence as its own exclusive preserve for exploitation. Therefore, it is more accurate to characterize the IMF (or, for that matter, the World Bank, other

---

[47] See, e.g., Kenichi Ohmae, *The End of the Nation State: The Rise of Regional Economies* (New York: Free Press, 1996).

regional banks, the WTO, etc.) as an instrument not of "U.S." imperialism but of transnational capitalist exploitation.

The continued existence of the national state is a central condition not for "U.S. hegemony" or a "new U.S. empire" but for the class power of transnational capital. The TCC has been able to use local core states to mold transnational structures and to impose these on distinct nations and regions. The real issue is not the continued existence of nation-states and of powerful national states in a globalized system – a fact that does not contradict the thesis of a TCC and a TNS – but *their function*. We must analyze U.S. foreign policy in relation to the structural role of U.S. state power in advancing neo-liberalism and global capitalism. U.S. policies such as the imposition of neo-liberal structural adjustment programs and the sponsorship of free trade agreements have by and large served to further pry open regions and sectors around the world to global capitalism. U.S. policies in the main have advanced transnational capitalist interests. The Bush administration, contrary to the rhetoric of some U.S. state managers, consistently ratified and pursued a policy not of national economic retrenchment but of neo-liberal global market integration. And an analysis of TNS apparatuses suggests that they act not to enforce "U.S." policies but to force nationally oriented policies in general into transnational alignment.

U.S. foreign policy is exercised behind the backs of the public by state managers as proximate policymakers and politicized corporate elites that constitute the ruling class in the formal sense of the term. Nevertheless, state policymaking is also a process in which different factions and institutions that make up the state apparatus have influence over varied quotas of decision making at given moments. Tactical and strategic differences as well as personal and institutional rivalries are played out at the level of proximate policymaking in disputes for control over policy. This diffusion of foreign-policy-making power within an elite and levels of (relative) autonomy among proximate policymakers can make moments of transition and redefinition appear highly contradictory and can confuse observers, especially when these observers take public discourse at face value or assume that social actors are not influenced by ideologies that may be inconsistent with interests and underlying intent. Policy analysis is conjunctural analysis and must be combined with structural analysis, and analysis of state policies and class practices must be based on the actual content of these policies and practices, not on what their agents claim them to be.

As we saw in the previous chapter, one of the fundamental contradictions of capitalist globalization is that economic globalization unfolds within the framework of a nation-state/interstate political system and its fragmented formal authority structures. The TNS can politically wield the structural power of transnational capital by, for example, imposing conditionality in lending, applying sanctions and financial embargos, issuing credit ratings, and so forth. But it does not have a coercive apparatus that is truly supranational. The U.S. state wields the only significant instruments of coercion on a world scale. This coercive apparatus is wielded, I have argued, in the interests of transnational accumulation. Nonetheless, such an institutional configuration presents significant contradictions because global elites as a whole do not have access to that apparatus in the way the U.S. contingent of that elite does. Even when there is ever-greater transnational consultation among global elites and transnational state managers, the transnational elite is unable, when it comes to the U.S. (or any national) state, to undertake the type of internal strategic debate, the consensus-building processes, the consensual mechanisms, and also the conspiratorial dimensions of policymaking that take place at the level of the national state. Moreover, the U.S. and other national states are subject to the pressures of internal (national) legitimacy and to particularlist interests.

There is little disagreement among global elites, regardless of their formal nationality, that U.S. power should be rigorously applied (e.g., to impose IMF programs, to bomb the former Yugoslavia, for "peacekeeping" and "humanitarian" interventions, and so on) in order to sustain and defend global capitalism. The U.S. state is a key *point of condensation* for pressures from dominant groups around the world to resolve problems of global capitalism and to secure the legitimacy of the system overall. In this regard, "U.S." imperialism refers to the use by transnational elites of the U.S. state apparatus to continue to attempt to expand, defend, and stabilize the global capitalist system. We are witness less to a "U.S." imperialism per se than to a global capitalist imperialism. We face an *empire of global capital*, headquartered, for evident historical reasons, in Washington. The questions for global elites are: In what ways, under what particular conditions, arrangements, and strategies, should U.S. state power be wielded? How can particular sets of U.S. state managers be responsive and held accountable to global elites who are fractious in their actions, dispersed around the world, and operating through numerous supranational institutional settings, each with distinct histories and particular trajectories?

The structural changes that have led to the transnationalization of national capitals, finances, and markets, and the actual outcomes of recent U.S.-led political and military campaigns, suggest new forms of global capitalist domination, whereby interventions such as those in Iraq, East Africa, Haiti, and the former Yugoslavia aim to create conditions favorable to the penetration of transnational capital and the renewed integration of the intervened region into the global system. U.S. intervention facilitates a shift in power from locally and regionally oriented elites to new groups more favorable to the transnational project. The result of U.S. military conquest is not the creation of exclusive zones for "U.S." exploitation, as was the result of the Spanish conquest of Latin America, the British of South Africa and India, the Dutch of Indonesia, and so forth, in earlier moments of the world capitalist system. The enhanced class power of capital brought about by these changes is felt around the world. We see *not* a reenactment of this old imperialism but the colonization and recolonization of the vanquished on behalf of the new global capitalism and its agents. The underlying class relation between the TCC and the U.S. national state needs to be understood in these terms. The U.S. state houses the ministry of war in a much-divided global elite cabinet.

The Case of Iraq

Most observers saw the 2003 U.S. invasion and occupation of Iraq as the premier example of the "new imperialism" – a U.S. attempt to control Iraqi oil in the face of rivals and to shore up its declining hegemony. In criticizing the theory of the TNS, Van der Pijl states that "the U.S. and the UK have used (in Iraq for instance) their military 'comparative advantage' to trump the Russian and French willingness to strike oil deals with the Saddam Hussein regime when it appeared that UN sanctions were unraveling."[48] Yet the very first transnational oil company to be assisted by the U.S. State Department in the wake of Washington's invasion and occupation was the "French" oil company Total, followed by Chinese oil companies that were able to enter the Iraqi oil market thanks to the U.S. occupation. The opposition of France, Germany, and other countries to the Iraq invasion indicated sharp tactical and strategic differences over how to respond to crisis, shore up the system, and keep it expanding. Baker has shown how the invasion of Iraq violently opened up the country to transnational capital and integrated it into new global circuits. The invasion resulted in a shift from the old nationally oriented to transnationally oriented elites cultivated and placed in power by the occupation force, the imposition of radical neo-liberal restructuring, and a change in the regional balance of forces in favor of the global capitalist power bloc.[49] As Klein has observed, "the architects of the invasion . . . unleashed ferocious violence because they could not crack open the closed economies of the Middle East by peaceful means."[50] In addition, the invasions of Iraq and of Afghanistan opened up vast profit-making opportunities for the TCC at a time when the global economy showed serious signs of stagnation, as I will discuss in more detail in the following chapter.

If the U.S. state has attempted to play a leadership role *on behalf of* transnational capitalist interests, it has been increasingly unable to do so due not to heightened national rivalry but to the impossibility of the task at hand given a spiraling crisis of global capitalism. This crisis has generated intense discrepancies and disarray within the globalist power bloc, which at best has been held together by fragile threads and may well tear apart at the seams under the

[48] Kees Van der Pijl, "A Theory of Global Capitalism: Feature Review," *New Political Economy* (2005), 10(2): 276.

[49] Yousef Baker, "Global Capitalism and Iraq: The Making of a Neo-Liberal Republic," paper presented at the international conference *Global Capitalism and Transnational Class Formation*, Center of Global Studies, Czech Academy of Sciences, September 16–18, 2011. Iraq, observes Naomi Klein, "was one of the last remaining holdouts from the drive to build a global market based on [Milton] Freidman's vision of unfettered capitalism." The invasion "was a rational policy choice. . . . [T]he architects of the invasion had unleashed ferocious violence because they could not crack open the closed economies of the Middle East by peaceful means, [so that] the level of terror was proportional to what was at stake." Naomi Klein, *The Shock Doctrine* (New York: Henry Holt, 2007), 326–7.

[50] Klein, *The Shock Doctrine*, 327.

pressure of conflicts internal to it and of forces opposed to its logic. The political coherence of ruling groups always frays when faced with structural and/or legitimacy crises as different groups push distinct strategies and tactics or turn to the more immediate pursuit of sectoral interests. Faced with the increasingly dim prospects for constructing a viable transnational hegemony, in the Gramscian sense of a stable system of consensual domination, the transnational bourgeoisie has not collapsed back into the nation-state. Global elites have, instead, mustered up fragmented and at times incoherent responses involving heightened military coercion, the search for a post-Washington consensus, and acrimonious internal disputes. The more politically astute among global elites have clamored in recent years to promote a "post-Washington consensus" project of reform – a so-called globalization with a human face – in the interests of saving the system itself.[51] But there were others, both from within and outside of the bloc, who called for more radical responses.

During the post 9/11 period the military dimension appeared to exercise an overdetermining influence in the reconfiguration of global politics.[52] The Bush White House militarized social and economic contradictions generated by the crisis tendencies in global capitalism, launching a permanent war mobilization to try to stabilize the system through direct coercion. The Obama White House followed suit, despite a distinct rhetoric. Was this evidence for a new U.S. bid for empire? Interventionism and militarized globalization has been less a campaign for U.S. hegemony than a contradictory political response to the crisis of global capitalism – to economic stagnation, legitimation problems, and the rise of counterhegemonic forces. As I will discuss in detail in the next chapter, despite the rhetoric of neo-liberalism, the U.S. state has played an almost unprecedented role in creating profit-making opportunities for transnational capital and pushing forward an accumulation process that, left to its own devices (the "free market"), would likely have ground to a halt well before 2008.

Some saw the billions of dollars invested by the U.S. state in the invasion and occupation of Iraq as evidence that the U.S. intervention benefits "U.S. capital" to the detriment of other national capitals. However, Bechtel, the Carlyle Group,

---

[51] See, e.g., Joseph Stiglitz, *Globalization and Its Discontents* (New York: W.W. Norton, 2003).

[52] By "overdetermination" I mean that an event or process – in this case renewed U.S. interventionism and militarization – is determined by multiple causes or conditions (determinations); the overdetermining condition is that which is singled out in concrete historical circumstances as an analytical explanadum. As further explanation: overdetermination in philosophical terms refers to an event or phenomenon whereby a single observed effect is determined by multiple causes at once, any one of which alone might be enough to account for – *determine* – the effect. In terms of social analysis, Althusser imported the concept from Freud and Mao. There may be a number of necessary conditions (determinations) of the event's occurrence; the *overdetermining* condition is that which is singled out in concrete historical circumstances as an analytical explanadum. Hence Althusser suggested that the economic level does not necessarily determine the event, process, or phenomenon – except, in his famous words, "in the last instance" – which can be overdetermined by political, ideological, or other levels. See Louis Althusser. "Contradiction and Overdetermination," in Althusser, *For Marx* (London: Verso, 1985).

and Halliburton, which were prime recipients of U.S. military contracts, are themselves transnational capital conglomerates. Carlyle, for example, is one of the largest private equity (holding) companies in the world, with investors from seventy-five countries and hundreds of companies around the world. Among its officials are former British prime minister John Major, former UN secretary general Javier Perez de Cuellar, former president of the Deutsche Bundesbank Karl Otto Pohl, former South Korean prime minister Park Tae-joon, the Saudi royal family (including members of the bin Laden family), Montenegran President Milo Djukanovic, the global financier George Soros, numerous officers from European-based businesses, and representatives from Nigeria, Dubai, China, Indian, Brazil, South Africa, and Singapore.[53] Rothkopf observes that defense firms around the world are becoming more and more integrated into a global network through strategic alliances, joint ventures, and cross-border mergers.[54] It is true that military, oil, and engineering/construction companies, many of them headquartered in the United States, managed to secure their particular sectoral interests through brazen instrumentalization of the U.S. state under the Bush presidency. However, these companies were themselves transnational, and their interests were those not of "U.S. capital" in rivalry with other countries but of particular transnational clusters in the global economy.

The "creative destruction" of war (and natural and humanitarian disasters) generates new cycles of accumulation through "reconstruction." And the military-energy-engineering-construction complex constitutes one of those sectors of global capital that most benefit from the "creative destruction" of crises, wars, and natural and humanitarian disasters. Transnational capitalists are themselves aware of the role of the U.S. state in opening up new possibilities for unloading surplus and creating new investment opportunities. "We're looking for places to invest around the world," explained one former executive of a Dutch-based oil exploration and engineering company, and then, "you know, along comes Iraq."[55]

The billions invested by the U.S. state in war and "reconstruction" in Iraq went to a vast array of investors and subcontractors that spanned the globe. Kuwaiti Trading and Contracting, Alargan Trading of Kuwait, Gulf Catering, and Saudi Trading and Construction Company were just some of the Middle Eastern–based companies that shared in the bonanza, along with companies and investor groups as far away as South Africa, Bosnia, the Philippines, and India.[56] Allawi writes: "In the early days of the occupation, it was Kuwaiti, Egyptian and Korean subcontractors, Saudi and Turkish transport companies, Jordanian

---

[53] Dan Briody, *The Iron Triangle: Inside the Secret World of the Carlyle Group* (Hoboken, NJ: John Wiley and Sons, 2003). See also the Carlyle webpage: http://www.carlyle.com/about-carlyle.

[54] Rothkopf, *Superclass*, 207.

[55] As cited in "Note from the Editors," *Monthly Review*, November 2004, inside front cover and 64–65, cited on p. 64.

[56] David Phinney, "Blood, Sweat and Tears: Asia's Poor Build U.S. Bases in Iraq," *CorpWatch*, October 3, 2005, downloaded from http://www.corpwatch.org/article.php?id=12675.

good brokers, Pakisani and Indian labor contracts, and Lebanese middle-men who ruled the subcontract world of the U.S. military."[57] Moreover, Iranian investors and merchants poured into Iraq under the canopy of the U.S. occupation.[58] The picture was one in which the U.S. state mobilized the resources to feed a vast transnational network of profit making that passed through countless layers of outsourcing, subcontracting, alliances, and collaborative relations, benefiting transnationally oriented capitalists from many parts of the globe. The U.S. state was the pivotal gear in a TNS machinery dedicated to reproducing global capitalism.

Imperialism and the Extensive and Intensive Enlargement of Capitalism

If the world is not divided into rival national economies and national capitals, do we still need a theory of imperialism? Is there any contemporary relevance to the concept? During the post–World War II period, and drawing on the tradition established by Rosa Luxembourg, Marxists and other critical political economists shifted the main focus in the study of imperialism to the mechanisms of core capitalist penetration of Third World countries and the appropriation of their surpluses. Imperialism in this sense referred to such exploitation and also to the use of state apparatuses by capitals emanating from the centers of the world system to facilitate this economic relation through military, political, and cultural mechanisms. If we mean by imperialism the relentless pressures for outward expansion of capitalism and the distinct political, military, and cultural mechanisms that facilitate that expansion and the appropriation of surpluses it generates, then it is a structural imperative built into capitalism. It is not a policy of particular core state managers (to see it as such was Hobson's fallacy) but a practice *immanent* to the system itself. The imperialism practiced by the Bush White House was nothing particular to a group of neo-conservative politicians and organic intellectuals in the United States. And the Obama White House continued such practices, notwithstanding particular conjunctures and distinct policies and strategies among elites.

We need tools in order to conceptualize, analyze, and theorize how this expansionary pressure built into the capitalist system manifests itself in the age of globalization. We need these tools *politically* so as to help make effective our confrontation with the system. I would agree to this extent with Kiely that a theory of imperialism "remains indispensable for understanding both the contemporary world order and the place of the South in that order."[59] Yet, even at

[57] Ali A. Allawi, *The Occupation of Iraq: Winning the War, Losing the Peace* (New Haven, CT: Yale University Press, 2007), 253.

[58] Edward Wong, "Iran Is Playing a Growing Role in Iraqi Economy, *The New York Times*, March 17, 2007, http://www.nytimes.com/2007/03/17/world/middleeast/17iran.html?pagewanted=all&_r=0.

[59] Ray Kiely, "United States Hegemony and Globalisation: What Role for Theories of Imperialism?," *Cambridge Review of International Affairs* (2006), 19(2): 205–221.

that, capitalist imperialism is considerably more complex under globalization than the facile North-South/core-periphery framework through which it is typically viewed. The class relations of global capitalism are now so deeply internalized *within* every nation-state that the classical image of imperialism as a relation of external domination is outdated. Failure to comprehend this leads to such superficial and misleading conclusions as, for instance, that popular projects failed to materialize under the rule of the Workers Party in Brazil or the African National Congress in South Africa because of a "sell-out" by the leaders of those parties or simply because "imperialism" undercut their programs. Imperialism is not about nations but about groups exercising their social power – through *institutions* – to control value production, to appropriate surpluses, and to reproduce these arrangements. The challenge for such a theoretical enterprise is to ask: how and by whom in the world capitalist system are values produced (organized through what institutions), how are they appropriated (through what institutions), and how are these processes changing through capitalist globalization? During the 500 years since the genesis of the world capitalist system, colonialism and imperialism coercively incorporated zones and peoples into its fold. This historical process of "primitive accumulation" is coming to a close.

The end of the extensive enlargement of capitalism is the end of the imperialist era of world capitalism. The system still conquers space, nature, and human beings. It is dehumanizing, genocidal, suicidal, and maniacal. But with the exception of a few remaining spaces (Iraq until recently, North Korea, etc.) the world has been brought into the system over the past half-millennium. The implacable logic of accumulation is now largely internal to worldwide social relations and to the complex of fractious political institutions through which ruling groups attempt to manage those relations. The effort by the U.S. state to design repressive immigration legislation to assure a cheap, repressed, and tightly controlled Latino workforce within U.S. territory is no different from the efforts of the TNS to impose intellectual property rights in Latin America, privatization in Southern Africa, or deregulated and flexiblized labor in the EU – all this, and more, is the ugly face of global capitalism. But it is not imperialism in the old sense either of rival national capitals or conquest of precapitalist regions by core states. We need a *theory of capitalist expansion* – of the political processes and the institutions through which such expansion takes place, the class relations and spatial dynamics it involves.

Yet this capitalist expansion is a process that generates capitalist crisis by its own internal workings. In the next chapter we return to the theme of crisis, examining the internal contradictions that are tearing global capitalism apart and that exploded with the economic collapse of 2008. In doing so we will further analyze the role of the United States in the global capitalist system, not as an empire but as a major axis or nodal point for this global system.

4

The "Great Recession"

Financial Speculation and Militarized Accumulation

Drug lords need banks. A glimpse: *Bloomberg Markets* magazine's August 2010 issue reported that drug traffickers who used a DC-9 jet to move cocaine from South America to Mexico had purchased the jet 'with laundered funds they transferred through two of the biggest banks in the U.S.: Wachovia Corp. and Bank of America Corp'. But banks also need drug lords. In 2008, drug money saved the major global banks from collapse and thus, stretching just a bit, saved capitalism from a devastating internal crisis when the speculative capital markets imploded. … Antonio Maria Costa, the head of the UN Office on Drugs and Crime [told *The Observer* in London] that he had seen evidence that the proceeds of organized crime were 'the only liquid investment capital' available to some banks on the brink of collapse.

Journalist John Gibler, in *To Die in Mexico: Dispatches from Inside the Drug War*[1]

PRESIDENT OF THE FIRST LOS ANGELES BANK: "How much [cash] are you shipping today?"

BCCI [BANK OF CREDIT AND COMMERCE INTERNATIONAL] CUSTOMER AND HEAD OF A BILLION-DOLLAR DRUG MONEY-LAUNDERING OPERATION: "How much? I don't know. I have no idea."

"Ship me all you got."

"Okay, everything's yours anyway."

DEA surveillance tape[2]

CAPITALISM AND CRISES

The "Great Recession" of 2008 was triggered by the collapse of the global financial system, but it has much deeper structural causes. It was not in essence

[1] John Gibler, *To Die in Mexico: Dispatches from Inside the Drug War* (San Francisco: City Lights Books, 2011), 33.
[2] As cited in George Winslow, *Capital Crimes: A Globe-Spanning Account of the Violence of Power and Money – from Street Crime to Corporate Crime* (New York: Monthly Review Press, 1999), 269.

a "financial" crisis, much less simply an institutional disorder. Moreover, it was – and is – a crisis of the world capitalist system and not of any particular country or region. As a *global* crisis it cannot be understood by limiting the focus to a particular country or region, as a number of studies have done.[3] How can we characterize the crisis? Is it cyclical, structural, or systemic? *Cyclical crises* are recurrent to capitalism about once every ten years and involve recessions that act as self-correcting mechanisms without any major restructuring of the system. The recessions of the early 1980s, the early 1990s, and of 2001 were cyclical crises. By contrast, the 2008 crisis, in my view, signaled the slide into a deep structural crisis. *Structural crises* reflect deeper contradictions that can be resolved only by a major restructuring of the system.[4] The structural crisis of the 1970s was resolved through capitalist globalization. Prior to that, the structural crisis of the 1930s was resolved through the creation of a new model of Fordist-Keynesian or redistributive capitalism, and prior to that the structural crisis of the 1870s resulted in the development of corporate capitalism and a new wave of colonialism. The current systemwide crisis will not be a repeat of earlier such episodes in the 1970s, the 1930s, or the 1870s, precisely because world capitalism is fundamentally different in the twenty-first century. A *systemic crisis* involves the replacement of a system by an entirely new system *or* leads to an outright collapse. A structural crisis opens up the *possibility* of a systemic crisis. But whether it actually snowballs into a systemic crisis – in this case, whether it gives way either to capitalism being superseded or to a breakdown of global civilization – is not predetermined and depends entirely on the response of social and political forces to the crisis and on historical contingencies that are not easy to forecast. This is an historic moment of extreme uncertainty, in which collective responses to the crisis on the part of distinct social and class forces are in great flux.

Capitalism is a system wracked by *internal contradictions* that generate crises. Crisis theory attempts to identify these internal contradictions and exactly how and why they generate crises. There is a vast literature and much debate on the nature of capitalist crises, too vast to take up here.[5] But those who approach crisis from the vantage point of Marxist political economy agree on two points:

---

[3] See, e.g., John Bellamy Foster and Fred Magdoff, *The Great Financial Crisis: Causes and Consequences* (New York: Monthly Review Press, 2009); Andrew Kliman, *The Failure of Capitalist Production: Underlying Causes of the Great Recession* (London: Pluto Press, 2012). Both these studies limit themselves to examining data from the "U.S. economy" and U.S. country-level data, which in my view makes them fatally flawed, despite their important insights.

[4] O'Connor writes: "The difference between the concept of crisis as periodic economic fluctuations and structural crisis is that the latter refers to long-term conjunctures and multiple contradictions in economic, political, and social life." James O'Connor, *The Meaning of Crisis* (New York: Basil Blackwell, 1987), 63–64.

[5] But see, inter alia, Michael F. Belany, *Underconsumption Theories: A Historical and Critical Analysis* (New York: International Publishers, 1976); Rosa Luxemburg, *The Accumulation of Capital* (New York: Monthly Review Press, 1971); Ernest Mandel, *Marxist Economic Theory* (New York: Monthly Review Press, 1968), and Mandel, *Late Capitalism* (London: Verso, 1978);

1) crises are immanent to capitalism, that is, crises are "normal" insofar as they are generated by the "normal" functioning of the system; 2) crises are generated by the many interrelated contradictions internal to capitalism, whether posited as the tendency for the rate of profit to fall, as the social antagonism between capital and labor, between use-value and exchange-value, forces and relations of production, value-production and value-realization – posed as the disjuncture between production and circulation, and termed overproduction or underconsumption – or as overaccumulation (overproduction of capital), and so on. I want to focus here on the latter two approaches.

What is meant by *contradictions* in reference to a social order (or to any phenomenon) is the existence of two dimensions inherent in the particular order that are incompatible and that make instability and change an intrinsic part of the order. What is meant by *internal* is that these contradictions are not anomalies but are part of the very logic of the system, how it functions and is reproduced. In political economy, analysis of the contradictions of capitalism draws on crisis theory and involves a focus on the tendency for the capitalist system to experience recurrent crises. In its political-economy dimensions, the crisis of global capitalism is one of *overaccumulation*. Capitalism produces vast amount of wealth but also generates social polarization. By definition, capitalists could not generate a profit if the workers who produce wealth were paid for the value of what they produce. Under capitalist production relations, workers produce more goods and services that they are actually able to purchase with their wages. Capitalists would have no incentive to invest their money if the price fetched for the goods and services produced were exactly equal to wages, that is, if they were not assured a profit by appropriating a portion of the value produced by labor in the form of profits (or surplus value, although these two terms are not synonymous). At a certain point, more goods and services are produced than can be purchased by the mass of laborers, and the economy enters a recession or a depression because capitalists cannot "unload" the surplus. This situation of "overproduction" or "underconsumption," or the "realization problem," means that in order for capitalists to make ("realize") a profit they must actually sell the goods and services produced; otherwise, it simply accumulates and the capitalist loses the money invested in the production process.

The notion of overaccumulation is a part of this general contradiction. Overaccumulation appears as an excess of capital relative to opportunities for investing that capital, so that it further accumulates, that is, so that it generates new surplus value and profits. Overaccumulation can be displaced though time – that is, postponed (e.g., through credit), which only – literally – buys time. It can be resolved through a change in the conditions of exploitation or through the devalorization of some portion of the total social capital. "*Devalorization*" here is understood as a reduction in the total social capital, variable as well as

David Harvey, *The Limits to Capital* (London: Verso, 2006 edition); James O'Connor, *The Meaning of Crisis* (New York: Basil Blackwell, 1987).

constant. This resolution can involve, in the short term, an increasing rate or intensity of exploitation (that is, a devalorization of variable capital through either a decrease in wages or an increase in productivity without an increase in wages; this includes an increase in the rate and intensity of exploitation via geographic relocation to lower wage zones, or spatial displacement). This resolution can also involve the reorganization of capital and devaluation of some portion of it (e.g., through cyclical recessions). But these resolutions only *postpone* or *displace* the contradiction. The *tendency* toward overaccumulation continues and in the modern history of world capitalism has generally culminated in structural crises that threaten permanent stagnation unless there is a much more fundamental reorganization of the system. The rise of a Fordist-Keynesian social structure of accumulation in the aftermath of the 1930s depression and the Second World War involved such a restructuring, as did the initial decades of neo-liberal globalization in the 1980s and 1990s.[6]

Crisis theory suggests that overaccumulation may be manifested in different ways.[7] How is it manifested in the current crisis? In the last major crisis, that of the 1970s, it took the form of a falling rate of profit, as "profit squeeze" theorists writing in that decade demonstrated.[8] But a "profit squeeze" does not explain the current situation as profits soared in the period leading up to 2008 (see Figure 4.1), and we should recall that savings is not equivalent to investment, either financial or productive. In the 1970s overaccumulation also took the form of stagflation, or inflation together with stagnation. In the early and mid-1970s working and popular classes fiercely resisted a transfer of the costs of the crisis to themselves.[9] Neither these classes nor capital were willing to shoulder the costs of crisis; this standoff is what, in my view, generated stagflation. But working and popular classes were able to put up resistance precisely because they faced capital within the confines of the nation-state. The gains these classes had made within nation-state capitalism and their ability to resist capital's impositions is precisely what led capital to go global in the first place, that is, to undertake a restructuring of the system through globalization. But stagflation and standoff does not characterize the current ongoing crisis, at least not as I write in early 2013. As has been amply documented, the portion of value going to workers has dropped sharply, and living standards have plummeted since the late 1970s. Instead, it seems clear that overaccumulation is now expressed, as it

---

[6] "As the most fundamental contradiction of capitalism is between the classes," according to Cleaver and Bell, "so the most fundamental role of crisis-as-solution is restoring the balance of class forces such that capital can resume its growth, i.e., growth in the control of the working class and society" See Harry Cleaver and Peter Bell, "Marx's Crisis Theory as a Theory of Class Relations," *Research in Political Economy* (1982), no. 5:257.

[7] See, inter alia, Harvey's discussion in *The Limits to Capital*; O'Connor, *The Meaning of Crisis*.

[8] See, e.g., Andrew Glyn and Bob Sutcliffe, *Capitalism in Crisis* (New York: Pantheon Books, 1972).

[9] Again Cleaver and Bell: "For workers the most important thing about capitalist crisis is that it is, for the most part, the consequence of their struggles. The rupture of accumulation by struggle is a moment of conquest." ("Marx's Crisis Theory," 258).

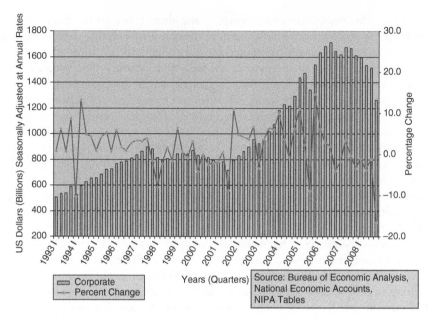

FIGURE 4.1. U.S. Corporate Profits, 1993–2008.

was in the 1930s crisis, as overproduction/underconsumption. In the wake of the 2008 collapse, for instance, the world press was full of images of car lots overflowing with vehicles that could not be marketed as factories shut down and production plummeted. In 2008 it was estimated that over 75 percent of China's industries were plagued by overcapacity.[10] And if there was a "credit crunch" it is not because bankers and investors did not have money to lend but because they could not do so profitably due to consumer insolvency.

Structural crises involve great social conflict and also evince political, ideological, cultural, and other dimensions, as I will discuss later.[11] Let us here retrace in brief the lead-up to the 2008 financial collapse. Crises of overaccumulation follow periods of hyperaccumulation. At the structural level, to reiterate, the current global crisis is above all one of overaccumulation, or the lack of outlets for the profitable absorption of surpluses. As we saw in previous chapters, the globalization stage of world capitalism itself evolved out the response of distinct agents to previous episodes of crisis, in particular, to the 1970s crisis of Fordism-Keynesianism, or of redistributive capitalism. In the wake of that crisis

[10] See Ho-fung Hung, "Rise of China and the Global Overaccumulation Crisis," *Review of International Political Economy* (2008), 15(2): 159.

[11] It is, however, worth quoting here James O'Connor: "The critique of the well-established dualism between objectivist and subjectivist approaches to crisis theory is based on the idea that modern economic, social, political, and cultural crisis interpenetrate one another in ways which transform them into different dimensions of the same historical process." (*The Meaning of Crisis*, 11).

capital went global as a strategy of the emergent transnational capitalist class and its political representatives to reconstitute its class power by breaking free of nation-state constraints on accumulation. These constraints – the so-called class compromise – had been imposed on capital through decades of mass struggle around the world by nationally contained popular and working classes. During the 1980s and 1990s, however, globally oriented elites captured state power in most countries and utilized that power to push capitalist globalization.

Global mobility gave transnational capital newfound structural power over nationally based working classes. Globalization and neo-liberal policies opened up vast new opportunities for transnational accumulation in the 1980s and 1990s. What took place, in broad strokes, during these decades? Privatizations facilitated a new round of primitive accumulation as public and community spheres were commodified and turned over to capital. These privatizations as well as the imposition of "intellectual property rights" opened up public sectors, community spaces, and cultural and knowledge production to commodification and hence facilitated new bursts of accumulation. Deregulation, liberalization, and free trade agreements allowed for a new wave of foreign direct investment, for a sharp increase in cross-border mergers and acquisitions, and for a heightened concentration and centralization of capital on a global scale. The incorporation of the former Soviet bloc and Third World revolutionary countries into global capitalism provided vast new markets and investment outlets. The introduction of computer and information technology (CIT) represented a new "Scientific and Technological Revolution" that triggered explosive growth in productivity and productive capacities, a disproportionate increase in fixed capital, and also the means for capital to go global – to coordinate and synchronize a globalized system of production, finances, and services, in distinction to a globalized market for goods and services that dates back centuries.

The revolution in CIT and other technological advances helped emergent transnational capital to restructure, "flexibilize," and shed labor worldwide. New modalities for mobilizing and exploiting the global labor force included a massive new round of primitive accumulation and the uprooting and displacement of hundreds of millions of people, especially from the Third World countryside, who became internal and transnational migrants. These processes, in turn, undercut wages and the social wage and facilitated a transfer of income to capital and to high-consumption sectors around the world that provided new market segments fueling growth. Crisis theory suggests that new phases of capital accumulation come on the heels of crisis and involve the introduction of technological innovations that become the leading edge of renewed rounds of accumulation. This certainly seems to be the case with regard to the generalized introduction of CIT in the wake of the 1970s crisis. Whether nanotechnology, bioengineering, 3-D printing manufacturing, or some other emerging technology will become a new leading edge of accumulation in the wake of the current crisis remains to be seen.

In sum, globalization made possible a major extensive and intensive expansion of the system and unleashed a frenzied new round of accumulation worldwide that offset the 1970s crisis of declining profits and investment opportunities. Global elites giddily declared "the end of History" in the heyday of global capitalism's hegemony in the early 1990s, following the end of the Cold War and the consolidation of the so-called Washington consensus around the neo-liberal model. But by the end of that decade the limits to expansion became clear as global markets became saturated. As privatization programs ran their course, the well of assets to privatize dried up. The initial boom in investment opportunities in the former socialist and revolutionary countries began to taper after they were brought into global markets. Once plants and infrastructure made the switch to computer and information technology, the remarkable rate of fixed capital turnover that the initial systemwide introduction of these technologies generated could not be sustained. Investment in high tech slowed greatly in the twenty-first century, and in 2008 telecommunication and computer orders were down 50 percent from their late 1990s high.[12] By the turn of the century it had become apparent that we were headed toward a structural crisis. The system was generating ever-more massive surpluses, yet the globalization generated ever-more acute inequality and pauperization worldwide. Opportunities for the profitable absorption of those surpluses diminished after the boom of the 1980s and 1990s. Global economic expansion and global market contraction reflect perhaps *the* fundamental contradiction of capitalism: overaccumlation.

The capitalist system, in sum, again faced the recurrent challenge of how to profitably unload surpluses. The system had been stumbling from one lesser crisis to another since the mid-1990s. The first was the Mexican peso crisis of 1995 and its "tequila effect" elsewhere. This was followed by the Asian financial meltdown of 1997–98 that also spread to Russia, Brazil, and other parts of the world. Then there came the bursting of the dot-com bubble and the recession of 2001. Between the Asian meltdown of 1997–98 and the recession of 2001 global elites began to sound alarm bells. The billionaire financier George Soros warned of the need to save the system from itself.[13] These elites came to be wracked by divisions and infighting as the more politically astute among them clamored for a "post-Washington consensus" project of reform – a so-called globalization with a human face.[14] The neo-liberal monolith began to crack, although it would be several more years before its downfall. By the new century two major mechanisms for unloading surplus capital would provide a perverse lifeline to the system: *financial speculation* and *militarized accumulation*.

[12] Peter G. Gosselin, "U.S. Economy May Sputter for Years," *Los Angeles Times*, January 19, 2009: A1.

[13] George Soros, *The Crisis of Global Capitalism: Open Society Endangered* (New York: Public Affairs, 1998).

[14] Joseph Stiglitz, *Globalization and Its Discontents* (New York: W.W. Norton, 2003).

THE GLOBAL CAPITALIST FINANCIAL COMPLEX

There are historically contingent forms of capitalist organization molded by secular tendencies in the system together with the struggle among social and class forces. The oscillating role that finance has played at different places and in different moments in the history of world capitalism is a reflection of this historical movement. The rise to hegemony of transnational finance capital is a major historical development of the late twentieth and early twenty-first centuries. Financial markets concentrate wealth; they appropriate value from other circuits that have, in turn, appropriated it from labor. With the deregulation and liberalization of financial markets worldwide in the 1980s and 1990s and the introduction of CIT, national financial systems have merged into an increasingly integrated global financial system – a monstrous global complex that allows for hitherto unknown concentrations of social power, including the ability to dictate to states and to other circuits of accumulation. The officers, directors, and owners of financial corporations (banks, insurance companies, securities firms, etc.) are usually at the center of interlocking directorates in the corporate economy. However, the concept of finance capital does not refer exclusively to individuals or institutions in the financial sector; it refers to the preponderant weight of the financial sector in relation to the capitalist economy overall. In this sense, transnational finance capital is at the center of the global capitalist economy and is the hegemonic fraction of capital on a world scale. Marazzi observes how the entire (global) economy has become financialized:

The process of financialization that led to the crisis we are living in now is distinct from all other phases of financialization historically recorded in the twentieth century.... Financial crises ... based on a contradictory relationship between real and financial economies, [is] a relationship that today is no longer expressed in the same terms. The financial economy today is pervasive, that is, it spreads across the entire economic cycle, co-existing with it, so to speak, from start to finish. Figuratively speaking, finance is present even when you go shopping at the supermarket and use your credit card. The automobile industry, to give only one example, functions entirely upon credit mechanisms (installments, leasing, etc.), so that the problems of a General Motors have just as much to do with the production of cars as, if not above all, with the weakness of GMAC, its branch specializing in consumer credit, indispensable for selling their products to consumers. This means that we are in a historic period in which finance is *cosubstantial* with the very production of goods and services (emphasis in original).[15]

The "revolution in finance" has included over the past few decades all sorts of financial innovations – a vast and bewildering array of derivatives, from swaps to futures markets, hedge funds, institutional investment funds, mortgage-backed securities, collateralized debt obligations, Ponzi schemes, pyramiding

[15] Christian Marazzi, *The Violence of Financial Capital* (Bellinzona: Switzerland: Edizioni Casagrande, 2011).

of assets, and many more.[16] The term "derivative" refers to a financial asset whose value directly depends (or derives from) that of another asset, such as homeowners' insurance, in which the insurance is the financial asset derived from the material asset, a house. But the recent explosion of derivatives involves something novel: the derivative is linked not to a material asset but to another financial asset or payment, such as a debt.[17] These innovations make possible a Global Casino, or transnational financial circuits based on speculation and the ongoing expansion of fictitious capital, that is, money thrown into circulation without any base in commodities or in production. Just as capital takes over and appropriates all spheres through the drumbeat march of commodification, the circuits of financial accumulation steadily take over in the capitalist system, since money capital is universally convertible to any other commodity form of capital. Marx observed:

> All particular forms of capital, arising from its investment in particular spheres of production or circulation, are obliterated.... It exists in the undifferentiated, self-identical form of independent value, of money.... Here capital really does emerge, in the pressure of its demand and supply, as *the common capital of the class* ... as a concentrated and organized mass, placed under the control of the bankers as representatives of the social capital in a quite different manner to real production.[18]

With the deregulation and liberalization of financial markets, money can now move virtually frictionlessly and instantaneously around the world; it knows no bounds. Capital has developed the ability to capitalize nearly anything and to absorb nearly anything into the circuit of money. Securitization makes every pile of money – pensions, for example – as well as debt itself, or negative money, a "tradable" and therefore a source of speculation and accumulation. The "revolution in finance" has allowed global speculators to appropriate values through new circuits that are in many respects irrespective of space and irrespective of "real" value or material production. Moreover, the freeing of currencies – the introduction of floating exchange rates and the lifting of exchange controls in most countries – has contributed to the derivatives boom in a major way. Global currency trading is not linked to underlying assets, so that it represents par excellence a severing of the "real" economy from the speculative economy.

What capital has achieved with the "revolution in finance" is the ability to transform any current *or future* stream of earnings (dividends, interest, mortgages, credit card payments, state and private bond maturities, commodity deliveries, and so forth) into an easily tradable capital asset. And then, in turn, it has achieved the ability to speculate further through trade taking place at a

---

[16] The nuts and bolts of the new financial system and all its "instruments" are well explained by William K. Tabb, *The Restructuring of Capitalism in Our Time* (New York: Columbia University Press, 2012).

[17] A useful glossary of the technical terms that became household words in the wake of the 2008 financial collapse was published in *Historical Materialism* (2009), 17: 109–113.

[18] As cited in Doug Henwood, *Wall Street* (London: Verso, 1998), 238.

second degree of separation of the original productive origin of the stream of earnings from the financial instrument being traded. In other words, most derivative trading is in financial derivatives themselves, that is, a doubling in of the derivatives on themselves, irrespective of the original link to assets. Theoretically, there can be endless degrees of separation of this speculation from the original productive generation of value, so that fictitious capital becomes ever-more divorced from the "real" (or productive) economy. That is, frenzied trading in money and paper – really, electronic trading – involves ever-greater degrees of separation from any underlying tangible values – assets or wealth produced by human beings. Money capital may be able to open or close the gates within the logic of capitalist accumulation (of exchange value) for the generation of wealth, but it does not in itself do anything other than have real values stick to itself; that is, fictitious capital cannot produce surplus value, but it can redistribute wealth. I will return to this matter momentarily.

Stock and credit markets have apparently been replaced at the apex of the hypertrophied global capitalist financial complex by markets in derivatives and in other exotic "financial instruments" that allow for the permanent and dizzying movement of speculative money capital from one instrument to another. What is known in the lexicon of the financial world as "over-the-counter" – that is, unregulated – derivatives began their stunning takeoff in the mid-1980s with the proliferation of new instruments worldwide, and with the rise of nonbank financial institutions taking over currency swaps and derivatives markets. Doug Henwood reports that in 1986 the principal invested in interest rate swaps was $400 billion, with another $100 billion in currency swaps. Just four years later, by the end of 1990, the figures were $2.3 trillion and $578 billion, respectively, to which had been added another $561 billion in caps, floors, collars, and swaptions. By 1997, these combined figures had reached a staggering $24 trillion.[19] And to put the relation between stock and derivative markets into perspective, by late 2008, the size of the world stock market was estimated at about $37 trillion, while the total world derivatives market has climbed to an unfathomable $791 trillion, eleven times the size of the entire world economy, although this is a notional (rather than actual) value (and moreover, the vast majority of derivatives "cancel" each other out because they are "bets" on an event occurring that are offset by a comparable derivate "bet" on the event not occurring).

Corporate profits are increasingly doled out, as dividends and interest, to shareholders and global financial investors and speculators – Henwood reports that dividends and interest as a percentage of profits in the United States went from 20–30 percent in the 1950s to 60 percent in the 1990s. Investors generate ongoing speculative bubbles by plowing their profits back into the stock and derivatives markets.[20] Financial holding companies that manage and also

[19] Ibid., 36.
[20] Ibid., 73.

organize these global transactions seem to be the gears of the global corporate economy. In the United States, these came into being in the wake of bank deregulation and the liberalization of financial markets in 1998 with the repeal of the Glass-Steagall Act, which had separated banking from other financial activities. These holding companies could now own banks as subsidiaries, engage in merchant banking, deal in securities and mutual funds, underwrite insurance, and manage portfolio investment.[21] At the institutional core of the global financial complex are these gargantuan financial holding companies such as Goldman Sachs and the Blackstone Group.

Some observers have posed the problematic as increased rentier power over corporate policy. Doug Henwood argues in his study, *Wall Street*, that "behind the abstraction known as 'the markets' lurks a set of institutions designed to maximize the wealth and power of the most privileged group of people in the world, the creditor-rentier class of the First World and their junior partners in the Third."[22] While there is some purchase to this notion of a creditor-rentier class, it must be tempered by several observations. First, the post–World War II banking conglomerates that political economists analyzed in reference to the U.S. economy,[23] which brought together competing groups or clusters of leading banks, corporations, and financial firms (especially insurance companies) in long-term relationships, clearly gave way in the late twentieth century to a very different structure in which long-term relationships have broken apart (such relations now appear ephemeral), ownership relations change with great rapidity and fluidity, institutional investor groups and investment and portfolio management houses have eclipsed traditional banking roles, and above all, for our purposes, various forms of capital became increasingly integrated and organized transnationally.

At the same time – and this is crucial – global corporations are often the main derivative traders, so that hedging is only one aspect of their financial activities, increasingly subordinated to pure speculative trading. Here there is a blurring of the lines between "industrial" and "commercial" with (transnational) finance capital. What has taken place is less the domination of financial over industrial and commercial capital than a general financialization of global capitalism. There has been a shift in the primary sources of wealth accumulation to finance. As Marazzi points out, "*Non-financial firms themselves* sharply increased their investment in financial assets relative to that in plants and equipment, and became increasingly dependent on financial sources of revenue and profit relative to that earned from productive activities" (emphasis in original). Indeed, Marazzi emphasizes Krippner's finding

---

[21] James R. Barth, R. Dan Brumbaugh Jr., and James A. Wilcox, "The Repeal of Glass-Steagall and the Advent of Broad Banking," Economic and Policy Analysis Working Paper 2000-5, April 2000, Office of the Comptroller of the Currency, U.S. Department of the Treasury.

[22] Henwood, *Wall Street*, 6–7.

[23] See, e.g. David M. Kotz, *Bank Control of Large Corporations in the United States* (Berkeley: University of California Press, 1978).

"that manufacturing not only dominates but *leads* this trend towards the financialization of the non-financial economy" (emphasis in original).[24]

Second, the deregulation and liberalization of national financial systems together with the freeing of currencies worldwide may have "caused" the derivative boom insofar as unregulated money could now move about the world practically instantaneously and friction-free, and operate in new ways relative to states and distinct social groups. However, the freeing of currencies and banking was in turn "caused" by a more fundamental restructuring of the global political economy, the liberation of capital from nation-state constraints and from the countervailing social power that popular classes had been able to accumulate, both in their direct confrontations with capital and through national states. The Global Casino could have come about only on the foundations of the more fundamental creation of a global production system dominated by transnational corporate capital. The world economy, in which nations were linked to each other via trade and concomitant financial flows, was not the foundation for the Global Casino. Its foundation was the global economy, in which national production circuits have been functionally integrated as components of a globalized system of production and services.

Stephen Hymer argued that the integration of national financial markets into a single global system – a process that was only beginning when he wrote in 1972 – developed in symbiosis with the growth of the multinational corporation. Hymer had written in 1972 that "the multinational corporation's need for short-term loans and investment arising from the continuous inflow and outflow of money from all nations, never quite in balance, has encouraged international banking and has helped integrate short-term money markets; its long-term financial requirements ... have broadened the demand for international bond and equity capital."[25] Henwood adds: "Production must be financed, and if all goes well, it throws off profits in money form, and globalized production is no exception, meaning that MNCs [multinational corporations] inevitably create financial flows alongside their productive activities."[26] At a certain point in the late twentieth century these financial flows became dominant within global accumulation circuits as hypertrophied global financial markets came to dwarf their real-world productive base. Money capital became the determinant of productive capital insofar as the level and allocation of real investment came increasingly to depend on financial markets and on the speculation that characterizes these markets.

We want to recall that money is the mobile and alienated embodiment of value and that, as such, it is a form of social power. Financial structures are in

---

[24] Marazzi, *The Violence of Financial Capitalism*, 32. He is referring to Greta R. Krippner, *Capitalizing on Crisis: The Political Origins of the Rise of Finance* (Cambridge, MA: Harvard University Press, 2012), 32.

[25] Hymer, as cited in Henwood, *Wall Street*, 112.

[26] Henwood, *Wall Street*, 112.

essence power relations – structures of legal and institutional control. Control over money becomes social control. The capitalists' class power is asserted over corporations and states – as well as over the popular classes via these institutions – through financial mechanisms. The generalization of exchange value that is a defining characteristic of capitalism presupposes that money embodies the whole set of capitalist relations, including social power relations and the exercise of social power through institutions, especially through the state. Under capitalism, production is always for profit, and the realization of that profit is always through exchange for money. Production and money are therefore in unity unless that unity is broken by crisis – both for the capitalist, who must turn production into money, and for the worker, who must turn labor power into money. The rise to hegemony of transnational finance capital is really the story of the rise to power of the TCC and the dictatorship of the TCC, in the literal sense of its having the social power to dictate.

As Henwood points out, "the exchange of [monetary] claims in the financial markets amounts to the social construction of ownership,"[27] that is, the financial system shapes class relations. The now-globalized financial system has become perhaps the cutting edge of global class relations insofar as property/ownership relations are structured on a global scale through the circuits of financial capital and insofar as globally mobile financial capital is able to invade, in vampire-like fashion, and snatch up values as they circulate through circuits that intersect with those of global financial capital. Many view Wall Street as the center of this global financial complex. It may be true that Wall Street is one command post (though even that is changing rapidly).[28] But institutional investor flows are transnational. Henwood observes that national capital markets join together fragmented surplus and deficit units that may be miles apart. We can argue, similarly, that the global market joins creditors and debtors around the world. It is important to emphasize the *transnational* – rather than *international* – nature of the class relations embedded in this global financial structure. Transnational capital invests in every direction across borders in the Global Casino, and as it does so it appropriates values from the global working class through manifold mechanisms.

Speculation in the Global Casino

Transnational finance capital has proved to be utterly predatory, seeking out one outlet after another for frenzied speculation. The sequence of speculative waves in

---

[27] Ibid., 11.

[28] The *New York Times* reports that "in today's burgeoning and increasingly integrated global financial markets – a vast, neural spaghetti of wires, Web sites and trading platforms – the N.Y. S.E. is clearly no longer *the* epicenter. Nor is New York. . . . [T]rading and money management are spreading globally. Since the end of the cold war, vast pools of capital have been forming overseas" (emphasis in original). Daniel Gross, "Money in New York: The Capital of Capital No More?," *New York Times*, October 14, 2007, on-line edition, http://www.nytimes.com/2007/10/14/magazine/14wallstreet-t.html?pagewanted=all.

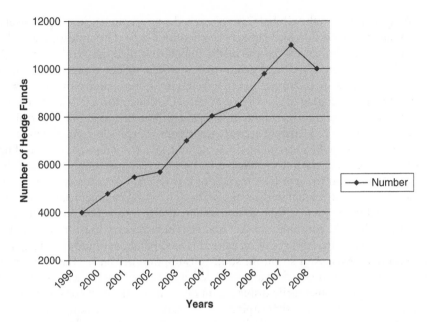

FIGURE 4.2. Global Hedge Funds, 1999–2008.

the Global Casino beginning in the 1980s included real estate investments in the emerging global property market that inflated property values in one locality after another; wild stock market speculation leading to periodic booms and busts, most notably the bursting of the dot-com bubble in 2001, followed by a massive shift to the mortgage market; the phenomenal escalation of hedge-fund flows and pyramiding of assets (see Figure 4.2);[29] currency speculation; one Ponzi scheme after another; and later on the frantic speculation in global commodities markets, especially energy and food markets, that provoked a spike in world prices in 2007 and 2008 (and again in 2012 and 2013) and sparked "food riots" around the world.

[29] "Nowhere is the concentration of wealth more astounding than in the case of hedge funds," writes Rothkopf:

In just a few years, hedge funds have grown almost exponentially in economic significance, from controlling $221 billion in 1999 to more than $2 trillion by mid-2007. But more important, given their active trading strategies – for example, making money from small movements in the daily prices of securities – these ten thousand funds are, according to some estimates, responsible for between 30 and 50 percent of the trading on most major equity and debt markets in which they participate. That means that the individuals controlling these funds' trading activities, along with a handful of other major institutional and professional investors, play the central role in determining the share price of the world's largest companies.

David Rothkopf, *Superclass: The Global Power Elite and the World They Are Making* (New York: Farrar, Straus and Giroux, 2008), 36.

As speculation in the Global Casino reached a feveri pitch following recovery from the 2001 recession, the gap between fictitious capital in this casino and the productive economy, or what the media popularly called the "real economy," grew ever greater. This "real economy" was kept afloat momentarily by a massive increase in consumer debt (largely credit cards and mortgages) and federal deficit spending in the United States. U.S. consumer debt climbed from $355 billion in 1980 to $1 trillion in 1994, $2 trillion in 2004, and $2.6 trillion in 2008, while the U.S. current account went from a surplus in 1992 to deficits of $100 billion in 1998, $700 billion in 2004, and $1.2 trillion in 2008, according to Federal Reserve data. Consumer credit and deficit spending converted the United States into the world's "market of last resort." As a result, China and other Asian countries that in the wake of the 1997–98 Asian financial meltdown had shifted to exports in order to accumulate dollar reserves could continue to export to the U.S. consumer market and also buy treasury bills. In turn, Latin American raw materials producers were able to expand their output and export, especially to Asia. And so on. In sum, consumption driven by U.S. consumer credit card and mortgage debt and state deficit financing sustained accumulation worldwide and momentarily displaced (in time) the crisis. Such consumer credit is one of the mechanisms that capital and the state have of breaking the barriers to accumulation. Overaccumulation thus typically leads to a perilous expansion of credit in order to sustain absorption of the surplus. But this is a temporary "fix" that ends up aggravating the problem by increasing the gap between real value and "fictitious" value and by generating "fictitious profits," meaning that sooner or later a mass of capital must experience devalorization.[30] As early as 2005 an IMF researcher warned that China's export-dependent economy and the United States' debt-financed and real estate bubble had induced a consumption spree, that these two intertwined processes accounted for nearly half of global economic growth, and that this unsustainable growth had created an alarming imbalance in the global economy.[31]

The Federal Reserve's decision to reduce interest rates to about one percent in 2003 as a mechanism to overcome the recession also triggered a wave of speculation in the U.S. mortgage market and prompted investors to begin subprime lending, including the infamous "teaser" interest rates aggressively sold to millions of people who would later be unable to meet their mortgage payments

---

[30] To summarize Harvey: During economic booms, credit money and fictitious capital tend to grow more rapidly than real capital, thus producing a twofold realization problem – the realization of fictitious values as well as values in the commodity form. Furthermore, during periods of economic expansion, interest rates rise, money capital is reallocated from industrial capital to interest-bearing capital, and capital as a whole tends to be undermined. See Harvey, *The Limits to Capital*.

[31] Raghuram G. Rajan, "Global Imbalances – An Assessment," IMF Research Department, 2005, http://www.imf.org/external/np/speeches/2005/102505.htm.

once the rates were adjusted upward.[32] By the time of the 2008 collapse the housing bubble was estimated at $8 trillion.[33] Moreover, mortgage and other loans were securitized. Securitizing loans means packaging a batch of similar loans (e.g., mortgages) and then selling them as bonds on the open market, where frenzied global speculation takes place. This activity had been going on since the 1980s and steadily accelerating, and then really took off in 2003 when Federal Reserve head Alan Greenspan reduced interest rate to just one percent. Already by 1993, the twenty largest U.S.-based banks had off-balance-sheet exposures equal to 39 percent of assets and 573 percent of their "core capital" (retained profits plus the proceeds of past stock sales), "meaning that if all hell broke loose many would be legally insolvent."[34] All hell did break loose, in fact, with the collapse of the global financial system in mid-2008, triggered by the collapse of the subprime mortgage market starting in 2007.

Rising consumer debt in the United States and elsewhere cannot be separated from increasing income inequality. As wages and family incomes decline, households borrow more to stay in place, so that consumption is more and more debt-driven, intermediated by transnational finance capital for which the act of consumption (the final phase in the circulation of capital) is not the source of profit. Rather, profits derive from the contracting of debt followed by speculation with that debt. Behind institutional relations are class relations: workers borrow from financial capitalists and wealthy investors, so that "the few lend to the many." The rich get richer as workers get poorer, through this upward redistribution of income invested in credit, contributing to the hypertrophy of the financial sector and, of course, to the contradictions of overaccumulation. However, the initial debtor-creditor relation is only the first part of this story, since consumer and other forms of debt are then bundled and resold endlessly in the global financial casino. Capitalists thus unload surplus through lending to workers and then further unload this accumulating money capital by throwing it into circulation in expanding circuits of the Global Casino, where it becomes divorced from original assets or the "real" economy.

The Perverse World of Predatory Transnational Finance Capital

In the perverse world of predatory transnational finance capital, private and public debt and government deficits themselves became new sources of financial speculation, bonanzas for finance capital. The massive increase in U.S. and Third World debt from the 1980s onward is closely associated with the development of the new "financial products" that made possible the worldwide trading in this debt and went hand in hand with the liberalization and transnationalization of

[32] For an excellent study on the housing bubble and its bursting, see Dean Baker, *Plunder and Blunder: The Rise and Fall of the Bubble Economy* (Sausalito, CA: PoliPoint Press, 2009).
[33] Ibid.
[34] Henwood, *Wall Street*, 83.

national financial systems. Debt leads the way to the transnationalization of the financial system as governments from First and Third World alike turn to investors worldwide to finance deficits. Marx noted long ago that this public debt becomes the most powerful lever of primitive accumulation. The growth of U.S. state deficits and debt, while it has sustained global accumulation by generating some of the mechanisms used to prolong surplus absorption, has also meant the growth of the power of finance capital. The historically unprecedented U.S. federal deficit represents a transfer of income from labor to transnational capital and also greatly heightens the power of finance capital over the U.S. state. The more government debt, the more states must adopt policies that satisfy the holders of bonds and other creditors. This "veto power" of transnational financial investors has been broadly observed in the literature, so that the credit rating agencies, acting in the service of this investment community, exercise enormous power over states, including the power to demand neo-liberal adjustment, the flexibilization of labor, austerity, and so forth. Sir William Ryrie, executive vice president of the World Bank's International Financial Corporation, was quite candid in this regard: "The debt crisis could be seen as a blessing in disguise."[35] The war of global capital against global labor is played out in the global capitalist financial complex.

The market in U.S. treasury bonds is the biggest financial market in the world. This must be seen in the context of the United States as the market of last resort and as a sink for investors globally. The class relation between the U.S. state and the TCC is in part manifest in transnational capital "lending" the U.S. state money, which means buying interest-yielding bonds (assumed to be guaranteed), as the U.S. state and its (expected) fiscal solvency is the lynchpin of the ability of the global economy to hold together and function. It was *transnational* – not "U.S." – capital that relied on U.S. debt and deficits to sustain profit making around the world. The subprime mortgage market, for example, attracted trillions of dollars from individual, institutional, and corporate investors from all continents. It is a mistake to see things in terms of "U.S. capitalism" rather than global capitalism. The U.S. state has acted as an instrument of global capitalism, and the United States as a major axis or nodal point for globalized accumulation. U.S. treasury bailouts of the Wall Street–based banks in late 2008 and early 2009, for instance, went to bail out individual and institutional investors from around the world, while the U.S. debt was itself financed by these selfsame investors. According to a 2011 report by the U.S. government's General Accounting Office, between 2007 and 2010 the U.S. Federal Reserve undertook a whopping $16 trillion in bailouts to banks and corporations from around the world that were not made known to the public.[36] Moreover, there has been an increasing fusion of private financial

---

[35] As cited in ibid., 295.
[36] General Accounting Office, *Federal Reserve System: Opportunities Exist to Strengthen Policies and Processes for Managing Emergency Assistance*, GAO-11-696, July 2011, Washington, DC.

institutions with TNS apparatuses. Some two-thirds of the bailout package of some $100 billion provided to Ireland in 2011, to take one example, came from the European Financial Stability Facility and the European Financial Stabilization Mechanism, both loan programs with funds originating in private banks but guaranteed by the EU central banks. In this way, the TNS provides global investors with publicly guaranteed investment outlets.

Financial speculation also fueled industrial production, in part, so that the Global Casino kept the Global Factory running for a while. But much credit went not to expanded production but to inflate the prices of assets already in place. The gap between the worldwide speculative economy and the productive economy grew to an unfathomable chasm. Capital is fictitious when money capital has no basis in productive activity, since productive capital is what actually generates values. Valorization, or the adding of new value to the total through human labor, takes place through production. A gap between the real value generated in the productive economy and fictitious value circulating in the financial system may well be intrinsic to the functioning of capitalism, but what is novel is the near-unfathomable gap between the two. In 2000, for instance, the worldwide trade in goods and services was less than $10 trillion for the entire year, according to IMF data, while *daily* movements in currency speculation stood at $3.5 trillion, so that in just a few days more currency circulated as speculation than the international circulation of goods and services in an entire year! Stephen Graham reports that in 2006 financial markets were trading more in a month than the annual gross domestic product of the entire world.[37] The outcome of such a gap can only be devalorization of the total global social capital. Such a devalorization can take the form of a shifting of quotas of wealth among capitalists and investors worldwide, so that some gain and others lose out; it may also result in a transfer of wealth from the mass of laboring people around the world to capital. Both of these seemed to be results of the 2008 crisis and its aftermath, but particularly the latter, leading to heightened rounds of austerity, and so on, as I will discuss later.

By the early years of the twenty-first century the massive concentrations of transnational finance capital were destabilizing the system, and global capitalism ran up against the limits of financial fixes. The bottoming out of the subprime mortgage market in 2007 that triggered collapse a year later of the global financial system headquartered in Wall Street was merely the "straw that broke the camel's back."

Subsequent to the collapse, the speculative frenzy shifted to the global bond market, as governments facing insolvency in the wake of 2008–9 turned to bond emissions in order to stay afloat. Global speculators used the U.S. state's bailouts to channel a new round of speculative investment into the market in state-issued bonds and into bank lending to these cash-strapped countries. Once the private

[37] Stephen Graham, *Cities under Siege: The New Military Urbanism* (London: Verso, 2010), 4.

banking and financial institutions recovered from the 2008 collapse – in large part thanks to government bailouts – they turned to unloading surplus into these sovereign debt markets that they themselves helped to create. The global bond market ("sovereign debt") climbed to some US$95 trillion by the start of 2011 and constituted the single biggest market for financial speculation in the wake of the 2008 collapse. In 2011 government bonds accounted for 43 percent of the value outstanding, up from 39 percent a year earlier.[38] Gone are the times when such bonds were bought and held to maturity. They are bought and sold by individual and institutional investors in frenzied twenty-four-hour worldwide trading and bet on continuously through such mechanisms as credit default swaps that shift their values and make bond markets a high stakes gamble of volatility and risk for investors. This explains, in part, the latest round of crisis as manifest in Greece, Spain, Portugal, Ireland, and elsewhere. Government debt is portrayed as "spending beyond means" and used to justify cuts in social spending and austerity. Yet this debt has become a major source of profit making for transnational finance capital – the latest financial fix – to the extent that social consumption continues to decline as a source of accumulation.

The austerity sweeping across Europe (and in the United States) from 2008 onward is particularly revealing; it represents an acceleration of the process of "Thirdworldization" of the First World, in which the wealth concentrated at some poles of accumulation in the world is no longer redistributed downward locally toward First World labor aristocracies. Regardless of the outcome of financial crisis in the case of each individual country, capital wins in both the short and the long term. In the short term, investors cash in on a would-be defaulter with higher bond rates and/or through state bailouts that are channeled into their coffers. In the long run, austerity intensifies the processes of regressive taxation, privatization, and the dismantling of the social wage. Behind massive cuts in education and increases in tuition in both Europe and the United States, for instance, is the steady march of the privatization and commodification of public education. In short, the toxic mixture of public finance and private transnational finance capital in this age of global capitalism constitutes a new battlefield on which the global rich are waging a war against the global poor and working classes.

Alongside the global bond market, investors shifted to speculation in global commodities markets. Worldwide investment in commodities markets rose from 2006 to 2011 by almost 300 percent, from $141 billion to $431 billion.[39] Wild fluctuations in commodity prices may become a fixed feature in unregulated global capitalism, so long as money capital can move in and out of markets with ease and transnational corporate capital can manipulate markets in search of

---

[38] For these details, see "Global Bond Market Up 5% in 2010 to Record $95 Trillion," *The CityUK*, internet blog, published online April 7, 2011. From http://www.thecityuk.com/media/press-releases/global-bond-market-up-5-in-2010-to-record-95-trillion-more-than-two-thirds-the-size-of-equity-market/.

[39] "Back to the Futures," *The Economist*, Sept. 17, 2011: 79.

windfall profits and other advantages. As Rosset observes, agricultural commodities experienced a twenty-five-year trend of low and stable prices, until prices began to rise in 2004 and 2005, and then to spike upward in 2007 and 2008, from 200 to 300 percent for staple commodities, only to fall by 55–65 percent later in 2008.[40] In 2007 and 2008 food protests and riots broke out in dozens of countries around the world, from Bangladesh to Brazil, Burkina Faso, India, Ethiopia, Myanmar, Panama, the Philippines, Pakistan, Russia, and Egypt.

The proximate causes of the global food crisis that first hit in 2007 were the ongoing shift in farmlands from food to biofuels production, prolonged droughts in several major agricultural regions, and rising demand for grains by China. But its more immediate cause was the wild speculation on commodities markets, especially by hedge funds gambling with futures markets, and private sector hoarding as financial capital shifted out of mortgage markets and other speculative circuits and into food and energy markets.[41] A torrent of new investment, as much as $300 billion, poured into these markets in the lead-up to the 2007–8 food crisis.[42] In Mexico, for instance, Cargill bought a major portion of the late 2006 corn harvest and then withheld inventory from the market in expectation of higher prices, creating an artificial shortage, which led prices to more than double the following year.[43]

Militarized Accumulation

Alongside frenzied financial speculation, the U.S. state took advantage of 9/11 to militarize the global economy. This militarization needs to be seen as a response to the crisis of global capitalism. CIT revolutionized warfare and the modalities of state-organized militarized accumulation, including the military application of vast new technologies and the further fusion of private accumulation and state militarization. However, before the dot-com bust the cutting edge of accumulation in the "real economy" worldwide shifted from CIT to a military-security-industrial-construction-engineering-petroleum complex that also accrued enormous influence in the halls of power in Washington.[44] An emergent power bloc that brings together the two complexes – the financial complex and this military-security-industrial-construction-engineering-petroleum

[40] Peter, Rosset, "Food Sovereignty in Latin America: Confronting the 'New' Crisis," *NACLA Report on the Americas* (2009), 42(3): 16–21.
[41] Melisa Pitts, "Rising Food Prices: The Role of Pension Funds," *The Guardian*, May 16, 2011.
[42] Rosset, "Food Sovereignty in Latin America," 20.
[43] Ibid.
[44] According to the U.S. Department of Commerce, by the late 1990s information technology had become the main engine of U.S. investment, accounting for over half of all newly produced business equipment, up from only 10 percent a generation earlier. Lynn Margherio, Dave Henry, Sandra Cooke, Sabrina Montes, and Kent Hughes, *The Emerging Digital Economy* (Washington, DC: U.S. Department of Commerce, 1998).

TABLE 4.1. *U.S. Military Spending, 1997–2012*

Year	Amount ($billions 2005)
1997	325
1998	323
1999	333
2000	360
2001	366
2002	422
2003	484
2004	544
2005	601
2006	622
2007	654
2008	731
2009	795
2010	848
2011	879
2012	902*

* Projected.
Source: *usgovernmentspending.com*, http://www.usgovern mentspending.com/spending_chart_1997_2012USb_13s1li1 11mcn_30t_30_Defense_Spending_Chart.

complex – appeared to be crystallizing in the wake of the 2008 collapse, with financial capital at its center.[45] U.S military spending skyrocketed into the trillions of dollars through the "war on terrorism" and the invasions and occupations of Iraq and Afghanistan (Table 4.1). The "creative destruction" of war acted to throw fresh firewood on the smoldering embers of the global economy. In 2003, for instance, military spending accounted for a full 70 percent of the rise in the U.S. GDP.[46] The Pentagon budget increased 91 percent in real terms between 1998 and 2011, and even apart from special war appropriations, it increased by nearly 50 percent in real terms during that period.[47] This spending has stabilized at levels significantly above Cold War peaks (adjusted for inflation) and far above the Cold War average in real terms.[48] In the decade from 2001

[45] As we shall see in the next chapter, I include within the notion of a "security" complex what has been referred to as the "prison-industrial complex," but a vastly expanded one that includes a global detention and interrogation complex and vast new systems of repressive social control.
[46] L. Randall Wray, "Let's Create a Real Job Czar for the Jobless," University of Missouri – Kansas City, Policy Note No. 03/01/2003, Center for Full Employment and Price Stability, accessed at http://www.cfeps.org/pubs/pn/pno301.html.
[47] Project on Defense Alternatives, "The Pentagon and Deficit Reduction," PDA Briefing Memo #47, Washington, DC, Commonwealth Institute, March 1, 2011: 1.
[48] Project on Defense Alternatives, "An Undisciplined Defense: Understanding the $2 Trillion Surge in US Defense Spending," Washington, DC, Commonwealth Institute, January 18, 2010.

to 2011 defense industry profits nearly quadrupled.[49] *Worldwide*, total defense outlays (military, intelligence agencies, homeland security/defense) were forecast to grow by roughly 50 percent from 2006 to 2015, from $1.4 trillion to $2.03 trillion.[50]

Spin-off effects of this spending flowed through the open veins of the global economy – that is, the integrated network structures of the global production, services, and financial system. In this way, the U.S. state mobilized vast resources and political pressures, taking advantage of the dollar's role as the global currency and therefore of the extraordinary power of the U.S. Treasury, in order to absorb surpluses and sustain global accumulation by militarizing that accumulation and creating a global war economy under the pretext of a "war on terrorism" and a "war on drugs" (note also that wars accelerate the turnover time of the circuit of militarized accumulation). The "war on terrorism" also has collateral political and ideological functions.

Neo-liberalism had "peacefully" forced open new areas for global capital in the 1980s and the 1990s. This was often accomplished through economic coercion alone, in particular, by the imposition of structural adjustment programs, neo-liberal policies, and free trade agreements made possible by the structural power of the global economy over individual countries. But this structural power became less effective as a means of sustaining global accumulation in the face of stagnation. Opportunities for both intensive and extensive expansion began to dry up as privatization ran its course, the "socialist" countries became integrated into the world market, the consumption of high-income sectors worldwide reached a ceiling, spending through private credit expansion could not be sustained, and so on. The space for "peaceful" expansion, both intensive and extensive, became ever-more restricted. Military aggression became an instrument for prying open new sectors and regions, that is, for the forcible restructuring of space in order to further accumulation, either on the heels of military force or through the state's contracting of corporate capital for the production and execution of social control and war. The train of neo-liberalism became hitched to military intervention and the threat of coercive sanctions as a locomotive for pulling forward the train of global capitalism. Wars, interventions, and conflicts unleash cycles of destruction and reconstruction and generate enormous profits. We are now living in a global war economy that goes well beyond "hot wars" such as those in Iraq or Afghanistan.

There is not a monocausal explanation for militarized accumulation or for particular interventions, as already indicated, nor is there a single "function" that it serves. The larger theoretical-conceptual framework here is one of *historical conjunctures* – less in the sense of the union of antecedent forces at

---

[49] Associated Press, "Defense Industry Faces Profit Loss as Golden Decade Ends," August 15, 2011, posted on *Huffington Post* at http://www.huffingtonpost.com/2011/08/15/defense-industry-profits-911_n_927596.html.

[50] Graham, *Cities under Siege*, 74.

a certain moment of history than of the unique historical configuration of a set of contingent factors or processes in the determination of outcomes.[51] Yet, once launched, the "war on terrorism" achieved a number of objectives for a global capitalism beset by structural, political, and ideological crises. It provided a seemingly endless military outlet for surplus capital, generating a colossal deficit that justified the ever-deeper dismantling of the Keynesian welfare state and locked neo-liberal austerity in place. It legitimated new transnational social control systems and the creation of police states to repress political dissent in the name of security. It allowed these states to criminalize social movements and "undesirable" populations, such as undocumented immigrants or the activists of Occupy Wall Street in the United States (see the next chapter).

Politically, the "war on terrorism" allowed the transnational elite to move from the defensive to the offensive. Neo-liberal hardships generated widespread, yet often spontaneous and unorganized, resistance around the world in the 1980s and 1990s. But everywhere there were also organized resistance movements. At a certain point in the 1990s popular resistance forces reached a critical mass, coalescing around an agenda for social justice, or "anti-globalization movement," and putting forward a counterhegemonic challenge. By the turn of century the transnational elite had been placed on the defensive, and a crisis of the system's legitimacy began to develop, symbolized by the creation of the World Social Forum (WSF) in Porto Alegre, Brazil, under the banner "Another World Is Possible." A global peace and justice movement emerged from the womb of a rapidly expanding transnational civil society, representing, in the words of the *New York Times*, the world's "other superpower." But 9/11 undercut its momentum. In the post-9/11 period the military dimension appeared to exercise an overdetermining influence in the reconfiguration of global politics. Militarization has involved not just the major U.S.-led interventions but the adoption by 144 countries of "counterterrorist" laws and the development of enhanced systems of policing, internal security, urban militarization, and social control to suppress dissent (and also to make

---

[51] For Althusser, the balance of unevenly developed social and political forces in society at a given moment is the conjuncture. My use here of "historical conjuncture" is closer to that of Max Weber, although not equivalent. Weber is invariably slippery to pin down epistemologically. In *The Protestant Ethic and the Spirit of Capitalism*, for instance, he suggested that the rise of capitalism was the chance outcome of historically distinct developments as they came together in a particular conjuncture. However, Weber also saw rationalization as exercising underlying historical determination, and this rationalization was not universal but unique to European societies. I see the laws and dynamics of capitalist development as exercising ultimate historical determination; yet such laws and dynamics are general/universal relations, and their original emergence in Europe was but by chance.

It is unlikely indeed that militarized accumulation as discussed here was the result of any intentionality, as distinct from the unplanned outcome of multiple intentionalities – the convergence of the political agenda of the "neo-conservatives" in the United States, the profit-making aspirations of TNCs, and so on.

profits).[52] These laws "include elements that raise grave human rights concerns including overly broad and vague definitions of terrorism – such as 'disrupting the public order' – as well as sweeping powers for warrantless search and arrest, the use of secret evidence, and immunity for police who abuse the laws," according to one Human Rights Watch report. The report observed that many of these laws authorize prolonged detention without charges, as is the case in the United States, where the National Defense Authorization Act of 2012 codifies indefinite detention without charges of "terrorism suspects."[53]

As we saw in the previous chapter, many interpreted militarization and renewed U.S. interventionism under the Bush administration through the lens of the "new imperialism" theories so popular during the Bush years because they allowed critics to identify a visible enemy – a state and its direct agents – responsible for the horrors of global intervention and domination. But this was a fundamentally flawed interpretation of militarized accumulation. Despite the rhetoric of neo-liberalism, the U.S. state undertook an unprecedented role in creating profit-making opportunities for transnational capital and pushing forward an accumulation process that, left to its own devices (the "free market"), would have ground to a halt much earlier than 2008. The interventionist wars of the late twentieth and early twenty-first centuries, from Yugoslavia to Afghanistan and from Iraq to Libya and Somalia, are *global wars* staged not by the United States but by the transnational elite.

Militarized accumulation now is not the same as previous "military Keynesianism," since much of warfare itself and the related processes of social control and repression have been privatized or semiprivatized. Well beyond the older linkage between state warfare and corporate capital – that is, the procurement of weaponry, equipment, and military technology – militarized accumulation now ranges from the replacement of state soldiers by mercenary armies ("private security firms"), to the subcontracting of reconstruction projects, military engineering, the construction of military and conflict-related installations, the supplying of food, consumer items, and services to occupation armies, the construction of private prisons and "security walls," and even the subcontracting of torture and interrogation.[54] The state organizes and directs warfare from above yet doles out the distinct activities directly and indirectly associated with warfare and with the global "security" establishment to transnational corporations. In other words, military interventions don't just open up new

[52] The figure 144 is from Human Rights Watch, "In the Name of Security: Counterterrorism Laws Worldwide since 9/11," released on June 29, 2012. See the summary on the Human Rights Watch webpage: https://mail.google.com/mail/?shva=1#inbox. On urban militarization in cities around the world, see Graham, *Cities under Siege*.

[53] Human Rights Watch, "In the Name of Security."

[54] On the privatization of warfare, see, inter alia, Jeremy Scahill's noted work, *Blackwater: The Rise of the World's Most Powerful Mercenary Army* (New York: Nation Books, 2008); Naomi Klein, *The Shock Doctrine: The Rise of Disaster Capitalism* (New York: Picador, 2008).

markets and investment opportunities in intervened countries; they *are in them-selves* markets and investment opportunities.

The privatization of warfare and repression is a crucial dimension of milita-rized accumulation in the twenty-first century. During thirty years of neo-liberalism and capitalist globalization much of what had been public sectors in the world economy became privatized or semiprivatized, from industry and finance to utilities, land, and health and education. The privatization of war became a new frontier in the juggernaut of commodification. In order for this to happen, wars and interventions must be launched and legitimated politically and ideologically, enemies need to be conjured up, and culture itself needs to be militarized and masculinized. In this process there is a fusion of the state with transnational capital. Those clusters among the TCC that benefit from the privatization of war, weaponization, policing, and social control have an eco-nomic interest in generating and sustaining conflicts independent of any ideo-logical or political concern, as we shall see in the next chapter.

In the first decade of the twenty-first century the U.S. government launched a so-called transformation project intended to restructure and privatize the mili-tary and systems of social control. The structure of chains of subcontracting and outsourcing that characterizes the global economy would now apply to the military establishment. "Why is the DoD [Department of Defense] one of the last organizations around that still cuts its own checks?," asked then secretary of defense Donald Rumsfeld in announcing the project. "When an entire industry exists to run warehouses efficiently, why do we own and operate so many of our own? At bases around the world, why do we pick up our own garbage and mop our own floors, rather than contracting services out, as many businesses do? And surely we can outsource more computer systems support?"[55] As Klein noted:

The Bush team created a whole new framework for its actions – the War on Terror – built to be private from the start. This feature required two stages. First, the White House used the omnipresent sense of peril in the aftermath of 9/11 to dramatically increase the policing, surveillance, detention and war-waging powers of the executive branch. ... Then those newly enhanced and richly funded functions of security, invasion, occupation and recon-struction were immediately outsourced, handed over to the private sector to perform at a profit. Although the stated goal was the creation of the disaster capitalism complex – a full-fledged new economy in homeland security, privatized war and disaster reconstruction tasked with nothing less than building and running a privatized security state ... [e]very aspect of the way the Bush administration has defined the parameters of the War on Terror has served to maximize its profitability and sustainability as a market.[56]

The Pentagon set up a Defense Venture Catalyst Initiative to feed security information to venture capitalists and the corporate sector to be used to start up surveillance, security, and related products, ranging from biometric identi-fication and video surveillance to Web tracking, data mining, motion sensors,

[55] As cited in Klein, *Shock Doctrine*, 287.
[56] Ibid., 298–300.

high-tech fence construction, and so on. In 2001 there were just two security-oriented lobbying firms in Washington. By 2006 there were 543.[57] According to a 2006 study, the CEO's of the top thirty-four defense contractors saw their average pay levels double in the wake of 9/11. And the Spade Defense Index, a benchmark for defense, homeland security, and aerospace stock went up every year from 2001 to 2006 by 15 percent.[58] In the decadent world of global capitalism, war, conflict, and instability generate an environment for permanent accumulation. "It was a truism of the contemporary market that you couldn't have booming economic growth in the midst of violence and instability," observes Klein. "But that truism is no longer true. Since 2003, the year of the Iraq invasion, the index found that spending has been going up on both fighter jets and executive jets rapidly and simultaneously, which means that the world is becoming less peaceful while accumulating significantly more profit."[59]

The global wars are increasingly fought by private armies paid for and contracted out by states. In the first Gulf War of 1990, one out of every 100 soldiers was a private contractor. A few years later, during the former Yugoslavia's wars, the figure was one in fifty. By 2006 it was one in every ten in Iraq and Afghanistan.[60] Blackwater (later renamed Xe) may be the most notorious of these companies, but there are dozens more. At the height of the U.S. occupation in 2006–7 there were more private contractors, in Iraq, military and civilian, than there were U.S. troops, 180,000 (among them 25,000 military contractors) and 160,000, respectively.[61] And while Iraq may have been the best-known case of the deployment of such mercenary armies, private security firms have also been contracted to fight in conflicts and conduct missions in Bosnia, Sierra Leone, the Congo, Afghanistan, New Orleans, Mexico, Colombia, and elsewhere. Military coercion becomes a commodity to be bought and sold on the open market, as Graham notes, with little import to the identity of suppliers and purchasers. In 2010, state contracted mercenary companies received an estimated $202 billion from the U.S. government alone.[62] In effect, the state renounces its monopoly of legitimate violence; it shares that monopoly with private transnational capital, and for the purposes of direct accumulation as much as for political purposes. With the Iraq and Afghanistan wars winding down, contractors turned their attention to generating profit out of border militarization and other social control systems. In the United States, "homeland security" became big business,

---

57 Ibid., 302.
58 Ibid., 311, 425.
59 Ibid., 424.
60 Jose Gomez, "The Mercenaries or the Corsairs of the XXI Century?," *Zmag* online magazine, July 1, 2006, accessed at http://www.zcommunications.org/the-mercenaries-or-the-corsairs-of-the-xxi-century-by-jose-gomez.
61 See T. Christian Miller, "Contractors Outnumber Troops in Iraq," *Los Angeles Times*, July 4, 2007, online edition, from http://articles.latimes.com/2007/jul/04/nation/na-private4. See also David Isenberg, *Shadow Force: Private Security Contractors in Iraq* (New York: Praeger, 2008).
62 Graham, *Cities under Siege*, 17, 75.

spawning an entire industry and a market that was expected to surpass $30 billion by 2014 (see the next chapter).[63] By the end of the first decade of the twenty-first century the market for "border security" goods and services was growing 5 percent annually and was estimated to become a $25 billion industry by 2020.[64]

The September 2001 attack on the World Trade Center in New York suggested the rise of new modalities of conflict between the weak and the powerful in global society. For the first time, acts of rebellion can be waged around the world regardless of space. The spatial separation of the oppressors from the oppressed as epitomized by the old colonial system is vanishing. Global capitalism is too porous for spatial containment. Just as progressive resistance to the depredations of global capitalism is less space-bound and more transnational than in the past, so too is reactionary resistance. Pentagon planners now talk of a "Long War" that projects an "arc of instability" caused by insurgent groups from Europe to South Asia that will last between fifty and eighty years.[65] This type of permanent global warfare involves low- and high-intensity wars, "humanitarian" missions, "drug interdiction operations," and so on; it appears to be the twenty-first-century variant of the external military conquests and formal territorial expansionism of the nineteenth and twentieth centuries. The social costs of such militarized accumulation are enormous, almost unfathomable. These include the direct victims of intervention – from millions of Iraqis killed and injured, four million Colombians terrorized and displaced by U.S.-backed paramilitary forces, and so on, to the social deprivation caused by the shift in resources, to cycles of destruction and social austerity, to the ecological devastation and the opportunity costs of not investing in social development.

CONCLUSION: WHO WILL PAY?

A crisis of overaccumulation means that the system's capacity for surplus absorption is exhausted and that a phase of the devaluation or destruction of capital surpluses has begun. In 2008 close to $7 trillion was wiped out on Wall Street through such devaluation.[66] A crucial point of departure between bourgeois economics and Marxism "is that within the latter tradition there is general agreement that capitalism is not only crisis-ridden but crisis dependent," notes O'Connor. Capital accumulates *through* crises, that is, "crises are the cauldron in which capital qualitatively restructures itself for economic, social, and political renewal and further accumulation."[67] Crises in capitalism are a mechanism

---

[63] Kim Murphy, "Has All the Spending Paid Off?," *Los Angeles Times*, August 28, 2011: A1, A14–15.

[64] Todd Miller, "Follow the Money: The University of Arizona's Border War," *NACLA Report on the Americas* (2012), 45(1): 23.

[65] See Tom Hayden, "War Never-Ending," *Los Angeles Times*, March 28, 2010: A31.

[66] Renae Merle, "Wall Street's Final '08 Toll: $6.9 Trillion Wiped Out," *Washington Post*, January 1, 2009: A1.

[67] O'Connor, *The Meaning of Crisis*, 93–4.

for restructuring and renewal of the system; they form part of the processes of its reproduction. The crisis is already resulting in a further concentration and centralization of capital worldwide, in hothouse fashion, in the hands of the TCC. This process was one of the great untold stories of the 1990s boom in the global economy.[68] It has accelerated since the financial collapse; to wit, the eight great Wall Street financial houses became only four just in 2008.

Historically, dominant groups attempt to transfer the cost of crisis onto the mass of popular and working classes, and in turn these classes resist such attempts. This is the global political moment. Crises are times of great uncertainty, so short-term predictions may be of little value. As I have noted previously, they are also moments in which political agency may prevail over structural determinations: depending on the elements of contingency and agency, crises may tilt the correlation of social and class forces in distinct directions. Transnational capital and its political agents have attempted to resolve the structural crisis by a vast shift in the balance of class and social forces worldwide – in effect, to deepen many times over and to consummate the "neoliberal counterrevolution" that began in the 1980s. In this respect, the 2008 financial crisis was a major turning point. The multibillionaire Warren Buffet, chairman of Berkshire Hathaway and one of the richest men in the world, famously stated in 2006 that "There's class warfare, all right, but it's my class, the rich class, that's making war, and we're winning."[69] In fact, the global crisis provided the TCC with an opportunity to intensify this war. The money mandarins of global capitalism and their political agents utilized the global crisis to impose brutal austerity and to attempt to dismantle what is left of welfare systems and social states in Europe, North America, and elsewhere. The crisis allowed transnational capital to squeeze more value out of labor, directly through more intensified exploitation and indirectly through state finances. Social and political conflict escalated around the world in the wake of 2008, including repeated rounds of national strikes and mass mobilization in the European Union, uprisings in North Africa, and so on, as I will discuss in the final chapter. While the TNS failed to intervene to impose regulations on global finance capital, it did intervene to impose the costs of devalorization on labor.

Once the private banking and financial institutions recovered from the 2008 collapse, they turned, as I noted earlier, to unloading surplus into sovereign debt markets that they themselves helped to create. Greece provides a textbook case of how this operated. Goldman Sachs led the charge of transnational investors into Greece, advising Greek financial authorities to pour state funds into derivatives in order to make national accounts look good and thereby to attract loans and bond purchases. Goldman Sachs then turned around and engaged in parallel derivative trading known as "credit default swaps" – that is, betting on the

---

[68] Robinson, *A Theory of Global Capitalism.*
[69] William K. Carroll, *The Making of a Transnational Capitalist Class: Corporate Power in the 21ˢᵗ Century* (London: Zed, 2010), 1.

possibility that Greece would default. This raised the country's cost of borrow-
ing, making huge profits for Goldman Sacks and increasing interest rates many
times over for Greece, while raising the prospect of sovereign debt default and
therefore justifying brutal austerity measures imposed by the EU and the IMF as
a condition for a series of bridge loans.[70] When a state issues interest-yielding
bonds, it is extracting surplus from working classes in order to turn it over to
capital, in the form of a claim on future wages along with pressure on the state to
reduce current wages and social spending. Speculation in sovereign debt is a
mechanism at work in the EU and the United States and more generally, worldwide (in this respect, the Eurozone sovereign debt crisis is simply the coming to
the First World of the debt crisis that the global South has experienced for several
decades).

Apart from the massive devalorizations of 2007 and 2008, the crisis has
therefore involved less a devalorization of capital than a further transfer of
wealth from labor to transnational capital and has set the stage for a new
round of deep austerity. The crisis has in part been displaced to state budgets –
bailouts, austerity, deficits, and so on – yet this needs to be seen in terms of class
relations. The bailouts of transnational capital represent in themselves a transfer
of the devaluation of capital onto labor. The budgetary and fiscal crises that
supposedly justify spending cuts and austerity are a matter of political decisions;
they are contrived, literally. They are a consequence of the unwillingness or
inability of states to challenge capital and their disposition to transfer the burden
of the crisis to working and popular classes. Mass unemployment, foreclosures,
the further erosion of social wages, wage cuts, furloughs, the increased exploitation of part-time workers, reduced work hours, informalization, and mount-
ing debt peonage – including capital's claim on the future wages of workers
through public debt – are some of capital's transfer mechanisms. Unless there is
effective resistance, global capital is likely to make permanent the further flexibilization of labor and other concessions it is wringing out of workers through
the crisis.

It seems clear that transnational finance capital was able to privately appropriate state bailouts and turn them into super-profits. In 2009 Wall Street
reported a resumption of massive profits, even in the midst of severe recession
and low levels of consumption, a decline in productive investment, and a sharp
rise in unemployment. By 2010 global corporations were registering record
profits, and corporate income escalated. After suffering losses in 2008, the top
twenty-five hedge-fund managers were paid, on average, more than $1 billion
each in 2009, eclipsing the record they had set in pre-recession 2007.[71] The Dow

---

[70] For these details, see William I. Robinson, "Global Capital Leviathan," *Radical Philosophy*
(2011), no. 165: 2–6.
[71] Chrystia Freeland, "The Rise of the New Global Elite," *The Atlantic*, January/February 2008,
from p. 4, internet edition, from http://www.theatlantic.com/magazine/archive/2011/01/the-rise-
of-the-new-global-elite/8343/.

Jones, which had dropped from 14,000 to 6,500 in late 2008 and early 2009, rose to 13,000 in early 2012 and to 16,000 in late 2013. In the United States, corporate profits in 2011 hit their highest level since 1950. Between 2008 and 2011, 88 percent of national income growth in the United States went to corporate profits, while just one percent went to wages. In comparison, in the recovery from the 2000–1 recession, 15 percent of income growth went to wages and salaries while 53 percent went to corporate profits, and in the recovery that began in 1991, 50 percent of the growth in national income went to wages and salaries while corporate profits actually fell by one percent.[72] According to Federal Reserve data from late 2010, companies in the United States held $1.8 trillion in uninvested cash, more than at any time since 1956 (adjusted for inflation) – a powerful indicator of the persistence of overaccumulation.[73]

Will popular sectors manage to forge a social solidarity of the oppressed, the exploited, and the subordinate majorities across ethnic and national lines? Dominant groups, especially in the heartlands of global capitalism, have tried to aggravate existing national and ethnic hierarchies of labor, to scapegoat immigrants and unemployed Black people, and so forth, as I will discuss in the next chapter. Gary Dymsky has shown how financiers shifted from red-lining African American communities in the United States to predatory lending to them, that is, from racial exclusion in mortgage lending to racial exploitation.[74] Following the subprime collapse, the dominant discourse attempted to shift blame to these African American families as "irresponsible borrowers." Similarly, anti-immigrant forces in the United States shifted from a blatant racialist anti-Latino discourse to an economicist discourse of "protecting citizens' employment." These discursive shifts underscore that a major dimension of the battles to come is *whose* interpretation of the crisis will prevail. How majorities in global society understand the threats to their security and survival will shape their social and political agency. In this regard, it is not foretold that the crisis will act as a steering or "corrective" mechanism for capital to resume accumulation and assert its domination rather than to strengthen fascist, anticapitalist, or socialist forces or the "mutual ruin of the contending classes." In the next chapter I will explore further the response of distinct agents to global crisis and alternatives futures, and then turn to the topic of a burgeoning of repressive social control systems around the world, both in response to real and potential resistance from below and as a mechanism for further profit making through conflict and coercion as stagnation in the global economy persists.

[72] Steven Greenhouse, "The Wageless, Profitable Recovery," *The New York Times*, June 30, 2011, online edition, from http://economix.blogs.nytimes.com/2011/06/30/the-wageless-profitable-recovery/

[73] As cited in Christian Parenti, *Tropic of Cancer: Climate Change and the New Geography of Violence* (New York: Nation Books, 2011), 228–229.

[74] Gary A. Dymsky, "The Political Economy of the Subprime Meltdown," paper presented at the symposium *Financial Crisis and Globalization*, Institute for Global Cooperation and Conflict (IGCC), University of California at Riverside, January 13, 2009.

5

Policing Global Capitalism

This is an extremely important moment: the point where, the repertoire of 'hegemony through consent' having been exhausted, the drift towards the routine use of the more repressive features of the state comes more and more prominently into play. Here the pendulum within the exercise of hegemony tilts, decisively, from that where consent overrides coercion, to that condition in which coercion becomes, as it were, the natural and routine form in which consent is secured. This shift in the internal balance of hegemony – consent to coercion – is a response, within the state, to increasingly polarization of class forces (real and imagined). It is exactly how a 'crisis of hegemony' expresses itself.... the slow development of a state of legitimate coercion, the birth of a 'law and order' society.... The whole tenor of social and political life has been transformed by [this moment]. A distinctively new ideological climate has been precipitated.

Stuart Hall and his colleagues, in *Policing the Crisis*[1]

RESPONSES TO THE CRISIS

How have social and political forces around the world responded to the global crisis? When we observe that the structural crises of the 1870s, the 1930s, and the 1970s had been resolved through a restructuring of the capitalist system, this does not mean that things necessarily got better for the mass of humanity. "Resolved" means that restructuring allowed for the resumption of sustained accumulation. As I have emphasized thus far, crises open up the possibility of change that can go in many different directions. How a crisis unravels depends, among other things, on the agencies of the constellation of social forces that come together in particular conjunctures, the correlation of force among classes

[1] Stuart Hall, Chas Critcher, Tony Jefferson, John Clarke, and Brian Roberts, *Policing the Crisis: Mugging, the State, and Law and Order* (New York: Holmes and Meier Publishers, 1978), 320–321.

in these conjunctures, distinct projects that are put forward in response to the crisis, political conditions, and contingency – all within the bounds of what is structurally possible. Here I identify three responses to the crisis that are in dispute, although this does not mean that there are not, or will not be, other responses not addressed here.

The first is a reformism from above aimed at stabilizing the system, or saving the system from itself and from more radical responses from below. Many global elites responded to the collapse in 2008, and even before, by pushing for a neo-Keynesianism. These elites articulated a project involving a shift from neo-classical to institutional economics, a limited re-regulation of global market forces, tax reform (e.g., the Tobin Tax), limited redistribution, and multitrillion-dollar state intervention programs designed to bail out transnational capital. The "new institutionalism" is a research agenda spanning the social sciences whose principal theoretical claim is that institutions have an independent and formative influence on politics, economics, and social structure. As well, prior institutional development establishes paths that shape and circumscribe present and future political, economic, and social processes ("path dependence").[2] Reformists among global elites such as Joseph Stiglitz, Jeffrey Sacks, Kofi Annan, and George Soros, among others – all previously adherents to the neo-liberal "Washington consensus" – espouse institutional over neo-classical economics as the intellectual scaffolding of a post-neo-liberal global capitalist order.[3] If neo-classical economics provided the theoretical and ideological foundation for the neo-liberal program, then institutionalism along with neo-Keynesianism is likely to provide such a foundation for reformist projects from above.

A global reformism appeared to be the dominant response from elites in the immediate aftermath of the 2008 collapse, but later it seemed to lose steam. There was no global elite consensus around such a reform project. It is entirely premature to predict or describe a new model of global capitalism, whether reformist along these lines or otherwise, as any project will be the outcome of a struggle among social forces that will be battling it out for a long time to come. Moreover, such a project must contend with the fundamental contradiction of a globalizing economy within a nation-state-based system of political authority and legal enforcement. In fact, global elites have been scrambling since the Asian crisis of 1997–98 to develop more effective TNS apparatuses, or institutions and mechanisms that allow for transnational coordination and supervision. These efforts have intensified since the collapse of 2008. As mentioned previously, for

---

[2] Perhaps the best-known academic associated with the New Institutional Economics is Douglass C. North. See *Institutions, Institutional Change and Economic Performance* (Cambridge: Cambridge University Press, 1990). See also John Harris, Karen Hunter, and Colin M. Lewis, eds., *The New Institutional Economics and Third World Development*, 2nd ed. (New York: Routledge, 1997).

[3] See, e.g., Joseph E. Stiglitz, *Globalization and Its Discontents* (New York: W.W. Norton, 2003). To his right is Jeffrey D. Sacks, *The End of Poverty: Economic Possibilities for Our Time* (New York: Penguin Books, 2006).

instance, the Chinese government, among one of many such proposals, has called for the creation of a new global reserve currency to replace the dominant dollar – a super-currency made up of a basket of national currencies and controlled by the IMF.[4]

A reversion to national protectionism in response to pressure from national constituencies to address the crisis is, in my view, highly unlikely. The integrated nature of the global production and financial system makes it difficult for it to be disassembled into national systems. Moreover, it is not in the interests of transnational capital to seal off any national territory, which would undermine transnational circuits of accumulation. A handful of apparent protectionist measures in late 2008 and early 2009 sought not to shield national capitals in rivalry with one another, as in the 1930s, but to bail out *transnational* capital within particular nation-states. National constituencies pressing for protectionism were not for the most part capitalist groups, which are transnational in character even when headquartered in one nation or another, but popular and working classes. U.S. trade unions, for instance, called for a "buy American" provision to be included in the early 2009 U.S. government bailout of auto firms, while the U.S. Chamber of Commerce and other business groups railed out against such provisions.[5] Such labor protectionism may be progressive in some cases, but in others it is clearly chauvinist – as in the United States and England, for example, where it has been directed by privileged, largely white, sectors of the working class against immigrants.

What are the prospects of a "new New Deal"? At the time of writing (early 2013) there were few signs that capitalist states could foment a shift back from financial to productive accumulation. As I have suggested, global capital has become a leviathan in which capitals from around the world are so deeply interpenetrated, not only across borders but through the overlap of productive and financial circuits, that it is not clear how meaningful it is to continue to distinguish, in the classical way, between the two. The giant global financial conglomerates draw in individual and institutional investors from around the world and in turn circulate unfathomable amounts of capital into productive, commercial, and service circuits. There did not appear to be the political will or even the notion among global elites and capitalist state managers in the years subsequent to the collapse to restructure the system in any way that would reestablish some boundaries between financial and productive circuits or that would modify the role transnational finance capital has played as the regulator of the circuit of accumulation and the proximate causal agent in the crisis. While some state officials called for a re-regulation of the global financial system none appeared to challenge in any fundamental way the very structure of the system

---

[4] Don Lee, "China Pushes for Bigger Role in Reshaping the World Economy," *Los Angeles Times*, April 2, 2009: A1.
[5] See Peter Wallsten, "Liberals Watch Obama, and Worry," *Los Angeles Times*, February 16, 2009: A1.

by which transnational finance capital exercises such utter domination over the world. Moreover, while such would-be reformers among the TCC as Warren Buffet, Carlos Slim, and George Soros have advanced a reformist-redistributive discourse, their eagerness to take advantage of the crisis to make profits prevents them from playing any significant reformist role. By way of example, even as Warren Buffet publicly criticized Wall Street for its role in the crisis he bought controlling shares in Citigroup, while Soros is a major shareholder in the same banks (e.g., Citigroup and J. P. Morgan) that he has condemned for their contributions to the crisis.[6]

In the 1930s reformist forces from above were able to restructure capitalism by curtailing capital's prerogatives without challenging its fundamental interests. Now, in distinction, I do not see any way a reformism from above could adequately address the crisis without a head-on collision with the interests of global capital – the transnational banks, the oil/energy sector, the military-security-industrial-reconstruction complex, and so forth. This is to say that in order to salvage the system from its own self-destruction the capitalist state would have to exercise a remarkable degree of autonomy not just from individual capitalists and investor groups but from the leviathan that is the inextricably entangled mass of global capital. Such a role would necessarily involve a change in the worldwide correlation of class and social forces in favor of popular and working classes. The principle underlying difference between the 1930s New Deal project of reform and restructuring and the twenty-first-century conjuncture is this correlation of class and social forces worldwide. There is currently no socialist-oriented bloc of countries that could exercise a critical counterweight to capitalist elites in response to the crisis, while mass socialist and worker movements, although they are burgeoning, are weak compared to the 1930s.

A second response, hence, is popular and leftist resistance from below. Although often in fits and starts, this resistance appeared to be resurgent in the wake of 2008, yet spread very unevenly across countries and regions. Although these forces are weaker in a comparative historical sense, they are also more coordinated across borders and regions in the new global age and reinvigorated by the crisis. To speak of a global justice movement is not mere rhetoric because resistance and counterhegemonic forces around the world are acutely aware, in a way that we have not previously experienced, that local resistance struggles and alternative projects acquire their meaning in the context of and in relation to transnational struggles and projects. Resurgent left, radical, and anticapitalist forces worldwide have again placed socialism on the world political agenda. At this time Latin America appears to be the "weakest link" in the global capitalist leviathan. The Venezuelan revolution is attempting to construct a twenty-first-century socialism and to stake out a radical anticapitalist pole in South America.

---

[6] See, e.g., "Soros's Firm Buys Shares of Morgan Stanley, Citigroup, JPMorgan," *Money News*, February 15, 2013, www.moneynews.com/InvestingAnalysis/soros-Morgan-Stanley-Citigroup-JPMorgan/2013/02/15/id/490537.

Everywhere popular forces are in ferment and mass struggles escalating. The organized left has had a renewed presence in many countries.

These counterhegemonic forces call for the resolution of the crisis through a more far-reaching transformation of the global social order. But severe fragmentation of the popular classes brought about by decades of global informalization and flexible accumulation continues to challenge counterhegemonic forces to find new ways to aggregate dispersed groups into collective projects of transformation. The anarchist-inspired aversion to struggling for state power and the illusion of being able to "change the world without taking power"[7] are under heightened challenge. At this time a radical response to the crisis from below lacks a "postmodern prince" or political vehicles and concrete projects for reordering the world, a deficiency that the global justice movement seemed to be more acutely aware of after the crisis than before. At the close of a 120,000-strong meeting of the World Social Forum in Belem, Brazil, in January 2009, representatives from social movements from around the world declared:

> We are facing a global crisis which is a direct consequence of the capitalist system and therefore cannot find a solution within the system. . . . In order to overcome the crisis we have to grapple with the root of the problem and progress as fast as possible towards the construction of a radical alternative that would do away with the capitalist system and patriarchal domination. We, the social movements, are faced with an historic opportunity to develop emancipatory initiatives on a global scale. Only through the social struggle of the masses can populations overcome the crisis. . . . The challenge of social movements is to achieve a convergence of global mobilization.[8]

In early 2009 the initiative seemed to pass back again from global elites to oppositional forces from below. Global elites meeting in January 2009 for the annual summit of the World Economic Form in Davos, Switzerland, appeared to be rudderless – confused and divided, unable to come up with coherent solutions to the crisis and on the defensive. By contrast, the 120,000 participants at the Belem World Social Forum meeting were clearly on the offensive. Could such a global mobilization from below push reformist-minded elites further to the left or even push beyond reformism? In my view, popular forces from below need to convert counterhegemony into hegemony within the gamut of social and political responses to the unfolding crisis. This hegemony must involve a radical critique of the crisis. Opposition to neo-liberalism needs to move beyond opposition to the mildly reformist proposals that do not challenge the power of the TCC. I will return to some of these issues in the concluding chapter.

But crises of state legitimacy and vacuums in institutional power open up space not just for popular forces from below but also for the far-right forces that compete with reformist and radical responses to crisis. Hence, the third response

---

[7] John Holloway, *Change the World without Taking Power* (London: Pluto, 2005).

[8] Declaration of the Assembly of Social Movements at the World Social Forum 2009, February 5, 2009, from www.globalresearch.ca/index.php?context=viewArticle&code=ASS20090204& articleId=12160.

is what I term twenty-first-century *fascism*. The need for dominant groups around the world to assure widespread, organized mass social control of the world's surplus population and of rebellious forces from below gives a powerful impulse to a project of twenty-first-century global fascism. Images in recent years of what such a political project would involve have ranged from the Israeli invasions of Gaza and ethnic cleansing of the Palestinians, to the scapegoating and criminalization of immigrant workers and the Tea Party movement in the United States, genocide in the Congo, the U.S./United Nations occupation of Haiti, the spread of neo-Nazis and skinheads in Europe as well as a surge in support for far-right parties, and the intensified Indian repression in occupied Kashmir. The crisis is resulting in a rapid political polarization in many parts of the world, and in the global system as a whole. Both right- and left-wing forces are resurgent. The remainder of this chapter will look at the increasingly coercive and militarized nature of global society, at and the rise of a proto-fascist right in the United States as one case study in twenty-first-century fascism.[9]

TWENTY-FIRST-CENTURY FASCISM

"The crisis consists precisely in the fact that the old is dying and the new cannot be born," Gramsci famously stated. "In this interregnum a great variety of morbid symptoms appear." The ultra-right is an resurgent force in many countries – in Latin America, for instance, in Colombia, Mexico, Honduras and elsewhere, in a number of EU countries, and – what concerns us in this chapter – in the United States. If reformism from above fails and if the left is not able to seize the initiative, the road may be open for twenty-first-century fascism, at least in some countries and regions around the world. This proto-fascist right seeks to fuse reactionary political power with transnational capital and to organize a mass base among historically privileged sectors of the global working class, such as white workers in the North and middle layers in the South experiencing heightened insecurity and the specter of downward mobility. The proto-fascist response to the crisis involves militarism, extreme masculinization, racism, the search for scapegoats (such as immigrant workers and Muslims in the United States and Europe), and mystifying, sometimes millennial, ideologies.

We should recall that fascism is a particular *response to capitalist crisis* that seeks to contain any challenge to the system that may come from subordinate groups. In this regard, central to the story of global capitalism and global crisis, as well as to the specter of neo-fascism, is a mass of humanity involving hundreds of millions if not billions of people who have been expropriated from the means of survival yet also expelled from capitalist production as global supernumeraries or surplus labor, relegated to scraping by in a "planet of slums" and subject

---

[9] The next section is a radically revised and expanded version of an article I co-authored with Mario Barrera, "Global Crisis and Twenty-First Century Fascism: A U.S. Case Study," *Race and Class* (2012), 53(4): 4–29.

to all-pervasive and ever-more-sophisticated and repressive social control systems, as I mentioned in Chapter 1 and will discuss in more detail later. From the vantage point of dominant groups the challenge is how to contain the mass of supernumeraries and marginalized and the resistance of downwardly mobile majorities.

Crisis of the Capitalist National State and the Impulse toward Neo-Fascism

To summarize what I argued in Chapter 2, the accumulation and legitimation functions of the capitalist state – always in tension with one another – cannot both be met in the long run. Globalization has sharpened this contradiction. Economic crisis intensifies the problem of legitimation for the dominant groups, so that accumulation crises appear as spiraling political crises. The juggernaut of the commodification of everything has aggravated crises of social reproduction, undermined the social bases for more stable forms of consensual domination, and provided further impetus for more coercive forms of social control. In essence, the state's ability to function as a "factor of cohesion" within the social order breaks down to the extent that capital has globalized and the logic of accumulation or commodification penetrate every aspect of social life – the "life world" itself – so that "cohesion" requires more and more social control in the face of the collapse of the social fabric. There is a shift from social welfare to social control or police states. This is a question less of public policy, in the first instance, than of class relations; the liberation of emergent transnational capital from the nation-state has undermined the material basis of the capitalist redistributive state – the particular correlation of forces between popular classes and capital that constituted the class basis of the social states of Fordist-Keynesian capitalism.[10]

In response, the state abandons efforts to secure legitimacy among broad swaths of the population that have been relegated to surplus labor. The system does not even attempt to incorporate this surplus population but rather tries to isolate and neutralize its real or potential rebellion, criminalizing the poor and the dispossessed, even tending toward genocide in some cases. States resort to a host of mechanisms of coercive exclusion: mass incarceration and prison-industrial complexes, pervasive policing, repressive anti-immigrant legislation, manipulation of space in new ways, so that both gated communities and ghettos are controlled by armies of private security guards and technologically advanced surveillance systems, and ideological campaigns aimed at seduction and

---

[10] Redistribution is still possible at the nation-state level when distinct class and social forces (as in Venezuela) take control of, and transform, the neo-liberal national state. Even then, however, the larger global system and the structural power that transnational capital is able to exercise over the direct power of national states severely constrain redistributive projects, unless, in my view, such projects 1) are transnational, as neither Keynesianism nor socialism is any longer possible in one country (something I have argued elsewhere at length), and 2) move beyond redistribution to effect a more fundamental transformation in class/property relations.

instilling passivity through petty consumption and fantasy. All this provides fertile bases for projects of twenty-first-century fascism.

Poulantzas makes a distinction between "normal" and "exceptional" forms of the state; the former corresponds to conjunctures in which bourgeois hegemony is stable and the latter to crises of hegemony.[11] To what extent are countries around the world moving into exceptional states? And how would such exceptional forms appear? The outlines of a twenty-first-century neo-fascism seemed to be congealing in the years of the Bush presidency in the United States, from 2001 to 2009, and more generally as an ascendant tendency in global society. A descent into barbarism, driven by military spending, multiple forms of repression, and wars waged to contain the downtrodden, seize new territories, resources, and labor pools, and maintain social control, has already begun – a veritable *global warlordism*. Could a neo-fascist project that moves in this direction organize enough support to put in place a hegemonic bloc? Some of the telltale signs of such a neo-fascist project, to reiterate, are the fusion of transnational capital and reactionary political power; escalating militarization and extreme masculinization; a mass base among economically insecure and socially disaffected sectors animated by a fanatical ideology, race/culture supremacy, and xenophobia embracing an idealized and mythical past; economic destabilization and concomitant social anxiety among privileged strata of the working and middle classes; a racist mobilization against scapegoats that serves to displace and redirect social tensions and contradictions; and charismatic leadership.

The division of the world into distinct, if inextricably interconnected, nation-states means that a wide variety of polities may appear in accordance with particular national and regional histories, social forces, and conjunctures, and within a larger global unity. Having said that, however, we must be clear that an investigation into twenty-first-century fascism in the United States is both a methodological simplification and an epistemological reduction, in that a twenty-first-century fascism cannot be understood as a nation-state project in this age of global capitalism. It is more analytically and conceptually accurate to talk of a *global police state* – or, applying Poulantzas's notion, an *exceptional TNS*. The global order as a unity is increasingly repressive and authoritarian and particular *forms* of exceptional national states or national polities, including twenty-first-century fascism, develop on the basis of particular national and regional histories, social and class forces, political conditions and conjunctures. Yet the militarization of cities, politics, and culture in such countries as the United States and Israel is inseparable from these countries' entanglement in webs of global wars and militarized global accumulation, or the global war economy, as I discussed in Chapters 3 and 4. The powers that be in the international system must secure social control and defend the global order in each particular national territory lest the global order itself become threatened.

---

[11] Nicos Poulantzas, *Political Power and Social Classes* (London: Verso, 1973).

In his brilliant yet chilling study, *Cities under Siege: The New Military Urbanism*, Stephen Graham shows how the structures and processes of permanent militarized social control systems and warfare constitute a global project that by definition is transnational. The "wars" against drugs, against crime, against terror, against insecurity itself incorporate "the stealthy militarization of a wide range of policy debates, urban landscapes, and circuits of urban infrastructure, as well as whole realms of popular and urban culture." They lead to "the creeping and insidious diffusion of militarized debates about 'security' in every walk of life. Together ... these work to bring essentially military ideas of the prosecution of, and preparation for, war into the heart of ordinary, day-to-day city life." [12] Every country has become enmeshed in policing the global crisis as the global economy becomes ever-more invested in warfare, social violence, and state-organized coercion and repression. Graham observes:

> The new military urbanism feeds on experiences with styles of targeting and technology in colonial war-zones, such as Gaza or Baghdad, or security operations at international sport events or political summits. These operations act as testing grounds for technology and techniques to be sold on through the world's burgeoning homeland security markets.... Israeli drones designed to vertically subjugate and target Palestinians are now routinely deployed by police forces in North America, Europe, and East Asia. Private operators of U.S. 'supermax' prisons are heavily involved in running the global archipelago organizing incarceration and torture that has burgeoned since the start of the 'war on terror.' Private military corporations heavily colonize reconstruction contracts in both Iraq and New Orleans. Israeli expertise in population control is sought by those planning security operations for international events in the West. And shoot-to-kill policies developed to combat suicide bombings in Tel Aviv and Haifa have been adopted by police forces and Europe and America. Meanwhile, aggressive and militarized policing at public demonstrations and social mobilizations in London, Toronto, Paris and New York are now starting to utilize the same 'non-lethal weapons' as Israel's army in Gaza or Jenin. The construction of 'security zones' around the strategic financial cores and government districts of London and New York directly import at overseas bases and green zones ... [m]any of the techniques used to fortify enclaves in Baghdad or permanently lockdown civilians in Gaza and the West Bank. ... [These techniques] are being sold around the world as cutting-edge and combat-proven 'security solutions' by corporate coalitions linking Israeli, U.S. and other companies and states. [13]

Twentieth- and Twenty-First-Century Fascism

If not all "exceptional states" can be considered fascist, is it justified to attach the term "fascism" to such trends toward exceptional states? In order to address this question, I specify here my understanding of fascism and explore what form a U.S. neo-fascism might take in this century. In addition to what I have just

---

[12] Stephen Graham, *Cities under Siege: The New Military Urbanism* (London: Verso, 2010), xiv.
[13] Ibid., xviii.

emphasized – that any such neo-fascism must be seen in terms of the unity of the global system – I do so with the understanding that fascism is not a simple, clearly demarcated phenomenon, and also that a twenty-first-century fascism, for reasons I will delve into, need not and would not resemble twentieth-century "classical" fascism in many respects, despite certain parallels.

In his detailed comparative analysis of the two historical cases – Italian Fascism and German National Socialism, or Nazism – Robert Paxton summarizes much of the earlier literature on fascism and describes classical fascism as a distinctively twentieth-century phenomenon based on the mobilization of a mass electorate that had emerged in nineteenth-century Europe.[14] Among the factors that contributed to their success were the economic dislocations produced in Europe by an increasingly internationalized economy, the social and economic disruptions that attended World War I, and fears on the part of traditional elites of strong socialist movements among the working class. Paxton identifies certain themes typical of classic fascist movements and regimes:

• a strong emphasis on nationalism and integration into a community, with a consequent deemphasis on the individual;
• mass political mobilization on the basis of strong emotional appeals;
• militarism and expansionist goals; imperialism;
• demonization of imputed enemies, often ethnic in character;
• a sense of victimization;
• authoritarianism; a hierarchical order with a supreme, charismatic leader;
• a desire for purification of society, with a glorification of violent means;
• a rejection of ineffectual or faltering democratic institutions.

It is important to see these "themes" of fascist movements that Paxton identifies in the context of the crucial link between capitalist crisis and fascist movements, and the fusion of capitalist interests with reactionary political power, as I will discuss, and as the classical Marxist and also some liberal treatises on fascism have highlighted.[15] At the same time, the scaffolding of classical as well as twenty-first-century fascism involves a major social-psychological and cultural component. In his classic 1941 text on European fascism, *Escape from Freedom*,[16] Erich Fromm argued that with the breakup of the medieval world Europeans had lost a settled social structure and a religious worldview that had

[14] Robert Paxton, *The Anatomy of Fascism* (New York: Vintage, 2005), esp. 78–80.
[15] Two classical Marxist texts on twentieth-century fascism are Franz Newmann, *Behemoth: The Structure and Practice of National Socialism, 1933–1944* (Oxford University Press, 1942, republished by Chicago: Ivan R. Dee Publishers in 2009 with an introduction by Peter Hayes), and R. Palme Dutt, *Fascism and Social Revolution* (1934, reprinted by Rockville, MD: Wildside Press, 2009).
[16] Erich Fromm, *Escape from Freedom* (New York: Henry Holt, 1941, 1969). Fromm is not alone in emphasizing the socio-psychological dimensions of fascism. Hannah Arendt and Wilhelm Reich, among others, have done so as well. See Arendt, *The Origins of Totalitarianism* (New York: Benediction Books, 2009 [1951]); Reich, *The Mass Psychology of Fascism* (London: Souvenir Press Ltd, 1997 [1933]).

provided them, despite its drawbacks, with a sense of having a place in society and in the universe, resulting in widespread anxiety and a loss of meaning. In many cases, this led to the creation of hierarchical and authoritarian solutions that represented an "escape from freedom."

These psychological stresses, according to Fromm, resulted in the creation of an authoritarian character, or personality, in those social sectors most affected. Fromm goes on to link these psychosocial dimensions of classical fascism to the early twentieth century crisis of capitalism, especially in Nazi Germany, and to the class bases of Nazism in the lower strata of the middle classes, composed of small shopkeepers, artisans, and white-collar workers threatened by capitalist displacement. "[The] psychological conditions were not the 'cause' of Nazism," says Fromm, in observing the confluence of rational and nonrational factors in explaining the triumph of the Nazi regime. The psychological conditions "constituted the human basis without which it could not have developed, but any analysis of the whole phenomenon of the rise and victory of Nazism must deal with the strictly economic and political, as well as with the psychological conditions."[17]

Clearly, many but not all of these dimensions of classic fascism are present or emergent in the United States. The emergence of a Christian Right since the mid-1980s, the explosion of the Tea Party movement, an escalation of social violence, the sharp increase in violent hate groups, the spread of a vicious anti-immigrant movement, and the psychopathology of white decline are some of the indications of the rise of fascist tendencies within U.S. civil society and polity. Later, I will discuss some of these developments. I conceive of a twenty-first-century fascism as an exceptional form of capitalist state and society that is not limited to movements in civil society and the polity such as these, insofar as it also involves tendencies within the state, the culture industries, the political economy, and capital accumulation. And I reiterate as well, following the classical Marxist studies on twentieth-century fascism, that whether in its classical form or in possible variants of neo-fascism in the twenty-first century, fascism is a *particular* response to capitalist crisis.

At the same time – *and this is crucial – a twenty-first-century fascism would not be a repetition of its twentieth-century predecessor.* In my public discussions on twenty-first-century fascism I have found much aversion to even raising the term. Such knee-jerk dismissal is unscholarly and not very useful politically. I suppose such dismissiveness is explained in part by the frequent misuse of the term these days to refer to any and every situation of state repression or an authoritarian system, or by the stereotypically rigid association of the term with images of Nazi Germany. Yet anyone who has spent time recently in Colombia and understands how that country is organized and operates, to mention just one example of an already existing and in-place system of twenty-first-century fascism, will no doubt recognize twenty-first-century fascism as discussed and

---

[17] Fromm, *Escape from Freedom*, 216.

analyzed here.[18] A twenty-first-century fascism would not be a repetition of its twentieth-century predecessor. The role of political and ideological domination through control over media and the flow of images and symbols would make any such twenty-first-century project more sophisticated and – together with new panoptical surveillance and social control technologies (see the following discussion) – probably allow it to rely more on selective than on generalized repression. These and other new forms of social control and modalities of ideological domination blur boundaries in such a way that there may be a constitutional and normalized neo-fascism – with formal representative institutions, a constitution, political parties, and elections – while the political system is tightly controlled by transnational capital and its representatives and any dissent that actually threatens the system is neutralized, if not liquidated. I agree, in this regard, with Bertram Gross, who in his 1980 modern classic, *Friendly Fascism: The New Face of Power in America*,[19] addressed some of these distinctions between classical fascism and neo-fascism. The element that Gross saw as central to all types of fascism is a strong interpenetration of large capitalist corporations with a repressive centralized government that serves corporate interests. He argued that such a state of affairs can develop gradually and incrementally, without a dramatic takeover of power by an overtly authoritarian party, and that control can be exercised through more subtle and sophisticated means than in the classic cases. Indeed, he believed that the evolution of such a system of friendly fascism in the United State is fully compatible with retaining a two-party and ostensibly democratic system. His statement in this regard bears great relevance to the current conjuncture:

> How would the elites respond if the masses began to ask the elites to give much more and gain much less – particularly when, under conditions of capitalist stagflation and shrinking world power, the elites have less to give. Some radical commentators claim that the powers that be would use their power to follow the example of the classic fascists and destroy the democratic machinery.... I see it ... as highly unlikely. No First World Establishment is going to shatter machinery that, with a certain amount of tinkering and a little bit of luck, can be profitably converted into a sophisticated instrument of repression.[20]

In Gross's view, the biggest success of incipient neo-fascist movements in the U.S. society and polity in the 1970s was that "many of [their] positions which first sounded outrageous when voiced during the Goldwater [presidential] campaign of 1964 are now regarded as part of the mainstream. This is not the result of Radical Right shifts toward the center. On the contrary, it is the result of a decisive movement toward the right by the Ultra-Rich and the Corporate

---

[18] See, inter alia, Jasmin Hristoy, *Blood and Capital: The Paramilitarization of Colombia* (Athens: Ohio University Press, 2009).

[19] Bertram Gross, *Friendly Fascism: The New Face of Power in America* (Boston: South End Press, 1980).

[20] Ibid, 230.

Overseers."[21] Needless to say, the ever-rightward drift of the "center" in the United States has continued unabated since Gross's time and has accelerated since the crisis exploded in 2008, pushed on by an array of far-right forces that I will discuss later. I *do not* assert that fascism has arrived in the United States, or even that it is likely. Rather, I suggest that fascist forces are insurgent in U.S. society and polity and that a twenty-first-century fascism in only one possible outcome of the crisis. Drawing in part on the classical and more contemporary studies of fascism as briefly discussed earlier, and in even greater part on my own propositions on the nature of a twenty-first-century fascism, I turn now to the twenty-first-century fascist impulse in the United States.

The Dictatorship of Transnational Capital and Reactionary Political Power

Fascism in the twentieth century involved the fusion of reactionary political power and *national* capital. Indeed, it was, in part, the inability of German and Italian national capital to successfully compete with the national capitals of other European powers in the imperialist conquests of the turn of nineteenth century and following the German defeat in World War I that led to a fascist response once the 1930s crisis hit full force. The major concentrations of what were national capitals have transnationalized under globalization. I do not see twenty-first-century fascism in the United States as a mechanism of competition with other national capitals but as an expression of the dictatorship of transnational capital. The fusion at the highest levels of the U.S. state of reactionary political power and transnational capital had been developing during the Bush years and could emerge or reemerge in the coming years.

Barack Obama's election to the presidency in 2008 and his reelection in 2012 made such an outright fusion more opaque. It also generated another set of conditions propitious for the development of neo-fascist forces in the United States. The Obama project from the start was an effort by dominant groups to reestablish hegemony in the wake of its deterioration during the Bush years. Obama's election was a challenge to the system at the cultural and ideological levels and shook up the racial/ethnic foundations upon which the U.S. republic has always rested, although it certainly did not dismantle those foundations. However, the Obama project was never intended to challenge the socioeconomic order; to the contrary, it sought to preserve and strengthen that order by reconstituting hegemony and conducting a passive revolution against mass discontent and spreading popular resistance that had begun to percolate in the final years of the Bush presidency, and that involved, among other things, the rise of a mass immigrant rights movement that peaked in the winter and spring of 2006 in a veritable "counter-hegemonic moment"[22]

---

[21] Ibid, 198.

[22] On this point, see Alfonso Gonzalez, "The 2006 Mega Marchas in Greater Los Angeles: Counter-hegemonic Moment and the Future of El Migrante Struggle," *Latino Studies*, 7(1): 30–39.

Gramsci developed the concept of passive revolution to refer to efforts by dominant groups to bring about mild change from above in order to undercut mobilization for more far-reaching transformation from below. Integral to passive revolution is the co-optation of leadership from below – that is, the integration of that leadership into the dominant project. Obama's 2008 election campaign tapped into and helped to expand mass mobilization and popular aspirations for change not seen in many years in the United States. The Obama project co-opted that brewing storm from below, channeled it into the electoral campaign, and then betrayed those aspirations, as the Democratic Party effectively demobilized the insurgency from below with more passive revolution. In this sense, the Obama project weakened the popular and left response to the crisis from below which opened space for the right-wing response – for a project of twenty-first-century fascism – to emerge. The Obama administration certainly appeared, in this respect if not in others, as a Weimar republic. Although the social democrats were in power during the Weimar republic of Germany in the 1920s and early 1930s, they did not pursue a leftist response to the crisis but rather sidelined the militant trade unions, communists, and socialists and progressively pandered to capital and the right before turning over power to the Nazis in 1933.

Transnational corporate capital financed both of the Obama presidential campaigns and would appear to have "purchased" the Obama presidency. At the same time, it has broadly funded such neo-fascist movements as the Tea Party as well as neo-fascist legislation such as Arizona's anti-immigrant law, SB1070. The far-right-wing billionaire brothers David and Charles Koch, whose combined fortune of some $40 billion is exceeded only by those of Bill Gates and Warren Buffet, are the prime bankrollers of the Tea Party and also of a host of foundations and front organizations, such as Americans for Prosperity, the Cato Institute, and the Mercatus Center, that have pushed an extreme version of the neo-liberal corporate agenda, including the reduction or elimination of corporate taxes, cutbacks in social services, the gutting of public education, and the total liberation of capital from any state regulation. Less well known is that the Koch brothers have raised funds for the Tea Party and other organizations from dozens of the largest transnational corporations operative on the U.S. political scene.[23] The actual programmatic content of the Koch brothers and the organizations and movements that they finance and help to lead is a deepening many times over of the neo-liberal "counterrevolution" of radical free market global capitalism, and converges perfectly with the interests of transnational capital. This convergence is irrespective of the fact that elements of the politicized

---

[23] See, inter alia: Jane Mayer, "Covert Operations: The Billionaire Brothers Who Are Waging a War against Obama," *New Yorker*, August 30, 2010, and the documentary *Billionaire Tea Party*, directed and produced by Taki Oldham and released by Larrikin Films, 2010, see website at www. billionairesteaparty.com.

leadership of the TCC have put forward political programs and policy proposals quite distinct from those of the U.S. far right.

Transnational capital and its political agents have been attempting to resolve the crisis by launching war on the global working class – in effect, an effort to consummate the "neo-liberal counterrevolution" that began in the 1980s.[24] While transnational capital's offensive against the global working class dates back to the crisis of the 1970s and has grown in intensity ever since, the Great Recession of 2008 was in several respects a major turning point. As I discussed in the previous chapter, Europe and the United States now face the same neo-liberal policies that have been imposed on the global South since the 1980s. It is worth noting as well that three sectors of transnational capital in particular stand out as the most aggressive in pursing this agenda and as the most prone to seek neo-fascist political arrangements to facilitate accumulation: speculative financial capital, the military-industrial-security complex, and the extractive and energy (particularly petroleum) sector (the core of Koch industries is oil). Capital accumulation in the military-industrial-security complex, for instance, depends on endless conflict and war, including the so-called wars on terrorism and on drugs, as well as on the militarization of social control directed against immigrants and oppressed groups such as African Americans and Palestinians (more on this to come).

We should recall that a key component of classical fascism was the smashing of trade unions (along with socialist and communist parties). In the United States, as elsewhere, the assault against unions has been going on for several decades. Gross had observed in his study on *Friendly Fascism* that corporate capital was financing strenuous efforts to contain labor unions in sectors already unionized and to keep other sectors and regions, such as the U.S. South, union-free through such tactics as decertification and "right to work" campaigns.[25] Indeed, while more than one-third of employed people belonged to unions in 1945, union membership fell to 24.1 percent of the U.S. workforce in 1979, to 13.9 percent in 1998, and to just 11.8 percent in 2011.[26] This tendency has had the effect of reducing the militancy of the labor movement and helping to move the Democratic Party in a more conservative direction. The assault on unions dates back to the 1970s, when corporations stepped up lobbying of government officials for changes in the labor laws that would make it easier for companies not only to sue unions, but also to prevent workers from organizing in the first place. Wage stagnation in the United States appeared starting with the economic crisis of 1973, has continued its steady march since then, and is positively

---

[24] On these details, see Robinson, "The Crisis of Global Capitalism," and also William I. Robinson, "Global Capital Leviathan," *Radical Philosophy*, 165: 2–6.

[25] For these details, see Gross, *Friendly Fascism*, 244–245.

[26] See About.Com.Economics, www.economics.about.com/od/laborinamerica/a/union_decline.htm, for the 1945, 1979, and 1998 figures, and for the 2011 figure, see U.S. Department of Labor, Bureau of Labor Statistics, press release dated January 27, 2012, from www.bls.gov/news.release/union2.nro.htm.

correlated with the decline in union participation. Stone observes that a central tactic of the anti-union ideological offensive was to blame unions for the 1970s crisis, and to publically equate unions with "socialism" and "communism." This tactic brought the religious right (see the following discussion) – which sees "communism" as atheistic and the work of the devil – squarely into the anti-union campaign. According to one Christian fundamentalist leader, "many Bible verses indicate that people may be eternally separated from God if they are members of evil organizations like the Trade Unions."[27] In 1981 the Reagan government launched an all-out siege on unions with the notorious firing of striking air traffic controllers.

Deunionization is also the effect of deindustrialization, the flexibilization of work, heightened competition among workers as unemployment and underemployment increase in the face of the threat of capital flight, and of corporate anti-union campaigns made notorious by the vicious tactics employed by Walmart.[28] Public sector unions – perhaps the last bastion of major union strength in the United State, with 37 percent unionized in 2011 – came under full-scale assault following the "Battle of Wisconsin" in 2010–11. There, the Koch-brother-financed Republican governor Scott Walker pushed through a bill in the state legislature that undermined labor's right to collective bargaining, severely curtailed public sector worker benefits, and paved the way for broader antiworker restructuring of the state's finances, including draconian cuts in social services together with corporate tax breaks. Even as workers and students fiercely yet peacefully resisted the assault, Walker ominously threatened to deploy the National Guard, and other states around the country introduced similar anti-union, antiworker legislation.[29]

Placing candidates such as Walker who are so beholden to the transnational corporate agenda and so committed to repressive and authoritarian means to achieve that agenda has been made much easier by the notorious 2010 U.S. Supreme Court *Citizens United* ruling. This ruling stipulated that corporations could not be restricted in their financial contributions to electoral campaigns and political parties. *Citizens United* is a bone-chilling legal precedent insofar as it lifts any restriction on transnational capital's ability to impose its overwhelming financial power on the political process in order to secure political outcomes without having to support extra-legal coup d'états or breaks with electoral process and constitutional order.

---

[27] Wade Stone, "The Decline of Trade Unions in the U.S. and Canada," *Global Research*, an online publication of the Montreal-based Center for Research on Globalization, June 7, 2011, from www.globalresearch.ca/the-decline-of-trade-unions-in-the-us-and-canada/25161.

[28] See, e.g., Nelson Lichtenstein, *The Retail Revolution: How Walmart Created a Brave New World of Business* (New York: Metropolitan Books, 2009), see esp. Chapter 5, "Unions Keep Out."

[29] See, e.g., Christian Schneider, "The Second Battle of Wisconsin," *National Review*, online edition, May 28, 2012, from www.nationalreview.com/articles/301640/second-battle-wisconsin-christian-schneider#.

Neo-Fascist Movements in U.S. Civil Society and Polity

The Great Recession of 2008 seems to have been the trigger for an outbreak of one the most significant right-wing populist rebellions in U.S. history. The neo-fascist insurgency can be traced back several decades, to the far-right mobilization that began in the wake of the crisis of hegemony brought about by the mass struggles of the 1960s and the 1970s, especially the black and Chicano liberation struggles and other militant movements on the part of Third World peoples, countercultural currents, and militant working-class struggles. Neo-fascist currents range from a fundamentalist Christian right and the Tea Party to the Oath Takers, the patriot movement, the militia movement, the Minutemen, the White Power movement, various Neo-Nazi and Klan organization, white nationalists, and so on. There is a growing cross-pollination between different sectors of the radical right that has not been seen in years. Space constraints allow for no more than a cursory review here.

There is not a single neo-fascist organization or movement in the United States, and the distinct strands of what constitute the stirrings of neo-fascistm in U.S. civil and political society are quite disparate. Moreover, mass charismatic leaders of a twenty-first-century fascist project have so far been largely missing in United States, although figures such as Sarah Palin and Glen Beck have appeared at certain moments as harbingers. Some have seen the Tea Party as a movement that could galvanize the distinct sectors, in particular, one that could bring together a tripartite convergence of the Tea Party movement with the Christian right and the political far right housed in the Republican Party, although I believe it is premature to make such a prediction. It is significant that both the Christian right and the Tea Party have sunk deep roots in the Republican Party, as any neo-fascist movement, in order to gain headway, would have to be grounded in parties and the political system.

The patriot movement and the militias that serve as its armed wing see the federal government as a plot to take away "liberties" and support a "one world government." It first came to prominence in the 1990s among people formerly associated with racially based hate groups. In recent years the patriot movement has experienced a dramatic resurgence, led by the fastest-growing patriot group, the "Oath Keepers." Founded in 2009 by Stewart Rhodes, a former aide to Republican Congressman Ron Paul, who is considered one of the intellectual fathers of the Tea Party movement, the militarized Oath Keepers movement has a core membership of men and women in uniform, including soldiers, police officers, and veterans. At regular ceremonies in every state, members reaffirm their official oaths of service, pledge to protect the Constitution, and vow to disobey – by arms, if necessary – "unconstitutional" orders from what they view as an increasingly tyrannical government that threatens the U.S. Constitution. By 2010 the Oath Keepers had at least one chapter in every state and was adding dozens of members daily, recruiting as well from active-duty police officers and members of the military.

The formation of a clear Christian right movement and its increasing identification with the Republican Party developed during the 1960s and 1970s around the 1964 anti–civil rights candidacy of Barry Goldwater, seen as a landmark in the rise of a new far right in U.S. politics, and around President Richard Nixon's 1972 "law and order" campaign discourse that took the place of overt racial appeals.[30] The Christian right also galvanized around opposition to the feminist movement, to gay rights, to abortion rights, to prohibition of school prayer, and in favor of the traditional patriarchal family. These "social issues" became the cutting edge of the so-called culture wars as a counterpart to the rising neo-liberal corporate agenda.

The most significant event in the consolidation of a politicized Christian right was the creation of the Moral Majority, also in 1979, which disseminated the Christian right's messages nationwide through Jerry Falwell's television network and began campaigns to register religious voters and encourage them to vote against liberal candidates.[31] The most important aspect of the Moral Majority was its role in the fusion of the Christian right with an emerging political far right, housed largely in the right wing of the Republican Party. Ronald Reagan's election to the presidency resulted in the consolidation of the Christian Right's role in the Republican Party, with a correspondingly decisive influence on future Republican Party platforms.

But the identification of a right-wing Christian fundamentalism with a political neo-fascist right lodged in the Republican Party – and in state institutions – reached a crescendo during the years of the presidency of George W. Bush, himself a declared "born-again Christian." A glimpse of the truly fascist nature of this fundamentalist movement became notoriously memorialized in the chilling 2006 documentary by filmmakers Heidi Ewing and Rachel Grady, *Jesus Camp*, which depicted evangelical Christian kids being trained as young soldiers in "God's Army" at a summer camp in North Dakota and being taught that they can "take back America for Christ" (in one scene, a cardboard cut-out of George W. Bush is presented to the children, who react by laying their hands on the figure and prostrating themselves as though in a religious procession).

The long-term politicization of U.S. Christian conservatives, and their increasingly entrenched influence in the Republican Party, has led some observers to see the Christian right as a centerpiece of a potential U.S. neo-fascism. Chris Hedges describes a fast-spreading network of influence in grassroots civil society through a rapidly rising and highly influential current known as "dominionism," which at the level of doctrine takes its name from Genesis 1:26–31, where God gives human beings "dominion" over all creation, and at the level of

---

[30] This section is a summary version of Mario Barrera and William I. Robinson, "The Christian Right, the Republican Party, and the Prospect of an American Neofascism," unpublished manuscript/work-in-progress, available by request to the authors, mbarrera@yahoo.com and wirobins@soc.ucsb.edu.

[31] Donald K. Williams, *God's Own Party* (New York: Oxford, 2010), 177ff.

politics calls for the radical right church to take political power and to replace secular law with biblical law. According to Hedges:

> Dominionism, born out of a theology known as Christian reconstructionism, seeks to politicize faith. It has, like all fascist movements, a belief in magic along with leadership adoration and a strident call for moral and physical supremacy of a master race, in this case American Christians.... It teaches that American Christians have been mandated by God to make America a Christian State.... America becomes, in this militant Biblicism, an agent of God, and all political and intellectual opponents of America's Christian leaders are viewed ... as agents of Satan.... Labor unions, civil-rights laws and public schools will be abolished.[32]

Meanwhile, the Tea Party movement exploded onto the U.S. political scene in early 2009 in the wake of Obama's election and has significant overlap with the Christian right and with other neo-fascist movements, especially the anti-immigrant movement.[33] The Tea Party is not just one organization. In fact, at the time of writing (early 2013) there were six major groupings. One was the *Tea Party Express*, which has supported Sarah Palin, has funded far-right Republican candidates for office, engages in anti-Islam activism, and promotes the "birthers" – the movement claiming that Obama was born abroad and is therefore legally prohibited from being president. A second was *Freedom Works*, which is heavily funded by corporate donors and provides support to its preferred right-wing candidates and to anti-immigrant activists. A third was *Tea Party Patriots*, a grassroots group claiming over 2,000 local chapters. The Patriots call for a repeal of the Sixteenth Amendment to the U.S. Constitution (which established the income tax), espouses a vitriolic anti-immigrant position, and is close to right-wing militia groups and such racist organizations as the Ku Klux Klan. Fourth was the *Tea Party Nation*, which organized a conference in 2010 featuring Sarah Palin and has strong ties to the Christian right, the "birthers," and the anti-immigrant movement. Fifth was the *Resistnet Tea Party*, which focuses on internet and social network organizing to push an anti-abortion, pro–traditional marriage, anti-immigrant, anti-Islamic, and anti-multicultural agenda. It also has overlapping membership with the Minutemen – the virulently anti-immigrant paramilitary hate group. Sixth was the *1776 Tea Party*, which also overlaps with the Minuteman and the Christian right.

---

[32] Chris Hedges, *American Fascists: The Christian Right and the War on America* (New York: Free Press, 2006), 10–12.

[33] Peter Montgomery, "The Tea Party and Religious Right Movements: Frenemies with Benefits," *paper presented at the Conference on the Tea Party Movement*, University of California at Berkeley, October 22, 2010: 9–10. Polling data presented by Montgomery shows that "47 percent of those who consider themselves part of the Tea Party movement, and 57 percent of Tea Partiers who identify as Christians, say they are also part of the Christian conservative or Religious Right movement."

Heavily funded by the Koch brothers, who in turn raise funds from a broad array of corporate donors, the Tea Party combines a program perfectly-suited to the transnational corporate agenda with an utterly irrational, fanatically anti-Obama, and often bizarre discourse about a secret "socialist plot" to take over the United States and about the need to restore a mythical past – cloaked in codes – of patriarchy, white supremacy, and the restoration of middle-class stability and conservative community. The Tea Party's programmatic themes include tax cuts for the rich and for corporations; lifting environmental and other government regulations on business; cutting and privatizing social services, including Social Security; anti-unionism, and especially attacks on public employee unions; and anti-immigrant attacks – and beyond them, a broader anti-Latino, antiblack, and antigay discourse, although often coded.

An overwhelmingly white movement, the Tea Party is the voice of the vulnerable Christian white lower and middle classes whose world is in crisis and collapsing around them. Their race/ethnic-based social privileges no longer provide protection against the ravages of global capitalism, and in response they are attempting to retreat into a soothing fortress of rage and alignment with the Christian right, with other neo-fascist organizations, and with an ideological fanaticism and moral absolutism promoted by their corporate sponsors. When decoded, Tea Party calls to "take back the country" should be read as taking back the caste privileges that Tea Partiers feel they have lost as a result of the breakdown of the traditional white race/culture supremacy that have underpinned those privileges. Tea Party rallies and Christian right events exude mass popular enthusiasm as well as anger characteristic of a neo-fascist movement that cannot be written off as manipulation by capital and the reactionary right.

The irrationality and lunatic claims of Tea Party members – for example, the claim that the Barack Obama presidency is both a socialist and a fascist conspiracy – bear some resemblance to the deep structures of what Fromm and the Frankfurt School termed the "authoritarian personality," including anti-intellectualism, anti-intraception, cynicism, and renunciation of critical inquiry and reflexivity.[34] Unlike the Frankfurt School's famous 1950 study, however, I would characterize such a personality structure not as a psychopathology originating in childhood experience as much as one induced by the ingrained authoritarianism of the hegemonic cultural and political order and its tendency toward irrational displacement of social anxiety. In an authoritarian hegemonic order those destabilized by crisis are more susceptible to interpretations of the causes of insecurity and anxiety put forth by dominant cultural and political agents, or organic intellectuals of ruling groups, even though such groups may be far from unified in terms of the discourses they advance.

---

[34] Theodor W. Adorno, Else Frenkel-Brunswik, Daniel J. Levinson, and R. Nevitt Sanford, *The Authoritarian Personality* (New York: W.W. Norton, 1993 [1950]).

"Anxieties, worries, concerns, discontents which ... have found not constant or clarifying articulation ... [do] not just disappear," observe Hall and his colleagues. "The impulse to articulate ... turns back on itself, and provides the seed-bed of 'social movements' which are collectively powerful even as they are deeply irrational, irrational to the point at least where any due measure is lost between actual threat perceived, the symbolic danger imagined, and the scale of punishment and control which is 'required'." But – and this is key – this defense of the traditional worldview, with its appropriate scapegoats, does not take place by magic: "The necessary connections have to be made, publicly forged and articulated – the sense of bitterness described by Seabrook has to be worked on to come to identify its scapegoats. Ideological work is necessary to maintain the articulation of the subordinate class experience with the dominant ideology. ... The devils do, indeed, have to be *summoned* [emphasis in original]."[35]

Nonetheless, The Tea Party, the Christian fundamentalist, patriot, and other far-right movements cannot be reduced to a displacement of the fear among white workers and middle-class layers to economic and social destabilization or to an effort to retain the "racial bribe," that is, "skin privilege." These instances represent an *authentic* rebellion against the destabilizing effects of capitalist globalization and crisis. There is a more deeply structured rebellion within the logic or the frame of reference of the dominant system. For this is the way in which hegemony functions; it establishes the outer bounds of opposition to the social order without the logical structure of that order, so that even though ideas may vary, their underlying structure becomes "common sense" – taken-for-granted assumptions about the world and its nature. Here we want to be clear that such "commonsense" assumptions do not represent a "false consciousness" (and it is worth noting that Marx *never* used such a phrase and that Gramsci, for his part, insisted that exploited classes have *not* a *false* but a *contradictory consciousness*). It is absolutely true that dominant ideas are grounded in the relations of material domination. As Marx noted long ago in *The German Ideology*:

> The ideas of the ruling class are in every epoch the ruling ideas, i.e. the class which is the ruling material force of society, is at the same time its ruling intellectual force. The class which has the means of material production at its disposal has control at the same time over the means of mental production, so that thereby, generally speaking, the ideas of those who lack the means of mental production are subject to it. The ruling ideas are nothing more than the ideal expression of the dominant material relationships, the dominant material relationships grasped as ideas; hence of the relationships which make the one class the ruling one, therefore, the ideas of its dominance. The individuals composing the ruling class possess among other things consciousness, and therefore think. Insofar, therefore, as they rule as a class and determine the extent and compass of an epoch, it is self-evident that they do this in its whole range, hence among other things rule also as thinkers, as producers of ideas,

[35] Hall et al., *Policing The Crisis*, 162.

and regulate the production and distribution of the ideas of their age: thus their ideas are the ruling ideas of the epoch.[36]

Yet the content of material social experiences that informs subordinate value systems is, in fact, very different from that which is expressed in "ruling ideas." This structured difference is concealed and harmonized under the tutelage of the dominant framework. It is through this unequal complimentarity that the hegemony of dominant ideas over subordinate ones is sustained. This complimentarity is the basis for *cross-class* alliances, where subordinate attitudes are mobilized and made active in support of interests and attitudes that reflect a quite different, antagonistic class reality. Hall and his colleagues observe, in this regard: "The world bounded by 'common sense' is the world of the subordinate classes. For the subordinate classes, ruling ideas tend to be equated with the whole structure of ideas as *such*. This does not mean that working class people 'think' the world with the same ideas as the ruling classes. . . . Subordinate classes maintain their autonomy, by struggle and by establishing their own defensive culture." But, *and this is the essence of hegemony as consensual domination*, "ruling ideas tend to form the outer limit and horizon of thought in a society. This is never simply a matter of mental subordination alone. Ruling ideas are embodied in the dominant institutional order; subordinate classes are bound by these dominant relations. Hence, in action as well as in thought, they are constantly disciplined by them."[37] The significance of these observations will become clear as we move forward through the next few sections.

SURPLUS LABOR, RACISM, SCAPEGOATS, AND THE NEW CONCENTRATION CAMPS: THE SOCIAL BASES OF TWENTY-FIRST-CENTURY FASCISM

One new structural dimension of twenty-first-century global capitalism is the dramatic expansion of the global superfluous population – that portion marginalized and locked out of productive participation in the capitalist economy and constituting some one-third of humanity.[38] To summarize what I argued in Chapter 1, crises provide capital with the opportunity to accelerate the process of forcing greater productivity out of fewer workers, and the processes by which surplus labor is generated have accelerated under globalization. Spatial reorganization has helped transnational capital to break the power of territorial-bound organized labor and to impose new capital-labor relations based on the fragmentation, flexibilization, and cheapening of labor. These developments,

---

[36] Karl Marx, *The German Ideology*, as cited in extracts published in Robert C. Tucker, ed., *The Marx-Engels Reader*, 2nd ed. (New York: W.W. Norton, 1978), 172–173.

[37] Hall et al., *Policing the Crisis*, 154, 156.

[38] The ILO reported that in the late twentieth century some one-third of the global labor force was unemployed. International Labor Organization (ILO), *World Employment Report 1996–97* (Geneva: ILO/United Nations, 1997).

combined with a massive new round of primitive accumulation and displacement, have given rise to a new global army of superfluous labor that goes well beyond what is traditionally considered a Reserve Army of Labor.

This mass of "supernumeraries" is of no *direct* use to capital. In the larger picture, however, such surplus labor is crucial to global capitalism insofar as it places downward pressure on wages everywhere – especially to the extent that global labor markets can be tapped and labor can be mobilized throughout the global economy – and allows transnational capital to impose discipline over those who remain active in the labor market. On the other hand, unrest, spontaneous rebellion, and organized political mobilization among the structurally unemployed and marginalized pose a potential threat to the system and must be controlled and contained. Criminalization and militarized control of the structurally marginalized is one major mechanism of preemptive containment. This drive to contain real or potential rebellion springing from the mass of the dispossessed and disenfranchised in twenty-first-century fascism replaces, in some respects, the drive to crush socialism springing from an organized working class that helped drive twentieth-century fascism. The state responds to those expelled from the labor market and locked out of productive labor not with expanded social welfare and protection but with abandonment and with repressive social control and containment strategies, including a *racialized* criminalization and the mobilization of the culture industries to dehumanize the victims of global capitalism as dangerous, depraved, and culturally degenerate Others, as criminal elements posing a threat to society.

In their classic 1978 study, *Policing the Crisis*, Stuart Hall and his colleagues show how the restructuring of capitalism in response to crisis led in the 1970s in the United Kingdom (and elsewhere) to an "exceptional state" characterized by an ongoing breakdown of consensual mechanisms of social order and an increasing authoritarianism.[39] They highlight, in particular, the highly racialized nature of policing and the criminalization of black and immigrant communities, deconstructing the complex ideological process of fabricating the criminalization of oppressed populations in function of social control. Here we see strong parallels between the incipient exceptional state in the UK in the 1970s and the current drift toward such a state in the United States (and elsewhere). In particular, we see the ideological and cultural construction of the "criminal" and the subsequent legitimation by the hegemonic discourse of criminalization as a process of racial and ethnic displacement of social tensions in times of crisis. This displacement of social anxieties to crime and a racialized "criminal" population in the United States dates back to the crisis of the 1970s. In the wake of the civil rights and black liberation movements, dominant groups promoted systematic cultural and ideological "law-and-order" campaigns as a way to legitimate the shift from a social welfare to a social control state and the rise of a prison-industrial complex. "Law and order" came to mean reconstructing and reinforcing racial hierarchies and

[39] Hall et al., *Policing the Crisis*.

hegemonic social order in the wake of the rebellions of the 1960s. Criminalization helped to displace social anxieties resulting from the disruption of stability, security, and social organization generated by the crisis onto a nonreflexive attribution of such destabilization to crime and an identification of crime with racially oppressed groups.

There developed multilayered associations of insecurity with hegemonic interpretations (often outright discursive constructions) of a series of phenomena – crime, terrorism, the empowerment of previously subordinate groups, and so forth. Moral panics are seen sociologically as intense collective sentiments over issues that are perceived to threaten the social order. But which issues are perceived as threatening the social order (and which threatening issues disappear from public perception) is not a chance process; these issues are socially constructed by powerful agents in the media, the state, and civil society. Moral panics serve to reorganize public opinion and "common sense" in ways that deflect attention from the sources of disruption and insecurity. Instead, caricatured and stereotypical "folk devils," to use the term coined by the sociologist Stanley Cohen in his classic 1972 study, *Folk Devils and Moral Panics*, are conjured up to focus the anxieties of a community.[40] Hall and his colleagues observe that "public opinion" about crime does not simply form up at random:

> It exhibits a shape and structure. It follows a sequence. It is a social process. Crime talk is not socially innocent. . . . The more such an issue passes into the public domain, via the media, the more it is structured by the dominant ideologies about crime. The more a crime issues on the public stage, the more highly structured it becomes, the more constrained by the available frameworks of understanding and interpretation, the more socially validated feelings, emotions, and attitudes are mobilized around it. Thus the more public – the more of a public issue – a topic becomes, the more we can detect the presence of larger networks of meaning and feeling about it; the more we can discern the presence of a highly structured, though by no means complete, or coherent, or internally consistent, set of *ideologies about crime.* . . . The intimate connection between the sources of crime news (the courts and the control culture) and the means of public dissemination (the media) served powerfully to structure and mould public knowledge about crime, and at the same time *to inflect that understanding with 'dominant interpretations'. . . . that is, 'public opinion' is something 'structured in dominance'* [first emphasis in original, second is mine].[41]

Reconstructing Hegemony around a "Law-and-Order" Police State

Hegemony in the Gramscian sense has to do with fundamental contradictions in the structure of capitalist relations. Hegemony ultimately secures the social conditions for the reproduction of capital. In Gramsci's words, it is the "theater" in which conflicts among social and class forces work themselves out as the

[40] Stanley Cohen, *Folk Devils and Moral Panics* (New York: Routledge, 2002 [1973]).
[41] Hall et al., *Policing the Crisis*, 136.

correlations of power among these forces become reaccomodated on an ongoing basis. The crisis of hegemony of the 1960s and 1970s, as we have seen, was "resolved" by the global restructuring of capitalism – but not just in terms of productive restructuring, global expansion, and new "flexible" capital-labor relations. This resolution also involved restructuring at the political, cultural, and ideological levels, inducing a shift from fight to flight (escapism, depoliticization) through consumerism and stoking multiple desires; multicultural identity politics; and a more thorough corporate penetration of cultural production and the mass media. There was a shift from consensual to more coercive modes of social control, for instance, in the spheres of policing and the legal and penal systems. In the United States, the right-wing offensive involved the expansion of the police state and the prison-industrial complex legitimated by the above-mentioned campaigns for "law and order" that eventually crystallized around the "war on drugs," launched all-out in the 1980s by the Reagan administration as "legitimate force" by the state.

Alexander notes that a huge majority of people in the United States did not identify drugs as a significant problem in the early 1980s.[42] Thus a "moral panic" had to be created, and it was. This "moral panic" involved the construction of blacks as drug criminals and of the "undeserving" poor. "To put it crudely," state Hall and his colleagues, "the 'moral panic' appears ... to be one of the principal forms of ideological consciousness by means of which a 'silent majority' is won over to the support of increasingly coercive measures on the part of the state, and lends its legitimacy to a 'more than usual' exercise of control."[43] The declared "war on drugs" and the "war on terrorism" as well as the undeclared war on immigrants, gangs, and youth clearly achieved the generation of moral panics for this purpose. "There is indeed in the latter stages" of a shift toward an exceptional state "a 'mapping together' of moral panics into a *general panic* about social order, and such a spiral has tended ... to culminate in ... a 'law and order' campaign," Hall and his colleagues continue. Such panics "now tend to operate from top to bottom" and effectively sensitize "the social control apparatuses and the media to the possibility of a general threat to the stability of the state. Minor forms of dissent seem to provide the basis of 'scapegoat' events for a jumpy and alerted control culture; and this progressively pushes the state apparatuses into a more or less permanent 'control' posture."[44]

The conservative backlash against radical black and working-class mobilization paved the way for the "war on drugs," launched in October 1982, which

---

[42] Michelle Alexander, *The New Jim Crow: Mass Incarceration in the Age of Color Blindness* (New York: New Press, 2010).

[43] Hall et al., *Policing the Crisis*, 221. They add: "The actual ideological passage into a 'law and order' society entails a process of a quite specific kind. Crucially, in the early years of our period, it is sustained by what we call a displacement effect: the connection between the crisis and the way it is appropriated in the social experience of the majority – social anxiety – passes through a series of false 'resolutions,' primarily taking the shape of a succession *of moral panics*" (322).

[44] Hall et al., *Policing the Crisis*, 222.

began the process of mass incarceration. This process coincided with an unprecedented surge in Latino immigration – the importance of which will become clear later. Alexander notes that "practically overnight the budgets of federal law enforcement agencies soared," increasing between 1980 and 1984 by over 1,000 percent for the FBI and the Drug Enforcement Agency (DEA) and by 3,000 percent for the Pentagon's war-on-drugs activity.[45] Between this launching of the "war on drugs" and 2010, the U.S. penal population soared from some 300,000 to close to 2.5 million, with drug convictions accounting for the majority of this increase. The United States came to have the highest rate of incarceration in the world and had a larger percentage of its black population caged than did South Africa at the height of apartheid – and, in fact, more black people were under the control of the penal system in 2010 than were enslaved in 1850, on the eve of the U.S. Civil War.[46]

The "war on drugs" ushered in a domestic militarization that expanded exponentially with the "war on terrorism." Thirty million people were arrested for drug offenses from 1982 to 2010, and the number of those imprisoned for these offenses increased by 1,100 percent. By 2007 more than seven million people were behind bars, on probation, or on parole, and some 650,000 were being released from prison annually. Roughly 65 million people now have criminal records, many of them given a social death sentences for life (see the following discussion). The conversion of the African American population into a tightly controlled mass of surplus labor cannot be overemphasized. Those swept up into the penal system are not included in employment figures. During the 1990s, 42 percent of noncollege black men were unemployed, and the figure was 65 percent among those who had not earned a high school degree.[47] While poor whites are victims of the drug war as well, studies show that people of all colors *use and sell* drugs at remarkably similar rates; if anything, according to the data, white youth are more likely to engage in drug crime than people from racially and ethnically oppressed groups. Yet in some states, Alexander points out, black men have been sent to prison on drug charges at rates twenty to fifty times greater than those of white men, and in major cities as many as 80 percent of young African Americans have criminal records and are thus subject to legalized discrimination for the rest of their lives.[48]

Among the many studies of the rise of a prison-industrial complex in the United States, Ruth Wilson Gilmore, in *Golden Gulag*, shows how California, perhaps the epicenter of the strategy of mass incarceration, has led the way in "the biggest prison building project in the history of the world." The number of people in U.S. prisons has skyrocketed despite a steady fall in crime rates. The

---

[45] Alexander, *The New Jim Crow*, 49. I have calculated these percentages on the basis of data provided by Alexander.
[46] Ibid., 6, 180.
[47] Ibid., 60, 147–148, 229.
[48] Ibid., 7.

defeat of radical struggles alongside the accumulation of surplus capital has led
to a strategy of caging surplus labor, made up of young people from racially and
ethnically oppressed groups ("people of color"),[49] in vast disproportion to the
population at large.[50] Gilmore demonstrates the correlation between the expansion of unemployment or relative surplus population and the massive increase in
the prison population, emphasizing, however, that this caged population has
grown much more rapidly than has unemployment.

Gilmore notes that about a million people in California, most of them blacks
and Latinos, were locked into isolated enclaves by virtue of being locked out
elsewhere as capitalist restructuring proceeded from the 1970s onward. "In the
rubble of extensive restructuring," she notes, "individuals and families have
developed alternative modes of social reproduction, given their utter abandonment by capital. These modes include informal economic structures for the
exchange of illegal and legal goods and services; social parenting, especially by
women, in extended families of biological and fictive kin; and the redivision of
urban spaces into units controlled by street organizations."[51] The criminalization of these alternative modes of social reproduction is not coincidental, and, as
Graham so disturbingly demonstrates, these urban spaces have become veritable
militarized war zones under the total and violent control of the state's repressive
apparatuses.[52] "African-American neighborhoods are usually cast as patholog-
ical places inhabited by non-white criminals, drug dealers and threatening
Others," notes Graham. These populations "are widely portrayed as shadowy
and monstrous, lurking beyond the normalized, mainly white and prosperous
exurban and suburban fringe. Although largely invisible in such locales, they
nonetheless pose a threat, and thus create a need for a massive ratcheting up of
fortification, militarization, securitization, and access control to generate feel-
ings of security among the white elites or middle class."[53] At the same time,
prisons depersonalize social control, "so that it could be bureaucratically managed across time and space," notes Gilmore, achieving in this way "partial
geographic solutions to political economic crises, organized by the state, which
is itself in crisis."[54]

As I discussed in Chapter 3, Neil Smith refers to the structural determinants of
the flow of capital through urban land as contradictory processes of centralization and equalization, in order to show how the movement of "capital rather

[49] The reader will note that I do not use the phrase "people of color." I am averse to this phrase for
    reasons I cannot take up here. I use the phrase "racially and/or ethnically oppressed peoples."
[50] Ruth Wilson Gilmore, *Golden Gulag: Prisons, Surplus, Crisis, and Opposition in Globalizing
    California* (Berkeley: University of California Press, 2007). See also, inter alia, Tara Herivel and
    Paul Wright, eds., *Prison Nation: The Warehousing of America's Poor* (New York: Routledge,
    2003); Alexander, *The New Jim Crow*.
[51] Gilmore, *Golden Gulag*, 74.
[52] Graham, *Cities under Siege*.
[53] Ibid., 45.
[54] Ibid., 11.

than people" is the leading indicator whose sociopolitical symptoms include both gentrification and what Gilmore terms "official racial class war" created through criminalization and policing.[55] In response to the mass struggles that began in the 1960s, state and capitalist discourse turned to delegitimizing the redistribution of income via the Keynesian welfare state, which involved, among other things, a regressive shift in the tax structure. This helped to generate state fiscal crises that were then used to further legitimate dismantling the social wage. In the wake of the general crisis of the early 1970s, surpluses were channeled by the state into the prison expansion project, resolving both the state's problem of "surplus capacity" and capital's problem of how to profitably unload surpluses in new accumulation activities, and removing surplus labor from the population. Finance capital, in particular, played a key role by investing in state and municipal bonds that raised funds for the expansion project. California alone constructed twenty-three major new prisons between 1983 and 2004 at a cost of $280–$350 million apiece; the state had built only twelve prisons between 1852 and 1964.[56] The state racked up an incredible 1,200 new pieces of criminal legislation, including "three strikes" laws and "gang injunctions," this latter part of a war on youth (especially poor black and Latino youth) that I am unable to discuss here.`

The turn to a "law-and-order" police state coincided with capitalist globalization, neo-liberalism, and the incipient dismantling of the welfare state. Far from coincidental, these two processes were mutually reinforcing and part of a singular project of reconstituting the mechanisms of social control and shifting the hegemonic discourse. In the late 1960s and early 1970s organic intellectuals in and out of the academy developed "cultural deficit" or "culture of poverty" theories. These theories advanced the proposition that the attributes of the poor – in particular, their cultural and behavior patterns – explain poverty and unemployment and that an end to these conditions would have to involve a modification of such attributes. This ideological construct expunged from the analysis racism and the larger social forces of power, inequality, and marginalization in attempting to explain the poverty of oppressed groups such as African Americans. One version of the thesis, dual labor market theory as elaborated by its more conservative adherents, the economists Peter Doeringer and Michael Piore, concluded that African Americans constituted a poorly rewarded and marginalized sector of the labor force because of their own cultural underdevelopment.[57] Hence, these groups constituted an "undeserving" poor who were engaged in social pathologies of crime, illegal drug use, and delinquency.

---

[55] Neil Smith, *The New Urban Frontier: Gentrification and the Revanchist City* (New York: Routledge, 1996), 70. See Gilmore, *Golden Gulag*, 64, for her discussion.

[56] Gilmore, *Golden Gulag*, 7.

[57] Peter Doeringer and Michael Piore, *Internal Labor Markets and Manpower Analysis* (Lexington: D. C. Heath and Company, 1971).

This ideological construct became a rationale for dismantling social services and rationalizing unemployment, particularly among blacks, reciprocal to the "law and order" campaign and efforts to generate a consensus around mass incarceration. Crime and welfare, referred to incessantly in racially coded language, were two of President Reagan's major domestic themes. He spoke of "welfare queens" and suggested that the food stamp program allowed "some fellow ahead of you to buy a T-bone steak [while] you were standing in a checkout line with your package of hamburger." He declared that the criminal is "a staring face – a face that belongs to a frightening reality of our time: the face of the human predator."[58] Yet we must be clear: there was no reduction in state resources directed to the poor; these resources were simply transferred from social spending to repressive social control of the poor. During the tenure of President Bill Clinton, for instance, funding for public housing was slashed by 61 percent and spending for the construction of prisons increased by 171 percent – "effectively making the construction of prisons," notes Alexander, "the nation's main housing program for the urban poor." And in the state of Illinois, there were more black men in prison just on drug charges than the total number of black men enrolled in institutions of higher education.[59]

Social Cleansing of the Poor; Racial and Ethnic Cleansing of Blacks and Latinos

A twenty-first-century fascism in the United States would have historical roots in the country's particular history of racialized class relations and religious evangelism, which have been central to the development of capitalism in the country. Historic blocs based on hegemonic domination, in order to achieve any stability, must involve material incentives for, and concessions to, those from the subordinate classes brought into the bloc. White labor in the United States, which has historically enjoyed caste privilege within racially and ethnically segmented labor markets, has experienced under capitalist globalization downward mobility, flexibilization, and heightened insecurity. This loss of caste privilege is problematic for political elites and state managers, since legitimation and domination have historically been constructed through a white racial hegemonic bloc. Organic intellectuals of the dominant groups operating in political and civil society have attempted to reconstruct such a bloc through, among other processes, the resubordination of the black population through criminalization and mass incarceration, the scapegoating of immigrant communities along with Muslims and other oppressed racial and ethnic groups, and by trying to draw in white workers with appeals to racial solidarity, xenophobia, and national chauvinism (the "nation" conceived as

---

[58] These citations appear in Alexander, *The New Jim Crow*, 49.
[59] Ibid., 57, 190.

white, Christian, and English-speaking) and through the outright, incessant manipulation of fear.[60]

These ideological campaigns obscure the sources of social deprivation. Combined with seduction into petty consumption and fantasy as an alternative to placing social or political demands on the system through mobilization, they channel the insecurities associated with capitalist globalization onto the marginalized groups. Within the nation-state these marginalized and/or superexploited groups become scapegoats that serve to symbolically condense and then redirect disorganization and destabilization anxieties and help the political representatives of the ruling groups to organize electoral coalitions and construct consensus around the new order (e.g., anti-immigrant and get-tough-on-crime campaigns). Internationally, the Third World victims of abandonment – viz, Somalia, Haiti, the Congo – are portrayed, at best, as passive and incompetent victims eliciting paternal sympathy, if not as inferiors to be dismissed and relegated to death and oblivion. Manipulation of economic crises in these ways helps channel mass frustrations and insecurity into highly coded racism, anti-immigrant sentiment, and so on, which deflects attention from the real causes of crisis.

As the level of anger and fear among the traditional, largely white working class and middle strata reaches unprecedented levels, what Hage calls a "psychopathology of white decline"[61] obscures the class dimensions of the crisis and lends itself to this scapegoating. What takes place is "nothing less than the synchronization of the race and the class aspects of the crisis," note Hall and his colleagues. "Policing the *blacks* [here "blacks" is a stand-in for the collective Other] threatened to mesh with the problem of policing the *poor* and policing the *unemployed*: all three were concentrated in precisely the same urban areas. ... The ongoing problem of policing the blacks had become, for all practical purposes, synonymous with the wider problem of *policing the crisis*" (emphases in original).[62] Those occasions when there is a radical discrepancy between the nature of the "threat" and the scale of "containment," or when the incidence of certain kinds of crime does appear, suddenly, to increase or assume a *new* pattern, or when the pace of legal repression and control rapidly increases – they observe – "coincide with moments of a wider historical significance than is contained by the play of normalized repression over the structure of normalized crime," an observation quite apropos to the discussion at hand. "Such moments of 'more than usual alarm' followed by the exercise of 'more than usual control' have signaled, time and again in the past, periods of profound social upheaval, of economic crisis and historical rupture."[63]

---

[60] See, generally on this topic, William I. Robinson, "Aqui Estamos y No Nos Vamos: Global Capital and Immigrant Rights, *Race and Class* (2006), 48(2): 77–91.

[61] Ghassan Hage, *White Nation: Fantasies of White Supremacy in a Multicultural Society* (New York: Routledge, 2000), 9.

[62] Hall et al., *Policing the Crisis*, 332.

[63] Ibid., 186.

Racism, and race itself as an historically constructed social category, cannot be separated from capitalist exploitation. Moreover, if race cannot be reduced to or subsumed into class, neither can it be seen as separate from class. It is *neither an immanent nor an organic category*. It has no existence independent of class. A reified notion of race as having some independent existence is widespread, both in mass consciousness and in the academic literature. There is a systematic conflation of culture with biology, on the one hand, and a conception of culture that is itself reified, on the other hand. These reifications become etched into the mass consciousness and, regrettably, into the dominant scholarly paradigms.[64] Class organization has been historically effected through racial stratification and the application of distinct forms of labor exploitation, state control, and institutional discrimination to distinct segments of the laboring masses, along with cultural, ideological, and even psychological processes, such as sublimation, associated with a racialized and racist social formation. The correct object of inquiry is *racialized class relations*.

The two dominant paradigms in the sociological literature on race and racism (especially in typically insular U.S. sociology), the "assimilationist paradigm" and "racial formation" theory, are deeply wanting on this count. As Greene notes, both emphasize the ideological and cultural construction of race and/or the formation of racial meaning and identity over the historical-structural roots of race and its material impacts. By extracting race from its historical origins in the accumulation of capital (especially through colonialism and imperialism) and its contemporary reproduction in capitalist exploitation, both formulations in the end reduce racial domination to discriminatory beliefs and behavior; they are at a complete loss to explain why certain attitudes and not others become a material force.[65] *Race*, As Hall and his colleagues assert, *is the lived experience of class*. I concur with their following statement, with the caveat that what they refer to as "black" can be generalized to racially and ethnically oppressed groups in the global capitalist system:

> [T]he general way in which class position and the division of labor is reproduced for the working class as a whole assumes a specific and differentiated form in relation to the stratum of black labor. There are specific mechanisms that serve to reproduce what almost appears to be a 'racial division of labor' within, and as a structural feature of, the general division of labor. Not only are these mechanisms race-specific; they have a differentiated impact on the different sexes and generations within the black labor force. Thus they serve to underpin and support the political fragmentation of the class into racially segmented classes or class fractions, and to set them in competition with one another. It is therefore important to see race itself as a structural feature of the position and reproduction of this black [and Latino

[64] I concur with Barrera that ethnicity is a more comprehensive concept that does not lend itself to such confusion and reification. Although I cannot take up the matter here, see Mario Barrera, "Are Latinos a Racialized Minority?," *Sociological Perspectives* (2008), 51(2): 305–324.

[65] I agree in this regard with the critique advanced by Kyra R. Greene, "Why We Need More Marxism in the Sociology of Race," *Souls: A Critical Journal of Black Politics* (2011), 13(2): 149–174.

immigrant, etc.] labor force – as well as an experiential category of the consciousness of the class. Race, for the black labor force, is a critical structure of the social order of contemporary capitalism.[66]

In her shocking expose of "the new Jim Crow," the U.S. law professor and civil rights activist Michelle Alexander documents how mass incarceration in the United States has emerged "as a stunningly comprehensive and well-disguised system of racialized social control." The entire collection of institutions and practices that comprise the criminal justice system functions as a *gateway* into a much larger system of racial stigmatization and permanent marginalization. Indeed, the racialized nature of the drug wars, caging, and social death sentences is so blatant that it shocks the senses. Human Rights Watch reported in 2000 that in seven states, African Americans constitute 80 to 90 percent of all drug offenders sent to prison. In at least fifteen states, blacks are admitted to prison on drug charges at a rate from twenty to fifty-seven times greater than that of white men. In fact, nationwide, the rate of incarceration for African American drug offenders dwarfs the rate for whites. When the war on drugs gained full steam in the mid-1980s, prison admissions for African Americans skyrocketed, nearly quadrupling in three years, and then increased steadily before reaching in 2000 a level *more than twenty-six times* the level in 1983. Whites have been admitted to prison for drug offenses at increased rates as well – the number of whites admitted for drug offenses in 2000 was eight times the number admitted in 1983 – but their relative numbers are small compared to blacks' or Latinos'. Although the majority of drug users and dealers nationwide are white, three-fourths of all people imprisoned for drug offenses have been black or Latino.[67]

Mass incarceration made "legal" by the war on drugs is a frighteningly effective system for sweeping up surplus labor, fragmenting the communities from which this labor comes, locking up those captured in cages, and then sentencing them to permanent social death upon release, thereby generating conditions that, at the very least, make collective rebellion many times more difficult. Virtually all constitutionally protected civil liberties have been undermined by the drug war. U.S. courts have approved mandatory drug testing of employees and students, upholding random searches and sweeps of public schools and students, permitting police to obtain search warrants based on anonymous informants' tips, expanding the government's wiretapping authority, legitimating the use of unidentified paid informants by police and prosecutors, approving the use of helicopter surveillance of homes without a warrant, and allowing the forfeiture of cash, homes, and other property based on unproven allegations of illegal drug activity, explains Alexander.[68]

"The term mass incarceration refers not only to the criminal justice system but also to the larger web of laws, rules, policies, and customs that control those

---

[66] Hall et al., *Policing the Crisis*, 345.
[67] Alexander, *The New Jim Crow*, 98.
[68] Ibid., 62.

labeled criminal both in and out of prison. Once released, former prisoners enter a hidden underworld of legalized discrimination and permanent social exclusion."[69] In what amounts to *social and civic death*, the incarcerated, once released, are subject to legalized discrimination in employment, housing, education, public benefits, and jury service. In many states they are also denied the right to vote in the same way the earlier apartheid system known as Jim Crow achieved this disenfranchisement and discrimination. "These laws operate collectively to ensure that the vast majority of convicted offenders will never integrate into mainstream, white society. They will be discriminated against, legally, for the rest of their lives – denied employment, housing, education, and public services. Unable to surmount these obstacles, most will eventually return to prison and then be released again, caught in a closed circuit of perpetual marginality."[70] Alexander concludes:

> What has changed since the collapse of Jim Crow has less to do with the basic structure of society than with the language we use to justify it. In the era of color-blindness, it is no longer socially permissible to use race, explicitly, as a justification for discrimination, exclusion, and social contempt. ... Rather than rely on race we use our criminal justice system to label people of color 'criminals' and then engage in all the practices we supposedly left behind. Today it is perfectly legal to discriminate against criminals in nearly all the ways that is was once legal to discriminate against African Americans. Once you're labeled a felon, the old forms of discrimination – employment discrimination, housing discrimination, denial of the right to vote, denial of educational opportunity, denial of food stamps and other public benefits, and exclusion from jury service – are suddenly legal. As a criminal you have scarcely more rights, and arguably less respect, than a black man living in Alabama at the height of Jim Crow. We have not ended racial caste in America: we have merely redesigned it.[71]

The "war on drugs" entails rapid and ongoing domestic militarization and, along with it, the particular patterns of militarized accumulation and repressive infrastructure that lend themselves to coercive modes of mass social control. By the 1990s police forces across the United States were acquiring millions of pieces of military equipment from the Pentagon for domestic operations, including aircraft for transporting police units, UH-60 Blackhawk and UH-1 Hewy helicopters (in the 2000s drones were added), M-16 automatic rifles, grenade launchers, bulletproof helmets, night-vision goggles, and even tanks and bazookas. Domestic militarization accelerated with the "war on terrorism." Paramilitary units known as Special Weapons and Tactics (SWAT) teams have been formed in virtually every major U.S. city, first to fight the drug war and then to fight "terrorism." In 1972 there were just a few hundred paramilitary drug raids per year in the United States. By the early 1980s there were 3,000 annual

[69] Ibid., 12–13.
[70] Ibid., 186.
[71] Ibid., 2.

SWAT deployments, by 1996 there were 30,000, and by 2001, on the eve of 9/11, there were 40,000.[72]

As police forces become paramilitary units they move from "community policing" to "military policing." The urban ghettos of the United States become war zones. "[In] drug raids conducted by SWAT teams [often acting on nothing but tips from anonymous informants] ... police blast into people's homes, typically in the middle of the night, throwing grenades, shouting and pointing guns and rifles at anyone inside, often including young children," notes Alexander. "In recent years, dozens of people have been killed by police in the course of these raids, including elderly grandparents and those who are completely innocent of any crime."[73] In what amounts to the military occupation of poor and inner-city communities, nearly everyone in these communities is directly or indirectly affected. "The nature of the criminal justice system has changed. It is no longer concerned primarily with the prevention and punishment of crime, but rather with the management and control of the dispossessed. Prior drug wars were ancillary to the prevailing caste system. This time the drug war *is* the system of control."[74]

These, then, are the *new concentration camps*, those of twenty-first-century fascism in the United States.[75]

Harnessing "White Pathology" into a Would-Be White Racial Hegemonic Bloc

Stepping back to observe the broader picture, the *spurious and entirely contrived* war on drugs was aimed at resubordinating the majority of the black population – the urban poor and working class – while absorbing a black middle and professional class into the hegemonic system through the lifting of legal discrimination, multiculturalism, affirmative action, and diversity policies. This re-subbordination came at a time when labor was rapidly radicalizing and when black labor was becoming the militant vanguard of labor struggles, as epitomized by the formation of the League of Revolutionary Black Workers in 1969. The League called for linking struggles at the workplace with mass community movements and building a movement that could combat capitalism.[76] As crisis gave way to restructuring and globalization, black unemployment both

---

[72] For these details, see various sections in ibid.
[73] Ibid., 74–75.
[74] Ibid., 188.
[75] My conception of historical outcomes is Weberian in inspiration, in that the outcomes discussed here were not (for the most part) the result of any conspiratorial plan or clear intentionality. Rather, certain outcomes fell into place as a configuration of the interactions among distinct processes (including the ways in which capital and the state came together) in the historical conjuncture of the crisis of the 1970s and the responses from dominant groups, in that decade and the ones that followed, to a palpable loss of ideological and political control.
[76] See James A Geschwender, *Class, Race and Worker Insurgency: The League of Revolutionary Black Workers* (New York: Cambridge University Press, 1977).

deepened and became more long-term and structural. Capital began to shift its labor recruitment from black to immigrant, particularly Latino, labor, as we shall see. The African American working class found itself moving from super-exploitation at the bottom rungs of segmented labor markets to expulsion from the labor market, exclusion and marginalization, what Gilmore, among others, terms "abandonment."[77]

The extreme racialized nature of the "war on drugs" as just described suggests that it was aimed, in particular, at control of the black population and may have helped reestablish consent among white working and middle classes. Stated as an ideal type, the system of domination bifurcated, so that coercive domination became, or remained, the principal mode of control with regard to the black and Latino working class and poor, while the reproduction of consent became, or remained, the principal mode with regard to the white population. Indeed, in Gramscian terms, the construction of hegemonic blocs involves material concessions to those subordinate groups brought into the bloc and repression of those unwilling to provide their consent or whom the system is unable or unprepared to materially incorporate. However, this analysis goes only so far because the attempt to construct a neo-liberal historic bloc has severe material limitations in that the mass of white workers as well are downwardly mobile and destabilized under global capitalism. Hegemony – that is, consensual domination – *cannot* be sustained on the basis of ideology and culture alone. The "racial bribe" tends to lose its material foundation. The agents of the social order have attempted to cohere the would-be neo-liberal hegemonic bloc through a reformulation of the racist construct as an outlet for the displacement of social anxieties and insecurities. "Law and order" and racialized criminalization become a mechanism for the social control both of the newly superfluous and marginalized population in the wake of global economic restructuring *and* of the downwardly mobile and flexibilized white working class.

"Crime control" under capitalism largely means the defense of private property and the suppression of any threat, whether direct or indirect, to the system of private property. Criminalization in this context constitutes the normalization of state repression. The "war on drugs" and the mass incarceration it has brought about are clearly out of any proportion to any manifest threat that drug use and distribution represents to the system. Indeed, drugs are a commodity like any other, produced and distributed worldwide just as a transnational corporation organizes its worldwide activities, with the exception that this peculiar commodity is made illegal. The "legal" global economy is actually dependent on the drug trade. U.S. drug consumption helps fuel global drug trafficking as an illegal form of transnational capital accumulation that becomes integrated into legal forms through numerous channels. The United Nations has estimated the annual profits worldwide from drug trafficking at $300–500 billion, that is, 8–10

---

[77] Gilmore, *Golden Gulag*. See also William Julius Wilson, *When Work Disappears: The World of the New Urban Poor* (New York: Vintage, 1997).

percent of world trade. The journalist John Gibler reports in his revealing study, *To Die in Mexico*, that in 2008 drug money saved the major global banks from collapse. According to a United Nations official he cites, a majority of the $352 billion in drug profits that year was absorbed into the economic system and was the only liquid investment capital available to some global banks prior to state bailouts.[78]

Police forces have been granted the authority to keep for their own use the bulk of the cash and assets they seize when waging the drug war and hence develop a vested interest not in its success but in its perpetuation, and in simply targeting any individual, family, or community in order to acquire such assets. This is especially so given that *property and cash can be seized on mere suspicion of drug activity; the seizure can occur without notice or hearing, and even if the property owner is never charged with a crime much less found guilty, he or she is subject to forfeiture.* This becomes even more frightening considering that the full weight of this repression and dispossession can be unleashed merely on suspicion of "probable involvement" in a drug crime, that such suspicion can be legitimated merely by a call from an anonymous tipster, and that "involvement" includes the use of someone's house or other property for a crime even if the individual is unaware or has no direct involvement.[79] In short, *the police as a coercive apparatus of the state develop a vested institutional interest in the profitability of the drug market itself and in unleashing state-organized terrorism against entire communities* – a terrorism that serves the function of removing surplus humanity from society and relegating it to the new concentration camps and social death processes while accumulating capital in the process.[80]

In analytical abstraction, I reiterate, mass incarceration takes the place of concentration camps, insofar as they conjoin with legal changes – such as anti–drug consumption and "three strikes" laws – that criminalize the marginalized, especially youth from racially and ethnically oppressed groups. So-called zero tolerance policies that criminalize and severely punish the slightest violation of a rule or even the suspicion of such violation through twenty-four-hour policing in and out of school have established what critics call a *school-to-prison pipeline*; poor black and Latino youth are channeled from schools, which are often themselves run in highly repressive, authoritarian, and prisonlike conditions, into the prison system, effectively locked away from their adolescent years into middle age and upon release subject to civic death.[81] The system subjects a surplus and potentially rebellious population of millions of people to concentration, caging, and state violence. The so-called (and declared) war on drugs

[78] John Gibler, *To Die in Mexico: Dispatches from Inside the Drug War* (San Francisco: City Lights Books, 2011), 33.
[79] Alexander, *The New Jim Crow*, 78–79.
[80] Ibid., 74–75.
[81] See, e.g., Victor M. Rios, *Policing the Lives of Black and Latino Boys* (New York: New York University Press, 2011).

and war on terrorism, as well as the undeclared "war on gangs," among others, must be placed in this context.

A Reserve Army of Immigrant Labor

During the 1980s eight million Latin American emigrants arrived in the United States as globalization, neo-liberalism, and global labor market restructuring induced a wave of out-migration from Latin America. This was nearly equal to the total number of European immigrants who arrived on U.S. shores during the first decades of the twentieth century, and it made Latin America the principal origin of migration into the United States. Some thirty-six million immigrant workers were in the United States in 2010, at least twenty million of them from Latin America. Repression and xenophobia against immigrants from Third World countries is ingrained in U.S. (and Western) history (and it must be stressed that while I focus here on Latino immigrant labor, analogous conditions exist for many immigrant workers from Africa, Asia, the Caribbean, and elsewhere). Transnational immigrant labor flows from traditional peripheries is a mechanism that has replaced colonialism in the mobilization of racialized labor pools. States assume a gatekeeper function in order to regulate the flow of labor for the capitalist economy. U.S. immigration enforcement agencies undertake "revolving door" practices – opening and shutting the flow of immigration in accordance with the needs of capital accumulation during distinct periods. Immigrants are sucked up when their labor is needed and then spit out when they become superfluous or potentially destabilizing to the system.[82] The 1970s crisis unleashed a "new nativism" and punitive state-sponsored controls over immigrants in many countries around the world. "The main problem is how to get rid of those six to eight million aliens who are interfering with our economic prosperity," declared then U.S. President Gerald Ford in 1976.[83]

The super-exploitation of an immigrant workforce would not be possible if that workforce had the same civil, political, and labor rights as citizens, if it did not face the insecurities and vulnerabilities of being undocumented or "illegal." Granting full citizenship rights to the tens of millions of immigrants in the United States would undermine the division of the U.S. – and, by extension, the global – working class into immigrants and citizens. That division is a central component

---

[82] In 1994, for example, the government launched "Operation Gatekeeper," which accelerated militarization of the U.S.-Mexico border (see Joseph Nevins, *Operation Gatekeeper: The Rise of the 'Illegal Alien' and the Making of the U.S.-Mexico Boundary* [New York: Routledge, 2002]). Two years later the Clinton government passed the Illegal Immigration Reform and Immigrant Responsibility Act (IIRIRA), which tightened requirements for asylum claims, increased penalties on undocumented immigrants, and led to a massive increase in deportations. In that same year, the Welfare Reform Act excluded even legal immigrants from unemployment or health benefits. And in 2005 the U.S. Congress approved the Real ID Act that prohibited undocumented immigrants from holding driver's licenses.

[83] Nevins, *Operation Gatekeeper*, 63.

of the new class relations of global capitalism, predicated on a casualized and "flexible" mass of workers who can be hired and fired at will, who are deunionized, and who face precarious work conditions, job instability, a rollback of benefits, and downward pressures on wages. It is the "revolving door" function of states in the era of globalization (see the following discussion) that makes it *appear* that state policy is contradictory. Neither employers nor the state want to do away with immigrant labor. To the contrary, they want to sustain a vast exploitable labor pool that exists under precarious conditions, that does not enjoy the civil, political, and labor rights of citizens, that faces language barriers and a hostile cultural and ideological environment, and that is flexible and disposable through deportation.

The *condition of deportable* must be created and then reproduced – periodically refreshed with new waves of "illegal" immigrants – since that condition assures the ability to super-exploit with impunity and to dispose of without consequences should this labor become unruly or unnecessary. Driving immigrant labor deeper underground and absolving the state and employers of any commitment to the social reproduction of this labor allows for its maximum exploitation together with its disposal when necessary. The punitive features of immigration policy have been combined in recent decades with reforms to federal welfare law that have denied immigrants – documented or not – access to such social wages as unemployment insurance, food stamps, and certain welfare benefits.[84] In this way members of the immigrant labor force become responsible for their own maintenance and reproduction and also – through remittances – for their family members abroad. This makes immigrant labor low-cost and flexible for capital *and also* costless for the state compared to native-born labor. *Immigrant workers become the archetype of these new global class relations – the quintessential workforce of global capitalism.* They are yanked out of relations of reciprocity rooted in social and political communities that have historically been institutionalized in nation-states. Latino/immigrant workers are reduced to a naked commodity, another flexible and expendable input into globalized production, a transnationally mobile commodity deployed when and where needed throughout North America. As one Canadian agribusiness representative from Ontario bragged: "We can take Mexican tomatoes and ship them up here, you can send a Mexican to California to produce tomatoes there and ship them up here, or you can send a Mexican up here and you grow the tomato here in Ontario."[85]

Labor supply through transnational migration constitutes in this way the *export of commodified human beings*. This commodification goes beyond the more limited concept first developed by Marx, in which the worker's *labor power* is sold to capital as a commodity. To Marx we must add Foucaultian

[84] Leigh Binford, "A Generation of Migrants: Where They Leave, Where They End Up," *NACLA Report on the Americas* (2005), 39(1): 32.
[85] As cited in Binford, "A Generation of Migrants," 36.

insights, in particular, the recognition that control reaches beyond the productive structure, beyond consumption and social relations, to *encompass the body itself* (hence "biopolitics"). In the classical Marxist construct, the worker faces alienation and exploitation during the time he or she sells this commodity to capital, that is, during the work shift. In between this regularized sale of labor power the worker is not a commodity but an alienated human being, "free" to rest and replenish in the sphere of social reproduction. In its archetypical form, the new immigrant worker as a mobile input for globalized circuits of accumulation is not just selling commodified labor during the time he or she is working; *the whole body becomes a commodity*, mobilized and supplied in the same way as are raw materials, money, intermediate goods, and other inputs. It is, after all, the whole body that must migrate and insert itself into the global accumulation circuits as immigrant labor. Hence, even when each regular sale of labor power concludes – that is, after each work period – the worker is not "free" to rest and replenish as in the traditional Marxist analysis of labor and capital, since he or she remains *immigrant/undocumented* labor twenty-four hours a day, unable to engage in the "normal" channels of rest and social reproduction due to the whole set of institutional exclusions, state controls, racialized discrimination, xenophobia, and oppression that the undocumented immigrant worker experiences in the larger social milieu. The worldwide immigrant labor regime becomes the very epitome of transnational capital's naked domination in the age of globalization.

Summoning the Devil: "Kill a Mexican Today"

If African Americans have been politically disenfranchised in large numbers through incarceration that also strips them of many political rights, then immigrants – in particular, Latino immigrants, who swell the lower rungs of the itinerant workforce – are entirely disenfranchised through the denial of citizenship rights and beyond that, in effect, the labor, social, and civil rights that, according to international (and U.S.!) law, are universal. The "war on terror" paved the way for an undeclared war on immigrants by fusing "national security/ antiterrorism" with immigration law enforcement, involving designation of borders and immigrant flows as "terrorism threats," the approval of vast new funding, and the passage of a slew of policies and laws designed to help undertake the new war.[86]

This war against immigrants has escalated in recent years, in part in response to the worldwide spread of an immigrant rights movement to fight back against

---

[86] See, inter alia, Tanya Maria Golash-Boza, *Immigrant Nation: Raids, Detentions, and Deportations in Post-9/11 America* (Boulder, CO: Paradigm Publishers, 2011); Joseph Nevins, *Operation Gatekeeper: The Rise of the 'Illegal Alien' and the Making of the U.S.-Mexico Border*, 2nd ed. (New York: Routledge, 2011); Deepa Fernandez, *Targeted: Homeland Security and the Business of Immigration* (New York: Seven Stories Press, 2007).

repression, exploitation, exclusion, cultural degradation, and racism. A major turning point in this struggle in the United States came in the spring of 2006 with a series of unparalleled strikes and demonstrations that swept the country.[87] Beyond making immediate demands, the emerging movement challenged the very structural changes bound up with capitalist globalization that have generated an upsurge in global labor migration and placed that segment of the global working class in increasingly direct confrontation with transnational capital.

The immediate trigger for the mass protests was the introduction in the U.S. Congress of a bill, known as the Sensenbrenner bill, that called for criminalizing undocumented immigrants by making it a felony to be in the United States without proper documentation. It also stipulated the construction of the first 700 miles of a militarized wall between Mexico and the United States, a doubling of the size of the U.S. Border Patrol, and the application of criminal sanctions against anyone who provided assistance to undocumented immigrants, including churches, humanitarian groups, and social service agencies. The bill underscored the extent to which elites in the United States, as elsewhere in global society, are willing to go to maintain a super-exploitable and super-controlled army of immigrant labor for the new global economy. Although the U.S. federal legislation was shelved in the wake of these protests, dozens of state and local governments around the country passed repressive anti-immigrant legislation in subsequent years, starting with Arizona's notorious SB1070, as I will discuss momentarily.

The protests defeated the Sensenbrenner bill and at the same time frightened the ruling class, sparking an escalation of state repression and racist nativism and fueling the neo-fascist anti-immigrant movement.[88] The backlash involved, among other things, stepped-up raids on immigrant workplaces and

---

[87] In one "day of national protest" on March 25, 2006, for instance, between one and two million people demonstrated in Los Angeles – the single biggest public protest in the city's history – and millions more followed suit in Chicago, New York, Atlanta, Washington, D.C., Phoenix, Dallas, Houston, Tucson, Denver, and dozens of other cities. Then on May Day of 2006 trade unionists and social justice activists joined immigrants in "The Great American Boycott 2006 / A Day without an Immigrant." Millions – perhaps tens of millions – in over 200 cities from across the country skipped work and school, commercial activity, and daily routines in order to participate in a national boycott, general strike, rallies, and symbolic actions. Hundreds of local communities in the South, Midwest, Northwest, and elsewhere, far away from the "gateway cities" where Latino populations are concentrated, experienced mass public mobilizations that placed them on the political map.

[88] The state's repression of the mass immigrant uprising of 2006 resulted in a significant split in the movement. In broad strokes, the Latino middle class and professional establishment found that their class interests were threatened by an uncontrolled self-mobilization of immigrant masses. Clustered in well-funded NGOs and in local, state, and federal elected and appointed government positions, the establishment attempted to demobilize the grassroots base, direct protest toward lobbying for legislative reform, and align with the Democratic Party. The Obama presidential campaign of 2008 effectively combined with the political aspirations of the establishment and the state's repression to co-opt and neutralize, at least momentarily, the mass movement. The radical

communities, mass deportations, an increase in the number of federal immigration enforcement agents, the deputizing of local police forces as enforcement
agents, the further militarization of the U.S.-Mexico border, anti-immigrant
hysteria in the mass media, and the introduction at local, state, and federal levels
of a slew of discriminatory anti-immigrant legislative initiatives. Anti-immigrant
hate groups had already been on the rise in the years prior to 2006. The FBI
reported more than 2,500 hate crimes against Latinos in the United States
between 2000 and 2006. Blatantly racist public discourse that only a few years
earlier would have been considered extreme had by 2005 become increasing
mainstream and aired on the mass media. The paramilitary organization
Minutemen, a modern-day Latino-hating version of the Ku Klux Klan, spread
in the first decade of the twenty-first century from its place of origin along the
U.S.-Mexicon border in Arizona and California to other parts of the country.
Minutemen claimed they must "secure the border" in the face of inadequate
state-sponsored control. Their discourse, beyond racist, was neo-fascist. Some
were even filmed sporting T-shirts with the emblem "Kill a Mexican Today?",
and others have organized for-profit "human safaris" in the desert. One video
game discovered in 2006 circulating on the internet, "Border Patrol," let players
shoot at Mexican immigrants as they try to cross the border into the United
States. Players in the game were told to target one of three immigrant groups
portrayed in a negative, stereotypical way as the figures rushed past a sign that
read "Welcome to the United States." The immigrants were caricatured as
bandoleer-wearing "Mexican nationalists," tattooed "drug smugglers," and
pregnant "breeders" who spring with their children in tow. Minutemen clubs
were sponsored by right-wing organizers, wealthy ranchers, businessmen, and
politicians, but their social base was drawn from the white working class.

As I have noted earlier, sustaining a reserve army of immigrant labor means
reproducing the division of workers into immigrants and citizens, which in turn
requires contradictory practices on the part of national states. The state must lift
national borders for capital but must reinforce these same national boundaries in
its immigrant policies, and in its ideological activities it must generate a nationalist hysteria by propagating such images as "out-of-control borders" and
"invasions of illegal immigrants." Racist hostility toward Latinos and other
immigrants may be intentionally generated by right-wing politicians, law-
enforcement agents, and neo-fascist anti-immigrant movements. Such hostility

grassroots camp was not against lobbying or attempting to penetrate the halls of power but
insisted on prioritizing a permanent mass movement from below that subordinates alliances with
liberals to the interests of the disenfranchised majority of immigrant workers and their families.
This camp has also insisted on the need to link the immigrant rights movement more openly and
closely with other popular, labor, and resistance struggles for global justice around the world.
These distinct strategies represent, in the broader analysis, two different class projects within the
multiclass community of immigrants and their supporters: the former, those middle class strata
who aspire to remove racist and legal impediments to their own class condition; the latter, a mass
immigrant working class that faces not only racism and legal discrimination but also the acute
labor exploitation and survival struggles imposed on them by a rapacious global capitalism.

may be the effect of the structural and legal-institutional subordination of immigrant workers and their communities, or simply an unintended (although not necessarily unwelcome) by-product of the state's coercive policies. Embodied in this structural condition is the rise and the ongoing recomposition of an internally stratified global working class controlled by political borders, state repression, criminalization, and militarization. The state's war on immigrants in the United States, including an escalation of workplace and community raids, detentions and deportations, racial profiling, police abuse, and so forth, has fed hate crimes against immigrants and hostility toward Latino/a communities. In these ways the state's repressive activities combine with corporate strategy to generate the spread of neo-fascist forces in civil society, as already discussed. One 2007 report by the Southern Poverty Law Center observed:

> There's no doubt that the tone of the raging national debate over immigration is growing uglier by the day. Once limited to hard-core white supremacists and a handful of border-state extremists, vicious public denunciations of undocumented brown-skinned immigrants are increasingly common among supposedly mainstream anti-immigration activists, radio hosts and politicians. While their dehumanizing rhetoric typically stops short of openly sanctioning bloodshed, much of it implicitly encourages or even endorses violence by characterizing immigrants from Mexico and Central America as 'invaders,' 'criminal aliens' and 'cockroaches.' The results are no less tragic for being predictable: hate crime statistics ... strongly suggest a marked upswing in racially motivated violence against all Latinos, regardless of immigration status.[89]

The Center also reported in 2011 that "three strands of the radical right" – hate groups, nativist extremist groups, and patriot organizations – increased from 1,753 groups in 2009 to 2,145 in 2010, a 22 percent rise, which followed a 2008–9 increase of 40 percent, and that these groups have expanded in part through anti-immigrant activity.[90] A 2010 Department of Homeland Security (DHS) report observed that "rightwing extremists may be gaining new recruits by playing on the fears about several emergency issues. The economic downturn and the election of the first African American president present unique drivers for rightwing radicalization and recruitment." The DHS report concluded that "over the past five years, various rightwing extremists, including militias and white supremacists, have adopted the immigration issue as a call to action, rallying point, and recruitment tool."[91]

"Gatekeeper" functions, super-exploitability, and super-controllability become more complex – and contradictory – as transnational capital becomes increasingly dependent on immigrant labor. By the turn of the century Latino/a immigrant labor had become structurally embedded in the North American

---

[89] Southern Poverty Law Center, "Immigrant Backlash: Hate Crimes against Latinos Flourish," *Intelligence Report* (Winter 2007), no. 128: 1.
[90] Southern Poverty Law Center, *Intelligence Report* (Spring 2011), no. 141.
[91] Department of Homeland Security, U.S. Government, *Rightwing Extremism: Current Economic and Political Climate Fueling Resurgence in Radicalization and Recruitment*, April 7, 2009.

economy. Although immigrant labor sustains U.S. and Canadian agriculture, by the 1990s the majority of Latino/a immigrants had been absorbed by industry, construction, and services as part of a general "Latinization" of the economy. Latino immigrants have massively swelled the lower rungs of the U.S. workforce. They provide almost all of the farm labor and much of the labor for hotels, restaurants, construction, janitorial and house cleaning, child care, domestic service, gardening and landscaping, hairdressing, delivery, meat and poultry packing, food processing, light manufacturing, retail, and so on.[92]

Historically, outside of the U.S. Southwest (where Chicanos/as have occupied this structural location), African Americans have been relegated to these lower rungs in the U.S. caste system. But as African Americans fought for their civil and human rights in the 1960s and 1970s they became organized, politicized, and radicalized. As discussed earlier, black workers led trade union militancy. All this made them undesirable labor for capital – "undisciplined" and "noncompliant." Starting in the 1980s employers began to push out black workers and massively recruit Latino immigrants, coinciding with deindustrialization and restructuring.[93] As one employer explained to a reporter, African Americans are "too expensive and, well, too activist." The article went on to portray such activism as damaging to black employment precisely because it is successful in bringing about "better wages, greater health care."[94] Blacks moved from super-exploited to marginalized – subject to unemployment, cuts in social services, mass incarceration, and heightened state repression – while Latino immigrant labor became the new super-exploited sector.

There is a broad social and political base, therefore, for the maintenance of a flexible, super-controlled, and super-exploited Latino immigrant workforce. The system cannot function without it. But if global capital needs the labor power of transnational migrants, this labor power belongs to human beings who must be tightly controlled, given the special oppression and dehumanization involved in extracting their labor power as noncitizen immigrant labor. The immigrant issue presents a contradiction for political and economic elites: from the vantage point of dominant group interests, the dilemma is how to deal with the new "barbarians" at Rome's door. The state must play a balancing act by

[92] See, inter alia, Golash-Boza, *Immigration Nation*; Robinson, "Aqui Estamos y No Nos Vamos!".
[93] Keeanga Y. Taylor, "Life Ain't Been No Crystal Stair: Blacks, Latinos and the New Civil Rights Movement," *Counterpunch*, May 9, 2006, from www.counterpunch.org/taylor05082006.html.
[94] Erin Aubrey Kaplan, "They're Our Jobs Too: A New Union Contract in L.A. Recognizes That Hotels Have to Hire More African Americans," *Los Angeles Times*, October 25, 2006; A17, as cited in Lisa Marie Cacho, "The Rights of Respectability: Ambivalent Allies, Reluctant Rivals, and Disavowed Deviants," in Rachel Buff, ed., *Immigrant Rights in the Shadow of Citizenship* (New York: New York University Press), 190–206 (citation from p. 195 and p. 204, endnote 16). Kaplan's article takes up the important topic of the tensions between the African American and Latino immigrant communities, include the way citizenship and noncitizenship have been used by the system to generate divide-and-rule dynamics that undermine cross-ethnic (and, we should add, working-class) unity.

finding a formula for supplying stable, of cheap labor to employers while at the same time providing greater state control over immigrants.

The twin instruments for achieving the dual goals of super-exploitability and super-controllability are 1) the division of the working class into immigrant and citizen, and 2) racialization of the former. In this way race and class converge. Racialization is an instrument in the politics of domination. It is incorporated into the strategies of ruling groups to manage resistance and maintain order in the face of uncertainty and crisis. The dilemma for capital, dominant groups, affluent and privileged strata is how to "have their cake and eat it" too: how are ruling groups to resolve the contradiction of assuring a steady supply of immigrant labor while at the same time promoting anti-immigrant practices and ideologies? Moreover, as we saw above in the case of "the new Jim Crow," the loss of caste privileges for white sectors of the working class is problematic for political elites and state managers in the United States, since legitimation and domination have historically been constructed through a white racial hegemonic bloc.

Hence, as with the "law and order" bloc, the anti-immigrant bloc also draws in white workers who have historically enjoyed caste privilege within racially segmented labor markets and who now experience downward mobility and heightened insecurity. Studies in the early 1990s, for example, found that, in addition to concentrations in "traditional" areas such as Los Angeles, Miami, Washington, D.C./Virginia, and Houston, Central American immigrants had formed clusters in the formal and informal service sectors in areas where, in the process of downward mobility, they had replaced "white ethnics," such as in suburban Long Island, in small towns of Iowa and North Carolina, in Silicon Valley and in the northern and eastern suburbs of the San Francisco Bay area.[95] Again we see the contradiction that the state and dominant groups must wrestle with: how to secure an historic bloc with which to stabilize hegemony in the absence, given the crisis, of a solid material base for such a bloc.

MILITARIZATION AS SOCIAL CONTROL AND AS ACCUMULATION

The Fusion of Capital and the State in the War on Immigrants

Criminalization and militarization increasingly drive undocumented immigrants underground, where they become vulnerable to intermediaries in the quest for survival – intermediaries such as gangs, shady temporary labor agencies, and unscrupulous employers. The array of state and other institutional controls over immigrants further drive down black and informal market wages, working and living conditions and give employers an ever-freer hand.[96] At the same time,

[95] Robinson, "Aqui Estamos y No Nos Vamos!".
[96] See, inter alia, Southern Poverty Law Center. "Center Exposes Exploitation of Immigrant Workers" (posted August 16, 2006) and "Rebuilding New Orleans" (posted August 19, 2006);

borders, in order to be effective instruments for regulating and controlling the supply of immigrant labor, must be militarized. The U.S.-Mexico border is one of the most militarized stretches of land in the world, with ten guards for every mile of the 2,000 mile border. Many stretches along the frontier are akin to a war zone.[97]

Supplying global capital with immigrant labor is now a multibillion-dollar industry. Globally organized networks of "migration merchants," or usurious middlemen, provide a full range of legal and illegal services needed for migration, including the supply of passports, visas, work permits, cash advances, safe houses, above-ground and clandestine transport, border crossing by *coyotes*, and employment opportunities in countries of destination, all for fees that can add up to tens of thousands of dollars and in many cases place the transnational migrant in a situation of indentured servitude for many years. But these illicit and often underground profit-making ventures are dwarfed by the accumulation opportunities opened up to transnational corporate capital by the war on immigrants.

The activities of the American Legislative Exchange Council, or ALEC, expose the inner connections between corporate interests, the state, militarization and policing, and anti-immigrant and other neo-fascist tendencies in civil society.[98] ALEC brings together state and federal elected officials and law enforcement and criminal justice system representatives with some 200 of the most powerful transnational corporations, among them, ATT, Coca Cola, Exxon Mobile, Pfizer, Kraft Foods, Walmart, Bank of America, Microsoft, Nestle, AstraZeneca, Dow Chemical, Sony, and Koch Industries, this last one of the biggest ALEC funders. ALEC develops legislative initiatives that advance the transnational corporate agenda, hammering out at its gatherings draft criminal justice, anti-union, tax reform, financial, and environmental deregulation and related bills that are then introduced by state and local elected officials associated with ALEC. These bills have included the notorious "three strikes law" that mandates twenty-five-years-to-life sentences for those committing a third offense (even for minor drug possession), and "truth in sentencing," which requires people to serve all of their time with no chance of parole.

SB1070 was first introduced into the Arizona state legislature by State Assemblyman Russell Pearce, an ALEC board member. In 2009 ALEC members,

---

Center reports are posted at the Center website found at http://www.splcenter.org/. There is evidence that as Latinos came to constitute the principal labor force for the reconstruction of New Orleans in the wake of the destruction wrought by Hurricane Katrina in 2005, employers turned to such practices as refusing to pay immigrant workers after they had rendered services, turning them over to immigration authorities for deportation, and employing them in an array of slave-labor-like conditions.

97 For details, see, inter alia, Nevins, *Operation Gatekeeper*.

98 For an excellent brief documentary on ALEC, anti-immigrant legislation, and the vested corporate interest in the war on immigrants, see "Immigrants for Sale," from http://www.youtube.com/watch?v=vuGE1VxVsYo. The documentary was produced by Brave New Foundation, found at http://www.bravenewfoundation.org/. See also http://www.mycuentame.org/immigrantsforsale.

including Pearce and representatives from the Corrections Corporation of America (CCA), drafted a model anti-immigrant law. Pearce then introduced the bill into the Arizona legislature with the support of thirty-six co-sponsors, thirty of whom received campaign contributions from CCA lobbyists as well as from lobbyists for two other private prison companies, Geo Group and Management and Training Corporation. The bill was signed by Arizona Governor Jan Brewer, who herself has close ties to CCA and to ALEC. The CCA has received lucrative contracts to run immigrant detention centers in Arizona.[99] SB1070 was passed in 2010. The law legalized racial profiling by instructing state law enforcement agents to detain and question anyone who appeared to be undocumented and authorizing anyone to sue police who fail to do so – requiring, in effect, everyone to carry proof of citizenship or legal residence at all times. Among other stipulations, it also required teachers to compile lists of suspected immigrant children and directed emergency rooms and social service agencies to deny care to those who cannot prove citizenship or legal residence. Although some of the most draconian provisions were later struck down by federal courts, the Arizona law became a model for "copycat" legislation that had been passed in five other states and introduced in several dozen more at the time of writing (early 2013). The magazine *Mother Jones* built a database of hundreds of repressive local and state-level anti-immigrant laws introduced around the United States in the wake of SB1070, including 164 such laws passed by state legislatures in 2010 and 2011 alone.[100] The database also uncovered the extensive interlocking of far-right organizations comprising the anti-immigrant movement, other neo-fascist organizations in civil society, government agencies and elected officials (local and federal), politicians, and corporate and foundation funders, lobbies, and activists.

The Commodification of Coercion and Repression

Let us now reexamine the theme first introduced in Chapter 3, that of militarized accumulation. Fascism in both its twentieth- and twenty-first-century variants is not just a political response to capitalist crisis but also *in and of itself a project in function of accumulation* and profit making that brings together the state and capital. Given the extensive and continuing privatization of war and state-sponsored social control and repression, it is in the interests of a broad array of capitalist groups to shift the political, social, and ideological climate toward

---

[99] For these details, see an October 28, 2010, report by National Public Radio (NPR), reported at the NPR website, http://www.npr.org/2010/10/28/130833741/prison-economics-help-drive-ariz-immigration-law. Also see *Mother Jones* magazine at http://www.motherjones.com/poli tics/2012/03/john-tanton-anti-immigration-laws. Note that after a number of media exposés of ALEC in 2012, some forty of these corporations withdrew their funding. The list of those corporations that withdrew as well as more details on ALEC can be found at the Sourcewatch website, found at http://www.sourcewatch.org/index.php/ALEC_Corporations.

[100] See http://www.motherjones.com/politics/2012/03/john-tanton-anti-immigration-laws.

the generation and sustaining of social conflict and the expansion of systems of warfare, repression, surveillance, and social control. The generation of conflict, the criminalization of the dispossessed, and the repression of social movements and vulnerable populations around the world is an accumulation strategy independent of any political objectives. While transnational capital may not yet have fused with reactionary political power at the highest level of the U.S. federal government, militarized accumulation as well as such instances as the Koch brothers' sponsorship of Wisconsin Governor Walker's far-right program and the broad corporate sponsorship of anti-union and anti-immigrant legislation underscore a broader feature of both classical and twenty-first-century fascism: reactionary political forces in the state open up accumulation opportunities for capital in crisis, and in turn capital develops an interest in a system of violence and coercive control.

The deep historical roots of U.S. militarization and neo-fascism would go back to the genocide and slavery that laid the very foundation of a racial republic, followed by territorial expansion, imperialist conquests, and interventions through the history of the country and the terror campaigns of the Ku Klux Klan and the Texas Rangers, among others. It was the September 11, 2001, attack on the World Trade Towers and the Pentagon that gave the greatest impulse to militarization in relation to the current crisis and spawned a military-security-industrial-construction-engineering-petroleum complex that has become a cutting edge of accumulation in the face of stagnation. The top military brass has become increasingly politicized and involved in policymaking.[101] As we have seen previously, military spending skyrocketed into the trillions of dollars through the "war on terrorism" and the invasions and occupations of Iraq and Afghanistan, acting to throw fresh firewood on the smoldering embers of the global economy.

The prison industrial complex and the immigrant repression-detention system in the United States are in this way multifunctional for the system. In any one year the prison-industrial complex removes several million surplus workers from the labor market and employs another several million workers to run the warehousing of those caged, generating billions in profits. The economic interests bound up with the complex are enormous and are vested in expanding the pool of people who can be held captive for profit. The interests of investors in a growing number of private prisons, suppliers to the complex, 2.4 million prison guards and employees, outsourcers using prison labor, and so on is enormous, estimated by Alexander at some $200 billion, and this does not include all sorts of ancillary activities such as prison construction itself or backward linkages to other economic activities. For-profit prison companies are responsible for caging some 12 percent of state and federal prisoners in the United States and 50 percent of immigrant detainees. In 2010 these companies were paid an average of $122 per day per detainee for several hundred thousand immigrants held in these

---

[101] See, e.g, Bruce Ackerman, "A Less Political Military," *Los Angeles Times*, June 21, 2010: A9.

facilities.[102] In the larger picture the complex must be seen as part of militarized accumulation, a social control economy – one domestic U.S. component of a global war economy and transnational police state.

The 2005 annual report of the Corrections Corporation of America (CCA), the largest private prison operator in the United States, stated with regard to the profit-making opportunities opened up by the prison-industrial complex: "Our growth is generally dependent upon our ability to obtain new contracts to develop and manage new correctional and detention facilities. ... The demand for our facilities and services could be adversely affected by the relaxation of enforcement efforts, leniency in conviction and sentencing practices or through the decriminalization of certain activities that are currently proscribed by our criminal laws."[103] The New York–based investment firm World Research Group welcomed investors at a 1996 conference on expanded opportunities for profit making in private prisons: "While arrests and convictions are steadily on the rise, profits are to be made – profits from crime. Get in on the ground floor of this booming industry now!"[104]

Similarly, immigrant labor is extremely profitable for the corporate economy in a double sense. First, it is labor that is highly vulnerable, forced to exist semi-underground, and *deportable*, and therefore super-exploitable. Second, the criminalization of undocumented immigrants and the militarization of their control not only reproduce these conditions of vulnerability but also in themselves generate vast new opportunities for accumulation. The private immigrant detention complex is a booming industry. Undocumented immigrants constitute the fastest-growing sector of the U.S. prison population and are detained in private detention centers and deported by private companies contracted out by the U.S. state. As of 2010 there were 270 immigration detention centers that on any given day caged over 30,000 immigrants. Under Obama, more immigrants have been detained and deported than at any time in the past half-century (it should be noted that in addition to an upsurge of immigrant detention and deportation, Obama approved in 2011 a law allowing for the indefinite detention without trial of anyone in the United States that the state considers to be a "terror suspect").[105] Since detainment facilities and deportation logistics are subcontracted to private companies,

[102] For these details, see James Ridgeway, "Private Prison Companies Strive to Keep Millions Behind Bars to Keep Their Profits Up," *Al Jazeera*, English Language online edition, November 28, 2011, from www.aljazeera.com/indepth/opinion/2011/11/201111127105458655442.html.

[103] Alexander, *The New Jim Crow*, 231.

[104] As cited in Ken Silverstein, "Introduction," in Tara Herivel and Paul Wright, eds., *Prison Nation: The Warehousing of America's Poor* (New York: Routledge, 2003), 3.

[105] Chris McGreal, "Military Given Go-Ahead to Detain U.S. Terrorist Suspects without Trial," *The Guardian*, 14 December 2011, http://www.theguardian.com/world/2011/dec/15/americans-face-guantanamo-detention-obama. The article quoted a spokesperson for Human Rights Watch observing: "It's something so radical that it would have been considered crazy had it been pushed by the Bush administration."

capital has a vested interest in the criminalization of immigrants and in the militarization of control over immigrants – and more broadly, therefore, a vested interest in contributing to the neo-fascist anti-immigrant movement.

It is no surprise that William Andrews, the CEO of CCA, the largest private U.S. contractor for immigrant detention centers, declared in 2008 that "the demand for our facilities and services could be adversely affected by the relaxation of enforcement efforts ... or through decriminalization [of immigrants]." A month after SB1070 became law, Wayne Callabres, the president of Geo Group, held a conference call with investors and explained his company's aspirations. "Opportunities at the federal level are going to continue apace as a result of what's happening," he said, referring to the Arizona law. "Those people coming across the border being caught are going to have to be detained and that to me at least suggests there's going to be enhanced opportunities for what we do." Nor is it any surprise that CCA and other corporations, such as GEO Group – both of which are listed on global stock exchanges – have financed and participated directly in the drafting of the spate of neo-fascist anti-immigrant legislation in Arizona and other U.S. states, while state officials pushing this legislation are themselves tied to the private immigrant prison-industrial complex, including Arizona Governor Jan Brewer and Arizona State Senator Russell Pearce, who actually introduced the notorious anti-immigrant law SB1070. While Arizona is ground zero for the war on immigrants – and possibly for the twenty-first-century fascist insurgency – in neighboring New Mexico the firm CSI Aviation is headed by retired Marine colonel Allen Weh. CSI is the largest contractor for Immigration and Customs Enforcement (ICE) flights that deport the undocumented. CSI has also financed and sponsored the SB1070 and similar legislation in New Mexico.[106]

It must be reiterated that this war and the conversion of criminalization and caging into a lucrative business is not specific to the United States. It is increasingly integral to the global economy and polity. The creation of a "detention-industrial complex," notes Bernstein, is "part of a pattern on three continents where a handful of multinational security companies have been turning crackdowns on immigrants into a growing global

---

[106] On the CCA-SB1070 link and related details, see the journalistic exposé by Laura Sullivan, "Prison Economics Help Drive Arizona Immigration Law," National Public Radio, Oct. 28, 2010, print version from http://www.npr.org/templates/story/story.php?storyId=130833741, and also Catalina Nieto, "The For-Profit Con to Criminalize Immigrants," January. 4, 2011, *Commondreams*, www.commondreams.org/view/2011/01/04-12. For the Andrews citation, see Tom Barry, "The National Imperative to Imprison Immigrants for Profit," Center for International Policy, Americas Program, posted at CIP Americas Program webpage on October 3, 2009, at http://www.cipamericas.org/archives/1662. For general analysis, see, inter alia, Tanya Golash-Boza, "The Immigrant Industrial Complex: Why We Enforce Immigration Policies Destined to Fail," *Sociology Compass* (2009), 3: 1–15.

industry."[107] G4S, a UK/Dutch-based "security" conglomerate, employs 600,000 people in 125 countries. The $10 billion portfolio of another global "security" conglomerate, Serco, includes air traffic control monitoring and visa processing in the United States, nuclear weapons maintenance, video surveillance, "immigration removal centers," "welfare-to-work" programs in the U.K., and immigrant prisons in Australia. The GEO groups runs dozens of facilities in South Africa, Australia, the United States, and the UK.[108] In 2011 there were some twenty million private security guards employed worldwide, according to a UN report, an increase of 200–300 percent over the past several decades, and twice the number of government-employed police offers around the world.[109] The Department of Homeland Security has awarded billions of dollars to leading military and security-oriented transnational corporations, among them Lockheed Martin, Northrop Grumman, IBM, Boeing, Halliburton, and private for-profit prison companies, for everything from constructing a "border security wall" between the United States and Mexico and related "border security" operations (e,g., drone surveillance) to the construction of immigrant detention centers and databases.[110]

It is clear that militarization and capitalist globalization have become singular, reinforcing, and synergistic, fusing the global economy with the TNS ideological and coercive apparatuses and with the global culture industry. Global production sites, transportation, communications and logistics chains and their associated residential, recreational, and commercial quarters are "secured" by the global military apparatus. At the same time these vast transnational networks in themselves constitute militarized accumulation through the production of martial "goods and services," including the global arms trade (the "weaponization" of the world), the cycles of "creative destruction" and reconstruction, the montage of a global detention and torture network, prison construction and the management of caging, building border walls, and so forth and so on – all part of a fused global war economy and police state. These archipelagos of social control exhibit "startling similarities to those that sustain global geographies of tourism, finance, production, logistics, military power and the lifestyles of elites."[111] The global arms trade alone is a $3.5 trillion business that conjoins the above-ground and

[107] Nina Bernstein, "Companies Use Immigration Crackdown to Turn a Profit," *New York Times*, September 28, 2011, internet edition, from http://www.nytimes.com/2011/09/29/world/asia/getting-tough-on-immigrants-to-turn-a-profit.html?pagewanted=all&_r=0.

[108] For these details, see ibid.

[109] The report was dated July 2011 and summarized by the United Nation's press office at the following website: http://www.un.org/apps/news/story.asp?NewsID=38957&Cr=small+arms&Cr1=#.UP8 ZAPLjGqI. Two million people were deployed as private security guards in the United States in 2007, compared to 880,000 police officers.

[110] See Golash-Boza, *Immigration Nation*, 153–154.

[111] Graham, *Cities under Siege*, 94.

the black economies.[112] Gentrification, for instance, has fused with militarization – what Klein calls "militarized gentrification"[113] – so that in the United States, to take one example, the mortgage market collapse has resulted in the eviction of several million families from their homes and an accelerated gentrification of cities. This dispossession by financial gentrification results in capital and the better-off reclaiming space from the poor and working class masses and then sealing off these spaces for upscale residential, commercial, or tourist zones (or simply for future speculation) through the new modalities of exclusion, enclosure, surveillance, and repression.

The dual functions of accumulation and social control that militarization satisfies are played out in the militarization of civil society and the crossover between the military and civilian applications of advanced weapons, tracking, security, and surveillance systems. This crossover is at the heart of what Graham terms "the new military urbanism." In considering such a new military urbanism, let us recall that by 2007, over half of the world's population lived in the world's cities. Mike Davis notes in his study, *Planet of Slums*, that at least one billion people live in the teeming slums of these global megalopolises, and that there are probably more than 200,000 slums on earth.[114] The distinction between wars within nations and wars between nations becomes ever less meaningful. The U.S. government has gradually reduced long-standing legal barriers to military deployment within U.S. cities. Urban warfare training exercises now regularly take place in U.S. cities. In fact, drones are being introduced into some 18,000 police departments in the United States.[115] "The Los Angeles riots of 1992; the various attempts to securitize urban cores during major sports events or political summits; the military response to Hurricane Katrina in New Orleans in 2005; the challenges of 'homeland security' in U.S. cities – all become 'low intensity' urban military operations comparable to conducting counter-insurgency warfare in an Iraqi city," writes Graham in reference to the United States. "High-tech targeting practices such as unmanned drones and organized satellite surveillance programs previously used to target spaces beyond the nation to (purportedly) make the nation safe are beginning to colonize the domestic spaces of the nation itself. Military doctrine has also come to treat the operation of gangs with in U.S. cities as 'urban insurgency,' 'fourth generation warfare', or 'netwar,' directly analogous to what takes place on the streets

[112] See Andrew Feinstein, *The Shadow World: Inside the Global Arms Trade* (New York: Picador, 2012).

[113] Noemi Klein, *The Shock Doctrine: The Rise of Disaster Capitalism* (New York, Metropolitan Books, 2007).

[114] Mike Davis, *Planet of Slums* (London: Verso, 2006).

[115] On the spread of drone warfare worldwide and in the United States, see Medea Benjamin, *Drone Warfare: Killing by Remote Control* (London: Verso, 2013). It is noteworthy that the United States recently established a military command for North America for the first time: the Northern Command. Previously this was the only part of the world not covered in this way.

of Kabul or Baghdad."[116] So apropos are Graham's observations that he is worth quoting at some length:

> [In] the United States this process [blurring the traditional separation of the military and the civilian spheres, local and global scales, and inside the nation–outside the nation distinctions] allows the nation's military to overcome traditional legal obstacles to deployment within the nation itself. As a consequence, the U.S. military's PowerPoint presentations talk of urban operations in Mogadishu, Fallujah, or Jenin in the same breath as those during the Los Angeles riots, the anti-globalization confrontations in Seattle or Genoa, or the devastation of New Orleans by Hurricane Katrina. Such a paradigm permits a host of transnational campaigns and movements – for social justice, for ecological sustainability, against state oppression or the devastating effects of market fundamentalism – to be rendered as forms of 'netwar.' Civil law enforcement agencies are becoming remodeled along much more (para)militarized lines. As well as reorganizing themselves to engage in highly militarized counterterrorist operations and the fortification of major conventions, sport events or political summits, they increasingly adopt the techniques and language of war to launch SWAT teams against a widening array of civilian events and routine call-outs. ... SWAT teams are called out in the U.S. about forty-thousand times a year, a rise from the three thousand annual call-outs of the 1980s.

Most of these call-outs, he observes, are executed to serve warrants on non-violent drug offenders. Graham continues:

> Military-style command and control systems are now being established to support 'zero tolerance' policing and urban surveillance practices designed to exclude failed consumers or undesirable persons from the new enclaves of urban consumption and leisure. What Robert Warren calls 'pop up armies' are organized transnationally to pre-emptively militarize cities facing major anti-globalization demonstrations. In addition, the almost infinite metaphorization of 'war' – on crime, on drugs, on terror, on disease – solidifies wider shifts from social, welfarist and Keynesian urban paradigms to authoritarian and militarized notions of the state's role in sustaining order[117]

It is hard to understate the significance of new technologies that allow state and corporate repressive apparatuses to exercise such a degree of surveillance and control over space that threats can be disarticulated before wholesale, mass repression becomes necessary. "Because networked electronic control and surveillance devices are now distributed throughout society, everyday urban life is now modulated by a sense of ever-present tracking, scrutiny, and electronic calculation," observes Graham.

> Thus an individual's movements between different spaces and sites within cities or nations often entails a parallel movement of what sociologists call the 'data subject' or 'statistical person' – the package of electronic tracks and histories amassed as a means of judging the individual's legitimacy, rights, profitability, security or degree

[116] Graham, *Cities under Siege*, 20.
[117] Ibid., 21–23.

of threat. The attempted social control increasingly works through complex technological systems stretched across both temporal and geographical zones. ... [B]ehind
every social movement operates a vast array of computerized calculations dispersed
through a global matrix of linked computers and computerized devices. Databases
communicate and their content is continuously mined across a diversity of sources,
scales and sites by advanced computer algorithms that assess a commensurate
diversity of bodies, transactions, and movements.[118]

Graham asks whether "urban securitization might reach a level in the future
which would effectively decouple the strategic economic role of cities as the key
drivers of capital accumulation from their historic role as centers for the mobilization of democratic dissent."[119] Such a future may already have arrived.
Heavily redacted FBI documents obtained through a Freedom of Information
Act (FOIA) request by the Partnership for Civil Justice Fund, a Washington-
based civil rights and legal defense fund, in the wake of the crackdown of the
Occupy Movement in the United States and uploaded to the organization's web
site (www.justiceonline.org/index.html) reveal that the violent repression of the
movement in the fall of 2011 – including violent arrests, infiltrations and group
disruptions, tear gas and grenade attacks, mass arrests, and detentions without
charge – by the state's repressive apparatuses, including the FBI, the Department
of Homeland Security, and local police, was coordinated with the banks that
were the target of Occupy protests, the New York Stock Exchange, and Federal
Reserve offices. The documents also ominously mention "sniper fire" to assas-
sinate OWS leaders, although the redacted documents gave no further details.
They highlight the coordination between the FBI, the Department of Homeland
Security, and the corporate sector. They include a report by the Domestic
Security Alliance Council, described by the federal government as "a strategic
partnership between the FBI, the Department of Homeland Security and the
private sector," discussing the OWS protests at the West Coast ports in order to
"raise awareness concerning this type of criminal activity." What becomes glaringly
clear in the Domestic Security Alliance Council report is the routine collaboration
between U.S. police and intelligence agencies and corporate officers. The document contains a "handling notice" that the information is "meant for use primarily within the corporate security community. Such messages shall not be released

---

[118] Ibid., 63–64. Cities around the world are starting to display startling similarities: hard, military-
style borders, fences and checkpoints around defended enclaves and 'security zones', superimposed on the wider and more open city, are proliferating. Graham discusses jersey barrier
blast walls, identity check points, computerized CCTV, biometric surveillance, and military
styles of access control designed to protect archipelagos of fortified social, economic, political,
and military centers "from an outside deemed unruly, impoverished or dangerous. In the most
extreme examples, these encompass green zones, military prisons, ethnic and sectarian neighborhoods and military bases; they are growing around strategic districts, embassies, tourist and
consumption spaces, airports and port complexes, sports arenas, gated communities and export
processing zones." (xxi).

[119] Ibid., xxii.

in either written or oral form to the media, the general public or other personnel."[120]

Such coordination resembles the fusion of capital with the state repressive apparatus characteristic of fascism. According to author Naomi Wolf there was "a terrifying network of coordinated DHS, FBI, police, regional fusion center, and private-sector activity so completely merged into one another that the monstrous whole is, in fact, one entity: in some cases, bearing a single name," the Domestic Security Alliance Council. "This merged entity [was revealed] to have one centrally planned, locally executed mission": to politically disable the Occupy Movement, which was designated by the government as a "terrorist threat."[121] In numerous cities, the OWS movement was targeted by "domestic terrorism" units of state agencies, even though the OWS was a peaceful movement.

Alongside the militarization of civil society and everyday life we are seeing worldwide the cultural, ideological, and political normalization of that militarization. During the U.S. invasion and occupation of Iraq, it should be recalled, Pentagon "perception management" and psychological operations involved the complete Goebbelsian fabrication of news stories fed to the U.S. and international media.[122] "Goebbelsian" refers to Nazi Minister of Propaganda Joseph Goebbels, who famously stated that if you repeat a lie ("the big lie") often enough, no matter how fabricated, far-fetched, or outrageous, it will eventually be accepted as truth.

The filmmaker Roger Stahl has coined the term "militainment" in reference to how U.S. state war making and militarism is now presented by "news" programs as an entertainment spectacle. News reporting on wars becomes indistinguishable from Hollywood film, video games, and reality television as the popular culture comes to normalize and glamorize militarization.[123] An all-pervasive war culture is a culture of violence and domination. So frequent are mass killings with firearms in the United States that death by social violence has all but become *infotainment*. Not since Roman citizens in the Coliseum feasted on the bloody carnage of warring gladiators has a general population come to be so fascinated with the unlimited use of power to dominate and dehumanize. Directing aggression against scapegoats or "foreign" enemies is predicated on internalized fear of those demonized by the propaganda machinery of state apparatuses and the dominant culture, which then reverberate this demonization in the mass media and popular Hollywood culture. The largely contrived wars on drugs, crime,

---

[120] See http://www.justiceonline.org/commentary/fbi-files-ows.html, which published the heavily redacted FBI documents obtained under the FOIA.

[121] See Naomi Wolf, "Revealed: How the FBI Coordinated the Crackdown of Occupy," *The Guardian*, December 29, 2012, from http://www.guardian.co.uk/commentisfree/2012/dec/29/fbi-coordinated-crackdown-occupy.

[122] This was underreported once it became publicly exposed. See Graham, *Cities under Siege*, 72.

[123] *Militainment, Inc.*, a 2007 documentary written, produced, and narrated by Roger Stahl, released by Media Education Foundation, Northhampton, MA.

immigrants, gangs, and terrorism serve to sustain an enduring internalized fear whose effect is to displace insecurities generated by the crisis and at the same time to legitimate militarization and boundless war, whether "hot" or "low-intensity." Ceteris paribus, the system functions as a mechanism for the preemptive control of those who would challenge the social order.

The masculinist and militaristic culture that accompanies militarized accumulation has reached unprecedented heights. The fusion of militarization and extreme masculinization – masculine fear of female power, misogyny, and homophobia, what Goff calls "martial masculinity" – has invaded the sphere of mass culture.[124] An increasingly fascistic pop culture combines this celebration of militarization and masculinity with fantasy, mysticism, and irrationality, as epitomized in the mass appeal of extremely violent computer games, the proliferation of reality TV shows, and the glorification of military aggression, social violence, and domination in mainstream Hollywood cinema. Hollywood cinema draws in enormous audiences, achieves record profits, and wins Oscar awards with "true grit" films such as *The Hurt Locker* that depoliticize and normalize, even glamorize, warfare even if they fall short of formal endorsement. Video-gaming of war and of state and interpersonal violence for pure entertainment – viz, the widely popular HAWX video game – normalizes and aestheticizes the militarization of culture and everyday life as never before.

The immense structural inequalities of the global political economy cannot easily be contained through consensual mechanisms of social control, that is, through consensual or hegemonic domination. Nonetheless, I reiterate that a twenty-first-century fascism would not look like twentieth-century fascism. Among other things, the ability of dominant groups to control and manipulate space and to exercise an unprecedented control over the mass media, the means of communication, and the production of symbols, images, and messages means, as previously noted, that repression can be more selective (as we see, e.g., in Mexico or Colombia) and also organized juridically, so that mass "legal" incarceration takes the place of concentration camps. As well, the vast new powers of cultural hegemony open up new possibilities for atomizing and channeling grievances and frustrated aspirations into escapism and consumerist fantasies. The fashion and entertainment industries market anything that can be converted into a commodity. With this comes depoliticization, at best, if not the ability to channel fear into flight rather than fight-back. The ideology of twenty-first-century fascism often rests on irrationality – a promise to deliver security and restore stability is emotive, not rational. Twenty-first-century fascism is a project that does not – and need not – distinguish between the truth and the lie.

---

[124] Stan Goff, "Sowing the Seeds of Fascism in America," *Truthdig* (internet magazine), posted on October 3, 2006, from http://www.truthdig.com/dig/item/200601003_white_supremacism_sexism_militarism/.

CONCLUSION: UNCERTAIN FUTURES

All of the conditions and the processes are present and percolating for a twenty-first-century fascism to take shape, and the social and political forces behind such a project are mobilizing rapidly. Nonetheless, the United States cannot be characterized at this time as fascist. What is to be done? I do not have that answer, nor is an attempt to provide such an answer within the scope of this study. I reiterate by way of concluding this chapter that times of crisis open up space for collective agency and for contingency to influence the course of history in ways not possible in times of stability, so that short-term predictions are of little value. Under these circumstances, how masses of people understand the nature of the global crisis becomes itself a critical battleground in the struggle for alternative futures. Hence, crucial to any struggle in the United States and in global society against neo-fascism and the war that has been unleashed on the global working class is to counter right-wing and neo-fascist discourse with a coherent explanation of the crisis and of possible solutions from a working-class, leftist, feminist, and democratic socialist–oriented perspective, a theme I will revisit briefly in the final chapter.

In the United States, the challenge for anti-neo-fascist forces is how to build an antifascist front that could bring together a grassroots fight-back with some of the reformist forces from above, yet in which *hegemony over such a fight-back is exercised by popular forces from below and not by elite reformers*. Beyond the United States, the counterweight to a twenty-first-century fascism must be a coordinated fight-back by the global working class that involves rebuilding working-class organizations, including independent trade unions and socialist movements, and extending cultures of social solidarity and transnational resistance. The only viable solution to the crisis of global capitalism is a massive redistribution of wealth and power downward to the poor majority of humanity along the lines of a twenty-first-century democratic socialism, in which humanity is no longer at war with itself and with nature. And the only way such redistribution can come about is through mass transnational struggle from below. Otherwise, humanity may be headed for what Chew, among others, has termed a new Dark Ages.[125]

[125] Sing C. Chew, *The Recurring Dark Ages: Ecological Stress, Climate Changes, and System Transformation* (Landham, MD: AltaMira Press, 2007).

6

Conclusions

Interregnum – A New Crisis of Hegemony

> It is easier to imagine the end of the world than it is to imagine the end of capitalism.
>
> Frederic Jameson, 2003[1]

> We do not attempt dogmatically to prefigure the future, but want to find the new world only through criticism of the old. But if the designing of the future and the proclamation of ready-made solutions for all time is not our affair, then we realize all the more clearly what we have to accomplish in the present – I am speaking of a ruthless criticism of everything existing, ruthless in two senses: The criticism must not be afraid of its own conclusions, nor of the conflict with the powers that be.
>
> Karl Marx[2]

In 2003 I co-organized a conference in Santa Barbara, California, titled *Towards a Critical Globalization Studies*. The conclave brought together some 100 leading scholars worldwide on globalization with leading activists and intellectuals from the global justice movement. Our objective was to explore what a critical study of global society involves and how such a study is related to struggles for social justice around the world. I argued that there is no such thing as free-floating academics and that all intellectual labor is *organic* in the sense that studying the world is itself a social act, committed by agents with a definite relationship to the social order. Intellectuals who consider themselves revolutionaries should have as their task analyzing the system of global capitalism, I continued, exposing its myths and lies, unmasking its legitimating discourses and ideologies, and identifying the forces that benefit from the continuation of this system. If we are to contribute to movements for social justice through our intellectual labor, then we should seek to aid those directly organizing mass

---

[1] Frederic Jameson, "Future City," *New Left Review*, May–June 2003: 21, as cited in Paul Mason, *Why It's Kicking Off Everywhere: The New Global Revolutions* (London: Verso, 2012), 27.

[2] Karl Marx, "For a Ruthless Crticism of Everything Existing" (Marx to Arnold Ruge), in Robert C. Tucker, ed., *The Marx-Engels Reader*, 2nd ed. (New York: W. W. Norton, 1978), 13.

struggles around the world to transform this system by applying our training and experience to elucidating the real inner workings of the social order and the contradictions therein. Central to this undertaking is putting forward a cogent and systematic critique of global capitalism.[3] For her part, the scholar-activist Susan George cautioned at the Santa Barbara conference that academics who wish to be relevant should study the rich and powerful, not the poor and powerless. "Although wealth and power are in a better position to hide their activities and are therefore more difficult to study, any knowledge about them will be valuable to movements for social justice," she argued. "Better a sociology of the Pentagon or the Houston country club than of single mothers or L.A. gangs."[4]

The present study has focused on power from above and on the ruling groups rather than on resistance and popular struggles from below. For my purposes that is just as it should be; I have attempted here and elsewhere to develop "an ethnography of 'Davos Man'." There is a caveat, however: the dominant groups exist only in relationship to subordinate groups, and so too their projects of domination are constructed in a permanent dialectic tension with struggles and projects from below. As this dialectic plays itself out in the midst of ongoing crisis, the challenge is how to reconstruct the social power of the popular classes worldwide in a new era in which such power is less mediated and organized through the nation-state. The universal penetration of capitalism through globalization draws all peoples not only into webs of market relations but also into webs of resistance.

Globalization disorganized the working and popular classes in the late twentieth century, acting as a centrifugal force for these classes around the world and as a centripetal force for transnationally oriented elites. Working classes were fragmented by restructuring as the intense competition that was forced on these classes in each nation debilitated collective action. In earlier periods of world capitalism the popular sectors were *brought together* as intersubjectivities and mounted collective challenges to the social order. To the extent that the old subjectivities were fragmented and dispersed and new subjectivities had not yet coalesced, capitalist globalization blunted the collective political protagonism of the popular classes. Yet the ongoing crisis appears to have helped generate new

[3] William I. Robinson, "What Is a Critical Globalization Studies? Intellectual Labor and Global Society," in Richard Appelbaum and William I. Robinson, eds., *Critical Globalization Studies* (New York: Routledge, 2003), 11–18. The larger matter of the intellectual in unjust societies is a crucial one here. My own comments on intellectual labor in global society are framed within this larger matter, as taken up in a number of classical works, among them Juilen Benda, *The Treason of the Intellectuals* (Piscataway, NJ: Transaction Publishers, 2006 [1927]); Karl Mannheim, *Ideology and Utopia: An Introduction to the Sociology of Knowledge* (Harcourt, CT: Harcourt, Brace & World, 1968 [1929]); Noam Chomsky, *American Power and the New Mandarins* (New York: Vintage, 1969).

[4] Susan George, "If You Want to Be Relevant: Advice to the Academic from a Scholar-Activist," in Appelbaum and Robinson, *Critical Globalization Studies*, 8.

bases for mass resistance as popular classes regroup. In this brief conclusion I refer to the crisis of hegemony in the global system and discuss the prospects and challenges for counterhegemonic projects from below in the face of global crisis as well as the threat of ecological holocaust and collapse. Further elaboration of these themes is properly the subject of another study.

THE BREAKDOWN OF CONSENSUAL DOMINATION

The worldwide crisis of hegemony of the late 1960s and early 1970s, we shall recall, opened the way for capitalist globalization. Are we entering a new crisis of hegemony at the world systemic level?[5]

I will draw here on several Gramscian concepts that are useful in attempting to understand the historic interregnum we face in the second decade of the twenty-first century: *restricted* and *expansive* hegemony; *historic bloc*; and *passive revolution*. Hegemony in the Gramscian sense refers not to the rule or domination of a country in the international system of nation-states but to a particular relation of social domination in which subordinate groups lend their "active consent" to the system of domination. Projects of hegemony involve not merely rule but political and ideological leadership based on a set of class alliances. Hegemony as a particular modality of ruling-class dominance is fragile; it must constantly be constructed and reconstructed because the possibility of hegemonic or consensual domination rests on both ideological and material foundations. Hegemony therefore requires a material base – what some social scientists have called a "moral economy,"[6] or the material conditions, institutions, and concomitant norms that allow for the social reproduction of a sufficient number of people among subordinate groups. No would-be ruling class can exercise hegemony without developing diverse mechanisms of legitimation and securing a social base – a combination of the consensual integration through

---

[5] Twenty years after the fall of the Berlin Wall, in 2009, one poll conducted across twenty-seven countries found widespread disaffection with free market capitalism and majority support for government intervention to redistribute wealth and regulate the economy, a powerful reflection of global capitalism's crisis of legitimacy. Nearly one-quarter of respondents believed the system was fatally flawed, a view held by 43 percent in France, 38 percent in Mexico, and 35 percent in Brazil. Only 11 percent across the twenty-seven countries believed the system was working well. The poll was conducted by the BBC. The BBC report was summarized by Julie Hyland, "BBC Poll Shows Widespread Disaffection with Capitalism," at the *World Socialist Web Site*, November 12, 2009, from http://www.wsws.org/en/articles/2009/11/bbcc-n12.html. Another poll conducted in the United States that same year found that only 53 percent of adult Americans believed that capitalism was better than socialism. Twenty percent said that socialism was better, and 27 percent were not sure which was better. Importantly, the younger the adult respondents – and therefore the greater the portion of their lives experienced under capitalism in crisis – the more likely they were to prefer socialism over capitalism. Craig Brown, "Poll: Just 54% Favor Capitalism over Socialism," *Common Dreams* website, April 9, 2009, https://www.commondreams.org/further/2009/04/09.
[6] See, e.g., James C. Scott, *The Moral Economy: Rebellion and Subsistence in Southeast Asia* (New Haven, CT: Yale University Press, 1977).

material reward for some, and the coercive exclusion of others whom the system is unwilling or unable to coopt.

Structural crises in the capitalist system upset existing material (class) arrangements. They throw social and class forces into states of flux and reorganization that involve struggles over hegemony. Subordinate groups and counterelites pursue projects of counterhegemony that compete with efforts by dominant groups to reconstitute their fractured hegemony. "One speaks of a 'crisis of authority' and this in fact is the crisis of hegemony, or crisis of the State in all its spheres," writes Gramsci.

> The crisis creates immediately dangerous situations, because the different strata of the population do not possess the same capacity for rapid reorientation or for reorganizing themselves with the same rhythm. The traditional ruling class, which has a numerous trained personnel, changes men and programmes and reabsorbs the control which was escaping it with a greater speed than occurs in the subordinate classes; it makes sacrifices, exposes itself to an uncertain future by making demagogical promises, but it maintains power.[7]

Dominant groups have indeed been striving to reconstitute hegemony. Emergent transnational elites set about in the 1980s and 1990s to construct a global capitalist historic bloc. An historic bloc is a social ensemble involving dominant strata and a social base beyond the ruling group, in which one group exercises leadership and imposes its project through the consent of those drawn into the bloc. The ruling group in an historic bloc is able to present its class project as being in the general interest and to gain the active support of those brought into the bloc through the combination of material reward and ideological leadership, thus achieving what Gramsci referred to as *expansive hegemony*. It appeared for a time in the 1990s that transnational elites would be able to establish this historic bloc, but efforts to cement the bloc proved elusive. The "neo-liberal counterrevolution" that rolled back the welfare, developmentalist, and social-democratic states of twentieth-century redistributive capitalism never won the active support of a majority of humanity. Elites and their organic intellectuals worldwide may have reached consensus around neo-liberalism and set about from within state and TNS institutions to restructure world capitalism through globalization. But the popular classes never internalized this neo-liberal worldview. If neo-liberalism appeared to achieve a broader consensus, this was because of the worldwide defeat of the left in the 1980s and the dramatically changed correlation of global class and social forces in favor of transnational capital and its agents in the late twentieth century. At best, such a globalist bloc achieved in the 1980s and 1990s a certain *restricted* as opposed to expansive hegemony, limited to building a global capitalist power bloc, based less on the consent than on the disorganization of the popular classes in the wake of the juggernaut of capitalist globalization.

[7] Antonio Gramsci, *The Modern Prince* (New York: International Publishers, 1957), 174.

As the crisis has deepened in recent years the globalist bloc has been unable to reproduce even this restricted hegemony. It has had to resort, as we saw in the preceding chapter, to increasing worldwide use of direct coercion in order to maintain its domination. The neo-liberal power bloc has been decomposing. As class and social forces regroup, new political projects and counterhegemonies are emerging. What social form may take the place of the neo-liberal project, as I have suggested, is in dispute and may be for quite some time. World politics will be driven by struggles linked to the reorganization of the world economy in the face of prolonged crisis. As I write these lines (early 2013) we are in the midst of the interregnum. Sustained crisis may open up opportunities for capital to restructure in ways that further its interests, but it also makes legitimation problematic insofar as political legitimacy is tied to the state's ability to manage crises.

Specifically, to the extent that neo-liberalism has done away with a moral economy it undermines the material base for a transnational hegemonic project. The logic of accumulation burst forth in past centuries as the negation of a social logic. But in the twentieth century fierce social and class struggles worldwide were able to impose a measure of social control over capital, what Karl Polanyi referred to as the "double movement" (the first movement being the rise of the capitalist market).[8] Popular classes, to varying degrees, were able to force the system to link social reproduction to capital accumulation. What has taken place through globalization is the severing of the logic of accumulation from that of social reproduction, resulting in the unprecedented growth of social inequality that I discussed in Chapter 1 and in intensified crises of survival for billions of people around the world.

It appeared in the wake of the 2008 financial collapse that neo-liberalism in its original incarnation, as a set of policies girded by the ideology of laissez-faire "free markets" and neo-classic and monetary economics, was giving way to "post-neo-liberal" policies involving new forms of state regulation and intervention intended to bring some stability to the chaos of unbridled accumulation or in some cases to allow the limited introduction of redistributive measures. It is not clear if such a post-neo-liberalism will manage to prevail. At the time of writing it appears quite the contrary – that global elites are pursuing a tenacious new round of neo-liberal restructuring coupled with new modalities of repression and social control to contain the discontent that austerity generates.

The present moment is therefore a time of ongoing and escalating conflict around the world without any clear resolution to a brewing crisis of hegemony. Extreme volatility appears to be endemic to the system. The structural causes of the 2008 collapse remain in place. Any number of new bubbles, such as those in global commodities and bond markets, or in the student loan market, could trigger further collapses whose social and political consequences are not

[8] Karl Polanyi, *The Great Transformation*, 2nd ed. (New York: Beacon, 2001).

possible to predict.[9] The IMF warned in a 2011 report that the extreme and growing gap between the rich and the poor worldwide could spark civil wars and throw the global economy into heightened instability. The uprisings in North Africa, warned the report, may be a prelude to what will take place around the world as 400 million youths join the workforce in the next decade. "We could see rising social and political instability within nations – even war."[10]

Conflict in global society is prone to occur at multiple levels: among transnationally oriented elites and those with a more local, national, or regional orientation; between agents of global capitalism and popular forces, within and among nation-states; among competing groups within the globalist bloc who may foment interstate or other types of conflict in pursuit of their particular interests; or simply among communities divided along ethnic or cultural lines in the face of economic destabilization and social stress. Specifically, challenges to the global capitalist power bloc may come from subordinate groups in transnational civil society or from individual nation-states when these states are captured by subordinate groups – as in the case of Venezuela since the start of the Bolivarian revolution in 1999 – as well as from dominant groups who are less integrated into (or even opposed to) global capitalism, such as, for example, the Baath Party/Iraqi state elite prior to the 2003 U.S. invasion, sectors among the Russian oligarchy, and some Chinese economic and political elites. The picture is further complicated by the instability wrought by the breakdown of social order and the collapse of national state authority in many regions. We can expect ongoing civil wars and international conflicts or, even more likely, conflicts that combine these two dimensions, as in Syria.

A WORLD TO WIN, A WORLD TO LOSE

The World Revolution of 20xx

Have we entered a new wave of popular revolts and revolutions? Since the crisis of global capitalism began in the final years of the twentieth century there seem to have been two waves of global rebellion. The first involved the rise of a global justice movement, the coalescing of numerous popular struggles and resistance movements from around the world into a critical mass in the late 1990s and the formation of the World Social Forum under the banner "Another World Is Possible." This wave reached its crest at the turn of the century and was in part derailed, in part transformed, by the events of September 11, 2001, and the counteroffensive of the transnational elite made possible by those events. The

---

[9] On the massively profitable student loan market, see Christian Deritis, "Student Lending's Failing Grade," *Moody's Analysis*, July 2011: 54–59.

[10] Ambrose Evans-Pritchard, "IMF Raises Spectre of Civil Wars as Global Inequalities Worsen," *The Telegraph*, February 1, 2011, on-line edition, from http://www.telegraph.co.uk/finance/globalbusiness/8296987/IMF-raises-spectre-of-civil-wars-as-global-inequalities-worsen.html.

second wave began in the wake of the 2008 financial collapse. It spread from 2009 to 2011. Among the flash points that most grabbed international headlines were repeated rounds of mass strikes and mobilizations in the EU countries (most notably in those hardest hit by austerity, including Greece, Spain, Cyprus, and Ireland); uprisings in the Middle East and North Africa; the Occupy Wall Street Movement in the United States; the Chilean student movement; ongoing strike waves among Chinese workers; immigrant rights struggles in many countries, and so on.

We need to theorize and conceptualize these diverse movements and their emancipatory potentials as well as limitations. The notion of a global justice movement, which in reality is not a single movement but hundreds – thousands – of movements, increasingly articulates an expansive and multifaceted global revolt, especially insofar as global communications and social networking bring to these movements, no matter how local, a sense of transnational connection and global consciousness. It is not clear at the time of writing if the momentum of this global revolt can be sustained or if it will be defused by passive revolution (see the following discussion). Nonetheless, as mass social movements around the world continue to struggle and to proliferate, a restoration of the hegemony of the global capitalist bloc is unlikely.

The sociologist and world-systems scholar Christopher Chase-Dunn has placed the current wave of revolts in historical perspective. He terms the wave "the world revolution of 20xx," the x's to denote that it is yet in formation. "The idea of world revolution is a broad notion that encompasses all kinds of resistance to hierarchy regardless of whether or not it is coordinated," he states. "Usually the idea of revolution is conceptualized on a national scale in which new social forces come to state power and restructure social relations." But it is the "world polity or world order that is the arena of contestation within which world revolutions have occurred and that world revolutions have restructured." World revolutions involve constellations of local, regional, national and transnational rebellions and revolutions that have long-term consequences for changing world orders. The years that symbolize the major world revolutions after the Protestant Reformation are 1789, 1848, 1917, 1968, and 1989. He concludes that "revolutionaries appear to have lost in the failure of their most radical demands, but enlightened conservatives who are trying to manage hegemony end up incorporating the reforms that were earlier radical demands into the current world order."[11]

While rebellion appears to have broken out everywhere in the aftermath of the 2008 financial collapse, it has been spread very unevenly across countries and regions and faces many problems and challenges. Resistance is fragmented, often spontaneous, lacking in structures, strategies, and programs as well as

---

[11] Christopher Chase-Dunn, "The World Revolution of 20xx," Institute for Research on World-Systems, University of California at Riverside, 2007, from p. 7, found at http://irows.ucr.edu/papers/irows35/irows35.htm.

sturdy organizations that can give both substance and continuity to popular upheavals. Part of the problem in sustaining a rebellion that could present a systemic challenge to global capitalism stems from the crisis of the twentieth-century left worldwide, its willingness to have bought into the neo-liberal ideological claim of the "End of History." This left became defeatist in the late twentieth century in the face of the ascent to hegemony of global capitalism, insisting that we had to be "realistic" and "pragmatic," to limit ourselves to putting a "human face" on the capitalist system. The quote by Frederic Jameson that opens this chapter was meant to draw attention to the mental paralysis and "postmodern cynicism" of the global left.

The bankruptcy of the strategy and program of much of this twentieth-century left – social democratic as well as self-declared socialist and communist – its dogmatism, vanguardist, hierarchial, and often authoritarian practices, left a generation of youth with an equally defeatist rejection of theory, of socialist organizations, programs, and strategies. The dominant tendency in many late twentieth and early twenty-first-century global justice movements and popular rebellions became variants of anarchism, syndic-anarchism, "horizontalism," "autonomism," and so on – varied approaches to struggle that have in common two notions above all. The first is that we can "change the world without taking power," that is, that we can create an alternative society in the interstices of the existing global capitalist one, without confronting the (capitalist) state, over-throwing it, and utilizing revolutionary state power as part of a broader trans-formatory project of emancipation.[12] The second is the idea that neither revolutionary theories and political organizations (whether called parties or not), nor socialist (or even any) programs, are necessary.[13]

---

[12] Among others, John Holloway, in *Change the World without Taking Power: The Meaning of Revolution Today* (London: Pluto, 2002), elevated to theoretical status the notion that capitalism can be superseded without confronting and overthrowing the capitalist state. I cannot take up the debate here, but see my critique in William I. Robinson, *Latin America and Global Capitalism* (Baltimore: Johns Hopkins University Press, 2008). Anticipating such an argument in the wake of the "identity politics" of the 1980s onward, A Sivanandan noted in 1990: "There may be all sorts of 'resistance to the system' in civil society, all sorts of new social movements and a 'politics of the family, of health, of food, of sexuality, of the body,' as Sivanandan observes. "And they may even succeed in pushing out the boundaries of individual freedom. But the moment they threaten to change the system in any fundamental way or go beyond the personal politics of health, food, sexuality, etc., they come up against the power of the state." It is only by challenging state power that "you expose the coercive face of the state to the people, sharpening their political sense and resistance, providing the temper and climate for the construction of more effective 'social blocs'. . . . It is inconceivable that we should go on talking about resistances in civil society and ignoring the power of the state. . . . How do you extend a 'politics of food' to the hungry, 'a politics of the body' to the homeless, a 'politics of the family' to those without any income?" *Communities of Resistance: Writings on Black Struggles for Socialism* (London: Verso, 1990), 42–43.

[13] In its extreme variant – which regrettably, in my view, has become a not uncommon attitude among youth – is the belief that social communication blurbs are a sufficient substitute for reading texts and studying society and history, as expressed to a reporter by one organizer of mass student

There is a glorification of spontaneous, yet rudderless, revolt. Spontaneous protest gives an illusion of power. Yet if social protest movements don't have their own agenda they end up negotiating that of those in power. The journalist Paul Mason quotes a UK protester against the privatization of higher education who declared, when asked what she reads and what influences the way she thinks and acts: "I don't like talking about what I think; it's bullshit. It's this action, this protest, Iraq, Palestine, Deptford."[14] Without theory, the much-maligned Lenin pointed out, there can be no revolution. Practice by itself becomes short-lived, rudderless, and susceptible to co-optation and passive revolution; theory by itself is meaningless, as "the point is to change the world." *Praxis* – the unity and synergy of theory and practice – is often lost in the new global revolts. Confronting the crisis also means confronting these political – or rather apolitical! – ideas and practices as illusions that are disempowering and self-defeating.

The commitment of youth, in particular, to "horizontalism" may generate a great many "prefigurative practices" indispensable to the development of counterhegemonic movements. Yet it is sometimes difficult to expunge the individualism of such practices from the social solidarity – fetishizing individual subjectivity contributes to the social fragmentation produced by global capitalism and, in the extreme case, to narcissism. Mason argues that "networked protests" made possible by new social communication technologies "reduce the level of commitment needed to be involved in anything. They allow users to adopt multiple identities, a pick-and-mix attitude to commitment, a kind of learned mercuriality. They allow instant concentration upon a target (as with Tahrir Square, or the Manet painting at London's National Gallery), but equally instant fragmentation and dispersal." They make every action, he observes, "the subject of negotiation between the participants; unlike with an infantry battalion."[15]

How viable are transformative strategies based on the notion that local communities can withdraw from global capitalism? The attempt to create alternative communities at the local level, to set up cooperatives, to decentralize circuits of food supply, to withdraw from the global agro-industrial regime, to decentralize energy distribution and consumption, and to construct cooperative enterprises and local solidarity economies are necessary and important. Yet they do not in themselves resolve the problem of power. In the absence of a strategy to confront the state and to transform the system *from within* we are left with the

protests in England in 2010 against the privatization of higher education: "I would rather read new stuff [not books and articles dealing with history, theory and analysis]: the old ideas are nice to know; they're context. But I would rather know what's happening now. I can't believe there are still those who read articles. If everybody had a Twitter feed you could just see the news as it happens. You don't need 100 words of background." As cited by Mason in *Why It's Kicking Off Everywhere*, 42.

[14] As cited in ibid., 57.
[15] Ibid., 81–82.

dangerous illusion that the world can be changed without resolving this matter of power. Global capitalism is now internal to practically all communities on the planet. It has spun webs of worldwide interdependency that link us all to a larger totality. Global capitalism is indeed *totalizing*. The notion that one can escape from global capitalism not by defeating it but by creating alternative spaces or islands of utopia ignores the unpleasant fact that no matter how one wills it to be so, these spaces cannot disengage from capitalism, if for no other reason than that capital and the state will penetrate – often forcibly – and continuously reincorporate these spaces.

Localized solutions are too piecemeal to confront the power of global capitalism – to change the global balance of class and social forces. There is no way to get around the fact that the TCC holds class power over humanity, and the TNS exercises multiple forms of direct, coercive power. *The state exercises power over us.* This fact will not go away by ignoring this power. It is illusory to suppose that it can be countered by constructing autonomous communities, which in fact are not autonomous because such communities cannot extricate themselves from the webs of global capitalism, and even if they could, in theory, the state would not allow them to; it would use the force of *its* law to reincorporate such communities. There is no getting around confrontation with the state, no avoiding a struggle to wrest state power away from capital, its agents and allies. The struggle to withdraw from global capitalism, no matter how important, must be coupled with a struggle to overthrow global capitalism, to destroy the transnational capitalist state.

On the other hand, what undergirds the global revolt are movements that are less "glamorous" and less likely to draw the attention of the international media, yet deeply grounded in the everyday struggles of the working and popular classes around the world. Such organizations as unofficial trade unions in Egypt and the Via Campesina peasant and small farmer movement have been patiently accumulating forces, building strong organizations and programs of struggle that can be sustained over many years. Mason, among others, reports on an insurgent working class in Egypt that from 2008 onward broke with official unions and launched sustained campaigns against privatization, neo-liberalism, and the dictatorship of Hosni Mubarak (see the following discussion). Via Campesina is one of the most transnationalized, largest, and best-coordinated mass social movements in the world, bringing together millions of peasants and rural workers from sixty-nine countries and every continent. The global agricultural system and its accelerated takeover by transnational corporate agribusiness is becoming a major site of transnational class and social struggles, and Via Campesina is at the vanguard of those struggles, with its agenda of "food sovereignty," agrarian reform, defense of smallholder land, and withdrawal from the agribusiness system. In Brazil, "peasants who in the past were accustomed to only fighting against large landowners and plantation owners have now transformed themselves into a principal actor against large transnational capital," observed João Pedro Stédile, a leader of the Via Campesina–affiliated Landless Workers

Movement in Brazil.[16] Similarly, the working class has been central to many recent struggles around the world even if it is absent from international media coverage of these struggles, which has tended to focus on middle-class urban youth and their savvy social media organizing.

Passive Revolution?

It is clear there is no single conclusion to be reached with regard to the content and direction of the worldwide revolt, which ranges from explicitly socialist revolutions in South America, to the well-organized social movements of peasants in the worldwide Via Campesina or the South African shack dwellers union, to the amorphous anticapitalism of the anarchist-inspired upheavals in Spain or of the Occupy Wall Street movement, to shifting coalitions of youth, workers, middle-class professionals, and neo-liberal technocrats in Egypt or Greece. The key question is whether these global revolts will succeed in altering the political and economic power structures or actually renovate them through combinations of mild reform and cooptation? Or worse still, will the global police state respond to mass uprisings that do try to transform the social order in favor of the poor majority by imposing twenty-first-century fascism?[17]

The Italian socialist Antonio Gramsci developed the concept of *passive revolution* to refer to efforts by dominant groups to bring about mild change from above in order to undercut mobilization for more far-reaching transformation from below. Integral to passive revolution is the co-optation of leadership from below, its integration into the dominant project. Gramsci also referred to this process as *transformismo*, whereby rule by the dominant groups is dependent

---

[16] As cited in Annette Aurelie Desmarais, *La Via Campesina: Globalization and the Power of Peasants* (London: Pluto Press), 29. See also Eric Holt-Giménez and Raj Patel, *Food Rebellions: Crisis and the Hunger for Justice* (San Francisco: Food First Books, 2009).

[17] One clear model for such an outcome is provided by Haiti. The country was shattered in January 2010 by a massive earthquake that killed or injured a half-million people. But Haiti had been experiencing the earthquake of global capitalism for decades. The popular classes have sustained a mass rebellion that began in the mid-1980s against the repressive social order and its violent inequalities. See Justin Podur's excellent study, *Haiti's New Dictatorship: The Coup, the Earthquake and the UN Occupation* (London: Pluto, 2012). See also Jeb Sprague, *Paramilitarism and the Assault on Democracy in Haiti* (New York: Monthly Review Press, 2012). All the machinations of power and domination have been brought into play since the 1980s to suppress this mass popular movement and turn the country into an open field for transnational corporate plunder, including state and paramilitary terrorism against the popular movement, systematic human rights violations, UN occupation, the orchestration of electoral shams, disinformation campaigns, economic blackmail, the dismantling of local state autonomy, and ever-deeper austerity and dispossession. Global elites took advantage of the 2010 natural disaster to accelerate this transnational agenda – a textbook case of "disaster capitalism" – turning the country into a virtual protectorate of the TNS, a giant sweatshop for the global economy, through "reconstruction," a concentration camp where utter desperation would subdue the population, impose discipline, obedience, and submission under the watchful control of a transnational political-military occupation.

on the ongoing absorption of intellectual, political, and cultural leaders of the subordinate majority into the ruling bloc and the resulting decapitation and disorganization of resistance from below. In the wake of the 1960s worldwide rebellions and the 1970s crisis, the transnational elite appeared to have carried out a "passive revolution" of sorts involving the reorganization of the world political economy and social relations ("revolution") while neutralizing the resistance of the subordinate majority. For Gramsci, a passive revolution involves what he calls "statisation," or restructuring from above so that popular projects from below are contained and undercut, combined with, in Gramsci's words, the use of "force, fraud, and corruption" as mechanisms of social control.[18] It appears as well that the TNS has responded to the revolt of 20xx with attempts at further passive revolution.

To illustrate the point, global elites, led by the U.S. state, seem to have set about fomenting passive revolution in the Middle East and North Africa (MENA) as a response to the Arab Spring. Popular struggles in the MENA region before and after the overthrow of Egyptian dictator Hosni Mubarak in January 2012 clearly could not be controlled by transnational elites. Yet Egypt's integration into the new circuits of global capitalism began in the 1990s, and in 2003 the U.S. government announced a broad program to "promote democracy" and "free markets" in the Middle East and North Africa.[19] U.S. and other transnational agents had been laboring together with local transnationally oriented business and political elites to bring the region more fully into these circuits and to undertake a more sweeping neo-liberal transformation. In Egypt this involved programs to bring about a transition to "democracy" that would replace the decadent Mubarak dynasty with more transnationally oriented elites who could assure more stable rule and dismantle what was left of a rentier state. The strategy was to bring about mild political reform from above in order to keep any potential popular rebellion within manageable boundaries. Political regime change was not just tolerated but actually encouraged – so long as Egypt's popular masses did not challenge the pillars of the Egyptian social order itself – domination by an increasingly transnationally oriented civilian-military elite and a neo-liberal program of integration into global capitalism.

"Successive U.S. administrations had made it clear that for economic and political reasons," observes Ramadan, "the region's dictatorships had to change as a necessary precondition for opening up Arab markets and integrating the region into the global economy."[20] In this respect, the Arab Spring has helped open up the region to global capitalism. In Egypt, leaders of the April 6

---

[18] Among other places, Gramsci developed the notions of passive revolution and transformismo, and discussed fraud and corruption, in his writings on Italian history. See, e.g., *Prison Notebooks*, 52–120.

[19] See, inter alia, Tariq Ramadan, *Islam and the Arab Awakening* (New York: Oxford University Press, 2012); Adam Hanieh, "'Democracy Promotion' and Neo-Liberalism in the Middle East," *State of Nature*, Spring 2006, from http://www.stateofnature.org/democracyPromotion.html.

[20] Ramadan, *Islam and the Arab Awakening*, 9.

movement of largely middle-class youth that played a critical role in convening the mass protests that led to the ouster had previously been brought to the United States for training by U.S. government–financed organizations in how to organize a movement against Mubarak. Transnational corporations with interests in the MENA region, together with U.S. government and quasi-governmental organizations, also provided broad training and resources to these youth. "In point of fact," notes Ramadan, "Google, Twitter, and Yahoo were directly involved in training and disseminating information on the Web promoting pro-democracy activism." These leaders in turn declared their support for Mohamed el-Baradei, the former director general of the International Atomic Energy Agency and the favored transnationally oriented technocrat to replace Mubarak.[21]

That transnational elites cannot control the social and political forces unleashed by the crisis became clear when the masses of protesting Egyptians resoundingly rejected al-Baredei as their would-be leader when he returned home from self-imposed exile in the midst of the anti-Mubarak uprising. The U.S. state and transnational elites have influenced but cannot control events or outcomes in the MENA region. However, the wild enthusiasm displayed by some international commentators ignored the fact that the Arab Spring uprisings were not anticapitalist, and indeed did not tend to question in any fundamental way the socioeconomic order. The outcome – or multiple outcomes – of the Egyptian revolution, of the Arab Spring, and more generally of the 20xx revolution will be shaped by ongoing struggles among distinct social/class forces and political agents.

Reflecting on these ongoing struggles, Bayat observes the "profound disjunction between two key dimensions of [twenty-first-century] revolution: *movement and change*" (emphasis in original).[22] The focus on "revolution as movement" that appears to predominate in the global revolt, he continues, "has served to obscure the peculiar nature of these 'revolutions' [in MENA] in terms of change, with little to say about what happens the day after the dictators abdicate. It may even serve to disguise the paradoxes of these upheavals, shaped by the new political times in which grand visions and emancipatory utopias have given way to fragmentary projects, improvisation and loose horizontal networks."[23] The neglect of revolution as change, or socioeconomic transformation, and together with it, or perhaps because of it, renunciation of the struggle for state power, paves the way for global elites to promote passive revolution. In Egypt and around the world, as I have discussed at length elsewhere, the strategy

---

[21] For these details, see ibid, 11–13. See also the detailed report by Edmund Berger, "Egypt and International Capital: Is This What Democracy Looks Like?," in Rebecca Fisher, ed., *Managing Democracy, Managing Dissent: Capitalism, Democracy and the Organization of Consent* (London: Corporate Watch/Freedom Press, 2013), p. 310–333.

[22] Asef Bayat, "Revolution in Bad Times," *New Left Review* (2013), 80: 47–60 (citation from p. 48).

[23] Ibid., 48.

of passive revolution seeks to channel mass rebellions into "movement without change," often through the rhetoric and policies of "democracy promotion," that is, promotion of polyarchic systems of elite rule.[24] Revolutionaries remained outside the structures of power because they were not planning to take over the state, while the TNS and global elites channeled and utilized revolts to catapult to power transnationally oriented elites and to promote passive revolution.

A New Dark Ages? The Specter of Collapse

It would be impossible to conclude this study of crisis, hegemony, and counter-hegemony without a discussion, no matter how brief, of ecological holocaust. The environmental sciences have shown that natural and social history – always a dialectical unity even though we have only just become cognizant of this unity – are converging in unprecedented ways. The Nobel Prize–winning atmospheric chemist Paul Crutzen coined the term *Anthropocene* to mark the coming of a new epoch in planetary history that has replaced the *Holocene*, which refers to the stable, interglacial geological epoch dating to 10–12,000 years ago. For Crutzen, humanity has become the chief driver of rapid changes in the earth system during this new epoch, and geological-scale change has suddenly entered into human history itself. There has always been a complex co-evolution of nature and human society (human production, to be specific), or of "earth systems" and "world systems." At this time, however, the world system is a truly global system, and the transformations in natural systems brought about by human activity have now begun, in the words of ecologist Peter Vitousek, to "alter the structure and function of Earth as a system."[25]

The notion of the *Anthropocene* "highlights that a potentially fatal ecological rift has arisen between human beings and the earth, emanating from the conflicts and contradictions of the modern capitalist society," in the words of Foster, Clark, and York. Marx had argued that capitalism produces a *metabolic rift* between human society and natural systems. Capitalist production, said Marx, "disturbs the metabolic interaction between man and earth," or the equilibrium of exchanges, the "metabolism" between human society and natural systems. Building on Marx's notion of a metabolic rift, Foster and his colleagues warn that "the planet is now dominated by a technologically potent but alienated humanity – alienated from both nature and from itself; and hence ultimately

---

[24] William I. Robinson, *Promoting Polyarchy: Globalization, U.S. Intervention, and Hegemony* (Cambridge: Cambridge University Press, 1996). Berger notes, in reference to the protest strategies promoted by U.S. and transnational elites, that these are "articulated rather simply as the toil of the subject/people under the ruler/government. Thus, [these] tactics are always geared towards oppression rooted in states. The exploitative system of capitalism is completely ejected" from the analysis and subsequent strategies. Berger, "Egypt and International Capital," 312.

[25] As cited in John Bellamy Foster, Brett Clark, and Richard York, *The Ecological Rift: Capitalism's War on the Earth* (New York: Monthly Review Press, 2010), 35.

destructive of everything around it. At issue is not just the sustainability of human society but the diversity of life on Earth." Indeed, "perhaps the greatest danger of climate change to life is the accelerated tempo of the change in the earth system, overwhelming natural evolutionary processes and even social adaptation, and thus threatening the mass extinction of species and even human civilization itself."[26]

It boggles the mind to comprehend that global capitalism now couples human and natural history in such a way as to threaten to bring about what would be the sixth mass extinction in the known history of life on earth (it is estimated that, at current rates, some one-third of the millions of species on the planet will have gone extinct by 2100).[27] *Yet this mass extinction would be caused not by a natural catastrophe such as a meteor impact or by evolutionary changes such as the end of an ice age, but by purposive human activity.* Seen in this light, the conclusion of Foster and his colleagues indeed seems to be an understatement:

> Ironically, most analyses of the environmental problem today are concerned less with saving the planet or life or humanity than saving capitalism – the system at the root of our environmental problem. . . . The structural significance and scale of the ecological crisis is not reflected in solutions of a corresponding significance and scale. This failure of both imagination and social practices is in many ways a product of a double alienation: from nature and within human society itself. Not only has this generated inertia with respect to social change – indeed a tendency to fiddle while Rome burns – but it has also led to the belief that the crisis can be managed by essentially the same social institutions that brought it into being in the first place. . . . By abandoning the critique of capitalism and increasingly dropping it from their analytical vision altogether, mainstream social scientists (even environmental sociologists in some cases) have removed from their analytical vision the essential problem now facing planetary society. Once the notion of 'green capitalism' is accepted – as if capitalism was not a system of self-expanding value, or that endless accumulation was somehow compatible with environmental sustainability – then the environmental problem becomes merely the question of management and markets.[28]

The three key questions that are of concern to us here are: *first,* can ecological holocaust be averted without superseding capitalism? *Second,* how is ecological crisis related to other dimensions of global crisis? *Third,* how do the popular and working classes combine struggle against the deleterious social effects of trans-national capitalist plunder with struggle against the deadly effects on the environment that result from this plunder?

[26] Foster, Clark, and York, *The Ecological Rift,* 14, 35.
[27] Richard Leakey and Roger Lewin, *The Sixth Extinction: Patterns of Life and the Future of Humankind* (New York: Anchor, 1996).
[28] Foster, Clark, and York, *The Ecological Rift,* 29–30, 37, although they note subsequently (p. 38) that "the only thing that can save us is a revolution in the constitution of society itself. Without such a revolution changes in the human metabolic relation to earth (in the material relations of production), the future of the world, like bourgeois human nature, will be 'nasty, brutish, and short'."

Regarding the first – can capitalism be reconciled more broadly with nature? – the accumulation imperative that is at the core of the capitalist system, the imperative for this system to constantly expand, which is the real meaning of "growth," means that a stationary state under capitalism is not possible. As Joseph Schumpeter observed, stationary capitalism "would be a *contradictio in adjeto*."[29] By definition there can be no resolution of the "metabolic rift" from within the system of global capitalism.[30] A global reformism or neo-Keynesianism, even if it could temporarily alleviate the sharpest social contradictions of neo-liberal globalization, is not viable because any project that seeks to resolve the crisis from within the logic of capital accumulation must by definition seek continued growth, that is, the continued expansion of the system (the *endless self-expansion of capital*).

Yet expansion is reaching its limits. As Foster and his colleagues note, "the essential problem is the unavoidable fact that an expanding economic system is placing additional burdens on a fixed earth system to the point of planetary overload."[31] Ecologically, the system draws ever more destructively on the limited resources and absorptive capacity of nature, as the economy continually grows in scale in relation to the planetary system. The depletion of resources, the destruction of the biosphere, and the impending collapse of agriculture make impossible a further expansion of the system, at least if we want to avoid a mass dying. Implosion may well be the eventual outcome to the drive for further expansion. Those that call for "pragmatism" and operating within "the limits of the possible" miss the point: it is more utopian to believe that the crisis can be resolved within the confines of the system than to believe the system can and must be overthrown.

Yet in attributing the ecological holocaust to capitalism, a 500-year-old system (and industrial capitalism a 250-year-old system), Foster and his colleagues, among others, ignore that precapitalist and ancient civilizations collapsed under the impact of their social forms on natural (environmental) changes, starting with the collapse of the very first known civilization, Sumer, due to oversalination of agricultural lands. The ruling elites of Easter Island or the Mayan city-states could not separate their imperative for domination from the destruction that their systems of domination and exploitation wrought on the environment, thus undermining the capacity of these societies for social reproduction. There are many historical episodes of such collapse, instances in which civilizations are unable to resolve the contradictions that tear

---

[29] Joseph Schumpeter, *Essays* (Reading, MA: Addison-Wesley, 1951), 293, as cited in Foster, Clark, and York, *The Ecological Rift*, 29.

[30] Among the many studies I have found invaluable from the "Marxist ecology" perspective, and from a deeper historical, world-system, and earth system perspective, is Sing C. Chew, *The Recurring Dark Ages: Ecological Stress, Climate Changes, and System Transformation* (Lanham: AltaMira Press, 2006).

[31] Foster, Clark, and York, *The Ecological Rift*, 17.

them apart.[32] When no social or political force is able to prevail and impose a stable system of domination, demise has been the outcome, from Easter Island and the Mayan states already mentioned to the collapse of the Roman Empire and several Chinese dynasties. However, it is now clear that social and political crises in these ancient civilizations combined with their contradictions with nature, so that ecological constraints played a role in their collapse. The domination of some human beings over others in class societies, whether capitalist or precapitalist, has historically been coupled with human domination over nature in a way that renders civilization unsustainable.

What makes capitalism unique in this sense is not that it is in fundamental contradiction with nature. Rather, it is *the scope and the magnitude* of this contradiction, such that human activity now threatens the earth system itself. The current moment is distinct in that this time the collapse would be that of global civilization. We face the prospect of a more far-reaching systemic implosion in the twenty-first century through ecological crisis – as suggested in global climate change; peak oil and other resource depletion scenarios; the spiral of species extinctions; and scientific predictions of a collapse of central agricultural systems in China, Australia, the U.S. Midwest, and other global breadbaskets in the coming decades. According to leading environmental scientists there are nine "planetary boundaries" crucial to maintaining an earth-system environment in which humans can exist, four of which are now experiencing the onset of irreversible environmental degradation, and three of which (climate change, the nitrogen cycle, and biodiversity loss) are at "tipping points," meaning that these processes have already crossed their planetary boundaries.[33] The ecological constraints on a resolution of the global crisis circumscribe the political possibilities for such a resolution. Even if global capitalism could manage to stabilize in the next few years, a recovery would be ephemeral without a resolution of the fundamentally unsustainable nature of the system.

The sociologist Sing Chew, who specializes in what he terms the "Nature-Culture relationship," has studied "recurrent Dark Ages" in world history, including mass dying, political chaos, and a regression in levels of social organization and productive forces as civilizations decompose. He has warned that we face the possibility now of a "new Dark Age" on a planetary scale:[34]

---

[32] See, for example, Jared Diamond, *Collapse: How Societies Choose to Fail or Succeed* (New York: Penguin, 2005).

[33] As reported by Foster, Clark, and York, *The Ecological Rift*, 14. These scientists are involved in a project led by Johan Rockstrom from the Stockholm Resilience Center that includes the participation of Crutzen and the U.S. climatologist James Hansen. The nine are: climate change, ocean acidification, stratospheric ozone depletion, the nitrogen and phosphorus cycles, global freshwater use, change in land use, biodiversity loss, atmospheric aerosol loading, and chemical pollution.

[34] Sing C. Chew, *World Ecological Degradation: Accumulation, Urbanization, and Deforestation* (Landham, MD: AltaMira Press/Rowman and Littlefield Publishers, 2001), and *The Recurring Dark Ages*.

> Dark Ages (as historical events and as a theoretical concept) are critical crises periods in world history over the course of the last five thousand years when environmental conditions have played a significant part in determining how societies, kingdoms, empires, and civilizations are reorganized and organized. They [Dark Ages] are periods of devolution of human communities, and as such from the perspective of human progress, a period of socioeconomic and political decay and retrogression. ... Over world history, such Dark Ages, or prolonged periods of widespread social and economic distress and ecological crisis lasting for centuries, are rare. Between 3000 B.C. to A.D. 1000, there have been identifications of only two or three such periods impacting Northwestern India, west Asia, the Mediterranean, and Europe.[35]

During these periods, notes Chew, more advanced technologies and material skills, even the written language, disappeared for generations, crafts and the arts declined, trade and commerce collapsed, disease spread, food production and living conditions plummeted, and population declined drastically. "As the world system evolved over time, the occurrence of Dark Ages extending over wider and wider geographic space revealed the interconnectivity of socioeconomic and political relationships. Places where Dark Ages have not been experienced or appeared later in time suggest to us that these locales had not been incorporated into the evolving world system at that particular point in time when a Dark Age was occurring."[36] Now, the world system of capitalism – a *global* system – suggests that any new Dark Age would encompass all of humanity.

Regarding the second matter, the relationship of ecological to other dimensions of global crisis, Christian Parenti and Gwynne Dyer, in their respective studies, *Tropic and Chaos: Climate Change and the New Geography of Violence* and *Climate Wars: The Fight for Survival as the World Overheats*, document the escalation of social and political conflicts around the world in the face of the effects of climate change, especially drought, resource depletion, and extreme weather events.[37] Escalating "climate wars" may be the most visible social manifestation of ecological holocaust. Extreme weather events further destabilize the social order and generate violent conflict, adding fuel to the fires of global crisis. Here we face what Walden Bello terms the "fatal intersection of the ecological crisis and the economic crisis,"[38] both of which are global in nature.

Parenti writes of a "catastrophic convergence of poverty, violence, and climate change" whose impacts on the biosphere include extreme weather events, desertification, ocean acidification, melting glaciers, mass extinctions, and

[35] Chew, *The Recurring Dark Ages*, xvi, 6–7.

[36] Ibid., 170.

[37] Christian Parenti, *Tropic of Chaos: Climate Change and the New Geography of Violence* (New York: Nation Books, 2012); Gwynne Dyer, *Climate Wars: The Fight for Survival as the World Overheats* (Oxford: OneWorld Publications, 2010).

[38] Walden Bello, speech at the Meeting of International Social Movements, Hotel Trang, Bangkok, August 31, 2012, transcribed and posted at the website of Focus on the Global South, from http://focusweb.org/content/challenge-asia%E2%80%99s-social-movements.

incrementally rising sea levels, bringing about widespread famine, proliferating disease, millions of deaths, and a projected 700 million climate refugees over the next few decades. Pentagon planners, he notes, call climate change a "threat multiplier" as extreme weather and water scarcity inflame and escalate existing social conflicts, leading to "militarized management of civilization's violent disintegration." One British government study he cites found that, if current trends, continue, fully one-third of the planet's land mass will be desert by 2100, while up to half the land surface will suffer drought. The study also predicted that during the same period the proportion of land in "extreme drought" will increase from the current 3 percent to 30 percent.[39]

Parenti argues that resolving the climate crisis – what he and many others view as the most urgent task of an environmental movement – cannot wait until capitalism is superseded, and that this can be accomplished through "mitigation" and "adaptation" strategies, at whose core is decarbonizing the global economy. I am not as sanguine as he, but I agree that policies, protocols, and politicies can mitigate climate crisis within the existing global order (which is to say that under certain circumstances the development of alternative energy sources may be profitable enough for capital to develop them on a larger, global scale), so long as there are mass environmental justice movements that are strong enough to force the TCC and its state agents to adopt them.

Hence the third matter of concern here is the centrality of a transnational environmental justice movement to any resolution of the crisis of humanity. Via Campesina may be a model for linking social and environmental struggles and for transnationalizing these struggles. As mentioned earlier, the key pillar of its struggle, for "food sovereignty," encompasses the demand that agricultural policy be for food self-sufficiency involving the deconcentration and democratization of land through agrarian reform and access to land and production resources, beyond individual ownership, thereby allowing more communal and collective forms of ownership that promote ecological stewardship. Via Campesina's struggle to transform agrarian social relations is inseparable from the struggle for environmental justice. To advance this struggle, Via Campesina organizes locally, nationally, transnationally, and globally and strives to link its activities to those of other traditional and new movements around the world. Beyond this inspiring networked organization, the imperative of a transnational environmental justice movement leads us back to the matter of power, the struggle against the very logic of global capitalism, and the need to replace it with a system in which humanity is no longer at war with itself and with nature.

Wither a Global Democratic Socialist Project?

Despite the dangers humanity faces, the current interregnum offers major opportunities for transformative, emancipatory projects. First, the system has lost its

---

[39] Parenti, *Tropic of Chaos*. See p. 47 for the British government report.

legitimacy. Second, neo-liberalism appears to be reaching material and ideological exhaustion. Third, the dominant groups worldwide look to be divided and often rudderless. Fourth, the "Thirdworldization" of the First World opens up new opportunities for radical globalized politics, for organic alliances across North and South. Nonetheless, a resistance movement is not necessarily a counterhegemonic movement, and the latter is not necessarily an anticapitalist movement. The negative of an anticapitalist movement does not necessarily involve the positive (Hegel's "negation of the negation") of an alternative post-capitalist or socialist project. A popular anticapitalist resolution of the global crisis requires not only political action but also an historical-theoretical understanding of world capitalism, its underlying structures and dynamics, its present incarnation.

What configuration of social and political forces could bring about a post-capitalist global order? A socialist alternative is not at odds with a struggle for global reformism, and in fact such an alternative would most likely snowball out of efforts to bring about a reform of the system. Reforming and transforming, or superseding, the system of global capitalism must be mutually reinforcing. People struggle around the conditions of their daily existence, to address the problems that disrupt and undermine that existence. These are, virtually by definition, reformist struggles. What is crucial is for popular, radical, and socialist-oriented forces in the global justice movement to put forward an alternative vision that goes beyond reformism and to have such a vision achieve hegemony within any global counterhegemonic bloc. Such a bloc must move from challenging the "fairness" of the market to *replacing* the *logic of the market* with a *social logic.*

The problem, therefore, is not to identify the rational or logical solution to global crisis, for such solutions correspond to distinct and competing rationalities and logics. Solutions and interests cannot be separated from one another. From the logic of the dominant groups, the solution that has been advanced by reformers is a redistributive project that could raise global demand, re-regulate transnational capital, and develop a "market-based" solution to the environmental crisis, such as making alternative energy sources profitable, that is, making them an attractive avenue for transnational capital accumulation. From the logic of the popular majority, the solution is systemic change, a change in the dominant logic, from an accumulative logic to a social logic, meaning ultimately that the global economy is organized in accordance with the needs of the world's people and not the imperative of accumulation. It is necessary to generate a *rupture* with the rationality or the basic logic of the prevailing order rather than generating counterpositions within that logic. This means overcoming the fragmentation that is itself, in part, the result of the global restructuring of capitalism; it also means breaking with what is "reasonable" and "pragmatic."

Only mass movements can generate counterdefinitions of the global order and its crisis. The Italian theorist (and admirer) of elitism Gaetano Mosca observed that the power of elites rests on an organized minority and a disorganized majority.[40] This majority does not control resources; its real or potential power comes from organization. Alternative solutions, that is, counterhegemony, arises from a change in the correlation of social forces, through mass organization and mobilization. Yet social movements and "civil society organizations" are not in themselves sufficient to confront the power of global capital. It is not enough to "speak truth to power"; those who seek to construct a more just world *must confront power with power*. Confrontation is inevitable. As Frederick Douglas insisted long ago, "power cedes nothing without a struggle; it never has and it never will."

"There are simple, basic connections to be made here within and between the various movements, argues Sivanandan.

> They are connections which are organic to socialism, but they can only develop if the new social movements open themselves out to the larger social issues and to each other; move out in a centrifugal fashion without losing sight of the centripetal – move out, that is, from their particularities to the whole and back again to themselves, enriching both, in an unending traffic of ideas, struggles and commitments; weave the specific and the universal into a holistic pattern of socialism which, so far from failing the parts, continues to be informed by them.[41]

However, in order to make such connections, in my view, we need political organizations that challenge the state. Mass social movements cannot resolve the matter of power absent their amalgamation into a powerful political force capable of contesting the TNS. Without such a political vehicle to link the countless struggles of communities to a larger goal, that of transformation, popular struggles cannot address the root causes of the conditions against which or for which they are struggling.

States, like political parties, are not monolithic institutions, in the sense that social forces and political groups struggle within state institutions. As crisis spreads throughout the global system, states and ruling parties become battlefields for contending forces and can be pulled in multiple and often contradictory directions. The state is also a site of permanent contestation. Popular classes have a disunified, fragmentary presence in the TNS. Struggles do take place within and against the TNS. Anticapitalist and socialist struggles need to forge a new, effective model of relationships among parties (or political organizations), mass social movements, and – when the popular classes are able to establish a presence in its institutions – states. In order to succeed, any emancipatory project requires renovated political vehicles that provide the popular classes in civil society with instruments for invading state structures.

As mentioned earlier, *vanguardism* and *horizontalism* are twin pitfalls. Vanguardism is the view that a mass autonomous struggles from below should

---

[40] Gaetano Mosca, *The Ruling Class* (New York: McGraw-Hill, 1960 [1896]).
[41] Sivanandan, *Communities of Resistance*, 33.

be subordinated to the struggle of a revolutionary party to take state power and to change society from that summit of power. Such a strategy proved to be a disaster in the twentieth century. *Horizontalism* is the view that majorities should organize from below with no need for leadership or political parties – or for that matter, with no unifying program or agenda. It is not necessary to confront the state and conquer state power; it is enough to create local spaces supposedly detachable from the system. To be against vanguardism does *not* mean to be against revolutionary political organizations, and to be against horizontalism does *not* mean to oppose autonomous mass struggles from below.[42]

As I discussed in Chapter 1, a novel feature of the global crisis is that we are reaching limits to the system's extensive and intensive expansion. As capital searches for new outlets of expansion it has turned ever-more aggressively to the commodification of the sites of social reproduction – households, communities, public spaces. Struggles at the points of reproduction become strategic to popular struggles as the spaces for respite from the commodification of social existence, of life itself, are closed off. Kees van der Pijl has identified three moments in the process of the subordination of society and nature to the reproduction of capital: original accumulation, the capitalist production process, and the process of social reproduction, each of which generates its own form of "countermovement" resistance and struggle.[43] It is to the social forces from below engaged in resistance at *all three of these moments* that we should turn in anticipation of any counterhegemonic impulse that could develop into an effective socialist alternative to global capitalism. This involves linking three fronts of struggle: labor struggles at the points of production, community struggles at the points of reproduction, and political struggles in political society. Important to such linkage is social movement unionism – organizing working and popular class communities at the points of social reproduction as much as, or even more than, at the points of production.

Just as "reform and revolution" were never mutually exclusive struggles or processes, neither are struggling to build power from below and struggling to take power exclusive or antagonistic projects. To the contrary, they are mutually reinforcing, part of a broader project of transformation. Participation in elections – when such participation can advance popular empowerment – is one crucial front of struggle and is not the same as *electoralism*, or the notion that mass socialist struggles are to be reduced to electoral campaigns and that capitalism can be overthrown through elections *in and of themselves*. If there can be no socialism without democracy in the twenty-first century, it is equally true that democracy is not possible without socialism. There are endless series of demands that would be part of a popular agenda, ranging from a halt to austerity; taxing

---

[42] See my discussion in Robinson, *Latin America and Global Capitalism*.
[43] Kees van der Pijl, "The History of Class Struggle: From Original Accumulation to Neoliberalism," *Monthly Review* (1997), 49(1): 28–44.

capital and the rich; expanding the social wage; nationalizing banks, utilities, basic services, and natural resources; abolishing prison-industrial complexes, repressive laws, and bogus wars (e.g., on drugs, terrorism); lifting borders for people and granting universal citizenship rights (borders are not in the interests of the global working class, and neither are "citizenship rights" in its interests when they are defined by legal status rather than as universal rights). Beyond specific demands, alternatives are defined in the heat of mass struggles, not beforehand and not deductively.

The key here is to achieve the hegemony of the global working class within a movement to reform and transform the global system. Yet the global working class of the twenty-first century is a far cry from the classical working class of the industrial revolution or the international working class of the twentieth century. Challenges to global capitalism require creative new forms of organizing and new ways of aggregating global working-class intersubjectivities. "[T]he center of gravity has shifted," notes Sivanandan, "to peripheral workers, home workers, *ad hoc* workers, casual, temporary, part-time workers – all bits and pieces of the working class that the new productive forces have dispersed and dissipated of their strength."[44] It has also shifted toward women and transnational immigrant workers. The axis of an anticapitalist and universalist struggle must be the new global working class, with its rainbow and heavily female face, one that is transnationally organized. The empowerment of the global working class involves a completely new conception of labor organizing and unions; it involves organizing informal sector workers, the unemployed, immigrant workers, part-time and contract workers, and so on. Resistance involves flexibly switching from interrupting accumulation by withholding labor to interrupting accumulation by disrupting the normal functioning of the system.

How do we awaken a socialist consciousness? How do people come to believe in utopian visions that inspire the belief that change is possible, desirable, and worth the sacrifice it requires? Structures and struggles – or structure and agency, subject and object – cannot be separated because it is only through struggle that structures are imposed, reproduced, or transformed. All social orders require legitimation. The legitimation of global capitalism rests fundamentally on the denial of the humanity of its billions of victims. Global capitalism seeks its legitimacy in countless ideological and cultural processes – through myths of democracy, liberty, equality, progress, growth, freedom, and so on, as well as through inverse constructs – the barbarity, irrationality, and inhumanity of those who refuse to acknowledge the legitimacy of the system. At the same time, global accumulation is increasingly reliant on symbolic and cultural exchanges that make possible the rapid circulation of commodities. More than ever before, political and economic processes are globalized, as Levine observes,

---

[44] Sivanandan, *Communities of Resistance*, 29.

to the extent that they are "culturized."[45] The struggle to break the legitimacy of global capitalism involves cultural and ideological confrontation as much as the organization of social and political movements and theoretical labor in combating "commonsense" hegemonic conceptions transmitted through culture and everyday life in the construction of counterhegemony for what Gramsci referred to as a "long march" through civil society. Such a march requires a renewal of critical and radical thinking along with a capacity to operate as much on the cultural and ideological as on the political terrain.

We have entered, to reiterate by way of conclusion, a period of turbulence, upheavals, collapse of states, political vacuums, and prolonged conflict as we step into the unknown. We are headed toward the frightening dystopia portrayed in the classic film *Bladerunner*, in which the rich have ensconced themselves in mile-high citadels while the rest of humanity scrapes by on the brink of demise. But such a future is *not* inevitable. A resolution of the crisis of humanity is possible. This resolution must involve a radical redistribution of wealth and power downward to poor majorities. Social justice requires a measure of transnational social governance over the global production and financial system as a necessary first step in this radical redistribution. Such redistribution would require a reversal of neo-liberal policies at the nation-state level. But redistribution is not enough. It must be linked to the transformation of class and property relations. Local class and property relations have global implications. Webs of interdependence link the local to the global. Bottom-up (local, national, regional) struggles and top-down struggles need to converge. What can forces in favor of social justice hope to achieve if and when poor people and popular sectors are able to win state power in particular countries, or at least to place into state agencies people who are responsive to their plight, aware of their needs, and willing to challenge the prerogatives of transnational capital?

This brings us full circle back to globalization and to what makes the early twenty-first century distinct from previous moments in the history and the crises of world capitalism. In this qualitatively new stage of global capitalism there are clear limitations to reintroduction of a redistributive project at the nation-state level. It is not clear how effective national alternatives alone can be in transforming social structures and resolving the crisis. If the (capitalist) state as a class relation is becoming transnationalized, then any challenge to (global) capitalist state power must involve a major transnational component. Struggles at the nation-state level are far from futile. They remain central to the prospects for social justice, to progressive social change, and to any resolution of the crisis. But any such struggles must be part of a more expansive transnational counterhegemonic project, including transnational trade unionism, transnational social movements, transnational political organizations, and so on. And they must strive to establish sets of transnational institutions and

---

[45] Mark Levine, *Why They Don't Hate Us: Lifting the Veil on the Axis of Evil* (Oxford: One World, 2005).

practices that can place controls on the global market and rein in some of the power of global capital as the first step in a resolution of the crisis. An alternative to global capitalism must be a *transnational* popular project. The popular mass of humanity in its struggle for social justice must develop a *transnational* class consciousness and concomitant global political protagonism involving strategies, programs, organizations, and institutions that link the local to the national, and the national to the global.

Index